Will Birch has long experience of the music business,
having been a drummer, songwriter and record producer.
Today he writes about music and performers and has
contributed to *Mojo* and other magazines. His first book was
No Sleep Till Canvey Island: The Great Pub Rock Revolution.
Married with one son and a record collection,
he lives in Essex.

Also by Will Birch

No Sleep Till Canvey Island:
The Great Pub Rock Revolution

Will Birch

IAN DURY

The Definitive Biography

PAN BOOKS

First published 2010 by Sidgwick & Jackson

First published in paperback 2011 by Pan Books
an imprint of Pan Macmillan, a division of Macmillan Publishers Limited
Pan Macmillan, 20 New Wharf Road, London N1 9RR
Basingstoke and Oxford
Associated companies throughout the world
www.panmacmillan.com

ISBN 978-0-330-51148-3

The acknowledgements on pages 368–70 constitute an extension of
this copyright page.

A CIP catalogue record for this book is available from
the British Library.

Printed in the UK by CPI Mackays, Chatham ME5 8TD

Visit www.panmacmillan.com to read more about all our books
and to buy them. You will also find features, author interviews and
news of any author events, and you can sign up for e-newsletters
so that you're always first to hear about our new releases.

For my old man

Contents

'Ian Dury always seemed to me to be an
exceptionally witty and concise singer-poet,
with an especially admirable talent for making
contemporary references and language
feel a part of the long tradition of
lyric writing and balladeering.'

Andrew Motion, Poet Laureate, October 2008

'I'm a well-known softie.
You know that, an old pudding.
It's a pack of lies what they say about me.'

Ian Dury, May 1998

Introduction

This is the story of a great man who battled severe physical setbacks to become a cultural icon of the late twentieth century. He inspired, loved and motivated nearly everyone with whom he came into contact in his various roles as husband, lover, father, artist, teacher, photographer, drummer, songwriter, pop star, stage and film actor, voice-over artist, television presenter, charity fundraiser, goodwill ambassador for UNICEF and perennial Teddy Boy.

He never really grew up. He never really *had to*. His sense of awe and wonder was frozen in time from the moment that the joy of childhood was stolen from him in a tragic twist of fate. Following the early trauma of polio, he became a warm and compassionate mentor to many and retained an almost child-like enthusiasm for the marvels of art and music. He *raved about* the paintings of Vermeer, the flamenco guitar of Segovia, the jazz saxophone of Ornette Coleman and the wild, rebel yell of Gene Vincent and the Bluecaps. He obsessed over the creative detail, wanting everyone to know about the images and sounds that rocked his world.

But genius is pain. And throughout his life he was a tightly wound ball of complex emotions, as his closest friends and relatives will attest in the story that follows. It is not the purpose of this book to describe a sometimes unpleasant man. Although he 'had his moments', he was somebody who most people felt they were glad to have known and who enriched their lives. As his former manager, Charlie Gillett, says, 'He had a fantastic smile, as if he was sharing an unspoken joke. And he was friendly, with a genuine look of affection.'

To his many fans he will always be 'the diamond geezer', a worthy subject for that vacant plinth in Trafalgar Square, but the scale of his celebrity was not unlocked until he died from cancer in March 2000. We may be some years away from a blue plaque outside one of the dozen or so addresses he called home at various times and from the full recognition his work undoubtedly deserves, but right now Ian Dury is *the* working-class hero, a household name whose drug- and booze-fuelled career, Bohemian lifestyle and deft 'wordsmithery' inspire admiration, fascination and fear.

The posthumous respect has been building for some time. In 2003, comedienne Linda Smith nominated Ian Dury for inclusion in the BBC Radio 4 series *Great Lives*, in which he swaggered in the unlikely company of Lord Nelson and Tchaikovsky. The following year, London mayoral candidate Simon Hughes chose 'Reasons to Be Cheerful' as his campaign song. The Internet is awash with celebrity tributes. Try this from Clive James: 'Ian Dury was a magic messenger straight out of Prospero's island.' Shortly after Ian's death, the Poet Laureate, Andrew Motion, described him as 'a remarkable English poet'.

Since his death, his work has grown in stature. Hardly a week passes without his name appearing in the media. As well as two previous biographies, numerous magazine articles and CD reissues, there has been a stage play, *Hit Me: The Life and Rhymes of Ian Dury*, written and directed by Jeff Merrifield, and London's Graeae (pronounced grey-eye) theatre company, its cast drawn from physically disabled actors, is planning a musical. A full-length feature film, entitled *Sex & Drugs & Rock & Roll*, starring Andy Serkis in the lead role, written by Paul Viragh and directed by Mat Whitecross, was released to critical acclaim in 2010.

At the end of his life, Ian was said to be a 'national treasure'.

He would have hated this somewhat patronizing term, often used to describe a lovable artiste of a certain vintage. But to many, Ian *was* a treasure. The differently abled community, whose causes he enthusiastically supported, adopted him as their poster boy, and when the BBC's 'Ouch' website conducted a poll of 'Great Disabled Britons', Ian was placed second with a credible 28.6 per cent of the vote (behind Professor Stephen Hawking, but some way ahead of Sir Winston Churchill!).

As probably the most famous victim of England's post-war poliomyelitis epidemic, his full-on life was a multi-faceted journey through a wild and colourful landscape. But did his unfortunate condition become 'the catalyst that sparked the revolution'? Did polio give him a psychological and emotional resilience that drove him ruthlessly towards stardom? *This* was the conundrum that compelled me to research Ian's life and write his biography.

We met on a number of occasions when I was researching *No Sleep Till Canvey Island – The Great Pub Rock Revolution*, primarily to talk about that era. I was apprehensive about our first interview session because I had once experienced the sharp end of his tongue. It happened in 1973, when Kilburn and the High Roads played the Zero 6 in Southend-on-Sea, and I foolishly wandered 'backstage' after the show. When I became a touring musician myself I found out how irksome it can be when fans insist on gatecrashing the dressing room within seconds of the encore, thus interrupting the inevitable post-show inquest and the privacy a musician requires when changing his trousers. Anyway, Ian was in a state of undress, dripping with sweat, and he told me to 'fuck off!' just like he would tell Chaz Jankel to fuck off some years later and, no doubt, many others since.

We bumped into each other from time to time. The Kilburns appeared on bills with my own group, the Kursaal Flyers, and I would occasionally see him in Dingwalls or up at Stiff Records and found him a little abrasive, but when we met in the 1990s, Ian gave me his full cooperation, and I am grateful to him for his generosity at a time when he was contending with serious illness. The interviews took place at his home in Hampstead. The living room was a picture of Bohemian chic, with large paintings, some of which were early Dury works, adorning the walls. On the dining table stood an unopened bottle of white wine amid a surreal array of bric-à-brac. At the back of the flat, overlooking the garden, was Ian's workspace. The small, narrow room housed a high-level desktop scattered with large sheets of layout paper. These contained meticulous handwritten notes, some of which would show up in future songs.

After one lengthy interview session, Ian summoned me back for more, saying he felt he had 'left it half unsaid . . . or something', so I returned for further riveting yarns. I've never kidded myself that the tales he treated me to were exclusive or indeed completely true; his anecdotes were finely honed, oft-repeated and told with dramatic purpose. But now that I was equipped with some 30,000 of his hugely entertaining words and a first-hand account of key periods in his life, I felt I had the basis for a biography of the man I regarded as an extraordinary entertainer and England's foremost lyricist, or 'wordsmith' to use Ian's preferred term.

My overriding impression from listening to Ian was how proud he was of his time at the Royal College of Art and his family's lineage. 'I met Betty, my late first wife, at the Royal College,' Ian told me. 'She was at Newport College of Art. Her dad went to the Royal College in the thirties. My girlfriend's [Sophy, later to become Ian's wife] old man, Joe Tilson, went there. We've got a little baby now [Bill] who's a third-generation Tilson. His dad and his granddad and his mum went to the Royal College of Art. All my three children's parents went to the Royal College of Art. If they go the other way and grow up to be vicars, I shall be gutted.'

When discussing his songs, Ian was able to recite every word and nuance of his earliest, unrecorded efforts, as if the distant couplets were meticulously archived in some huge mental filing cabinet. He also had perfect recall of seemingly trivial events, dates and places. He savoured the detail and, as he reminisced, I could sense him mining his impressive memory vaults to summon up the minutiae. If ever I was in doubt about a certain biographical detail, it was Ian's version of events, where available, that I relied upon.

The detail that peppered his stories would have informed a great autobiography, had he chosen to write one. 'I did once speak to Robert [McCrum] at Faber,' he told me. 'To me, a title's important. I had "It's All Lies" or "On My Life" – it implies it's true, but it ain't. But my kids might read it, so I could only put half of it in, and then it would be a very boring book. Then I thought of getting all my mates round and have a few bevvies and take notes. Then I thought I'd like to do a book of anecdotes, like the David Niven books, with about 800 stories, but I don't really want to get into the forty-five-year plod. Does the world need another book? It's a lot of work.'

So it has been left to others to reconstruct Ian's life and decide what to include and what to omit. Ian seemed concerned about his family 'reading the truth'. He also didn't wish to appear ungrateful to his 'Aunt Moll', who augmented his mother's efforts and often came to the rescue when times were tough. 'My mum always wanted the best for me when I was a kid,' said Ian. 'Chailey was a fine place to be. Those four years made me strong enough to get out in the world again. But if I wrote my side of a certain scenario, my family might see that in the wrong light. I didn't enjoy High Wycombe, but I couldn't put that in the book because my auntie would read it and she helped me to go there. I'll wait 'til I'm about sixty before I write about that.'

Tragically, Ian was not to live to see sixty, or even fifty-eight, and it seems we will have to get by without his memoirs. Does the world need a new book about Ian Dury? It's a question I have often asked myself, but whenever I got a little disillusioned during my ten-year 'plod', a new batch of research material materialized! I'm sure there is more out there, and I'd love to hear from anyone who might wish to contribute to a possible future revision, or correct any factual errors. From Sydney to Tel Aviv, the stories are endless, and it pains me to think I may not have heard them all! Can there be another popular entertainer to match Ian for disgraceful, yet often hilarious, behaviour in public? Oliver Reed or Keith Moon spring to mind, but it seems you can only ever scratch the surface of Ian's vast catalogue of misdemeanours.

But hey! This was the man who wrote:

> Skinny white sailor the chances were slender the beauties
>   were brief,
> Shall I mourn your decline with some Thunderbird wine
>   and a black handkerchief?
> I miss your sad Virginia whisper, I miss the voice that
>   called my heart,
> Sweet Gene Vincent, young and old and gone ...

For this and other lyrical gems, all of the memorable shows and his stoic 'triumph over tragedy', there are reasons to be thankful indeed. And if it hadn't been for his chance encounter with the polio virus, we may not have enjoyed 'Sex and Drugs and Rock and Roll' or had 'Reasons to Be Cheerful' – two of Ian's phrases that appear in various dictionaries of quotations and still constantly feature in newspaper headlines.

His life was one of extremes, from the euphoria of the hit parade to daily, debilitating physical pain. It was no wonder he craved adoration, recognition and approval, the key drivers in his pursuit of fame. As his former minder, Fred Rowe, says, 'Ian simply wanted to be loved.' When he became a success, he was adored by his public, but when the hits dried up, mass adulation was swiftly followed by bitter rejection, all against the backdrop of severe disability. And throughout his wild years, there were voices in the back of his head, reminding him of his genteel family background and his mother's and aunts' efforts to educate and equip him for great things. His life was both tragic and charmed in equal measure, frequently eventful, always intense. If we're talking about the 'emotional roller coaster', Ian's seat was reserved at birth. This is the true story of Ian Dury and his life-long struggle for acceptance.

Prologue

Hammersmith Odeon, London, 1979. Through a door ajar we see the star, meticulously applying mascara to a pantomime visage with razor-blade earring and a head full of jet-black curls. Like the boss of a travelling circus, he is often miles away from home, distanced from reality and once again preparing to 'give' for his people. There are two men in the room. 'Come on, you tart,' says the bald one. 'You can't hurry art,' replies the star, leaning into the mirror to position a beauty spot on his left cheekbone. 'Ready are we?' asks the bald one. 'Ready,' says the star as he completes his nightly routine, although no two nights are ever the same.

Another ritual is taking place in an ante-room, where the musicians are tuning up and hurriedly discussing the fine detail of chords, keys, tempos and sound effects. As the dying echo of the opening act swirls around the backstage corridors, the star emerges from his dressing room on the arm of his minder. He shuffles past the band, oblivious to their technical discussions. 'Awright Davey?' he grunts self-consciously, making minimal eye contact with the wiry saxophonist. The troupe commences its long walk towards the stage, the pace of which is dictated by the star's painful gait.

A gangly youth in gorblimey trousers makes his announcement. 'Here they are, all the way from the Goldhawk Road, Ian Dury and the Blockheads!' The band settles into a familiar groove, and the star reaches for the arm of the bald one, gesturing towards the stage with his walking cane. He purposefully limps into position and croons his saucy opening line: 'I come awake, with a gift for womankind . . .'

It's show time, and all the comic-strip characters are on parade: 'Billericay Dickie' (who is *not* 'a blinking thicky'); the terminally uncertain 'Clevor Trever' and 'Sweet Gene Vincent', he of the 'lazy skin and ashtray eyes', a tragic role model for the artiste now in the spotlight. For seventy-five minutes he entertains with unexpected gestures, off-the-wall introductions and a carrier bag full of novelty items including a magic walking stick on an invisible wire. His best prop of all is the rubber-band-powered paper parrot that he will wind up mid-set and release from his good arm.

Some nights, the toy bird flaps its wings and soars high into the gods, guaranteeing a round of applause. Other nights, it misbehaves and hits the wall. Tonight, however, will be special. Standing at the edge of the stage and carefully judging the trajectory, the star releases the parrot with great care. It glides upwards and gracefully circles the auditorium. Then, sensationally, it returns like a boomerang and comes to rest in the star's outstretched hand. Magic! Thunderous applause, then a loud and immediate 'Rhythm Stick'! The audience is enthralled, showering their hero with love.

PART ONE

TRAGEDY

1

It's a Boy, Mrs Walker, It's a Boy

Belsize Park, London, 1937. Cigarette smoke fogged up the bar of the Adelaide Club where thirty-one-year-old Bill Dury was presiding over a game of dominoes. The voice of Bing Crosby – 'the new American singing sensation' – wafted from the Bakelite radio. In Germany, Adolf Hitler was tinkering with a map of Europe, but Bill paid little attention to politics. Under the dull illumination of a 40-watt light bulb, he lit another Craven A and amused his friends with a sly conjuring trick. When he looked up, he noticed that three ladies had entered the room. They were neatly attired in tweed and laughed amongst themselves as they ordered soft drinks, but Bill couldn't take his eyes off them. They came from another world.

When the dapper Bill Dury spotted twenty-seven-year-old Peggy Walker it was lust at first sight. Peggy, the long-legged daughter of an Irish country doctor, had flunked college and worked as a health visitor for Camden Council, whilst Bill, the dashing bus driver of immense charm, came from Kentish working class-stock, but their contrasting backgrounds were no bar to courtship. Magnetically attracted from the outset, their love affair would be fuelled by two overriding factors: Peggy's yearning for children and Bill's desire to rub shoulders with toffs.

William George Dury was born on 23 September 1905 at 18 Speldhurst Road, Southborough, near Tunbridge Wells in Kent. His parents, William Ernest and Mary Dury, already had four daughters when Bill arrived, and a second son, Victor, was born in 1911. To avoid confusion at home, the family referred to William junior as 'Will', whilst to his nieces and nephews he became 'Uncle Billy'. Personally, he preferred 'Bill'. His father had worked as a school caretaker and general labourer, but became too ill to work by the time Bill turned thirteen, leaving the young boy no option but to quit school and seek employment to help support the family.

A keen amateur boxer, Bill took a series of menial jobs, ending up at the Royal Blue Coach Company, where he learnt to drive. When Royal Blue became part of Western National in 1935, Bill found himself driving coaches between London and the West Country. Occasionally his journey called for an overnight stop in Winchester, where he would visit his cousin, Bert Tipping, an army man who lived with his family in the drill hall. 'Bill Dury was very suave,' recalls Bert's son Leslie Tipping. 'He would sometimes bring his girlfriend, and they'd stay with us. On one occasion we all went to see Dury Street in Winchester and had our photograph taken there.'

Bill was curious about his family name. Later in life, he researched its origins and discovered that Dury was part Scottish, part French. He thought about visiting the town of Dury in northern France, but never got round to it. He learnt that in Scotland, the name was spelt 'Durie'; that Robert Louis Stevenson devised a character called Henry Graeme Durie for his novelette *Master of Ballantrae*; and that in 1868 the French had a minister of education named Victor Dury. The history books tell us that in eighteenth-century Kent, smugglers Thomas and William Dury, from Biddenden and Flimwell respectively, were members of the notorious Hawkhurst Gang, but Bill decided that his immediate forebears were all born and raised in Southborough.

In stark contrast to her suitor's humble background, Peggy Walker was descended from the sprawling bloodline of an Irish Protestant land-owning dynasty that farmed County Donegal throughout the nineteenth century. It was said that her branch of the Walker family could be traced back as far as the Reverend George Walker, joint governor of Derry, who in 1689 helped defend his town against the besieging Catholic forces of King James II. Reverend Walker was later to die at the Battle of the Boyne. His famous monument, erected by the Protestant 'Apprentice Boys' in 1826, was blown up by the Irish Republican Army in 1973.

Peggy's grandfather, William Walker, was a wealthy dairy farmer who had inherited from his parents a 300-acre estate in the Finn Valley between the twin towns of Ballybofey and Stranorlar. In 1866, aged twenty-three, William set sail for Scotland, where he found a wife, one Margaret Ferguson Cuthbertson of Helensburgh, Dunbartonshire, some 30 miles north-west of Glasgow. William and Margaret married in Scotland in 1867 and settled at 46 Charlotte Street, Helensburgh. They would frequently commute to County Donegal in Ireland and stay at Kilcadden, a substantial family home that provided accommodation for their vast family. Five sons and two daughters were born between 1868 and 1880. In 1881, William and Margaret returned permanently to Ireland, where three further children were born. Most of the Walker children rejected the farming life and moved to England as quickly as possible to pursue professional careers in civil engineering, journalism and, in the case of their second son, John, medicine.

John Cuthbertson Walker was born on 5 March 1870. Upon leaving school, his medical studies took him to England, where he qualified as a general practitioner. In 1894, he secured a post in Mevagissey, a fishing village on the south coast of Cornwall, where he became a partner at the surgery of Doctor Charles Walker Monro Grier. He would frequently return to County Donegal, where at the turn of the century he met Mary Ellen Pollock of Finneederk, whom he married in Londonderry. He brought his bride back to England, and they lived for a year in a rented cottage at 106 Church Street, Mevagissey. As soon as he had established himself as a medical practitioner, thirty-two-year-old John designed and built a new house with an adjoining surgery for himself and Doctor Grier at the top of School Hill, Mevagissey. John Walker named the double-fronted property 'Pentillie' (the original name for Mevagissey) and employed a domestic servant, one Elizabeth Blight, to assist Mary in running the home.

John and Mary Walker's first child, William Cuthbertson Walker, was born at Pentillie on 7 February 1904. Two years later, there was much excitement in Mevagissey when the celebrated author George Bernard Shaw rented a room in John Walker's house to carry out background research for his new play, *The Doctor's Dilemma*. On 5 June 1906, the Walkers' second child, Doris Elisabeth Cochrane Walker, was born. She would grow up to detest the name Doris and asked everyone to call her Elisabeth.

In 1909, following a financial disagreement with Doctor Grier, John Walker moved his family to the north of England. William and Elisabeth were five and three years old respectively when their parents moved into 188 Milnrow Road in Rochdale, Lancashire. It was there that Peggy was born on 17 April 1910 and christened Margaret Cuthbertson Walker. A fourth child, Mary, was born on 8 September 1913, also at Milnrow Road. Mary, who would become known as Molly, remained the youngest of the Walker children, none of whom inherited their parents' Irish accent. In fact, they would all speak impeccable Oxford English. But although the Walkers were outwardly upper middle-class, they were far from wealthy. 'Money was a very difficult thing for my father,' says Molly Walker. 'He wouldn't have anything to do with borrowing it. An overdraft was as far as he would go. He thought banks were respectable, but this wretched overdraft pursued us all throughout our childhood.'

In 1914, the entire family left Rochdale and returned to Mevagissey, but two years later John Walker was enlisted into the army and posted to Stockport, Lancashire, to work at the military hospital, from where he would write a number of lively letters to the *British Medical Journal*. Throughout the First World War, William and Elisabeth were away at boarding school, and Peggy and Molly were sent to Ireland to stay with their grandmother at Kilcadden. Upon returning to Mevagissey in 1918, Peggy and Molly were sent to the local primary school, while William and Elisabeth continued their secondary education further afield. All four children gained the grounding that would equip them for university and, in most cases, excellent qualifications.

In 1923, seventeen-year-old Elisabeth entered University College London for three years of preclinical studies, resulting in a degree in medicine. Eight years after Elisabeth's graduation, Molly also went to University College and studied French, gaining a Bachelor of Arts degree in 1938. Peggy, however, was overshadowed by her sisters' academic achievements and, although she attended University College, left after one year, having failed her exams.

In 1935, Peggy and Molly pooled their resources to rent a small flat at 29 Adelaide Road, Chalk Farm, later moving to 1b Belsize Road, near Swiss Cottage, where Peggy was living when she met Bill in 1937. Peggy's work as a children's health visitor chiefly involved calling on families with small children and keeping an eye out for head lice. As she cycled the streets of Camden, she dreamed of having children of her own but first needed to find a husband, marriage being a prerequisite for parenthood in polite 1930s society. In contemplating wedlock, however, Peggy knew she would be breaking with family tradition; none of her aunts or female cousins ever married and her two sisters continued the trend. 'The Walker girls,' recalls a descendant, 'didn't go in for that sort of thing.'

There was, however, a somewhat apocryphal explanation for such rampant spinsterhood; it was said that several generations earlier, within their Irish Presbyterian family, a young

Walker girl had married a Catholic man against the wishes of her father. The father was so outraged by what was a very public ceremony that he placed a curse on all Walker women. From that day on, he declared, they would all die as spinsters. Peggy was having none of it. 'She was fed up with all this business about us Walker women never getting married,' remembers Molly. 'She had been visiting Kilcadden and heard that our uncle Arthur was going up to the little place where they used to live, the place where the father had cursed all the Walker women. Peggy said to Arthur, "I'd love to come with you," and she followed him up the hill. I never heard the details of what happened next, but I do know that a few months later Peggy got engaged to Bill and quite soon after a lot of her cousins got engaged.'

Just as Peggy had a weakness for children, Bill Dury had a weakness for class. His niece, Margaret Webb (née Dury), observes, 'A gulf existed between Auntie Peg's side of the family and ours. There wouldn't be a gulf now because we're all on an equal standing, but back then Mummy said, "Uncle Billy married Auntie Peg because he had aspirations to be a gent." He used to come and stay with my auntie and walk around in a sort of smoking jacket and wear silk dressing gowns. He also spoke very nicely. He liked to think of himself as a gentleman. They said that's why he married Peggy. He was marrying someone of a different class.'

At thirty-two, Bill Dury had charmed his way into many a girl's arms but had always retained his independence. Settling down was not really on his agenda, but, like many couples of the day, Bill and Peggy were thrown closer towards marriage by the threat of war with Germany. It seemed like it really could be the end of the world, and the usual courtships were often dispensed with. But the conflict was almost a year away when Peggy and Bill announced their plans to marry at All Souls Church in Loudoun Road, South Hampstead on 23 December that year. Peggy's mother, Mary, travelled alone from Cornwall to attend, her husband, Doctor John Walker, having died just weeks before the ceremony.

The turnout was small, since both families regarded the marriage as an unwelcome event. The Dury families, their men manual workers, their women housewives, looked on the Walkers as non-family-orientated, middle-class intellectuals. In turn, the Walkers dissociated themselves from the Kentish clan. Bill's nephew, Leslie Tipping, says, 'Peggy wasn't accepted by some members of the Dury family, and they didn't have a lot to do with one another. Amongst Peggy's family, the consensus was that she should never have married.' After the wedding and a small reception back at their flat, Bill and Peggy got down to the business of starting a family. Bill had left his own lodgings at 103 Finchley Road and moved in with Peggy at Belsize Road. Molly also shared the accommodation. 'I just sort of flopped about and worked in various places and finished up with a job in education,' says Molly Walker. 'My particular interest was children who needed special help.'

Elisabeth, now a paediatrician, was a frequent visitor to 1b, much to Bill's irritation. The three Walker sisters were inseparable and found much to discuss about their complementary professions and shared interests. Molly, in particular, was passionate about Eastern philosophy and the teachings of her 'guru', Basanta Kumar Mallik, a renowned Indian thinker who, in 1937, settled in Oxford, where Molly would later work as a director of Nuffield College. With the Walker sisters' skills clearly focused on the welfare and education of sick or disadvantaged children, their family infrastructure was such that, if they were to ever encounter a child with special needs, he or she would be guaranteed the best possible support.

Early in 1939, Peggy announced that she was pregnant. The flat in Belsize Road had already become too cramped for its three occupants, and, with a baby due, Bill and Peggy sought to move to a larger home. Bill had heard about some new rentable housing that was being built at Harrow Weald,

Middlesex, specially designed for young families who wished
to escape the centre of London. The first dwellings in Weald Rise
had been built in 1927, but even by the summer of 1939, when
Bill and the pregnant Peggy arrived at number 43, the thoroughfare was still unmade and without pavements. The end of
their road tapered off into a muddy field. 'I went along with
them,' recalls Molly Walker. 'It was a funny house on a kind of
estate. You didn't get to know people very well and there was
no social life. I was working at the time and what I objected to
was when all the lights went out and I had to get home on the
bus. It was a difficult journey in the dark.'

From their new semi-detached home, Bill made friends with
Tom Johnson, also a bus driver, who lived next-door-but-one.
Maurice Cattermole, who lived three doors down and was still
a resident of Weald Rise over sixty years later, remembers: 'Mrs
Dury loved children. There were always kids playing in the
street and they had a big English sheepdog [named Bella] that
used to join in. If any of the parents in the street had trouble
with their children, Peggy went over to help.' But the idyllic
street scene was to be shattered by the outbreak of war and,
more profoundly, a family tragedy. The pressure of moving
home had put great strain on Peggy's pregnancy, and her first,
longed-for baby was stillborn. Molly remembers: 'It must have
occurred a short time after we moved to Harrow. The moving
may well have had something to do with that. I suppose they
thought I was just a kid and I wasn't to be worried about any
details of it, but I know that it happened pretty soon after they
moved. Peg was very fond of children and must have been
very upset.'

In September 1940, Britain's city centres became prime tar-
gets for the Luftwaffe, and thousands of small children were
evacuated to escape the bombing. Harrow, a suburb of London,
was considered a safer area, and the childless Peggy was quick
to take in two children named Richard and Jill, who would stay
with her for the duration of the war. 'They weren't strictly evac-

uees,' says Molly. 'It was a private arrangement, but Peggy treated them just as other evacuees were treated. They were pretty young, not yet in long clothes, they hadn't quite started school.'

Now in his mid-thirties, Bill Dury might have been pressed into one of the armed services but was exempt from conscription owing to his reserved occupation, that of bus driver for London Transport. In 1941, Peggy fell pregnant for the second time and at 9 a.m. on Tuesday 12 May 1942 gave birth, at home, to a healthy baby boy. Peggy had bought a three-year diary in anticipation of the momentous event, and her entry for the day of the birth reads: 'Weight 7lb 6ozs – marked by forceps – slight facial paralysis – Tuesday's child.' Within forty-eight hours, the proud parents registered the birth at Hendon Register Office and, incorporating Bill's mother's maiden name, called their son Ian Robins Dury.

'I was conceived at the back of the Ritz and born at the height of the blitz,' Ian quipped some fifty-three years later when we met to discuss, amongst other things, his early years. It was a typically colourful couplet to describe his world debut. He went on: 'My mum was a health visitor, and her sister was a doctor, and her other sister an education officer. My dad was a bus driver. He was bright, but he wasn't educated. He left school at thirteen. He came from a long line of bus drivers, as they say. They were proud of it.'

Despite Ian's amusing claim, there is no record of any of Bill's relatives having been employed on the buses. In fact, Ian's grandfather was a general labourer who died at the age of fifty-three, and Bill himself was considering a career change. His marriage to Peggy was threatened from two standpoints: her literary leanings and his line of work. In the early days, he would arrive home after a hard day navigating his bus through the ponderous London traffic, only to find Peggy and her two sisters sitting at the kitchen table, embroiled in deep, intellectual discourse. With the intelligentsia at close quarters,

Bill began to resent his exclusion from conversations that took place under his own roof. Possessing only the bare bones of an education, he felt humiliated and incompatible. In an attempt to re-establish himself in Peggy's eyes, he started taking steps towards self-improvement, but Peggy was already thinking about departing the capital. The war forced her hand.

In the autumn of 1943, with a sky full of enemy bombers, the suburbs of London had become hazardous at best. Peggy suddenly announced that she was leaving Harrow and taking the three children to the safety of Penmellyn, a house on the Portmellon Road in Mevagissey, where her mother had lived since becoming widowed in 1938. Bill's job with London Transport prevented him from joining his family in Cornwall, and he stayed in Weald Rise. At Penmellyn, Peggy nurtured the infant Ian, devoting every spare moment to his early learning. Although he would remain an only child, Peggy's two foster-children provided Ian with excellent company as he started to toddle. Molly recalls: 'Peggy said it was absurd that she couldn't send them to the local school, so she said, "I'll teach them." Ian didn't like being left out of things, as you can imagine, so he came and joined in.'

Peggy and Bill's marriage was effectively over, but certain events would reunite the couple. On 26 May 1944, Ian was baptized by the Reverend Charles Whitworth Phillips at St Goran Church, in the parish of St Goran, Mevagissey. Bill made the 540-mile round trip from London. While in Cornwall, he witnessed his wife's diligent effort to educate their son. He noticed that Ian's development had become an almost obsessive project for Peggy, who was perhaps driven by her own academic under-achievement and the realization that Ian might remain her only child. The memory of her first son's stillbirth haunted her, and Bill's work-related absence made matters doubly difficult. But these factors guaranteed that Ian would receive Peggy's full attention. The house was crammed with books and other visual stimuli, which, combined with a mother's guiding hand, encouraged Ian's love of words and images. He responded well to the continual nurturing, and the hours that Peggy dedicated to him formed the basis of his education.

By the age of three, Ian could read many two-syllable words and simple stories. His vocabulary grew, and he became quite talkative. 'The story went that Ian picked up a nursery rhyme book and began to fit words to a rhyme he knew,' says Molly Walker. 'He said, "I can read, mum." He knew that the words fitted into the tune, he was quite bright in that way.' Mother and son also kept scrapbooks, and Ian could often be found sitting in a sea of tiny paper clippings. An assortment of pencils and crayons was never far from reach, and his imagination was fired at every turn.

Shortly after the war ended, Peggy decided that she and Ian should leave Cornwall so she could resume her career as a health visitor and accepted an offer to stay with her sister Elisabeth, who now lived in a cottage at 90 Front Lane, Cranham, near Upminster in Essex. Foster-children Richard and Jill had been returned to their mother, leaving Elisabeth, Peggy and Ian living at the cottage. Like Peggy, Elisabeth also loved children, but she had never married. She'd long ago decided that, if she was childless by the age of forty, she would try to adopt. Although Elisabeth was single, adoption was straightforward, as the war had left thousands of fatherless children whose widowed mothers were unable to cope. In 1946, Elisabeth adopted a baby boy named Martin, who would one day provide company for Ian. A few years later, Elisabeth would also adopt a baby girl, Lucy Catherine.

By the summer of 1947, Ian was nearing school age. For someone who had been heavily doted upon for five years, he was always going to find formal education a wrench. Compared to the security and warmth of home, where he received tuition from his mum, the daily trudge to Upminster Infants School was too grim for Ian to even contemplate. Confident of his reading ability, Ian questioned why he should go to school – what was the point if mum was providing all the education he would ever need?

December's severe weather with its heavy snowdrifts and icy pavements provided Ian with the perfect excuse for a spot of truancy. He was starting to taste the joy of rebellion, wondering how far he could push the boundaries. English law required all children over the age of five to attend school, but the wily Ian contrived ways to buck the system, including feigning illness and, his favourite trick, simply removing all of his clothes in the middle of the room and throwing a tantrum. Despite threats of a visit from the dreaded School Board man, Ian became a serial malingerer. 'I was taken to the head-shrinkers because I refused to go to school,' Ian told me. 'They said I was disturbed because my parents had split up. Some quite loud arguments used to take place between them, but I could read before I went to school. I suppose you could say I was semi-precocious.'

Ian's education was not much affected by prolonged absences, but he wasn't a complete homebody. He also enjoyed typical children's pursuits and would often play outside with Barry Anderson, whose family owned the Plough public house nearby. 'We were about five,' recalls Barry. 'The pub had a long corridor, and I remember seeing this little boy watching me from the doorway. It was Ian. He lived up the road and we became close friends.' In the summer of 1948, Barry was invited to join Ian and Peggy on a trip to Cornwall, where they would stay with Ian's grandmother. As 'best mates', this was the first of many holidays or day trips Ian and Barry would enjoy together. 'Ian used to read me stories,' says Barry. 'The books were a little beyond my understanding, but Ian could read them in a way that he made me understand. These were books about history or politics. He'd pick one out and say, "Would you like to hear about George Washington?" Even before that he was reading me *Rupert the Bear*. His mother got him the books. He had *Rupert the Bear* everywhere. She put this into him.'

While Ian was wriggling out of school, Bill's career was gaining momentum. In 1945 he had seen a newspaper advertisement, placed by Rolls-Royce, offering advanced driving courses for trainee chauffeurs. He quickly imagined himself behind the wheel of a prestigious motor car, rubbing shoulders and exchanging conversation with some distinguished client, perhaps a politician or a film star. Upon joining Rolls-Royce he quickly rose to the position of chauffeur for the company chairman, Lord Hives. He was also hired out by the famous motor company to drive businessmen all over England and occasionally across Europe. When his work took him to Switzerland, he arranged for his family to join him, perhaps hoping for a reconciliation with Peggy. The Swiss trip of 1948 provided Ian with a typically amusing story in later life. Reminiscing in his Hampstead work den, he told me, 'I lived in Switzerland once, when I was six, for six months. My dad had a job driving a rubber millionaire called Ellerman. My mum said he got the sack for cavorting with the geezer's missus . . . could have done, my dad was a bit of a chap. I've never been able to get this quite right, but we lived in a little village of chalets called Les Avants, near Montreux. In 1958 Noël Coward, as a tax exile, went to live in the same place, and I think it was the same house, called the Villa Christian. I was there ten years before Noël Coward! He probably found some of my notes! . . . and knocked out a couple of musicals on the strength of it, the old bastard!'

Ian returned from Switzerland with a musical box for Barry and a longing to see more of his dad, but his parents were unable to square their incompatibility and chose to permanently live apart. Ian may have assumed as a child that his father had deserted him, but it was his mother who had chosen not to return to the family home in Harrow at the end of the war, preferring to move in with her sister in Cranham. Bill returned to

central London and in between trips to Europe, rented rooms at
82 Ebury Street, Victoria. The accommodation was shared with
a 'lady friend', disparagingly referred to by the rest of the family
as 'Lulu'.

Despite their break-up, Peggy and Bill would never divorce,
and Ian continued to benefit greatly from their individual attentions, especially when Bill turned up to take Ian and his friends
out in the Rolls-Royce. The usual meeting place was the car park
of the Plough. Ian glowed with pride when Bill arrived and
people poured out of the pub to admire the gleaming automo-
bile. Ian was beginning to feel he was in some way special,
different perhaps from other children, most of who were un-
accustomed to fancy cars or the simple pleasures of being
tutored by mum. At the age of seven, he was Upminster's very
own 'Little Lord Fauntleroy'. He had a doting mother who
fed his imagination; two aunties who provided him with additional attention and a dad who drove aristocrats around in a
Rolls-Royce. To top it all, he only went to school when he felt
like it. What more could he want? He may have wished for a
few more friends, but he was also quite content with his
own company; Peggy had seen to that. In the spring of 1949,
Ian Dury was king of the hill, but his life was about to take a
dramatic turn.

2

Cruel Summer

Southend-on-Sea, 1949. August was one of the hottest months on record, with temperatures in the south of England frequently hitting the high eighties. In the midst of the heat wave, seven-year-old Ian and his friend Barry Anderson took a day trip to the seaside, accompanied by Barry's mum. They had been to Southend before, in the Rolls-Royce with Bill, but today they would travel by rail and visit the open-air pool on the Western Esplanade, situated close to the town's pleasure pier, renowned as 'the longest in the world'.

Westcliff swimming baths, built in 1915 high above the beach, had a raised viewing area around its perimeter and tiny changing cubicles that opened onto a blue-tiled pool full of mildly chlorinated water. Overhanging the deep end were some diving boards and a water-slide, into the surface of which – according to local folklore – a young tearaway had secretly inserted a razor blade in the misguided belief that it would cut through and completely remove one or two of the young girls' swimming costumes. This may have been some juvenile fantasy, but in truth a far greater danger lurked at the pool – the deadly poliomyelitis virus.

Oblivious to the invisible menace, Ian and Barry splashed about in the shallow end for an hour. Full of excitement, Ian accidentally took a gulp of the icy water. Its harsh saltiness stung the back of his throat and made him want to vomit. He spat out as much of it as he could, but in that split second his life was changed for ever. Within hours, the poliovirus was quietly raging through his otherwise healthy body.

Ian went home happy that evening. It had been an enjoyable day, and he could now look forward to a holiday at Penmellyn with Aunt Molly and his grandmother. Molly recalls, 'Peggy knew I was going away for a fortnight's holiday in Mevagissey, and asked if I could take Ian because she only had a short holiday herself and Ian had the whole school holiday. She asked, "What is he going to do with himself?" I agreed to take Ian, and we set off for Cornwall. The only thing I remember about the journey was that I asked him to go and have a wash before we ate. He said, "I don't need a wash." My mother had moved from our old house at the end of the village after my father died. Because she didn't have room for all the furniture we had, she got a big barn. We used it as a sleeping place. Ian and I slept out there on this particular occasion, and I remember reading a chapter or two to him at bedtime, and the next night he told me he'd finished the book. Then he had an awful headache.'

Ian's grandmother immediately sent for the doctor, who tapped Ian's knees to test his reflexes, but the reaction was worryingly poor. The doctor concealed his fears, but when he returned later that afternoon, he matter-of-factly announced: 'I'm afraid it's polio.' An ambulance was called, and Ian was rushed to Truro hospital, accompanied by Molly, who had telephoned her sister and suggested she should get the night train. 'My mum came down on the milk train, and they told her I was going to die,' recalled Ian. 'I was very ill. We were in Nissen huts. She wasn't allowed in, but she could see me from outside and she said my face was the same colour as the sheet. The idea had been that I was going to go to some sort of school where children who were a bit precocious went, to be together. I was fucking glad I didn't go there, but I got polio instead, as a sort of alternative route.'

Poliomyelitis is an infectious viral disease that attacks the central nervous system. The highly contagious virus is easily transmitted between humans or by the ingestion of contaminated water, particularly in warmer weather. In a small percentage of cases, it leads to muscle weakness and the destruction of nerve cells. This can result in the asymmetrical paralysis of limbs, in Ian's case his left arm and leg. The world had seen a number of polio outbreaks in recent years. On the other side of the Atlantic, the epidemic of 1949 had claimed over 40,000, with some 2,720 deaths. At the University of Pittsburgh, Doctor Jonas Salk, a thirty-five-year-old virologist, was taking an obsessive interest in the poliovirus, hoping to create a preventative. Salk's famous 'killed-virus' vaccine would arrive in 1954, sadly too late to immunize sufferers such as Ian.

About his life-altering experience, Ian told me, 'When my mum died I went through her papers and found some correspondence between the medical officer at Southend and her. There were nine cases [of polio] reported in August, during the heatwave. I got a heavy-duty fever and I had to have a lumbar puncture, for fluid on the spine. I spent six weeks in an isolation hospital in Truro, because I was infectious. My dad sent me a postcard every day, and my mum gave me a toy farm animal every day. I had a farm on my bedside locker with a mirror for the duck pond, a bit of fencing, a cow . . . I was encased in plaster – both arms and both legs. I rallied round after six weeks in the Royal Cornish Infirmary.'

During the time that Ian was in Truro, encased in plaster, Peggy was in constant touch with the health authorities, urging them to allow her son to be moved to a hospital nearer home. At one point the doctor at Truro wrote to Peggy stating that, although he couldn't legally prevent Ian leaving Truro, such a move would be ill-advised. Quite simply, Ian was not expected to live, but he miraculously pulled through. 'When I left the isolation unit my farm animals had to stay there,' said Ian. 'I was choked. They took me back to Essex on a stretcher, to Black Notley Hospital near Braintree.'

Ian's friend Barry Anderson had a close call. His family

worried that he too may have caught the poliovirus and kept him in bed with regular visits from the doctor, but Barry wasn't told about Ian. 'I kept asking, "Where's Ian?"' says Barry. 'I didn't see him for six months, but when he was in hospital in Braintree I went with his mother to visit him every few weeks. We'd be in tears from laughter, joking about, but I didn't really understand what was wrong with him.' Ian spent eighteen painful months in Black Notley Hospital, by which time he was nearly nine years old. The polio epidemic – cruelly arbitrary in its choice of victims – had stolen two years of Ian's childhood and designated him for a lifetime of physical discomfort. Although Ian put on a brave face, the early years would hit him hard. He became understandably bitter and physically off-balance, the loss of equilibrium making him irritable and stroppy, but his disability would render him effectively immune from physical retaliation if he chose to lash out with his tongue. Thus, polio was to become *the* major factor in Ian's existence and greatly influence his thoughts, words and deeds.

It had been a devastating blow for Peggy, whose dreams of Ian passing his exams and becoming a doctor or lawyer seemed to be dashed. She'd now been separated from Bill for three years. While Ian was in hospital, she and Elisabeth moved from the cottage in Cranham to a large corner house at 12 Waldegrave Gardens, Upminster. From there, the tireless Walker sisters would plan Ian's rehabilitation.

When Ian emerged from hospital in the spring of 1951, his left leg was supported by a steel and leather calliper. The left side of his body was now slight, his arm thin, his hand twisted and small. By contrast, the right-hand-side of his body displayed no abnormalities, and was quite strong. Physiotherapy sessions in hospital ensured that he would have the strength to move around virtually unaided, but would require a wheelchair for trickier journeys. Peggy turned to her younger sister for advice. Molly was now working in education and suggested placing Ian in a special school that would cater for his needs.

She knew of one such establishment in East Sussex, where disabled children were given occupational therapy by learning a trade such as book-binding, carpentry or shoe-repairing. Peggy had envisioned none of these occupations for Ian, but, given his condition, it seemed a better option than returning to school in Upminster. She nodded her agreement, and Molly quietly made the arrangements.

In April 1951, one month before his ninth birthday, Ian started at Chailey Heritage Craft School, a former workhouse that would become his home for the next three years. Chailey was founded in 1903 by Dame Grace Kimmins, a pioneer of education for disabled children suffering from diseases such as rickets, tuberculosis and malnutrition. In 1894, Dame Grace had established the wonderfully named 'Guild of the Poor Brave Things' to help disabled boys become productive in society, but she could not possibly have foreseen the coming maelstrom that was Ian Dury. *He* had no intention of becoming a street-corner cobbler and proceeded to hang tough. What were his choices, after all – to be a nice, polite boy from a posh family and risk a kicking or to become a leader of gangs?

In the grim, Dickensian atmosphere of the Craft School, Ian had no option but to fight. Combat would take place in various positions depending on impromptu 'rules' that took account of his adversary's disabilities. If his opponent was severely disabled, with two callipers, fighting would take place on the ground. If he had only one calliper, they would fight seated on a bench. Those who were calliper-free could brawl standing up. 'I don't remember fighting with an ordinary person,' Ian would tell BBC Radio 4's Frances Donnelly thirty years later. 'I mean by that, having two arms. There weren't many of those there. I would start a fight sitting next to somebody. They'd have to sit on my left-hand-side 'cos my right arm wouldn't give him no digs if he was sitting on my right-hand-side, I couldn't get near him. We'd usually end up on the floor, I'd use my right leg as well, do a bit of kicking.'

Ian would also recall his experiences in an aborted auto-biography. 'He wrote a chapter about Chailey,' recalls future manager Andrew King. 'It was the funniest, blackest thing I've ever read. It was called "The Night We Hung Charlie Young". They just about killed this guy, and you're pissing yourself with laughter. They were drowning him in the lavatory, hanging him upside down from the cistern by his legs, with his head in the pan. It was just terrifying.'

Many of the Chailey inmates were in a far worse state of health than Ian, with either physical or mental afflictions. Some had no lower limbs and were wheelchair-bound. Others had breathing difficulties and were confined to an iron lung, a mechanical device designed to assist sufferers of respiratory paralysis. One such pupil who experienced the iron lung was Paul Bura, who, when he met Ian later in life, joked: 'You're not the bastard who used to beat me up, are you?' To which, Ian replied, 'No I'm fucking well not!' and limped off in a huff. Bura later wrote a poem about the hardships of Chailey, which caused Ian to comment: 'This geezer tells it the way it was.' The two worst aspects of Chailey for Bura, and of course Ian, were missing their parents and being bullied or beaten up. Some children were less susceptible to bullying than others, but the harsh regime taught Ian not to take things 'lying down'. Molly Walker confesses, 'I thought it was a clever idea for Ian to go to Chailey, but they were too fierce there altogether. Ian used to say that if you fell down you had to get up. There was no running to help you. You were left to struggle. It was carried too far, I think.'

There had always been a no-nonsense philosophy at Chailey, and the regulations were tough. The ethos was one of self-sufficiency, fresh air and cheerfulness, and the habits of hard work and a strong moral fibre were drilled into the children. New arrivals were given the task of building a toy ladder that, however crudely assembled, would become a symbol of the 'ladder of life'. Most pupils would never physically get beyond the lower rungs, but they could aspire to reaching the top with their head held high. Most of their day was spent in the open air, year-round. Only during a thunderstorm – the outdoor beds were metal-framed – would the children be moved inside. An inspirational sign over the doors read: 'MEN MADE HERE'.

There is no doubt that the system at Chailey had a monumentally positive influence on Ian, but the school also had a dark side. As Ian later told me: 'Chailey made me strong . . . it was all right, although some terrible things went on there. There were some really evil sadistic fucking bastards and bullies amongst the teachers. Anything I saw, I told my mum. If I was being sexually abused by anybody, she tried to put a stop to it. I didn't hear of anything like rape or forced oral sex, mainly just wanking. There were a few pervy teachers there, but only on a wanking level. If there was any shagging going on I think I would have known.'

It seemed to me that Ian was making light of the more sinister side of life at Chailey, where, as he later admitted to friends, he had been 'forced to masturbate bullies'. Perhaps these incidents were rare, but such abhorrent abuse of a young, defenceless child was bound to leave its mark on Ian's psyche, and even though he could now shrug it off with commendable humour, how much of this contributed towards the 'difficult' side of his adult personality? In addition to the sexual abuse, Ian also witnessed the occasional violence. 'I saw some heavy-duty sadism a couple of times with a bloke hitting a kid with a stick, kids who were small and disabled and mentally not on the case. But there were wonderful things there. Bear in mind that the National Health Service had only been going for one year. Prior to that, Chailey had been a charity institution. It was a healthy place. We were outdoors most of the time. We were all tough little fuckers, it was a bit like Wandsworth, D-Wing. Once I got strong, I became quite a little tyke.'

As Ian would one day tell journalist Steven Fuller: 'Being in that place is one of the reasons I talk the way I talk. Before that

I talked not quite BBC. A third of the kids were funny in the head as well as being disabled. It was a very tough place, very cold and very brutal. The law of the jungle reigned . . . thinking about it [Chailey] now, I realize it was fuckin' heavy. It was like a hospital in one way, like a school in another way and like a prison in another way. It was very uncomfortable. Guys would die there.' Ian then went on: 'The third day I was there I woke up and discovered I had shit myself in the night. There was a guy called Hargreaves who had a big boot, he was an orderly . . . I was lyin' on it and didn't know what the fuck to do, and he came in and said, "Why haven't you got up yet?" He says [to the other children], "Come 'ere, everybody." They all came around the bed . . . I'm lyin' there in the shit, and he says, "Now roll over."'

For Ian, being away from home was the worst aspect of Chailey life, as he would tell BBC Radio 4's Peter White: 'I remember crying, waking up in the morning and hearing the bell ringing and facing the wall and knowing you were not at home. I missed my mates and my home and family.' Ian looked forward to visits from his parents and the occasional outing. In May 1951, Peggy took Ian to London's South Bank to visit the Festival of Britain, a 'tonic for the nation', which was slowly recovering from the ravages of war. There would also be trips back to Upminster in the school holidays. On one such break, Ian was taken to visit his paternal relatives in Southborough, Kent. With Peggy pushing Ian in his wheelchair, they travelled by train from Upminster to Tilbury and caught the ferry to Gravesend. The 122 bus then took them to Southborough. The arduous journey fatigued Ian, and he arrived at his destination in a mischievous mood. 'He was a little "basket" that day,' recalls his cousin, Margaret Webb. 'He was so naughty, and I was so good, being a girl. He did naughty things that I found difficult to handle, because I wasn't used to big naughty boys. He was bolshy, partly because of the reaction to what he was going through. He'd make silly faces and I found him a bit intimidating. When they were leaving that day, everyone said to me, "Give Ian a kiss goodbye," but I wouldn't. It worried me for years afterwards.'

Barry Anderson visited Ian at Chailey and regaled him with tales of life on the outside. 'I used to go to Saturday morning pictures at the Gaumont in Upminster where I would sing and do a silly act,' says Barry. 'Once they asked me to go up on stage in front of all the other kids. I got my courage up and did it. When I told Ian about it, he asked me a lot of questions: "What was it like being on stage? Did they cheer? Could you see them? Were you scared?" Ian was very interested in my experience.'

In late 1953, Peggy arranged for Ian to take the eleven-plus examination, which he passed with ease. But on reflection Ian felt that his education at Chailey was poor. Unlike many of the children, however, he was able to read and write, thanks to his mother's early tutoring. 'Eighty per cent were affected mentally, mostly hereditarily,' he told me. 'Those that could write would have a queue of boys behind us asking us to write their letters home. "Did you get a parcel this week? A letter?" My mum thought if I stayed at Chailey until I was sixteen I would suffer education-wise. Only twelve out of 120 boys passed the eleven-plus.'

With a grant from Essex County Council, Ian gained entry to the Royal Grammar School in High Wycombe. Once again it was Aunt Molly, now working in the Education Department of Buckinghamshire County Council, who was instrumental in securing the place. Molly Walker recalls, 'Peggy wanted Ian to have a good start so he could get a position in the world, and she knew that it meant you had to have a certain amount of wit to get into further education. That was what she had in mind.'

In May 1954, Ian made the journey by rail from Upminster to commence his secondary education at the Royal Grammar School in High Wycombe. There, he would board alongside 150 or so of the school's 900 boys. The 400-year-old seat of learning, founded during the reign of Elizabeth I, was divided into three houses: Terriers, in an annex 4 miles away in Haslemere; Uplyme, which occupied several temporary structures, one of which contained the music room; and School House, which abutted the quadrangle of the main building and into which Ian was placed. The school was surrounded on three sides by built-up areas, but on its fourth was a large sports field with rugby pitches, tennis courts and a running track, none of which of course held any interest for Ian.

On his first day at the school, he roamed the wood-panelled corridors, where portraits of former headmasters adorned the walls. He had been asked to report to the matron's office, where a metal-framed sick bed and a comprehensively stocked medicine cabinet sent a chill through his bones. Had he brought all his school kit? Peggy had been issued with a checklist of mandatory items including 'grey suit – short or long trousers at parent's discretion', or alternatively 'grey flannel trousers with School blazer; shirts, white or grey'; 'raincoats should be of navy blue'. Boys were expected 'not to wear open-necked shirts at School except when a white flannel shirt is worn with a School blazer and flannel trousers'. Those taking chemistry in the upper school would be 'expected to wear overalls to protect their suits'. The next item, sadly not applicable to Ian, called for 'Gym shorts, towel and rubber-soled shoes; Rugby Football shorts, maroon and white jerseys, stockings, boots; Cricket: white shorts, white shoes or boots, flannel trousers'.

Shortly after arriving at his new school, Ian was dragged to the surgery of one Doctor Agerholm, a specialist in matters of physical disability. With Ian accepted into the Royal Grammar School, the local education authority had seen an opportunity to put Agerholm's medical skills to the test, but Ian steadfastly refused to undergo the foot lock operation recommended by the doctor. Instead, in a rare act of conformity, he joined the School House boy scout troop, at the suggestion of house-master Reginald Howard. Although his time in the scouts was mercifully short, Ian would attend one summer camp, at Looe in Cornwall. 'It rained incessantly,' recalls fellow scout Graham Watson. 'A few of us took it in turns to push Ian in his wheelchair, but he never stopped moaning and whingeing.'

Back in school, the other pupils peered with morbid curiosity at the iron calliper that ran the full length of Ian's left leg. Revealed by the short trousers of his school uniform, the device was designed to bend at the knee, if he chose to unlock it, but usually this would only occur at bedtime. In class he would sit with his leg out straight to one side. Bicycles were prohibited anywhere in the school grounds, but Ian was permitted to ride his customized tricycle on the playing field. This and other special dispensations singled him out, forcing him to contend with persistent taunts and jibes, some of which may have arisen because of the over-protective behaviour of the school matron, a Miss Toulson, known to the boys as 'Toolbag'. 'People did stupid things,' says Molly Walker. 'I only heard about this afterwards but I was horrified. The very first night Ian was at High Wycombe, the matron tucked him up in bed and bent over and kissed him goodnight. Well . . . there was a start for a boy in his teens. The other boys must have thought, "My God, what have we got among us here?"'

The dormitory itself was a danger zone for younger pupils, who were often at the mercy of over-zealous, sadistic prefects and teachers of dubious propensity. And whereas day-boys would come in each morning freshly scrubbed, boarders only got their underwear changed after their weekly bath. Consequently, Ian and the other boarders could be easily identified by their smell. For Ian, living away from home had become bearable, but, in every other respect his time at the Royal Grammar School would be pure, unmitigated hell.

3

The Magnificent Severn

High Wycombe, 1954. The dormitory bell rang at 8 p.m. sharp, followed by the cry: 'Juniors up!' As the command echoed around School House, the first-form boys washed their hands and faces, brushed their teeth and lined up in front of an imperious prefect who carried out his inspection. Ian, being a little slower than the rest, struggled to get in line before his absence was noted. Then it was all into bed and lights out. In the dark corridor the prefect crept about, listening for the sound of voices. Suddenly, he burst into the dorm. 'Who was that talking?' It was Dury, as usual, reciting a dirty joke.

In September, after Ian had been at the Royal Grammar School for four months, a fresh intake of boys arrived. Among them was Warwick Prior, whose family hailed from nearby Aylesbury. For the next five years, Prior would live cheek-by-jowl with Ian, experiencing every nuance of his developing personality. Today, he has mixed emotions about Ian's behaviour at school, ranging from reluctant admiration to outright loathing, but is generally of the opinion that a school that groomed rugby players for England was a strange environment in which to find a disabled boy like Ian. 'He was not popular because he was not nice,' says Warwick Prior. 'You could argue that being there in his circumstances led to him not being nice, but he turned up there not being nice.'

Ian had in fact turned up at the school still bearing the scars of Chailey, where a culture of bullying existed, from ward orderlies humiliating children who had soiled their underclothes to pupils picking on each other because of their tragic deformities. To such children, bullying was the norm and Ian brought the behaviour with him. Ensconced in his new surroundings, he began picking on the odder characters in the junior dorm, including a Jewish boy and a chronically asthmatic lad, whose wheezing kept everyone awake on a nightly basis. Both boys were unpopular and taken out of the school within a term. Although Ian wasn't the ringleader, he had tagged on to their bullying because he'd seen an opportunity to deflect his own shortcomings.

None of the others pupils could be bothered to walk with Ian because they found him incredibly surly, foul-mouthed and possessing a verbal style that was ill-suited to the public school environment. Fellow scholar Michael Claridge remembers his 'slow and lurching gait' being painful to watch. Consequently, Ian had few friends and spent much of his time alone. Claridge once attempted to help him when he appeared to have mobility problems walking over the clinker patch, but Ian just said 'fuck off' and stuck the worn metal end of his crutch into Claridge's back. 'He did it with an extraordinary force for someone with his disability,' says Claridge. 'In short, my perception of Ian Dury was that he was a thoroughly nasty piece of work.'

Nasty or not, Ian was simply using whatever ammunition he could summon to survive under difficult circumstances. His unfortunate predicament didn't help, but he did possess an undeniable charisma. Realizing this – and it was an important turning point – Ian began to exploit his special powers. Like some first-form Fagin he formed a gang, into which he enlisted two particularly impressionable boys to form a 'terrible trio' that frequently set on smaller pupils to extort money or tuck. Although violence was only threatened, Ian's menacing presence, heightened by the flash of the leg iron, was usually enough to do the trick. As he and his crew moved up the school they became the persecutors, rather than the persecuted, emboldened by each little victory. But mugging boys for biscuits was fairly mild. Ian's behaviour hit rock bottom when a lad named William Busby came into the school. Busby was tall and crippled with rheumatoid arthritis, in a far worse state of health than Ian, but he immediately became another victim. Ian would physically set upon him, force him to the ground and beat him. At last, Ian had found someone physically weaker than himself, whose life he could make hell and force to share his suffering.

A sexual undercurrent exists at any boarding school where teenage pupils are thrown together to sleep in dormitories. The Royal Grammar School was no exception, and Ian dabbled in the mild homosexual behaviour that is common amongst twelve- and thirteen-year-old boys. Discovering masturbation ahead of the pack, he revelled in discussing the sensation of orgasm with his room-mates. 'He tried to jump into my bed more than once,' says Warwick Prior. 'He found sex quite early on and had a hell of an "old man" compared to the rest of us. The fact is, he had an extremely strong personality and if he'd had all his faculties he could have become anything he wanted, but he chose to go the thug route.'

Ian's educational opportunities, it seems, were excellent. Perhaps he could have now become the doctor or lawyer that Peggy dearly wished for, but he preferred to obscure his background and play the cockney barrow boy for all it was worth. In truth, Ian was suffering from a massive identity crisis and chose to side with his working-class dad, deliberately assuming the role of an East End villain with all the attendant behavioural quirks. But despite his thuggish tendencies, it is generally agreed that he was 'saved' by his artistic ability. 'He could draw like a saint, even at twelve,' admits Warwick Prior.

With his classmates watching in awe, Ian would produce

drawings of big-chested pin-up girls for everyone's amusement. Confident of his sketching skills, he mailed one of his cartoons to *Punch*, in the hope that they'd reproduce it. It depicted a Teddy Boy with a pick axe. In the first picture his luxuriant hair is swept back, but in the second frame his quiff has fallen over his eyes, making his work impossible. Ian received a kind rejection letter from the magazine. Nevertheless, he became celebrated around the school for his drawings of sexy females, many of which were painstakingly copied from magazines such as *Reveille*, *Titbits* and *Parade*. Even more exciting for Ian was that holy grail of adolescent titillation, *Health and Efficiency*, also known as 'the nudist bible'. Published under the ethos of physical fitness and a vigorous outdoor lifestyle, this dubious publication was the one place where young boys could legitimately enjoy photographs of the naked female form, even if the pubic hair had been airbrushed out.

Another source of inspiration for Ian was the paperback novel and, in particular, the works of Mickey Spillane and Hank Janson, whose lurid detective thrillers epitomized the genre of 'pulp fiction'. Janson's output in particular was prolific during the 1950s. In addition to the story, which usually contained some racy text, there was the bonus of a colour jacket illustration by the artist Reginald Heade, often depicting a vulnerable, scantily clad blonde. Priced at half-a-crown (12½ pence), Janson's books were perfect pocket money fodder for teenage boys, and Ian devoured them. Heade's illustrations informed Ian's improving drawing skills, and Janson's stories fired his imagination, but it was a novella entitled *Two Murders, One Crime* by Cornell Woolrich that had the greatest impact. The book's central character, 'Gary Severn', was a three-time loser, charged with a murder he didn't commit. Ian was captivated by the name. Seeking respect and tired of being referred to as 'Spastic Joe', Ian suddenly announced that forthwith he was to be known as 'Severn', perhaps failing to appreciate that a successful nickname is usually one that is given to you by others.

Returning to Upminster in the school holidays, he insisted that he was now 'Severn' and gave his local friends nicknames as well. 'He had to give everybody a bloody name,' says Barry Anderson, 'I was called "Lucky"; Dave Fry was "Spick". We went to the pictures to see films like *Blackboard Jungle* and go to Upminster recreation ground and hang about in the park-keeper's hut, pretending to be gangsters.'

Ian's friends and classmates were not about to start calling him 'Severn' just because he fancied the idea, and the name failed to catch on. In his frustration, Ian pushed himself even further into the character and persistently promoted himself as a hoodlum. Becoming ever more resourceful, he turned to petty crime. 'I was an outlaw at High Wycombe,' insisted Ian. 'I was as hard as nails, as tough as fuck. Resilient. I got a reputation as being a naughty boy, smoking, nicking. I had keys to every room in the school. I used to raid the desks for porno, 'cos nobody's gonna grass up that the porno's gone missing, and put it back in the desks again on Sunday night.'

A contemporary of Ian's at the Royal Grammar School was Ed Speight, later to become a dependable sideman in various musical ventures. One episode that stuck in Speight's mind was when he and Ian broke into the Officers' Training Corps signals hut to steal a long-wave radio set. 'I would never nick anything like a thief,' said Ian, 'it was more like nicking a radio for the weekend, so I could listen to [Radio] Luxembourg.' A long-wave set also enabled Ian and Ed to listen to *Voice of America Jazz Hour* and introduced them to New Orleans jazz and the music of Louis Armstrong and Jelly Roll Morton. 'In that closed society of boarding school,' observed Ian, 'you get people, complete nutters, who are interested in one narrow little area of music. I got the bug for music.'

One record that made a big impact on Ian and a few other boys at the Royal Grammar School was Lonnie Donegan's frantic recording of 'Rock Island Line', which topped the UK hit parade in January 1956. Donegan, who was famously crowned

'The King of Skiffle', played the kind of music that offered Ian and musical lightweights everywhere a viable alternative to more demanding styles. Skiffle music placed its emphasis on the rhythmic and vocal elements of the song, the only 'real' instrument deployed being a lightly strummed guitar. Ian went skiffle-crazy and fancied himself as a singer. School House already boasted a couple of budding musicians, so what could be simpler?

Envisaging a future in showbiz, Ian engineered a school skiffle group but was quickly relegated to washboard, which he scraped rhythmically alongside guitarists Warwick 'Rocky' Prior and John 'Jack' Dawes. Robin Sackett plucked the ubiquitous tea-chest bass. 'Dury had rhythm, no question,' says Warwick Prior. 'He could drum his fingers on the billiard table cover in a way that I quite admired, but he could not sing in tune. He was lucky to be in.' Considering Ian's love of word-play, it is surprising that this incarnation of the skiffle group never acquired an official name. Perhaps they couldn't agree on one, but the group became quite popular around the school, performing such songs as 'It Takes a Worried Man (To Sing a Worried Song)' and their 'tour de force', 'Jesse James'.

By May 1956, when the traditional school photograph was taken, Ian, just fourteen, was sporting a full 'Tony Curtis' hairstyle and a defiant expression. It is quite possible that he had just glimpsed a photograph of Elvis Presley, who was electrifying the hit parade that week with 'Heartbreak Hotel'. With the advent of Elvis, Lonnie Donegan had a serious rival and the music-obsessed boys of School House a new hero. If Presley's 'Heartbreak Hotel' lit the touch-paper for Ian and his closest chums, 'Jailhouse Rock' would create an explosion. 'The others didn't all get it – they were busy playing football,' says Prior, 'but Dury and I did. It threw us together in a weird way because we weren't particularly fond of each other.'

Ian was a huge fan of Presley's early records, but in order to establish an identity he needed to find his own Elvis – someone who was not quite as famous, not quite as handsome and not quite as good. That summer, when a skinny American underdog named Gene Vincent struck gold with 'Be Bop a Lula', Ian discovered his personal rock 'n' roll idol and future role model. Gene Vincent became Ian's crusade, and he championed Vincent's music with evangelical zeal. The twenty-one-year-old Vincent had all the credentials that appealed to Ian: his hair was a mess of black curls, he had a light mournful voice and, co-incidentally, a gammy left leg, although Ian claimed to be unaware of this crucial detail at the time.

'I bought all his singles until he got a saxophone,' said Ian. 'I went off him after "Say Mama". Same as when Elvis Presley got a saxophone. "King Creole?" Funny how you know when you're that young. Elvis Presley and the saxophone didn't go together, nor with Gene. I loved saxophones with Little Richard, but not with Elvis and Gene. Maybe it's something to do with rockabilly purity. It sounded like a moody addition, the wrong instrument. Later I got into rockabilly music, and you very rarely hear a saxophone, not with that Norfolk Virginia vibe.'

The merits of various rock 'n' roll singers were frequently debated by Ian and his cohorts. 'I remember arguing with Dury about Gene Vincent,' says Warwick Prior. 'I thought he was OK, but a bit empty and leftfield. I was more turned on to Elvis and Little Richard. Only a few of us had discovered records in 1956: me, Ian and a boy called Robert Trick. It was a minority thing.' Ian spent his free time going through the racks at Percy Prior's record shop in High Wycombe. Short of cash, he had to be selective about his purchases, but it was quite possible for the obsessive fan to build a collection in other ways in the days before record shops separated sleeves and discs, storing the latter behind the counter to deter theft. Enlisting day boy C. D. 'Seedy' Leach to purloin for him only the choicest rock 'n' roll platters, Ian increased his collection. When he returned to school with the latest Gene Vincent LP under his arm, the music master was only too pleased to grant Ian access to the school record player so he could 'listen to music'.

Rock 'n' roll provided Ian with an outlet. In the school summer holiday of 1956, he went home to Upminster with the sound of 'Be Bop a Lula' ringing in his ears, planning to form yet another skiffle group. This time, he would recruit his Upminster friends and personally alternate between washboard and tea-chest bass. Long-term buddy Barry Anderson, whose credentials included entertaining the kids at Saturday-morning pictures, would play guitar and sing lead vocals. A friend named Martin played second guitar, and Jo Dobson, who was head girl at the local Gaynes Secondary School, was called in to sing the popular 'Freight Train'. The entire group, again name-less, cruised around Upminster in a lilac Austin 7 that belonged to a friend and made their debut in a church hall by the Wantz Bridge in Cranham. It was Ian's first public performance.

Flash clothes, fast cars and all things American obsessed Ian, but nothing sparked his adolescent imagination quite as effec-tively as the Teddy Boy scene. Resplendent in their Edwardian-style draped jackets and drainpipe trousers, 'Teds' ushered in the first significant youth uprising of post-war Britain, and the public were duly warned about these 'juvenile delinquents' who carried bicycle chains and flick-knives and would cut you up as soon as look at you. When their rebellious antics made the news, Ian was impressed. Much to his delight, his corner of Essex boasted a sizeable Teddy Boy population. One can only imagine his emotions as he gazed in awe at the youthful arro-gance of these young, strutting peacocks commanding attention in Romford's market square. He hero-worshipped them and quickly attempted to ape their stance and echo their rhyming slang, much to the embarrassment of his pal Barry, who still remains pissed off for being thrown out of the local cinema because Ian, aged fourteen, was making too much noise during

Rock Around the Clock. Or perhaps, as Ian would later claim, releasing pigeons from underneath his overcoat and 'disrupting the performance'.

To have been ejected from the cinema, especially during a rock 'n' roll movie, was hard currency for Ian. He traded on it for weeks. Many years later, in a book entitled *Cool Cats – 25 Years of Rock 'n' Roll Style*, in a chapter entitled 'Razors Out at Rock Riot', Ian would write:

> The sideburns are coming on: less bum fluff, more little black ones. Anzora white preparation for the haircut. Water on first – sides only if the grapes look healthy. Dreadful Randolphs [Randolph Scott(s) = spots] round the corners of the mouth . . . grey worsted trousers with 12" bottoms done on my mum's hand-drive Singer, yellow and black check shirt and horrible one button jacket bought by mistake in Romford market when the geezer put his arm across the door and convinced me the pale green cardboard was just as smart as grey Donegal tweed . . .

Returning to the corridors of School House with a bootlace tie secreted in his kitbag, Ian creatively embellished his holiday experiences, including the story of being 'barred from the Ritz, Romford'! No one doubted him when he described his first, furtive sexual experiences in Upminster Park with a girl named Susan Herrick who refused to let him 'go all the way', but his tales of being accepted into a local Teddy Boy gang were taken with a pinch of salt. 'He had a "Tony Curtis" with a DA ['duck's arse'], an outrageous haircut in Great Britain at that time,' recalls Ed Speight. 'The headmaster, Mr Tucker, could never pronounce Ian's name properly; he would roar, "Doer-reee, you wretched boy!"'

With his hair combed into a greasy quiff, Ian persisted with the image, maintaining he was now a fully fledged 'Ted', a claim made plausible by his density of beard. Even at fourteen, Ian was able to cultivate a convincing pair of 'sideboards', and belittled those of a fairer complexion. When he encountered Warwick Prior and a friend in the gym changing rooms, Ian exclaimed, 'Ah! Pat Coates and Rocky Prior! I could hear your highfaluting conversation from around the corner. It's a shame your voices haven't broken! No pubic hair yet?'

Despite his often tiresome behaviour, Ian did exert a certain influence over his contemporaries. He told them about the little tailor's shop in High Wycombe where they could get their trousers tapered; the cinema at the back of town that showed the sleazy movies and the precise location of the dirty book-shop. 'Here was clearly a chap who recognized style,' says Prior. 'He once returned to school in what he called a "denim rock suit". It was a pair of jeans and a short jeans jacket, which were very rare in those days. He'd slip it on occasionally, if he got the opportunity. I grew my hair quite long, significantly under his influence. I learnt about it all from Dury.'

When Prior introduced Ian to an Aylesbury friend by the name of Tim Francis, who had an old drum kit he wanted to offload, Ian scraped up the money and set about practising the rhythms of his beloved rock 'n' roll records. With Ed Speight and John Owen Smith on guitars and Ian on drums – one of which, he told the others, was 'made from human skin' – the school skiffle group of the previous year evolved into the Black Cat Combo. Brimming with pride, Ian had momentarily become bigger than the polio that had dogged his childhood, but his accomplishment would be supplanted by a new strain of torture – the relentless punishment meted out by the school prefects.

The dormitory after dark provided Ian with a captive audience for his saucy tales and inspired narrations. These were usually stories from a book called *Ghostly Tales to Be Told*, which contained the scary story of 'The Wendigo', a favourite of Ian's. He had now found his forte as a narrator and raconteur, 'brilliant, without parallel in School House,' says Warwick Prior. But when the prefects burst in and disturbed Ian's midnight court, he was in trouble. Summoned to a prefects' meeting, Ian was made to stand on the stairs while they deliberated. 'The main reason for it all was so they could beat the shit out of him,' adds Prior. 'It wasn't uncommon for a strapping rugby player to run across the room with a leaded slipper to beat you on the arse six times. Life is different today, but back then you could be liberally slippered without any kind of regulation. Dury did garner some kind of sympathy for his situation, but he got beaten with the rest of us, even though he had a calliper up to his bum, which they had to avoid.'

To be ritually beaten by boys not much older than himself was an affront to Ian's dignity. To be asked to 'bend over' at the age of sixteen was incredibly humiliating and it had an enormous emotional impact on him. Possibly the prefects had been waiting for years to exact their revenge, and it was not until Ian was out of short trousers – and his calliper was no longer on display to serve as a reminder of his disability – that they felt they could let fly with the slipper. But the more Ian was bullied and abused by the prefects, the more he became unperturbed by physical violence. Compared with the trauma of polio and those early years at Chailey, being beaten was relatively tolerable. When his tormentors realized this, they turned to psychological torture. Ian cracked. 'The prefects decided that hitting me didn't hurt me,' recalled Ian, 'although I found it mentally pretty mind-fucking. I had a strange time with them. 800 boys, I was the only disabled one. Every Wednesday night they had a thing called the prefects' meeting, which is seventeen-year-olds sitting round in their study. They'd give you a trial and sentence you to the slipper, the size-eleven gym shoe. You'd bend over an armchair, and they'd whack the fuck out of you. Well, it hurt like fuck, but nothing hurts that much that you'd give up the ghost for it, or cry. Pain of that kind wasn't particularly frightening to me, although it was still frightening. That went on and then they went to the headmaster and they said, "Look, he doesn't feel pain, he's got polio. We can't beat it out of him, so can we mind-fuck him instead please?"'

According to Ian, the prefects now punished him with impositions, such as being forced to learn and recite long pieces of poetry. Any slip on Ian's part would result in the punishment being extended, and he would have to start reciting the poem all over again. 'Basically what they said was, "Can we give him essays and learning tasks rather than hitting him all the time? Like sentencing him to a week of sitting in the box room learning poetry, and if he gets it wrong, he adds that on to the end of his sentence." So they sentenced me to seven days of learning the poem . . . "Seasons of mist and mellow fruitfulness, close bosom friend to the maturing sun . . ." The other one was: "In Xanadu did Kubla Khan . . ." They're the only two fucking poems I know! I got it wrong after fourteen lines, and they added it on to the end of the sentence. This went on for days. I was thinking I had a life stretch ahead of me. They'd got me. I felt fucking bad.'

One night, after a particularly distressing detention, sitting amongst the suitcases and packing trunks in the box room, a tearful Ian encountered Alan 'Taffy' Davis, housemaster of Uplyme. 'I went over to the main school,' recalled Ian. 'I had a key to get in . . . and I was walking down the corridor while everyone was sleeping, crying my eyes out. The bastards had got me. They'd fried my head. I thought it was going to be going on and on and on, and these cunts were sitting there going: "Go on, what's the next bit?" With the headmaster's sanction . . . a teacher found me. Nice chap, family man, totally unperverted, always wore a red tweedy jacket, he didn't always wear his gown, bit of an item. He came out of a room and saw me crying. He said, "What's the matter?" I said, "They've got me." He put his arm round me and hugged me. Then he put a stop to it.' Ed Speight believes that the prefects' message to Ian was: 'Don't open your big mouth so much.' Taffy Davis was reckoned to be 'quite a nice bloke', and shortly afterwards the word went round: 'Lay off.'

The prefects' punishments had become too much for Ian, and at the age of fifteen he ran away from school. Peggy and her sister Molly were astonished when he arrived on the doorstep one afternoon, having made the rail and bus journey from High Wycombe to Upminster unaided. After welcoming him home, they told him he should phone the headmaster to explain his whereabouts. Molly Walker offered to drive Ian back to school the following Monday. 'The head didn't dare to say anything to me,' says Molly. 'I wasn't exactly formidable but I happened to work in the local education office, and he didn't quite know what position I held.'

Ian's relationship with the headmaster was further soured by an incident that occurred in the dining hall one Friday. Fish, which Ian hated, was being served, and the headmaster's wife, who assisted with lunch, handed Ian his plate of food. When he pushed it away, Mrs Tucker chose to imagine that he had thrown the fish at her and immediately called for her husband. Edmund Tucker had already had more of Ian than he could stand. Fuming, he entered the dining hall, roaring 'Doer-reee!' As Ian looked up, Tucker hit him hard, sending him flying across the room. Fellow pupils looked on in disbelief as the school's high-profile cripple lay writhing on the floor. When Peggy and Molly heard about the incident, they resolved to make an official complaint against Tucker, but Ian asked that the matter be dropped. 'I want him to live with it,' was Ian's rationale.

Coming on top of the harsh treatment he had received from the prefects, the fish episode crowned the unhappiest period of Ian's life, but it gave him something to hate and strengthened his resolve for the difficult times that lay ahead. 'I hate those bastards, those guys,' said Ian. 'I can still remember some of their names. I was fifteen, it was horrendous, it really did my head in. They were seventeen-year-old proto-fascists, guardians of Thatcherism, before it began. But I beat 'em. I saw them as the enemy. I knew they were wrong. I was seen as the figurehead of some imaginary gang.' In his mind, though, Ian *was* the leader of a juvenile gang. It was the image he promoted, and any sympathy he might have merited due to his disability was wiped out by his obstreperous behaviour. Although his knowledge of rock 'n' roll did earn him a smidgen of credibility, nobody believed his wild tales of running with the Upminster crew. He was generally regarded as pathetic, but the more others dismissed him, the more resourceful he became.

Ian's final, harrowing year at the Royal Grammar School was relieved by isolated moments of pleasure, particularly when Bill Dury created a stir by showing up in the Rolls-Royce. Ian was so proud of his dad. In 1958, at the time of one of his visits to the school, he was looking after the car driven by Danny Kaye in the movie *Me and the Colonel*. This enabled Ian to obtain Kaye's autograph, which he proudly displayed in his wallet. Bill's involvement with film industry work would culminate in a driving role in the 1964 movie *The Yellow Rolls-Royce*, but for now the Kaye association was enough to fuel Ian's dreams.

Ian kept a mental note of the famous lives that had fleetingly or indirectly touched his family. George Bernard Shaw . . . Noël Coward . . . Danny Kaye … the list grew. Of course, Ian never met any of these legends, but he imagined they had somehow played a part in his own destiny. Any tenuous association with celebrity would be exploited whenever the opportunity arose. He never forgot the time he saw Richard Burton in *Othello* from the front row of the Old Vic at the age of fifteen. Many would get to hear of it. It was as if Burton had entered Ian's life.

It was Peggy who arranged this and other theatre visits during the school holidays, including a concert by 1950s heart-throb Johnnie Ray at the London Palladium. She always allowed Ian to take a friend, usually Barry Anderson. For Ian's 1958 Christmas treat, Peggy obtained tickets to the London production of *West Side Story* at Her Majesty's Theatre, Haymarket, starring George Chakiris and Chita Rivera. 'Ian loved it, obviously,' says Barry, 'gang fights and music!' That evening, the two sixteen-year-olds made arrangements to meet Peggy, who was already in town. In a pub near the theatre, Ian struck up a conversation with various members of the cast who were on a break. An American actor asked Ian if he was going to the show. 'He's a nice bloke,' observed Barry, to which Ian replied, 'Fucking queer.'

Peggy was still hoping that Ian would pass his GCE exams and go on to university. He certainly possessed the brains, but lacked the inclination. 'Ian didn't see the point,' says Ed Speight. 'German, for instance, you'd think Ian would have been good at languages, but he didn't like the teacher. He took it at O-level but didn't pass. Thank God! I couldn't bear to have heard Ian mouthing off in German!'

'There were some nice teachers there,' conceded Ian. 'Runswick was a nice geezer, one or two more. If there hadn't have been, I might have got slung out. It was touch and go a few times.' It was housemaster 'Beaky' Runswick who on one occasion caught Ian demonstrating his much-acclaimed ability to spit. 'Ian could gob in an arc over telegraph wires,' recalls Warwick Prior. 'Runswick shouted: "Dury! I hope my eyes deceived me!"'

Ian was rebelling against education because he could. 'I think they knew I was fairly bright and I wasn't conforming to the rest of it,' said Ian. 'I just didn't do anything in any of the other classes. There was nothing they could do. It was difficult for them.' Frustrated by his lack of progress, the school authorities sent Ian to a psychiatrist who would try to fathom his under-achievement. At a surgery in Grays, Essex, a Miss Boniface subjected him to a number of tests and concluded that he was definitely not lacking in grey matter. 'You're very intelligent,' she told him. 'I know,' Ian replied, 'what's the problem?' Miss Boniface explained that she had to do her tests for Essex County Council. Ian told her, 'I'm not particularly disturbed, I'm quite happy, but I'd much rather be at home.'

'Mum never discouraged my artistic side,' said Ian, 'but I think she was disappointed about my school career. She couldn't understand that at all.' Years later, Ian found his school reports and wasn't surprised to discover teachers' comments such as 'extremely weak'. But his mother had only wanted 'the best' for him and hoped he'd do well. 'There's no blame attached. My mum's whole hopes in her heart were that I would be a lawyer or something, that I would go and use my brains. It was an academically brilliant school, I could have done well, I could have been a lawyer, but I wanted to go to art school.'

'I'm a Mockney, in the sense that my mum spoke beautifully and my dad didn't,' continued Ian. 'Dad would always tell me to sound my aitches, because he would worry about it, whereas my mum's lot, who were Bohemians, didn't. "Art school?" they would say. "Lovely!" My dad came to see me in hospital when I was seventeen, to have my appendix out. He was worried about my hair. I had big sideboards down here. He bought me an electric razor. He wanted me to be straight, but my mum's family didn't give a shit.'

Ian's 'Aunt Moll', who had helped him get into the Royal Grammar School, harboured a certain amount of regret about Ian's time there. 'Like Chailey, it was also my suggestion. Neither of them was very successful. I thought Ian would get a decent start at High Wycombe, but other things went against it. They never said much to me about it at the time, but afterwards I felt terrible. It was unfortunate.'

Ian passed three GCE O-level examinations: Art, English Literature and English Language, just enough to get him to art college. Just before his exit from school, there was one final, dramatic incident. His old sparring partner, Warwick 'Rocky' Prior, had been in trouble. 'The headmaster wrote to my father,' recalls Prior, 'saying, "I believe your son may be a Teddy Boy." He was reluctant for me to come back, but, before I left, I punched Dury's lights out. He'd been at it again, bullying, something to do with that poor bugger Busby. It was the end of term, we weren't coming back, so I gave Dury a sharp uppercut, and he went down like a sack of coals. That was the last time I saw him, except for one occasion on Highgate Hill many years afterwards, around 1969. He was coming up the path, limping. I stepped into the bushes.'

4

Nude Books and Aunties

Walthamstow, 1959. The 1950s had been a bleak, black-and-white decade, but Ian's London was about to explode with colour, although not officially 'swing' for a while. Within three months of leaving the Royal Grammar School, he had become a student at Walthamstow School of Art, an annex of South West Essex College. It was a tiresome, daily journey from Upminster by public transport, but worth every mile. In early October, just three weeks into his course, he sat in the life class, drawing a naked girl named Julia. He considered her to be gorgeous, not unlike Brigitte Bardot and just as unattainable. However, in the interval, as he was quietly shading his drawing, Julia approached. 'Do you want to come and play with me this evening?' she asked. Ian's pencil snapped in two. 'Not many!' he replied.

At the age of seventeen, after a long period of anguish, he had fallen into a world that he'd always suspected did exist but now he was sure. 'I went to Walthamstow School of Art as quickly as I could,' Ian told me. 'It was partly the lifestyle that attracted me. Van Gogh, Lautrec, Renoir. I knew about the Bohemian lifestyle. I used to draw all the time and I knew I wanted to go to art school. I didn't harbour ideas about being a painter as much as drawing and having that lifestyle. It was very easy to get into Walthamstow with three O-levels.'

In the post-war years, Britain's art colleges brought together students from all strata of society in a way that the universities did not, helping to create a social mix that would revolutionize popular culture. By the early 1960s, 'art school' had become a right of passage for the aspiring pop musician, including Lennon, Townshend et al., and Ian was similarly attracted. College discipline was often lax, affording the opportunity to knock off early for group practice sessions and enjoy a lie-in the morning after. Artists and musicians also shared an obsession with 'image', and Ian was more obsessed than most. Most importantly, the appreciation of art and music was conveniently subjective. Anyone could hold an opinion, and those of a more forceful personality could hold court.

At Walthamstow, Ian and his arty chums maintained a high profile and gently mocked those studying more prosaic courses. Ian's friend Barry Anderson, who attended the college to study the hotel and catering trade, was equally as excited as Ian about the prospects the new decade offered. 'It was our new world,' says Barry, 'rag weeks, jazz concerts and of course the girls were starting to wear sexy clothes . . . and at the same moment everything was becoming more radical with the protest movement. It was the birth of a social revolution.' But Barry noticed that Ian and his paint-smeared gang ruled the roost. 'He was usually sitting in the refectory with his arms around two girls,' recalls Barry. '"Hey Gus," Ian would shout, "this is Bumbly Number One and this is Bumbly Number Two!"'*

Ian met like-minded people at Walthamstow to whom his physical disability was irrelevant. They were more infatuated with all things modern: art, jazz, marijuana – 'the cosa nova' as Ian would later refer to it. This was 'the Beat Era', and the influence of American 'beat generation' writers like Jack Kerouac and Allen Ginsberg was now reaching young, free-thinking col-

---

* Ian took the name from *The Bumblies*, a 1950s BBC television puppet series for children, devised by Michael Bentine, an early star of *The Goon Show*. The Bumblies were triangular-shaped aliens known simply as One, Two and Three. Ian would have watched the programmes just prior to starting at the Royal Grammar School in 1954.

lege students and arty types on this side of the Atlantic. Ian soaked it all up and immersed himself in the lifestyle, becoming spellbound by the secret corners of Soho where Bohemian style flourished. Acting on a tip, he visited a café bar in Old Compton Street in search of 'Ironfoot Jack',* a legendary Soho character. 'I met him,' recalled Ian. 'He was a real Bohemian: long white hair, cape, iron foot. I fell in love with the whole idea of being a Bohemian, before they said "beatnik".'

Inspired by 'Ironfoot' Jack Neave and certain French painters, Ian began to refer to himself as 'Toulouse' (Lautrec). This time his self-appointed nickname would catch on. It actually suited his diminutive stature and latest accoutrement, a gnarled walking cane. His twisted body and strange gait, enhanced by a streetwise sense of humour, won him many admirers amongst fellow students of both sexes. He liberally dished out the rhyming slang, and, as his confidence increased, his emotional anguish evaporated. He was no longer a freak; he was the one who cracked the jokes and got the laughs. Thus he became an influential member of the clique, proposing outings to far-flung pubs where live jazz held sway.

The creatures Ian encountered on the art/jazz/beat circuit furthered his obsession with 'looking good', or at least unconventional. He recalled going out with one girl who was 'a Modernist'. 'We used to go down the Two Puddings Club in Stratford. She had eighteen buttons down her herringbone coat and an astrakhan collar, Lebanese points. That kind of sartorialism I thought was really brilliant. Yellow stovepipe trousers. Yeah, I'll fucking 'ave some of that.'

Back in the leafy enclave of Waldegrave Gardens, an outpost of the commuting pinstripe and umbrella brigade, Ian's appearance was unusual. His hair was quite long for the time, and with

---

* Professor J. R. Neave, known as 'Ironfoot Jack' on account of his metal-soled orthopaedic boots, was a lapsed academic who bought and sold household tat around Soho throughout the mid-twentieth century.

his straggly beard, duffel coat and bell-bottom jeans he was bound to raise eyebrows as he limped to and from Upminster tube station. Peggy grew tired of avoiding neighbours who enquired: 'Mrs Dury, is your son a tramp?' Ian's behaviour was also becoming progressively more bizarre; when the house became too small to accommodate his eccentricity, he was consigned to the attic. Fascinated by petty crime, he developed a penchant for stealing signs. 'He would walk in somewhere and, if there was a sign or a notice, anything with words on, it would disappear under his coat,' recalls Barry Anderson. 'Road signs, London Transport signs, the attic was full of them. It was his den until his mother found out, and she went absolutely mad. The attic was made out of bounds.'

Peggy decided that Ian had to be annexed. Ever the pragmatist, she acquired a two-wheel Bluebird caravan for 400 guineas and parked it in the back yard. In it, Ian would be allowed to create his own world. He installed a portable oven and a wind-up gramophone and stuffed old socks into the air vents in an attempt at soundproofing. He would be called into the house for meals and the occasional bath, but he otherwise lived the life of a crazy art student, playing rock 'n' roll records and making a mess. West Essex became his turf, and London Underground his favoured mode of transport. The District Line, which terminated at Upminster, provided access to a string of social hot spots along its route into the East End.

In February 1960, aged seventeen, Ian popped into the Elm Park Jazz Club, where he met a fifteen-year-old aspiring beatnik by the name of Patricia Few. In her hand-knitted 'sloppy' pullover and tight black jeans, Pat certainly looked the part. As Terry Lightfoot and his Jazzmen pumped out the traditional jazz, Ian summoned up the courage to ask her for a dance. Initially, Ian's advances came to little, but that Easter he bumped into Pat again, on the third annual Aldermaston march. As members of the Campaign for Nuclear Disarmament, Ian and Pat were fully paid-up pacifists, although Ian's commitment to the cause may have had as much to do with collecting the badges as any strong political conviction. Due to his limited mobility, he covered most of the CND march to Trafalgar Square on the back of his friend Terry Malloy's scooter. Pat followed close behind on foot.

Pat Few would become Ian's girlfriend and close companion for the next three-and-a-half years. She lived in Dagenham with her mother, 'a real East Ender' who impressed Ian with her rhyming slang and would refer to him as either 'Knitty Crutch' or 'Old Mr Shagnasty', which were actually terms of affection. Ian and Pat would hang out in beatnik pubs like Finch's in Goodge Street and the Duke of York in Rathbone Street and visit cafés such as the Nucleus, the Gyre and Gimble and the House of Sam Widges. 'We just did mad things on the street,' says Pat, 'then we got drunk and went home on the tube. I was a little cockney girl, and Ian was posh. I became posh later, and he became a cockney!'

Despite his boasts,* Ian had still not fulfilled his number one teenage priority, but the waiting was almost over. It happened that summer, on a camping trip to Cornwall with Pat. As weekend ravers, they were drawn to the West Country by the romantic notion of sleeping rough and, as Ian recalled, 'hanging about in bushes, being ejected by the council.' In Newquay, Ian and Pat lost their virginity to each other under a crude tent that was little more than a piece of old canvas nailed to a tree, but it afforded them just enough privacy.

Cornwall was home to the burgeoning music scene of the new left. Acoustic folk and blues, which supplanted the now-dead skiffle scene, provided the soundtrack for a generation of roaming radicals. In the environs of Newquay, Ian bumped into two prominent exponents of the acoustic vibe – banjoist Clive Palmer, later to found the Incredible String Band, and Wizz

---

* In 1998, Ian told the *Independent*'s Deborah Ross: 'I lost me virginity at fourteen on Upminster Common. Gorgeous it was.'

Jones, a precocious guitar talent – both of whom entertained the weekend beats who made the journey to the West Country by hitching lifts. 'When I was with Ian we never walked anywhere,' recalls Pat. 'I would be at the kerbside wiggling my hips, and Ian would be hiding behind a tree until someone stopped to pick us up. It would take twenty-four hours to get back to London, but it was all fun. We were madly in love.'

Ian invited Pat back to Waldegrave Gardens to meet Peggy and the aunts and show her his caravan. Within a few weeks Ian and Pat had devised a routine whereby Ian would enter the house by the front door and divert his mother's attention while Pat crept round the back and entered Ian's two-wheeler world. Then Ian would say 'goodnight' to his mum and join Pat for a night of passion in the caravan. The following day, usually a Sunday, Pat was invited for lunch. The two teenagers pretended that Pat had just arrived at number 12, but in fact she had simply freshened up in the caravan and knocked on the front door. It was, of course, a charade. Pat would then sit in the drawing room and Peggy would hand her a *Sunday Mirror*, saying, 'Here we are, Patsy, would you like to read this?' while Elisabeth and Molly fought over the *Observer*. If Pat didn't know the meaning of a word, Peggy would make her look it up in the dictionary. As a guest of Ian's mother and sisters, Pat minded her Ps and Qs and quietly observed them discussing cultural topics while coping with the onset of menopause. 'They were all wondering what they would do about Ian,' says Pat. 'He could be a bit of a pig.'

In 1961, the Pop Art exponent Peter Blake commenced teaching at Walthamstow School of Art. Born in Dartford, Kent, in 1932, Blake had studied at the Royal College of Art and become a part-time teacher at various colleges, including St Martin's School of Art, to supplement his income as a painter. 'What I did was very contrived and particular,' says Blake. 'By having three strings to my bow, being a painter, a part-time teacher and a graphic designer, it kept me independent of any one of them. I straddled the three. If I wanted to stop teaching, I could do design. I never had to paint, I never had to teach and I never had to do graphic design.'

Blake's artistic influence would soon be acknowledged in a BBC TV documentary about Pop Art, entitled *Pop Goes the Easel*. On his first morning at Walthamstow he was charged with taking an outdoor sketching class. Unable to locate his students, Blake walked out of the college and up the hill, where he found Ian and others in the Bell public house. Ian was expecting a bollocking, but instead, Blake bought them all drinks. At once, he formed a common bond with his students, which was to become an important factor in their progress. It was no longer a case of young students versus the establishment – their mentor was right there alongside them, and, for Ian, the feeling was righteous.

'I was still only twenty-nine,' recalls Peter Blake, 'and I would be at Ronnie Scott's the night before, turning up with a hangover, not much older than the students. What was exciting was that they were working-class ruffians. Joe Snowden . . . Bill West . . . these were tough characters, big hard youths. One of the students was a market trader in Walthamstow. It was a fascinating mix, very much a social phenomenon after the war ended. Suddenly after the ditch of no art, when people went to the war, a generation had a chance to get a grant and go to art school. Ian would never have had the opportunity before the war. It was as if someone was opening a book and saying: "This is a possibility." Ian's crowd was the extension of this phenomenon.'

Ian's imagination was certainly triggered by Blake's teaching methods and also those of another tutor at Walthamstow, Fred Cuming, who would say, 'If you're into football, draw footballers, if you're into car racing, draw cars. Draw whatever you're into.' Another key influence was Bill Green, the artist who coached Tony Hancock in *The Rebel* and showed him how to use a bicycle to paint with. Green was a big action painting star whose art 'performances' reinforced Ian's belief that entertainment was an integral factor in good art and that rules were made to be broken. A particular favourite of Ian's was Green's huge painting 'Billy Bunter Promenades Himself in Normandy'.

Peter Blake confirms Green's influence: 'Bill became famous for riding a bicycle over a picture, which was parodied in *The Rebel*, but in fact he didn't ever ride a bicycle over a picture; he laid a board on the floor, spread bitumen on it and held the bicycle over the board, manoeuvring the back wheel to spray the paint – action paintings. When the press got hold of it they said, "Would you ride your bike over it?" and of course Bill obliged, and the myth built up. At St Martin's, he set light to one of his pictures at the bottom of the deep stairwell, which became like a chimney. Flames would shoot up four or five storeys! Eventually, the fire became part of the work, but the idea was to burn the surface of the canvas.'

'Peter Blake and I are good mates,' said Ian in 1995. 'The kind of work a few of us were into related to being able to enjoy things that were popular rather than going down the bleeding library all the time. Pop Art, I suppose you could call it. Jazz was involved. It was OK to be rude or common in our art. Nobody was aiming to be academically clever. I was into jazz then, more than anything – the Johnnie Burch Octet at the Plough in Ilford with Ginger Baker and Jack Bruce, Don Rendell, Tommy Whittle at the Bell in Walthamstow, the local pub for the art school. At the Ship in Bermondsey we used to see a drummer called Lenny Livesey – he was really good. I was always into checking it out. All of us were insane about Ornette Coleman. My tastes were towards modern, free-form jazz, Albert Ayler, Don Cherry, Pharoah Sanders . . .'

Although Ian clearly loved jazz, this complex, demanding music was not easily replicated. He was still keen to be in a band, but learning the saxophone would require dedication, so

Ian decided to stick to rock 'n' roll, quite happy to try and emulate the style of Gene Vincent or Eddie Cochran. But even rock involved a certain level of commitment if the guitar, for example, was to be mastered. Although it is doubtful whether Ian's left hand could have coped with the fretboard, he was not about to submit himself to months of practice. He wanted a more immediate result and chose to concentrate on drums and vocals. But whilst Ian's rudimentary percussion skills were OK, he was unfortunately not a natural singer. 'Every time I tried to do a bit of skiffle, they told me my singing was out to lunch,' confessed Ian. 'It was in another key or whatever. So I did a little bit of bongos. We used to have these mad voodoo ceremonies. I hung out with Terry Day.'

Terry Day was a Dagenham rascal with an eye for the girls. Arriving at Walthamstow in February 1962, he made a big impression on Ian. Heavily into modern jazz and the action paintings of Jackson Pollock, Terry had started his record collection at the age of five. With help from his older brother, he learnt to play an assortment of musical instruments by the time he was fifteen. His first love was drums, and he found himself giving Ian some early tuition. 'We were always hitting things with paint brushes, bashing out rhythms and making a noise,' recalls Terry, who would go on to be one of Ian's closest pals.

Ian spent four years at Walthamstow, during which he received a travelling grant to enable his commute from Upminster. For the first two years, Peggy kept him in meals and clothing, but he later enjoyed an income from part-time teaching, as the Essex education authority insisted students gained some practical experience by taking four-week teaching courses in local schools. Ian was despatched to Culverhouse Secondary Modern School for Boys in South Ockendon, where he would teach art two days a week, qualifying him for a grant to continue his studies at Walthamstow, where he had his eye on an Intermediate Arts and Crafts Diploma. Peggy was proud of Ian's status of 'student teacher' and bought him a smart sports jacket and slacks from local clothiers Meakers. While at Culverhouse he befriended fellow teachers Barry White and Gordon Law, the piano-playing head of the art department who was about to experience the tweedy, academic ambience of 12 Waldegrave Gardens.

Ian had been trying to persuade his mother and aunts that he had enough talent to continue with his training. The formidable Aunt Elisabeth – the dominant Walker sister – summoned Gordon Law to give his professional assessment of Ian's artistic talents. Law, who remembers first seeing Ian 'rocking down Upminster High Street, supported by Pat Few and looking like a diminutive Captain Morgan, with flowing hair and maybe a beard', was interviewed as an 'art education expert'. He confirmed that Ian did possess a natural talent for painting. Somewhat encouraged, Peggy allowed Ian to use the attic as a makeshift studio. 'I used to think it was somewhat unjust that Ian had to limp up flights of stairs to a pokey garret,' says Gordon, 'while his cousins romped freely around the more accessible parts of the house.'

Gordon became a good friend, and he and Ian spent hours listening to jazz and reciting poetry. They made tapes for imaginary radio shows and dreamed of finding an outlet for their off-the-wall improvisations. When Gordon acquired a second-hand Bolex cine camera, they would spend Sundays making whacky black-and-white home movies in Peggy's back garden or the fields close to Barry White's house in Brentwood. 'Ian would stumble on the rugged terrain,' recalls Barry. 'I once tried to help him up, not in a patronizing way, but he gave me a mouthful. "I can fucking get up!" he roared. Ian was totally independent.'

Gordon Law's silent 8mm films were much in the style of Richard Lester's *The Running Jumping & Standing Still Film* (1959), featuring Spike Milligan and Peter Sellers. Law's troupe comprised himself and wife Ann, Barry and Barbara White, Mike Price and Ian and Pat. The films had no real plot, and the action consisted of the players running around and falling over repeatedly. Title boards were held up to the camera, announcing improvised sketches such as 'The Great Tortoise Hunt'. Ian was photogenic throughout and provided a couple of inspired Chaplinesque moments. Chubby and be-suited, he assumed the role of principal actor and could be seen giving direction to the other players. In one section of the film, he acted out the part of a western gambler, loading bullets into a six-gun. In another, he played a New York taxi driver in flat leather cap and was seen dashing in and out of the bushes in defiance of his disability.

Early in 1963, Walthamstow School of Art proposed over two dozen of its most promising students to the Royal College of Art. Walthamstow was a prime source of raw artistic talent and, largely due to the persistent networking of its tutors, was a principal conduit to the Royal College. The list of students put forward that year included: Alison Armstrong, Valerie Wiffen, Paul Babb, Joe Snowden, Bill West, Stanford Steele, Laurie Lewis, Terry Day and Ian Dury. Neither Ian nor Terry had much idea about the direction they wished to take, but they were sent for interviews during the three-day induction process. It was during that week that Ian first met Geoffrey Rigden, an art student from Somerset, also trying for one of the thirty available places. 'Where are you from, then?' Ian asked Rigden. 'Taunton,' he replied. 'Very well, then,' said Ian, 'I shall call you Taunton.'

The mid-1960s would represent a high-water mark in universal artistic expression, not to mention a social and sexual revolution. In Britain, it was an era that started with the Profumo scandal, the 'great train robbery' and, according to poet Philip Larkin, the birth of sexual intercourse 'between the end of the "Chatterley" ban / And The Beatles' first LP'. As acting social secretary at Walthamstow, Ian had already turned down the Beatles for a live appearance at the college dance in favour of jazz musician Tubby Hayes. 'We got heavily involved with rhyming slang and jazz,' said Ian. 'The little team we had going at Walthamstow carried on as a little team [at the Royal College]. They called us the Walthamstow Cockneys. A load of us got in – fourteen into the painting school, let alone the dress design department. There was a mass exodus for a further three years of jollification.' If Walthamstow had been Ian's creative kindergarten, the Royal College of Art would be one giant playground.

PART TWO

ASCENT

5

Swinging London

'Walk! Not bloody likely. I am going in a taxi.'
G. B. Shaw, *Pygmalion*, Act 3

Kensington, 1963. On 2 October, Ian began his studies at the Royal College of Art, working in the painting school, then housed in an annex adjacent to the Victoria and Albert Museum. Pop Art was still prominent, and Peter Blake, Ian's mentor from Walthamstow, was a part-time teacher at the college. Blake told his students 'to paint what they liked' and Ian obliged with a succession of 6B pencil drawings of nude pin-ups, dolly birds and Laurel and Hardy. Getting into the Royal College was the only thing Ian had aspired to in his life. 'It's the only achievement I've ever felt,' he said, 'a bit like going to the university of your choice. I'm really pleased I went there, I'm proud of it. I wouldn't have been able to learn about how to live as a person doing what they want to do if I hadn't gone there, allowing your determination and output to control the way things go – my nine and my five.'

For Peter Blake and his students, influences ranged from the American modernist painter Jasper Johns – famed for his many variations on the stars and stripes of the American flag – to the abstract expressionism of artists such as Larry Poons and Morris Louis. As one might expect, Ian took the opposite stance and favoured figurative paintings. Many hours were spent debating the merits of abstract versus figurative, as Geoff Rigden recalls: 'Ian and I were rivals in terms of taste, but we more than liked each other. We used to argue a lot. Ian was a good bloke to have an argument with. In fact, he was an argumentative cunt. He knew how to wind you up. And he'd end up agreeing with you and then he would say, "See, I was right!"'

Ian acknowledged Blake's influence and the 'American vibration' that was prevalent. The students' minds were open to enjoying themselves in common or garden ways; it was OK to paint pictures of your heroes, 'heroes' being the big word that Blake introduced. Popular entertainers such as Elvis Presley or Brigitte Bardot were typical subjects, in much the same way as American artist Andy Warhol had immortalized Marilyn Monroe on silkscreen and would later iconize Presley. 'I think that I opened a door for them and gave them licence to paint something other than a couple of apples on a plate,' says Peter Blake. 'It probably wouldn't have occurred to them to paint Elvis. It would have been banned subject matter, too vulgar.'

Ian was now desperate to leave home and live as close as possible to the Royal College. With Peggy's blessing, he clubbed together with his East End pals Terry Day and Alan Ritchie, a student in Dagenham but still part of the gang. They were joined by a second-year sculpture student from Blackburn by the name of Derrick Woodham. Together, they looked around for somewhere to rent. First stop was an estate agent in Notting Hill Gate, from where they were directed towards 144 Elgin Avenue, Maida Vale. The ground- and lower-ground-floor flat would become Ian's home for the next three years. For a fairly agreeable £42 a month, Ian and the lads could enjoy their independence and play jazz records at ear-splitting volume. 'Drums, clarinets and marijuana!' was how Ian described the cacophonous atmosphere, with the music of Charlie Mingus and Albert Ayler blasting out of every room. 'The bloke upstairs worked at London Airport,' recalled Ian. 'He used to wear those ear defenders they use to bring the planes down with. It was quite a noisy flat for some years.'

The room allocation at 144 reflected the social pecking order. Alan Ritchie was consigned to the basement; the reticent Derrick Woodham was given the small, middle room; Terry Day, perhaps the cheekiest member of the quartet, claimed the nice back room that overlooked the BBC studios in Delaware Road, where he laid polystyrene floor tiles, which Ian would frequently trip over. Ian, whether through sympathy or his forceful personality, was assigned the large, magnificently appointed front room with its bay-window overlooking the tree-lined Elgin Avenue. 'Nobody minded,' says Terry Day. 'We were all happy to be where we were.'

Geoff Rigden was a frequent visitor and would accompany Ian to the West End, where they would hang around the pubs of Fitzrovia and visit nightspots such as Ronnie Scott's and the Flamingo. Ian was Geoff's guide to Bohemia in London. 'I was from Somerset, and Ian knew Soho a bit,' says Rigden. 'In me, he got someone whom he could guide. If you were prepared to hang with Ian, he would lead the way. Because he couldn't get around fast, you had to sort of wait for him. Because I liked him, I was prepared to go at his speed. He always made it entertaining.'

London was now in full swing, and Peter Blake was a considerable influence on Ian and his chums in the area of sartorial style, flaunting the American 'college boy' look, achieved by shopping at Austin's in Shaftesbury Avenue – renowned purveyors of American button-down shirts and Ivy League jackets. Blake set the pace and Ian, who up until then was never seen without his duffel coat, tried to keep up. 'We went through a Bohemian phase, long hair, in the art school days,' said Ian, recalling the look he and his mates strove for at Walthamstow. 'By the time we were at the Royal College of Art we all dressed as much like bricklayers as possible: Tuf boots, checked shirts, rolled-up jeans and nice macs, rugged "working man today".

We looked more like an American painter would like to look. Not long hair and moustaches, not hippiefied.'

Soaking up diverse influences, Ian attended key concerts and cultural happenings as the lines between entertainment and art became blurred. One of the first shows he and his pals experienced was 'An Evening of British Rubbish' at the Comedy Theatre, featuring the 'madcap music' of the Alberts with 'Professor' Bruce Lacey, whose bizarre 'inventions' were certain to amuse the art school crowd. In October 1964, jazz saxophonist Roland Kirk's fourteen-night residency at Ronnie Scott's club in Gerrard Street was another crucial attraction, for which Ian and Terry Day managed to secure front-row seats. 'Kirk was swinging his saxophone backwards and forwards, almost touching our noses,' recalls Terry. 'In the interval we approached him and shook his hand – you have to remember Kirk was blind – he said, "I know you, you're the cats in the front row!" Ian was made up.'

In June 1965, Ian and his friend Barry White made their way to the Royal Albert Hall for 'Poets of the World', a galvanizing event at which leading American beat writers Gregory Corso, Allen Ginsberg and Lawrence Ferlinghetti performed. En route, Ian and Barry visited a number of pubs, including the Hoop and Toy, close to the Royal College. Meandering through Knightsbridge in search of a lavatory, Ian remembered that actress Kim Novak and her husband – the Upminster-born actor Richard Johnson – were honeymooning at the Hyde Park Hotel. 'I'm Kim Novak's brother,' Ian told the commissionaire as he unsuccessfully attempted to cross the threshold. Desperate to urinate, Ian and Barry turned into a quiet mews nearby, where they came across an antiques shop displaying a giant silver urn in its window. Finding the premises momentarily unguarded, Ian and Barry pissed into the urn before hot-footing it to the Albert Hall.

Throughout his time at the Royal College, Ian was an avid letter writer and often confided in his friend Gordon Law, who had now moved to Rayleigh in Essex to teach at Southend Art

College. Ian's letters to Gordon are full of rambling, abstract prose, but in between the whimsy they provide an insight into Ian's melancholic state, especially when *sans* girlfriend. In his careful lower-case printing, Ian pleaded to Gordon:

> Please forgive my apparent don't give a damn attitude. I do give a lot of damn. I am writing this and I don't know for sure even if I'll post it. I don't think you will condemn me outright for faults that I wish I didn't have, but sometimes the act of getting things done is beyond me. I have no chick at the moment and life in general is rough. I think perhaps the summer will bring a life worth living back to Dury. I have been working and thinking but without a dolly to be with, all I do comes back to me as shit. I am not as bad as I sound, but a big hangover and a lot of guilt is exaggerating the situation. I am looking forward to the future and the holiness of activity.

Wishing to escape the serial man-eaters who would 'invite you round for a spag-bol and a shag', Ian was desperate for a permanent girlfriend. Although Pat Few was still on the scene and often visited Ian at Elgin Avenue, her days as his girlfriend were numbered. Various women whom he thought might make a suitable partner were mentioned in further letters to Gordon Law. Prospective girlfriends included Sylvia and the previously courted Alison Armstrong, whom he referred to as 'Alice':

> Sylvia is ex- teacher of me at Walth I told you about before. She has young girl brat and husb. [who] has gone away with first year RCA potter name of Dawn. Goodly riddies (I think) but what of lovely Sylv? I see her a lot and snap her out with talk of my lust and other fantasies.

> . . . perhaps Alice will help. She is my friend of six years, through Walthamstow and now in the painting school with me. We suddenly took off our trousers last week and I have

a permanent stomach ache for she lives with an Indian
gentleman at Stewart Ray's house, and time must pass
before she can see me clearly, however. I will show you my
Alice of whom I am proud, by bowling down to Rayleigh
with her.

When told about this cryptic correspondence some forty
years later, Alison Armstrong was touched by Ian's affectionate
remarks. 'Hearing Ian saying "my Alice" was very pleasurable,'
says Alison. 'I've never heard the expression "took our trousers
off" before. It is nice to know he was proud of me. We never did
bowl down to Rayleigh.'

I would very much dig to bring Alice down to Rayleigh but
I may have to miss out there because her mean fellow may
not relinquish his cruel hold over her and I'm not going to
force the scene because then me and she won't be equal-
Stevens. I shall move down anyway, to see youse and it will
be soonly. Write and say when you will definitely be there
and I'll tell you when I'll definitely come. The thing is I
must finish 2 pictures to 'ease my mind' and I must also get
this magazine cheque to ease my ability to feel equal in the
eyes of men and also to have the satisfaction of getting you
stinking pissed on my money.

I had a long letter from Sylvia two days ago and she
says much of me and her. Ever so sad but bloody beautiful
and it scares me stiff. She's in Scotland at the moment
with her kid . . . before she went away, she came over here
and, as much for a giggle as for anything else, I gave her a
haircut. She began a dreadful weeping scene and to stop
all that we had a grand Hollywood type clinch . . . me
standing holding scissors and comb . . . her all hairy
shoulders and towels sitting near the wardrobe mirror . . .
a real gor blimey, but it cheered her up and I didn't even
feel soppy.

Ian's letter continued with reference to 'Janet Fagg', whom he had 'loved and lost', despite taking her to 'the wrestlies' [wrestling] at the Albert Hall. Ian closed his letter with: 'what is all this bloody Lennon Language? (It's really foul Will Burroughs influence). Mind it.'

Ian was feeling a little bit sorry for himself and expressed his money worries:

> I wrote a sad letter the last week, but I didn't post it as certain situations changed, then changed again. I'm up to the neck, or was until yesterday in terrible shits and monetary owings and dolly hang-ups . . . I got a council cheque yesterday at long last, which will see me through for a spell. Living out of other people's pockets always shits me up something terrible and until this loot arrived I was £30 in schnook. I have assets of around £50 to still arrive for an illustration I did and for major tasky holiday work.

In the autumn of 1965, Ian was pulled out of despondency when he met his future musical collaborator, Russell Hardy. Some years earlier, Russell had worked as a laboratory technician at South East Essex Technical College, where he had befriended Terry Day. The painfully shy Russell, who used to spend his meal breaks putting the college's Bechstein piano through its paces, went one night to see Ginger Baker play the Candlelight Club at the Plough public house. He struck up a conversation with Terry Day and before long they had formed a jazz trio with double-bassist Terry Holman, another 'mad' laboratory technician. Terry Day dragged Russell along to Elgin Avenue, where Ian was busy working on an illustration for *London Life* magazine, a commission that had been passed to him by Peter Blake. 'He was making a collage with drawings of famous musicians,' remembers Russell. 'It was meticulously set out. I talked to him and, Ian being Ian, I didn't have to say much. I felt at ease with him.'

Russell Hardy, then twenty-four and prematurely balding, worked in the East India Docks as a tally clerk and was 'often in a disgustingly pissed state', specially if there was an export shipment of Scotch Whisky going out. Every other Friday, Russell would visit Ian at Elgin Avenue. Eventually, Ian asked Russell, 'Can you give us a lift up the college?' It was the start of Russell's long career as Ian's unofficial chauffeur. If Russell wasn't around, Ian's preferred mode of transport was a taxi to Kensington, funded by his freelance drawing work. To avoid attention on arriving at the Royal College, Ian would have his cab stop at the Victoria and Albert Museum, so he could sneak into the adjoining Royal College painting school through a staff entrance. Occasionally, he would visit the V&A canteen, where a dinner lady by the name of Geraldine would supply free food and make a fuss of him.

Whenever Russell gave him a ride to college, Ian would drum on the dashboard and sing 'Tutti Frutti'. Russell had taken no previous interest in rock 'n' roll but quickly became familiar with the songs of Little Richard and Eddie Cochran. In return, Russell would enthral Ian with tales from the docks. 'My grandfather also worked there and he told me all the wrinkles,' says Russell. 'Ian was fascinated by the criminal fraternity, a bit like a schoolboy, so I told him stories about the bonded warehouses; how the dock workers would cleverly stack the lorries to conceal shortages; how the Customs officers would all be playing cards and say to me, "Come in, Mr Clerk, and have a waxer!" It was a huge tumbler of Scotch at nine o'clock in the morning, on the dockside. By lunchtime I was paralytic.'

Ian and Russell complemented each other perfectly and became almost mutually dependent. Ian was the front man, whose boisterous exterior opened doors at social gatherings, thus helping to draw Russell out of his shell. Russell, car at the ready, was Ian's mobility. 'Russell's motor was a terribly useful thing,' says Geoff Rigden, 'because Ian always wanted to go somewhere. We once went to the British Grand Prix at Goodwood. On the way back, Ian said, "Let's go to a party, it's in Romford!"' On many occasions, Russell was also Ian's legs, carrying him on his back up flights of stairs at parties that the gang gate-crashed. 'Ian grew up with a bunch of hooligans,' says Terry Day. 'We were all in our twenties, drinking and having a good time, but Ian's disability was no problem. We were coming home in the snow one night and he fell over, so I put him on my back and carried him home. He hated snow, but we would always help him if he slipped, though sometimes we would wind him up. "Stay down there you bastard!"'

The conversation frequently turned to music, and Ian would fantasize about making it big, promising Russell that he would be able to play his grand piano all day long on a big yacht when they become millionaires. 'That was our dream,' says Russell. 'Ian really liked the idea of becoming financially successful.' Ian was still dreaming of stardom when he had his first brush with a real rock star. Terry Day was again the catalyst. Terry had first met Charlie Watts in 1963, when he and Derrick Woodham bumped into the Rolling Stone coming out of a cinema in Shaftesbury Avenue. Watts was dating his future wife Shirley Shepherd, who had been at Hornsey College of Art with Woodham. Terry persuaded Charlie to come along to the Royal College to hear the Hardy-Holman-Day jazz trio. When Ian was introduced to Watts, he quizzed him mercilessly about his experiences with the Stones, then second only to the Beatles in the music popularity polls. Later on, when Watts bequeathed a Gretsch drum kit to Terry, Ian saw this tenuous connection with the Rolling Stones as a possible future benefit. But, for now, he was preoccupied with getting his diploma.

Students at the Royal College were assessed on a combination of practical and written work. Ian's life-size drawing of Gene Vincent, which consumed over two dozen 6B pencils, was an impressive effort. For his written work, he prepared a thesis on one of his favourite topics. Entitled 'Chicago Hoodlums', it profiled Al Capone and the gangsters of the prohibition era, much of it lifted from *The Lawless Decade*, a treasured tome by legendary New York journalist Paul Sann. 'Ian's thesis was brilliant,' says Bill Ellis, a student contemporary. 'Ian knew all about the gangsters.'

'I was right into gangsters,' Ian would tell journalist Steven Fuller some years later, revealing his major literary and cinematic influences. 'I was drawin' them and readin' about them . . . Ed McBain's and Ross MacDonald's. I don't like crap writers like Agatha Christie and Margerie Allingham. I like crime documentaries about America. I like James Cagney films when he's not going completely crackers. *Kiss of Death* with Richard Widmark and Victor Mature . . . *Key Largo* is an incredible film . . . *The Wild One* just took my head apart . . . *Somebody Up There Likes Me* is great, there's a knife fight on the roof with Steve McQueen . . . Tony Curtis I really dig. *The Vikings*, fuckin' 'ell!'

Peter Blake continued to pass magazine commissions to Ian including illustrations for *London Life*, depicting the stars of the 1965 Royal Variety Show. For this, Ian collaborated with Alison Armstrong and Stanford Steele, who drew the costumes and background respectively. Ian's contribution was a series of distinctive caricatures of the stars, including Peter Sellers and Spike Milligan, Shirley Bassey, Jack Benny, Peter, Paul and Mary, Peter Cook and Dudley Moore, Dusty Springfield, and Johnny Hallyday and Sylvie Vartan. His portrait of Tony Bennett adorned the front cover. Although Ian welcomed the work, getting paid was another matter, as he complained in a letter to Gordon Law:

> I have been eating drinking and sleeping lately. I have done this and that but it's never enough. People owe me money for a drawing and some grant for holiday work is due. I am writing on lined paper because I'm tired and it's 2.30 morningwise. I've been asleep already out of lackaday. Derrick's Lithuanian lady has just made me a big meal. I have not used African tobacco for some time now, but the booze is eating into my overdraft.

As well as encouraging his students to paint what they liked, Peter Blake helped to broaden their social horizons by inviting them to exhibition openings on the London art circuit. At the hottest galleries, there was always the prospect of bumping into a Beatle or a Stone and quaffing copious quantities of champagne. Geoff Rigden recalls, 'Peter used to casually say, "I'm going to a private view tomorrow evening, would you boys like to come along?" We'd turn up, very gauche, and stand there with our mouths open. Ian and Terry were very close and equal in their ability to chat up girls. Terry was impish, whilst Ian wasn't so mobile, but they were a double act; they both had that brightness.'

At a showing of Blake's work at the Robert Fraser Gallery on 20 October 1965, Ian looked dapper in 'a navy blue suit with white chalk stripe, a shirt with a pin through the collar and natty tie'. Terry Day's legendary chat-up technique was put to the test, as he was goaded by Ian. 'Oi, Tel, see that bird over there . . .' Terry looked round to see a stunning oriental girl and quickly started a conversation, while Ian and Geoff looked on, marvelling at the Dagenham Casanova, working his magic. As Terry was about to slip the girl his telephone number, she added, 'You're very kind, but I'm here with my friend,' and gestured towards a blue-suited gentleman in the corner. 'We looked round and it was Marlon Brando!' says Rigden. 'Terry went, "Streuth!" He definitely had panache with the girls. Ian loved it.' Terry remains modest about his pulling powers, crediting Ian and Geoff with much of the action. 'Tony Curtis was also there that night,' he recalls, 'with the actress Kristine Kauffman, so we all started chatting her up and slobbering over her, getting drunk on red wine. Brando leaned over and said, "You seem to be getting on all right there boys."'

Ian's fleeting glimpse of Marlon Brando was yet another notch on his social CV, but despite the presence of 'the beautiful people' on the London art circuit, the Royal College itself was rather less fertile for joint predators Day and Dury. In their male-dominated year group, girls were outnumbered five to one, and in the close confines of the college former Waltham-stow students such as Valerie Wiffen and Alison Armstrong continued to receive the boys' attentions. But it was twenty-three-year-old Elizabeth Rathmell, known to friends as Betty, who turned the heads of Ian and Terry. Born on 12 August 1942 in Leamington Spa, Warwickshire, Betty was the attractive third daughter of Thomas and Lilian Rathmell. Thomas Rathmell was a noted figurative painter who had moved from Cheshire to Wales after the war to teach at Newport College of Art. Betty studied at Newport, as did her boyfriend Dave Parfitt, before they both came to London in 1963, having won places at the Royal College of Art.

Ian and Terry were intrigued by Betty's gentle personality, sense of fun and the trace of a Liverpudlian accent in her soft voice, not to mention what some considered her slightly old-fashioned portraiture taken from photographs and drawn in coloured pencils with muted grey tones. The style would regain favour a few years later with the advent of 'photo-realism'. In her early days in the capital, Betty stayed in a students' hostel opposite the Natural History Museum but now lived in a studio flat above a shop at 103b Westbourne Grove. Betty's head had been turned by London life and she outgrew her relationship with Dave Parfitt. 'She was surrounded by lots of amoral, liberal hooligans,' says Terry Day, who won her affections in 1966. However, their romance was not to last and when it ended, Ian was ready to pounce.

The mid-1960s witnessed the gradual liberalization of British society. Ian and his friends were pleased to see many of the old taboos being quashed and progressive new legislation introduced. Although thousands campaigned in vain for the legalization of cannabis, 1965 had seen the abolition of the death penalty, and within two years abortion would be legalized and homosexuality decriminalized. The summer of 1966 – memorable for England's football victory in the World Cup and the release of the Beatles' *Revolver* LP – also saw some significant changes in Ian's life. The flat in Elgin Avenue was vacated, and the art school gang dispersed. Peggy and Aunt Elisabeth, both now retired, left Upminster for Barnstaple in Devon and settled at Higher Brockham, a National Trust cottage in East Down, where their pet tortoises, Homer and Chloe, could roam free. Although Ian would make many trips to East Down, his mum was no longer 'just around the corner'.

Ian was now courting Betty and missed her terribly when she went on holiday to Spain with Alison Armstrong that summer. Betty and Alison returned via Paris, where they found Ian waiting. 'This was really the first I knew of their romance,' says Alison. 'They kept it a bit quiet as they thought I'd be upset.' By October, Ian had moved into Betty's Westbourne Grove bedsit. Although it was not unusual for young couples to 'shack up' in the newly permissive society, this was Ian's first experience of cohabiting with a girlfriend.

Betty continued to paint but was uncomfortable with the schmoozing and marketing aspect of being an artist and sold few of her works. Ian was slightly more commercial in outlook and received illustration commissions from *The Sunday Times Magazine*. He also landed a part-time teaching assignment at Barnfield College, Luton. Although he had graduated on 8 July with a second-class honours diploma as an Associate of the Royal College of Art, Ian had to accept that, whatever his talent, he was unlikely to earn a living from painting. Perhaps encouraged by Peter Blake, he decided that teaching art would be an acceptable compromise.

'I wanted to teach,' Ian told me. 'There are only ten painters in this country who make money. As a fine art lecturer the bread was good, £20 a day, a shit load of money if you're doing two days a week. That was enough to live on, plus it involved me in running it on with the younger ones. If you're a full-time teacher you end up sharpening pencils and doing the register, but part-time teachers are expected to be working painters. That's what they wanted. It was a lovely life, but it was hard in the holidays. I had to sign on. I don't always know if sacrifice is a good thing. Peter Blake once said to me that a lot of his life he sacrificed other things for his art, which ultimately hadn't made him happy. He then developed the belief that happiness was an important element in art. It's not necessary to be in a garret with rats gnawing at your heels.'

Ian and Betty were in love and less than twelve months into their relationship they married. The ceremony took place on 3 June 1967 at Barnstaple Register Office. Signing the register, Ian gave his profession as 'painter and freelance illustrator', while Betty described herself as an artist. Later that year, Betty's parents gave the couple a belated wedding present in the form of the first year's rent – a generous £500 – on a home in Bedford Park, Chiswick. This architecturally notable area was home to an established artists' community, an enclave where young painters might meet and develop their artistic skills.

Kara Lodge, at 14 Newton Grove, London W4 was designed and built in 1880 by Maurice B. Adams, for the artist J. C. Dollman. Since Dollman's death, the building had been divided into flats, but retained many of its original Arts and Crafts features. Number 2, on the ground floor, contained Dollman's purpose-built studio with its high ceiling, a large window and a minstrel's gallery overlooking the central area, with bathroom and kitchen off to one side. This was now Ian's home. He had a telephone installed, which was handy for keeping in contact with the *Sunday Times*, for whom he continued to freelance. He also found time to befriend some of his neighbours, including Tom Affleck Greeves, a former architect and Slade-trained artist who had formed the Bedford Park Society in 1963, and one Geoffrey Stutfield, 'a distressed gentleman in reduced circumstances'.

•

Bill Dury had for some years been a chauffeur for the Western European Union (the defence organization), driving diplomats and politicians to and from London Airport in his Mercedes limousine, but on 25 February 1968 he died from acute bronchitis and emphysema in his small flat in Victoria. He was sixty-two years old. He had spent the previous Christmas staying with his sister Florence in Southborough, where he had complained of severe chest pains, and, although word had reached Ian that his father was not in the best of health, they had seen nothing of each other in recent years. Ian agreed to identify Bill's body and register his death at Caxton Hall, thus protecting Peggy from the grim task. 'Ian phoned me when his dad was dying,' remembers Barry Anderson. 'He said, "I'm out of my head over this. I've been a proper bastard." He felt guilty, but he was very proud of his dad. I remember Bill as a wonderful, funny guy who used to buy us copies of *Esquire*, in between giving us rides in the Rolls-Royce.'

Bill bequeathed Ian and Betty a modest amount of money, providing the couple with the financial security they felt they needed to start a family. Their first child, Jemima, was born on 4 January 1969 at Chiswick Maternity Hospital. Bringing Jemima back to Kara Lodge, they placed her cot behind one of the dividing screens that Ian had erected to separate sleeping and living areas. Their cosy domesticity, however, was often disrupted by Ian's social agenda. Russell Hardy recalls, 'Ian and I went out in the car, to pubs or parties, but I used to feel a bit sorry for Betty, stuck indoors with Jemima, whilst we were out getting pissed.' Geoff Rigden, who lived in nearby West Kensington, was also a regular visitor. 'We had days to fill in,' says Rigden. 'Ian acquired a small billiards table, and we spent hours playing on it and listening to recordings of Woody Allen. Ian kept on painting, and we did some teaching. That was the system.'

Some years earlier, Rigden had introduced Ian to his West Country pal Clive Davies, a writer and journalist who became an occasional member of the gang. Davies and his wife Jennifer lived in a Victorian mansion block near the Oval cricket ground but were keen to leave London. By the middle of 1969, when lack of funds was threatening to force Ian and Betty out of their distinctive Chiswick home, they joined forces with the Davies family and viewed inexpensive rental properties in rural locations as far apart as Wiltshire and North Essex, but none were suitable.

'I was signing on in Acton,' recalled Ian. 'They were giving me the fucking run-around. They sent me to a chap – I looked at the sign on his door – "Disabled Resettlement Officer" – I said, "I'm outta here."' Now broke and unable to pay the rent at Kara Lodge, Ian avoided Mrs Garmston, the old landlady who kept a room in the building. Before long, local estate agents Whitman Porter began marketing the unique property, and a string of prospective tenants arrived to inspect it. These included the artist John Plumb, who had first learnt about the Durys' imminent eviction from Andrew Clarke, a pupil of Ian's at Barnfield College. Plumb, who had just returned from teaching in the USA, remembers: 'When I first visited Kara Lodge, Ian was working on a portrait of Marilyn Monroe and listening to an LP by the American comedian Murray Roman. I've been indebted to Ian ever since for introducing me to that style of comedy.' Plumb arranged to take over the flat, and Ian and Betty were faced with homelessness, but were heartened by news from Aunt Molly, who was about to come to the rescue once again.

6

The Death of Gene Vincent

Marylebone Station, London, 1970. As Ed Speight approached the ticket hall, he spotted the little chap leaning into the window, shouting: 'I wanna get to Aylesbury!' Speight immediately recognized him as the fellow pupil he'd befriended at the Royal Grammar School but hadn't seen for more than a decade. Speight, now living in Aylesbury and working in London, greeted Ian, and they reminisced about the Black Cat Combo before swapping addresses. It was a chance meeting that brought Ian one step closer to his rock 'n' roll dream, Ed little suspecting that he would be called upon to bail Ian out at every dodgy musical juncture in the years that lay ahead.

Ian was on his way to Buckinghamshire to view an unusual property that was to let. It was Aunt Molly who had found the vast, sprawling vicarage in the village of Wingrave and suggested it might make a good home for the young Dury family. Its previous incumbent, an alcoholic parson, had left hundreds of empty sherry bottles that Ian discovered when he dug over the garden. 'I was very broke 'cos I wasn't teaching that much then,' said Ian. 'You can live extremely cheaply if you want to. A vicarage for a fiver a week! Two acres of ground and eight bloody big rooms – the condition was I had to decorate it, which took six months.'

Fired up by his enthusiasm for music, Ian would often make the arduous journey from Wingrave to Eastern Avenue, Dagenham, where Russell Hardy was lodging with Alan Ritchie, who had been part of the Elgin Avenue set back in 1966. They were all mad about jazz and rock 'n' roll and would spend hours spinning and discussing the latest records. One evening Ian told Alan and Russell about his recent reunion with Ed Speight and suggested they had the makings of a group. 'Ted's a good guitarist,' proclaimed Ian, 'he can sight-read.' Russell was immediately despatched to Chappell Music in Bond Street to get some sheet music and returned with 'The Cat Came Back', which he picked out on his Kembal Minx,* while Ian added a few of his 1950s favourites, including 'The Ballad of Davy Crockett'.

'The three of us used to rehearse with a Baldwin Burns amp and a Reslo microphone,' recalled Ian. 'We had loads of songs to give us confidence. We had a repertoire.' Ed Speight remembers, 'I would always wind Ian up at those sessions. I would shout, "Union break! Time for a pint!" Ian was very anti-drink at that point. He'd go through these phases. He could be quite moral, almost holier than thou. He had this work ethic and maintained that you shouldn't go to the pub when you're at work, but actually he didn't fancy the walk.'

Before long, Russell was invited to stay at Wingrave, and it was there that Ian's earliest attempts at songwriting occurred. 'I knocked out a couple of tunes with Russell,' said Ian, 'with my words – not lyrics – words, and Speight said, "You're quite good at that." It's a facility I'd always had, to knock out something that rhymed, but Speight gave me the encouragement. He said, "You should do more of that; a couple of people have read these and they think they're very funny."'

While Ian was sporadically teaching at Luton, his erstwhile companion Geoff Rigden had secured a part-time post at Canterbury College of Art. The college's head of painting, Thomas Watt, had asked Rigden to help him find new teaching talent. 'I suggested Ian,' says Geoff. 'You want your mates in, don't you?'

---

* A miniature 7 octave piano.

BILL AND PEGGY DURY (WITH BELLA THE SHEEPDOG) AT WEALD RISE, HARROW, 1940

LITTLE LORD UPMINSTER, 1945

ON THE BEACH: BARRY ANDERSON AND IAN, CORNWALL, 1948

KING OF THE HILL: CRANHAM, 1948

IN CAPE AND CALLIPER:
CONQUERING ADVERSITY, CHAILEY, 1951

A TONIC FOR THE NATION: PEGGY
AND IAN VISIT THE FESTIVAL OF BRITAIN
ON LONDON'S SOUTH BANK, 1951

'HE WAS A LITTLE BASKET THAT DAY':
BRIAN AND MARGARET DURY WITH IAN,
SOUTHBOROUGH, 1951

THE LADDER OF LIFE: BILL
VISITS IAN AT CHAILEY, 1951

AT THE PANTOMIME, 1953: (BACK ROW L–R) PEGGY, BILL, ELISABETH WALKER;
(FRONT ROW L–R) IAN, BARRY ANDERSON, MARTIN WALKER, ROGER WALKER, LUCY WALKER

THE NEW BOY: ROYAL GRAMMAR SCHOOL,
HIGH WYCOMBE, 1954

ELVIS HAS LANDED:
RATHMULLAN, IRELAND, 1956

ROAMING RADICALS, NEWQUAY, 1960:
(STANDING L–R) IAN, 'PETE', PAT FEW, WIZZ JONES

THE 'COLLEGE BOY':
MAIDA VALE, LATE 1964

'WE'RE ARTS AND CRAFTS':
IAN AT KARA LODGE, BEDFORD PARK, 1969

HUMPHREY STEPS OUT OF LINE; IAN GLOWERS, 1973: (L–R) RUSSELL HARDY, DAVID ROHOMAN, KEITH LUCAS, HUMPHREY OCEAN, IAN, DAVEY PAYNE

'GENTLE, DISCIPLINED, SELF-CONTAINED': IAN'S FIRST WIFE, BETTY (ELIZABETH RATHMELL)

THE SORCERER'S APPRENTICE:
PETER BLAKE IS TRANSFIXED, BRISTOL, 1974

IAN WINDS DOWN AFTER A SWEAT-SOAKED
PERFORMANCE, BRISTOL, 1974

STIFF'S STABLE OF STARS, 1977: (L–R) ELVIS COSTELLO, NICK LOWE, WRECKLESS ERIC, LARRY WALLIS, IAN DURY

IAN SUMMONS THE MUSE; GENE VINCENT HOVERS: OVAL MANSIONS, 1978

Mr Watt made the journey to Wingrave to meet Ian and was immediately impressed with the portraits adorning the walls, most of which were Betty's paintings. 'Ian got the job at the rate of £30 a day plus travelling expenses,' continues Geoff. 'We took it terribly seriously. We got up early and did the job.'

In September 1970, Ian commenced teaching at Canterbury, initially working two days a week and staying in Kent overnight with either Geoff Rigden or another fellow teacher, John Williams. Thomas Watt had told the students that the college was getting a new tutor from London, who was 'a bit rum-looking, crippled with polio but forthright . . . spoke his mind, a bit of a cockney.' But 'one shouldn't worry because he'd been to the Royal College of Art' and was therefore OK. 'We'd been forewarned,' says student Keith Lucas, 'but when Ian came in we got on with him straight away.'

On the first day in his new role, Ian greeted his students wearing a multi-coloured Fair Isle cardigan that had been made for him by a Mrs Kelly, the mother of one of his Luton pupils. He also wore an earring – bold for the time – and his hair was combed into a Teddy Boy quiff, with long ringlets hanging over his collar. It was an image that made an immediate impression on first-year student Humphrey Anthony Erdeswick Butler-Bowdon (or 'Humphrey Ocean', as he would later become). 'Ian came limping in, his fantastic cardigan like a coat of many colours,' recalls Humphrey. 'His body became part of the room, and the dynamics changed. He made me see that painting the things I liked was the most modern activity that I could possibly be involved with. We got on very well and socialized beyond the art class, talking about Gene Vincent. He was this intriguing kind of cockney, who was not only very bright but veered giddily between middle class and working class.'

At Canterbury, Ian sought to emulate Peter Blake's teaching methods by aligning himself with the students, as opposed to his staff colleagues. He was determined to get the most out of his pupils, not wishing to be mistaken for a figure of authority.

He started by extending the standard one-day life class to four days, hammering home his Protestant work ethic and begging the students not to cop out. The lessons were extreme, as Humphrey recalls: 'It was like an outward-bound course. There were twelve of us in Ian's life class, but only seven survived the four days. All of us were in tears at some point. Ian got us together and said, "Look! You're not looking! You're just being art students, you're just producing drawings! You're making that bit up between her crutch and her big toe. The proportion isn't right, it's full of lies!" Ian was right, it was full of lies.'

Ian's teaching style was impassioned, but it paled beside the intensity of his social behaviour. His spare time in Canterbury was spent hanging out with students of both sexes, and he often pestered the girls with light-hearted sexual innuendo, but none would succumb. Ian found it hard to take 'no' for an answer and on one occasion, when shunned by a female student, simply unzipped his jeans, pulled out his penis and pleaded, 'Look, there's nothing wrong with it!' Germaine Dolan, then a student in Ian's class, recalls, 'He was always trying to get us girls involved in stuff, and I frequently found myself backing off. He would send me letters, always written in pencil, with lots of rubbing out. The first line of one letter talked about "opening a nice little space and finding out a whale wants to come in". He was quite a heavy guy.'

Ian had fantasized about becoming an entertainer ever since his childhood friend Barry Anderson had recounted his experience of performing a song at Saturday-morning pictures. 'I did always want to be a pop st . . . in a band!' said Ian, quickly correcting himself. He had already made several attempts to join 'a band'; at the Royal Grammar School he had been the unwelcome washboard player in the skiffle group and later, drummer in the Black Cat Combo; at Walthamstow he was the failed singer turned bongo player in assorted amateur groups. Earlier in the year, he'd practised a few novelty songs with his mates and started to dabble in songwriting with Russell Hardy. It was now time to get serious.

In 1970, the progressive rock era was at its height. In the UK the leading practitioners were the groups Yes and King Crimson, whose technically proficient musicians concocted complex arrangements designed to dazzle their young audiences. In the USA, brass-driven bands such as Blood, Sweat and Tears and Chicago would insert light jazzy interludes into their bluesy songs, giving their players an opportunity to 'stretch out'. Consequently, younger jazz musicians on both sides of the Atlantic spotted a new commercial opportunity and started rubbing shoulders with rockers and chasing record deals. Ian had little interest in these developments, preferring pure jazz or 1950s rock 'n' roll, but he did know a number of proficient players who might be persuaded to 'rock out'.

At the 100 Club in Oxford Street, the 'musos' would gather to hear jazz saxophonist George Khan, whom Ian had known since the mid-1960s. Slightly drunk and in awe of Khan's go-ahead improvisation, Ian mingled with the audience one evening and bumped into multi-instrumentalist Charlie Hart. Ian talked excitedly about his plans to form a new band, telling Hart he was going to ask George Khan to help, knowing that Khan ran a rehearsal room at Jubilee Studios in Covent Garden. Hart related the plan to Khan, who was sceptical about Ian's talents, but he soon relented. 'I suppose we'll have to do it,' Khan told Hart. The two musicians recognized that Ian was 'a heavy-duty music fan' and decided to give it a go.

In November, Ian assembled a rehearsal group at Jubilee. Most of the musicians were pleased to accommodate him, perhaps hoping that a distinctive front man might help to bring their far-out music to a wider audience. It certainly looked good on paper: George Khan was a well-connected jazz face, whilst guitarist Ed Speight and pianist Russell Hardy were excellent musicians who were both aware of Ian's foibles. Multi-instrumentalist Charlie Hart and drummer Terry Day, who was Ian's closest friend from college, both came from the People Band, a loose assemblage of 'free jazz' musicians whose 1968 album had been produced by Charlie Watts.

They all recognized that Ian had something to offer: drive and ambition, creative talent and an indefinable uniqueness. There was no one else like him on the music scene, and, even though he was a 'crap singer', it was impossible to write him off. Russell enjoyed the line-up more than anyone, describing the mix of players as 'fantastic, mind-blowing', but he knew that Ian was out of his depth. 'There were too many cooks and not enough bottle washers,' he says. The group failed to get beyond a few practice sessions, but the exercise was an invaluable experience for Ian, who now realized that, if he was to succeed in the music world, he needed to develop a personal vocal style and make himself indispensable.

He started by incorporating elements he knew and understood – a broad knowledge of cockney humour and rhyming slang, an appreciation of sartorial excess and wide-boy imagery in general. Building on his Teddy Boy alter ego, he fashioned a unique and compelling character that audiences would find hard to ignore. Most importantly, he discovered a latent talent – the ability to write words for songs. 'Ian was making up words all the time,' says Humphrey Ocean. 'He was very good at arguing, and it became increasingly apparent to him that words were his strong point. His terms of reference kept one constantly on one's toes. I know that, bitterly, from experience. When everything was going your way, Ian would come in from behind and question you. He had an intellectual ability to move round a subject and look at it from different viewpoints, whereas in his art he'd been trying to paint like Peter Blake or Betty, who was a supremely wonderful painter. He felt he wasn't good enough. He wasn't as good as Betty; he could see that, but when he started doing words, it got out of hand.'

One of Ian's earliest opening lines – 'I consummated Linda, on a bench in Tufnell Park' – encapsulated the best of his writing, containing, as it did, a reference to sexual conquest, an everyday object and a bit of local geography. 'They were nutty-ish words, cathartic,' said Ian. '"She's sweeter than a horsefly on an arm, her tender smile secretes a rancid charm"; "I need you like a bandage needs a cut". I wrote one called "The Flasher Express", about a trainload of perverts hurtling down the track. "The ticket inspector with a secret smile drops his Y-fronts on the track."'

His early attempts at songwriting were based on little scenarios or whimsical phrases he found amusing. Often obscure and bordering on the surreal, they revealed a broad range of influences, from the humour of the Goons and Edward Lear, through John Lennon and William Burroughs, via the American beat poets whose London recital Ian had attended in 1965. He had soaked it all up during his college years and now had the facility to roll it out at will. His early efforts offered a fore-taste of the dazzling lyrical skills that would one day emerge, but one early song was far too sinister for broad public scrutiny. The disturbing 'I Made Mary Cry' described sexual, physical assault in graphic detail. He would later perform it brandishing a knife to act out the terror.

> *I made Mary cry in a lonely bus shelter*
> *By putting my flick-knife in the back of her leg,*
> *Severed a hamstring in the lonely bus shelter,*
> *I paid no attention but I made Mary beg . . .*
> *Sleep for tonight in a white dormitory,*
> *I'll dream my dreams in a cold iron bed,*
> *Fourteen more days in a white dormitory,*
> *I'll catch up with Mary, I'll chop off her head*

As well as developing his songwriting, Ian began dabbling in photography, under the alias 'Duncan Poundcake'. He tried out his photographic skills on a much-needed holiday with his family in Devon. Russell Hardy drove them down to Higher Brockham, where they stayed with Peggy. 'Aunt Molly and Aunt Elisabeth were there and they waited on us hand and foot,' recalls Russell, 'but Ian was so off and rude to his mum.' Ian had often shown off by being abrupt with Peggy or his aunts when his mates were around. Back in Upminster in the 1960s, it could have been put down to teenage tantrums, but Ian was now twenty-eight. Possibly embarrassed by the Walker sister's genteel ways, he felt obliged to rebel, as if to demonstrate that his background wasn't all about nice china and Oxbridge accents; people needed to know there was also a tough side that came from his dad's branch of the family tree.

But Ian wasn't so mouthy when he was out of his comfort zone. During the stay in Devon he had wanted to take some photographs near the sea. Russell got the map out, and they set off in the car, eventually driving through an open gate and along a track that led to the cliff edge, where Ian spent two hours taking his photos. When they got back to the gate it was shut and locked with heavy chains. Russell offered to drive through it, but Ian wasn't keen on the idea. 'I don't mind,' said Russell, 'I'll just crash through it, it'll be quite easy.' Suddenly three burly farmers appeared in the distance. 'We walked over to them for help,' recalls Russell, 'but they wanted us to buy our way out. It took them half an hour to unlock the gate. Ian was quite frightened.'

When college broke up in the summer of 1971, Ian was able to spend more time at Wingrave, where he had been exercising his DIY skills. In anticipation of bringing musicians there for practice sessions, he soundproofed what was to become the rehearsal room by nailing egg boxes to the walls and installed a secondary door to keep the noise in. On the weekends he would invite his musical chums up for a jam session, or to simply hang out. They were usually ferried around by art student Colin Thomas, whom Ian dubbed 'Larry Lilacs', owner of a gleaming Rover 90. 'He was like Ian's chauffeur,' says Paul

Tonkin, a friend and student at Canterbury. 'Ian had an amazing gift for recruiting people to help him.'

Jemima's earliest childhood memory is of 'bearded men walking round the garden all the time'. It was, according to Humphrey, an idyllic period. 'We were living a sort of flat-cap, Brideshead life. We'd do some painting then go out for a drink with Russell in the baby Austin. It wasn't going to last for long, it had to move on, but it was very much to do with painting and I got on well with Betty. It moved in a natural way, and Ian pulled me over towards rock 'n' roll. When I came up, it wasn't like there was suddenly a load of long-haired rockers around, it was more like a family, and the shift was gradual. It evolved. People came in and went out.'

Humphrey acknowledges Russell's unique mix of musical reference points that Ian would enjoy. 'When Russell started playing he made it sound like Erik Satie, it was a beautiful thing, utterly different . . . he's like Snooks Eaglin, who was blind and learnt music from the radio . . . he would listen to the Mike Sammes Singers – "Sing Something Simple" – and start playing around it. Nothing was beyond his ken. Russell hated performing in public, but he looked so good – like some kind of Victorian sailor, or a genie we'd picked up on our way from the docks.'

Humphrey took some LPs to Wingrave – Taj Mahal's *A Giant Step*; Rod Stewart's *Every Picture Tells a Story* and James Taylor's *Sweet Baby James*. Ian wasn't at all into James Taylor, but he hummed along to 'Fire and Rain' and sang fragments of it as he walked down the lane with Humphrey. 'Despite himself, he'd just come out with it,' recalls Humphrey. 'One moment he slagged it off, but the next moment, with that democratic quality in music, he wasn't worrying about class. It was either good or bad. He would never admit it, but his heart told him it was good music. He might have found himself singing 'Fire and Rain', but Ian would never say he liked James Taylor.'

•

By 1971, Gene Vincent was no longer the magnificent string-bean that Ian had idolized back in '56. Since his rock 'n' roll heyday, Vincent had been made to suffer all sorts of indignities, including one famous occasion when TV producer Jack Good ordered him to exaggerate his disability with the immortal command: 'Limp, you bugger, limp!' Vincent had also been a passenger in the motor accident that killed fellow legend Eddie Cochran. Gene was now a damaged, broken man. Living and working in England, he had become alcoholic, overweight and tetchy. Following a brief period signed to John Peel's Dandelion record label and a disastrous European tour backed by the House Shakers, his career was in ruins. Suffering from cirrhosis of the liver, he went home to California and drank so much liquor that his stomach exploded and he collapsed in a pool of blood. Lying in his mother's arms on 12 October, Vincent reportedly whispered, 'Mama, you can phone the ambulance now.' He was dead at thirty-six.

Gene Vincent's death shook Ian. Sensitive about his fast-approaching thirtieth birthday, he was beginning to think he was too old for rock 'n' roll, but his idol's demise was the pivotal moment, a call to action. It would one day inspire his rocking lament 'Sweet Gene Vincent', but for now the tragedy of the Virginian's wretched end gave Ian the motivation to consolidate his own group while there was still time. 'I really rated Gene Vincent,' said Ian. 'The visual aspects of him as much as the sound of it, but I loved that as well. This was before Jack Good got hold of him, 1956 and '57. *The Girl Can't Help It*, he's in that for about nineteen seconds. I had no idea that he had a bad leg until after he was dead, that was a sort of coincidence. I ended up looking a little bit like Gene for five minutes in the early seventies. There was no thought in my mind of copying him, but I did know all his tunes. When he died, he was only the same age as Van Gogh. I remember thinking I'd get a band together. I knew a lot of jazz musicians, so I gathered all my mates together. I had the name "Kilburn and the High Roads"; I thought it was very funny.'

The southern end of Kilburn High Road in London is literally a stone's throw from his parents' first marital home in Belsize Road. It is also one of the main arteries into the capital from Ian's Middlesex birthplace and the route that Bill and Peggy, then pregnant with her first, soon to be stillborn, child, must surely have taken when they carted their meagre chattels to Weald Rise in 1939. This area of north-west London is also home to a large Irish community and an eclectic mix of cultures . . . did the enchanted thoroughfare hold some special appeal for Ian, perchance? 'Nothing personal,' he replied, when I posed the question. 'I've driven through it. Nothing to do with being Irish but it's very cosmopolitan. Indian shops, Caribbean. It existed in my imagination for about three years, since 1969 probably, when I was teaching at Luton.'

Russell Hardy often chauffeured Ian around the area and remembers being the 'getaway driver' when Ian and Joe Snowden stopped off to score dope at the El Rio club in the Harrow Road. 'I had to sit in the car with the engine running,' recalls Russell. 'We would often see signs directing us to "Kilburn High Road". I think it was a factor.' Seeking advice on how best to launch his new group – at this point more of a concept than a musical unit – Ian turned to the one famous rock musician in his address book, Charlie Watts, then a tax exile in the South of France. Russell Hardy agreed to drive Ian from Wingrave to the Watts residence near Arles in Provence. It was an arduous trip in the Austin A35, 'broken only by stops for coffee, cognacs and not much else,' admits Russell. 'Ian was seeking advice and possibly money from Charlie. Ian was a bit mercenary in some respects.'

'I was asking more for his ideas than his fivers,' Ian told me, referring to the supposedly wealthy Stones drummer. 'I said I wanted to start this band and he replied, "What you wanna do that for? You're a fucking good painter. It's all been done before . . . Chuck Berry . . ." I told him, "I fancy it. I think I'd be quite good at it," to which Charlie replied, "If I help you and you get off, it's because I helped you. If I don't help you and you don't get off, I'm a cunt." I said, "OK," and he didn't help.'

The line-up of Kilburn and the High Roads would fluctuate wildly over the next four years, but Ian's confidence as inspirational leader was never in doubt. From the small pool of potential 'Kilburns' who populated the early line-ups, the most promising gravitated towards their leader, underscoring a broad consensus that humour and style were at least as relevant as musical ability. Those who 'got it' – that is to say, were on Ian's wavelength – would thrive. Those who failed to endorse his vision would be dropped. There was no room for an obstinate musician who refused to change. Even Humphrey Ocean, who was totally attuned to Ian's artistic vision and possessed a high style quotient, would be sacrificed at the opportune moment. 'It was "The Ian Show",' says Humphrey. 'In fact, throughout, it was "The Ian Show".'

In late 1971, the Kilburns consisted of Ian's jazz-inclined sidekick Russell Hardy (piano); law student Ian Smith, who also worked in a Canterbury health food restaurant (bass), and three Canterbury art students 'who said they liked Chuck Berry and the Rolling Stones'. These were guitarist Keith Lucas, who resembled a young Anthony Perkins, the long-haired Chris Lucas (no relation) on drums and the lofty, softly spoken Humphrey Ocean (on unamplified electric guitar). Occasional members included student Paul Tonkin (on 'out-of-tune violin') and fellow tutor Geoff Rigden (blues harmonica). Ian Smith and the Lucas duo lived at 114 Northgate in Canterbury, a typical student lodging house that became the Kilburns' first HQ and a crash pad for Ian.

They were all poor and bought most of their clothes from charity shops, resulting in the wide array of previously enjoyed overcoats that shaped the group's early image. Ian amusingly described this as 'Oxfam Chic'. 'Yeah, we got into a lot of gear that was old, because it was nicely made,' said Ian. 'When Humphrey joined the band it was because it was extremely unusual looking. It was loose in those days. It was always important to us that it was funny, not that we pushed it. I was Humphrey's tutor and Keith's tutor as well in the year above Humphrey, who added his styles and ideas, but they were already buzzing through the group.'

Like Ian, drummer Chris Lucas had contracted polio as a child. This brought about 'a kind of polio bond', but created tension; Chris had more run-ins with Ian than the others because of their common experience. 'He was more disabled than I was,' remembers Chris, 'but I used to wonder how he managed to get people running around doing things for him. He was the best personal manipulator I've ever met, big on cuddles and telling us everything was all right. He would dispense advice on women and how to handle certain situations. I've come around to the idea that, although he was controlling, it wasn't without understanding. He got Terry Day to come along and coach me on the drums. He was trying to help me become a better drummer. He always tried to support us despite being a tyrannical band leader.'

Guitarist Keith Lucas was a little more experienced, having played since his teens in groups such as Pentagon, Frosty Jodhpur and C-Stream, the latter being a name that particularly appealed to Ian. Keith remembers that Ian came along to the early Kilburns practice sessions with his 'traps set' – a box with wood blocks, skulls and tambourines that he played with sticks. Humphrey Ocean: 'If Ian could walk into that Canterbury studio and change the room in a small way, or somehow colonize that room, the shift towards going on stage in front of hundreds of people was a small step. He once said to me, "You want to be ready for when the thing comes along, so you don't miss it. You're already there and you make the thing happen." He talked about the Kilburns and said, "We're famous already." We weren't, but with Ian's self-assurance we'd walk in as if we were Muhammad Ali.'

In November, at the onset of the party season, the Kilburns

secured not one, but three live engagements, all at art colleges. The group's all-important debut was set to occur at Canterbury on 9 December 1971, with the Magic Rock Band and headliners Skin Alley, but this was preceded by an eleventh-hour booking at Croydon School of Art on 3 December, opening for Thunderclap Newman. Medway College of Art and Design in Rochester would follow in the New Year. At Canterbury, Ian persuaded art student and social secretary Allan Upwood to give them the date. 'Do you want a good result in your assessment at the end of the year?' Ian asked Upwood. 'You do a college dance, don't you? Put us on the bill.' Upwood agreed and offered a fee of £40. 'That's more than I got for another three years after that,' said Ian. 'I gave him excellent marks as well. Three art school gigs in one week, there was a reason to rehearse, to work towards. We started taking it a bit more seriously.'

With the Canterbury gig in the bag, it was Genevieve Dolan, sister of Canterbury student Germaine, who arranged the Croydon date. Ian asked the Dolan sisters to augment the group as dancers and christened them 'the Roadettes', from his latest lyric 'The Roadette Song'. 'It was actually Kilburn and the High Roads and the Neasden Roadettes,' says Germaine. 'My dad lived in Neasden, and Ian came there a few times with Russell. We did energetic dancing and rehearsed our routines at the group's practice sessions.'

Ian told the Roadettes what to wear and asked graphics student Mick Hill to design 'Roadettes' lettering that would be sewn across their T-shirts. 'Ian fancied both of them,' says Chris Lucas. 'He was fantastic at seducing people, men or women, and used that charm. If he wanted you to love him, he could make it happen. It's what he did with everyone for ever. If he wanted people on board, he would go out of his way to convince them into thinking it was a good idea. With Germaine and Genevieve, it was: "we need a couple of pretty girls to dance", and sure enough they did it.'

Ian still had a crush on Germaine, and enrolling her as an auxiliary Kilburn guaranteed proximity. 'Ian told me that he started all those bands for Russell Hardy,' says Germaine, 'because Russell was really shy. It was as if Ian was trying to rehabilitate lost souls, but I think that really he was trying to make himself seem nice for my benefit. Ian even asked me to make him a pair of trousers. He sent me off to a factory in Epping to buy tarpaulin because his calliper used to wear his trousers out, so he needed a really strong pair. I got the material and made them and then I thought, "God, how did he get me to do that?" He knew all about tarpaulin; he'd checked it out. He did everything in great detail. Ian turned being scruffy and tatty into a new kind of glamour. He dressed carefully and would deliberately wear a sweater that ended up being totally ragged, like the "Dennis the Menace" sweater, a black-and-rust striped jersey with holes in the elbows. All that scruffiness was very calculated. Ian wanted to wear it. It wasn't like he couldn't afford one without holes.'

Of the Kilburns' first gig, Humphrey Ocean says, 'It was bad, but just good enough. At Canterbury, we were on home ground, and our clique loved us, mainly because we had the temerity to get up on stage. Something happened. We couldn't go back to what we were doing before, painting.' Student Mick Hill, who was roped in as roadie, recalls Ian's first brush with stardom at Rochester. 'At half time, Ian said, "Right, let's go and pick up some birds." He sat next to this girl, and she shrieked and ran away.'

While Ian paraded the Kilburns around the college circuit, Betty was at Wingrave, heavily pregnant. On 18 December the group returned to the vicarage for a rehearsal, during which time Betty, assisted by her midwife, gave birth within earshot of the Kilburns at full volume. During a break, Ian nipped upstairs to see his new-born son, quickly returning to the session exclaiming:

'It's a boy – right, let's play some rock 'n' roll!' An hour later, Betty stuck her head round the door and pleaded: 'Do you think I can have a bit of peace please?' The Kilburns shrivelled up.

Ian hung around Wingrave over the Christmas holidays, doting over his new-born son, who would be christened Baxter. He was also giving serious thought to the Kilburns' rhythm section. Already a pattern was emerging – Ian needed to be at ease with his musicians, so whenever he felt he was losing control it was time for a shake-up. Following January's Rochester date and an appearance at the Royal College of Art supporting artist Bruce McLean's conceptual 'pose band', Nice Style, Kilburns bassist Ian Smith was fired because, according to Mick Hill, 'he was an incessant geezer, just like Ian'.

Chris Lucas, who had 'missed a crucial practice session', would also have to go. 'I met some floozy in London and didn't turn up at Wingrave,' recalls Chris. 'It was an opportunity for Ian to dispense with me, but when I was elbowed I was pissed off because it wasn't done to my face. It was a message conveyed to me by other band members.' Despite his ejection from the Kilburns, Chris has mainly warm memories of Ian at that time. 'He was going to be our passport to a rock 'n' roll nirvana. He had a few years on us and was streetwise. He knew people and had credibility. He was mesmerizing and charismatic from the beginning, and we believed in him.'

Ian's 'first reserves' Charlie Hart and Terry Day, both of whom had been part of the 1970 Covent Garden rehearsal group, were recalled to replace Ian Smith and Chris Lucas respectively. 'There was this constant playing-us-off-against-each-other thing, between the poor Canterbury students and the London professionals,' says Charlie Hart, who had been a classically trained child prodigy. 'We'd get disillusioned with Ian, and he would threaten to get these other guys in. He was quite good at always having these art students breathing down our necks. "I've got your replacement sorted out," he would imply. But he was very persuasive and brilliant at pushing people.'

'Early '72 we started digging in deep, and I got Terry back in on the drums,' recalled Ian. 'He brought Charlie Hart and Davey Payne. Davey came to the first gig we did at Rochester. I said, "You brought your saxophone with you? Why don't you come and join us, it's only twelve-bars." When he joined us he said he didn't know what a "bar" was! He was free-form, a serious player. Charlie Hart, Terry Day, Davey Payne, which was, in fact, the People Band. A few gigs we did you'd have three jazzers on, the People Band, then they'd say "Kilburn and the High Roads", and three more geezers would wander out and join them. Wacky.'

Davey Payne, two years younger than Ian, hailed from north London, but grew up in the seaside town of Clacton in Essex. As a teenager he learned woodwind instruments and took an interest in jazz, eventually joining the People Band in 1969. 'I didn't know what Ian meant by "twelve-bars",' confesses Payne, 'but I remember Ian walking around smoking a big Havana cigar, wearing a home-made glitter jacket. I was a free-form jazz musician, into John Cage and Stockhausen. I went home and practised [playing twelve-bar blues] in the main keys. I went up to Wingrave and, when I played my solo – the twelve-bar blues I'd been practising with some free-form jazz thrown in – Keith said, "Wow! Great man! Ian Underwood, Frank Zappa, brilliant!" Ian was going, "Yeah!" That's how I joined the Kilburns.'

When the group made its second appearance at Canterbury College of Art, in February 1972, the performance was captured on a reel-to-reel tape recorder. The recordings survive and provide evidence of a well-drilled rock 'n' roll group, its repertoire comprising a dozen standards and a smattering of original compositions. Despite the criticism that had been levelled at Ian's voice, he is heard to sing confidently on rockers such as 'Johnny B Goode' and 'Blue Suede Shoes'. Unintentionally or otherwise, a number of the songs have a 'walking' theme, for example, Fats Domino's 'I'm Walking', Jimmy McCracklin's 'The Walk', and 'Twenty Flight Rock', Eddie Cochran's paean to the girl-friend 'who lives on the twentieth floor up town, but the elevator's broken down', so he has to 'walk one, two flight, three flight, four . . .'

As Easter 1972 approached, Charlie Hart departed for Holland with the People Band, leaving a vacancy in the Kilburns for a bass player. Guitarist Humphrey Ocean, who had recently been sacked from the group, received a phone call. 'It was Ian,' recalls Humphrey, 'saying to me, "Charlie Hart's gone to Holland. I don't think he really likes being in the Kilburns. You can play guitar." What Ian really meant was, "I don't think I can control Charlie, do you fancy playing the bass?" I was up at Wingrave, and Ian and I were very close. The next thing I knew, I was at an address in Lordship Lane, Wood Green, interviewing a very nice Fender jazz bass guitar I'd found in *Melody Maker*.'

Ian recalled that Humphrey's new bass guitar had been 'doing a summer season in the Canary Islands on fluorescent cushions with two camp geezers'. He acknowledged that Humphrey 'could play a bit' and looked the part on stage. Humphrey said, 'We started playing "Tea For Two" cha-cha, with Ian on the drums, then free jazz. I found I had a feel for it. Charlie Hart came back from Holland. He walked in and saw my bass, and we both went bright red. Charlie knew he was the bass player – it was his life – whereas I was just a painter. I was a guitarist who had bought a bass.'

Charlie Hart skulked off and, for now, Humphrey remained the Kilburns' bass player, during which time a demo tape was made with the assistance of People Band guitarist and future Hollywood film director Mike Figgis. Noting that the People Band obtained regular work in Holland, Humphrey and Davey organized a trip in search of gigs and dragged Ian and Russell along too. Arriving in Amsterdam in Humphrey's Morris Traveller, armed only with a Grundig tape recorder and the name of a Dutch booking agency, the ragged quartet would proclaim:

'We're the Kilburns; we're a dance band!' When they attempted to play their tape to the Dutch agent, however, the local voltage differential caused the machine to run at half speed, emitting lifeless music. Unable to find work, the luckless Kilburns spent three days in an Amsterdam squat before returning home. To make matters worse, Humphrey contracted viral meningitis.

'It was a slightly serious moment,' says Humphrey, 'and Ian took it as a sign that I was out of my depth. As I was getting better and improving on the bass, playing along to *Blonde on Blonde*, I received a letter from Ian, telling me I was out of the group. I was very moved by it but I remember thinking, "You bastard," and – this is a tactic of mine – I went up to Wingrave with a cake I'd made, arriving as if nothing had happened. I was in serious denial. I knew that I was out, but I was determined to show that I wasn't in tears. Ian liked that. His letter was fantastic. It was the only letter he ever wrote me and it contained the reasons why I should carry on at art school and not be in the group. He told me I had allies at Canterbury. What he was doing was being my responsible tutor and not taking me out before I got my diploma.'

Ian had now turned thirty and had decided that music, not painting, was where his future lay. He reckoned that Davey, Terry, Russell, Keith and Charlie Hart, who had quietly rejoined the Kilburns following Humphrey's most recent departure, comprised the band with which he would conquer the world. They sat up late into the night at Wingrave, listening to Ian selling them the idea that they would play a few clubs to begin with, before swiftly transferring to the Royal Albert Hall. 'The first million we get,' Ian announced semi-seriously, 'I'll split with you guys. We won't have a manager and we won't give the publisher more than twenty per cent.' Ian had been swotting up. 'He was absorbed in it,' says Charlie Hart. 'He was envisaging a point where he had made it. Today, it would be like a beggar on the street, prophesying his first Porsche.'

Ian found the group an agent, but only one booking (at

Luton Airport Social Club) transpired. Despite frenetic inactivity, the Kilburns were mildly encouraged after a 'works outing'
to see Roxy Music at Friars Club in Aylesbury. Humphrey went
along too. 'They were an art school band with a few quiffs,' he
recalls. 'The verdict was that there were slightly too many quiffs,
but we convinced ourselves that Roxy Music were no opposi-
tion whatsoever, and were sort of on our side. The arrogance!
We also liked Slade. I remember Ian saying, "What I like about
them is they're not art school boys. If they were, they'd never
in a million years call themselves Slade!"'

Kilburn and the High Roads, much like the Bonzo Dog Doo-
Dah Band – captained by Ian's old Walthamstow contemporary
Vivian Stanshall – were a classic art school combo, made up of
enthusiastic amateurs and the odd pro, strong on in-humour
and sartorial flair. But with just half-a-dozen gigs under their
belts, the Kilburns were square pegs unlikely to find favour
in the round hole of UK pop, either musically or visually. Their
eclectic mix of rock 'n' roll, reggae and calypso was quite a challenge for audiences. A look at the 1972 music scene underlines
their incongruity. Glam Rock was the big noise; Marc Bolan was
already established, and David Bowie was poised for stardom.
Old warhorses like Gary Glitter and Roy Wood had reinvented
themselves and become regulars on *Top of the Pops*, decked out
in outlandish attire and make-up. The Kilburns, on the other
hand, looked like a bunch of musical misfits who had just been
refused entry to a tramps' convention. But in Ian's mind the
Kilburns possessed an alternative kind of glamour that went
way beyond the superficiality of early 1970s pop.

7

The Sacking of Charlie Hart

Margaret Street, London, 1972. On a sunny October afternoon, Ian popped into the Speakeasy, a West End music biz hang-out, accompanied by Keith and Russell. Frequented by roadies and record company dogsbodies, very few of whom were interested in live music *per se*, 'the Speak' was a tough gig for an unknown act, but Kilburn and the High Roads would be grateful for anything. As they entered the club, Leo Sayer and his band were rehearsing the Lovin' Spoonful hit 'Summer in the City', providing Ian with some light entertainment while he waited for club manager Laurie O'Leary – a former associate of the Kray twins – to emerge from his office. When O'Leary eventually appeared, Ian made his impassioned pitch, and the Kilburns were immediately booked to appear there on 11 November.

Ian didn't yet know that an alternative to venues like the Speakeasy existed, namely the London pub rock circuit, then in its infancy. 'We knew we would die a death down there,' said Ian, recalling his London debut, 'but after the first set, they all clapped. We thought: "Fucking hell!"' By an amazing stroke of luck, the night the Kilburns made their isolated Speakeasy appearance, two of pub rock's leading lights were in the audience – Nick Lowe, the singer, songwriter and bass player with Brinsley Schwarz, and his manager, Dave 'Robbo' Robinson, a buccaneering thirty-year-old Irishman who had cut his teeth road-managing Jimi Hendrix in 1967.

It was Robinson who, in 1970, masterminded the preposterous launch of Brinsley Schwarz by flying a plane load of UK journalists to New York to witness the group's US debut, supporting Van Morrison at the Fillmore East. It was a PR disaster, not least because a series of logistical nightmares resulted in the press contingent's arrival in the Big Apple being delayed by twelve hours and the fact that 'the Brinsleys' were somewhat ill-equipped to impress a stoned-out New York crowd. But there was an upside. As a reaction to the failure of 'The Hype', as it became known, the group took a strong anti-commercial stance. They simplified their music and retreated to the pubs of north London, where they played snappy sets with minimal equipment – the start in fact of the 'pub rock' movement, from which Ian and the Kilburns would mightily benefit.

'I think that I discovered the Kilburns,' says Nick Lowe. 'They were unbelievable, but Robbo wasn't having it.' Interestingly, Dave Robinson's own version of events contradicts Lowe's. 'I couldn't take my eyes off the Kilburns,' he says. 'I thought, "Geronimo!"' Robinson made a point of capturing Ian's telephone number and was in touch within a matter of days, swiftly followed by a visit to the Dury home at Wingrave, where he stressed that pub rock was 'all about taking music out of the hands of the music business and its sharp operators and bringing it back to the people'. Ian recalled, 'Dave sat on the floor, had a bowl of rice and said he thought that music would grow by word-of-mouth, if you had an environment where it could develop in one locality. He said we'd get a reputation in a locality that would sustain us. Dave made it sound very logical. I wasn't thinking of a career thing at all, although it had started occupying a great deal of the time. I had no idea of making a living out of it. No plot whatsoever.'

In truth, Ian had been formulating his master plan for months, his ideal venue for the Kilburns being a large concert hall with unencumbered access. The prospect of playing pubs unnerved him, but Robinson presented a strong case for the grass-roots approach. Dave's intervention also brought about a further personnel change; when he casually described the group's rhythm section as 'wobbly', Ian took this to be a criticism of Terry Day's jazz-tinged drumming and sacked his friend of ten years. Ian's ruthless streak was starting to emerge. 'As soon as Dave Robinson came in, I was out,' says Terry Day. 'When Terry got the boot it really affected me,' adds Charlie Hart. 'I felt it wasn't right and I became less tolerant of the whole thing after that.'

As one might expect, Ian already had Terry's replacement in mind – an unlikely candidate by the name of David Newton Rohoman. Ian had always craved a black drummer but not necessarily one who was unable to walk without the aid of crutches. Born in Guyana, South America in 1948, Rohoman had been disabled since birth and came to England as a teenager. He took up the drums initially as a form of exercise and eventually joined the group Kripple Vision and later the Magic Rock Band, who had appeared on the bill with the Kilburns at Canterbury. It was after that show that Ian first met Rohoman. 'He was sitting on cases putting his drums away,' recalled Ian. 'I had no idea he was disabled. I asked him for his number and tried to find out what he was up to 'cos I thought he'd be a great guy to have in the band. I said I'd give David a ring in the New Year. Then he stood up and he was on fucking crutches, then I thought, "Oh God, I won't phone him, two cripples in the same band is fucking stretching it a bit." It would have looked like it was on purpose. Anyway, that's how I met Rohoman. He was sitting down, otherwise I wouldn't have asked him.'

Rohoman's light, swinging style suited the Kilburns, and after a few rehearsals at Wingrave, Dave Robinson arranged for the group to play the Tally Ho, a prominent pub rock venue in Kentish Town, where they made their debut on 10 January 1973. It was a cold night, and the entire group wore overcoats on stage. London listings magazine *Time Out* had trouble with their unusual name, billing them as 'Kilburn High Road'. The following week, matters improved a little when readers were informed that they could see 'Kilburn and the High Road'.

'Dave made it sound very logical,' said Ian. 'The pubs . . . it was free to get in, thruppence on a pint, you'd have local radio supporting it, which had just started up then, plus this vibe you'd create, and the most important thing – playing three hours a night – an excellent way of learning your trade. That appealed. Up to point, what Dave said was true. It didn't go into the realms of, "Yee-ha, here we go! We're all on one!" It was harder than that, but it had the potential and doing six a week, not feeling like a band that said [snide voice], "Hello, this is our new one written by Ron our guitar player, it's called 'Wintry Day'." I saw a geezer in Canterbury with a bouffant barnet say that. I said, "Fucking hell, I'm going home in a minute!"'

Ian kept it snappy. Rock 'n' roll classics were interspersed with original compositions and the odd novelty song, such as Alma Cogan's 'Twenty Tiny Fingers'. The audience was sparse, but a handful of zealots positioned themselves in front of the stage and made approving noises. 'Ian was very clever at having a layer of cheerleaders, a couple of mates in the front row going bananas,' says Charlie Hart. 'Really, he was very vulnerable and always needed people to tell him he was great.' Ian loved it when members of the audience heckled him, recalling, 'There used to be these two girls in rolled-up trousers and seaman's jerseys, shouting "Sexist!" when I sang "I'll have you . . . girl of fifteen . . ." I used to say, "This is for all you fifteen-year-old-girls hanging round the toilets." They shouted back, "You fucking cunt, I'm eighteen, not fifteen." There was a Caribbean geezer called Jerry, at the Tally Ho. He used to put his head in the bass drum. He said, "Ian, Gary Sobers was born with a cricket ball in his hand, you were born singing." Jerry! He was lovely.'

The Kilburns hammered the pub rock circuit throughout the spring of 1973, with frequent appearances at the Tally Ho, the Kensington near Olympia and the Hope and Anchor in

Islington. None of these venues offered much in the way of facilities for the musicians, and the money was always meagre, but working these London venues made Ian feel important. As he recalled, 'The dressing room facilities were somewhat . . . fourteen-year-old junkies shooting up and you're three inches deep in piss and water . . . but we still pretended we were at the Albert Hall even though it was the Tally Ho. It was possible to feel ambitious, not that I was that ambitious, but it wasn't just some old pub gig. We played all our own gear, plus Bill Haley and obscure b-sides. I wanted each song to be unlike the song that went before it and came after it, stylistically. It was a deliberate policy not to play all the same kind of music. Reggae, calypso, the rhythms and the colours of the keys would change. It was hard to pin it down. Mostly to make it interesting so I wouldn't get bored.'

Gradually, the music press began to take notice of the Kilburns, with an early article appearing in *Time Out*, written by John Collis, the journalist credited with coining the term 'pub rock'. The Collis review was encouraging, but the group's next piece of press forecasted great things. Written by a London-based American student named Stephen Nugent, the article appeared in *Let It Rock* bearing the caption: 'Taking The Low Road – a potential supergroup have so far chosen the path of righteousness and small rewards.' In his article, Nugent predicted that before long the pubs would be too small to comfortably hold the number of people that wanted to hear Kilburn and the High Roads. 'The pub rock scene was not extraordinary to me,' says Nugent. 'In America, it had been going on for years. I didn't have any sense of what the path of a successful musician would be in London, but the place was packed and they weren't just there to have a drink. They were definitely there to see what was happening on stage.'

Ian had his own ideas about pub rock: 'The bands I saw in the pubs were all good musicians, but it was a bit samey. 'The Ducks had a certain rocking element; the Bees were pretty mellow; the Brinsleys had that organ-dominated Band sound, but a sameness about their tunes. Mostly, it helped to get those gigs if you played in that style, mellow, then you ended up doing "Brown Sugar". It was a little too mellow for my taste in music. We wanted to be a little more brittle than that, plus most of us had been to art school, and we thought of ourselves as being a bit snappy. It was actually second-hand gear, but we thought we were well turned out. My idea about being in a band has always been a little bit of Tommy Cooper, a little bit of Chuck Berry.'

It was Dave Robinson's custom on Monday mornings to systematically telephone every contact in his address book. 'What's happening?' he would enquire, with seemingly genuine interest. Acting as the Kilburns' unofficial manager, he spread the word and alighted upon thirty-one-year-old writer and broadcaster Charlie Gillett, who was then preparing to launch his own independent label, Oval Records. Gillett and his business partner, Gordon Nelki – a dentist by profession – had recently been to Louisiana and come back with a suitcase full of records including Johnnie Allen's 'Promised Land', but were not averse to the idea of also working with home-grown talent. Robinson encouraged Gillett to go see the Kilburns at the Tally Ho, and the next week Gillett mentioned the band on his BBC radio show *Honky Tonk*. 'I said, "There's this amazing bunch of anarchic musicians you should see,"' recalls Gillett. 'Three weeks later at the Tally Ho the singer limped up to me and said, "You keep going on about how good we are on the radio, why don't you come and fucking manage us?"'

Charlie and Gordon were sufficiently flattered and bemused. Having checked out the Kilburns, they both recognized that Davey Payne was a musician of the highest level and that pianist Russell Hardy had 'an amazing range of references, from Charlie Kunz to Fats Waller and everything in between'. They also considered Ian to be a unique entertainer and clever lyricist. 'For better or for worse, Charlie and Gordon became our managers,' said Ian. 'I'd seen Charlie's reviews in *Rolling Stone* magazine. He was a pretty cool geezer. He knew what he was on about. He played us Dr John and "Small Town Talk" by Bobby Charles . . . a lot of records he played I would really dig. He knew I liked jazz. I may have turned him onto some of it, but I loved that New Orleans stuff he played that I'd never heard. A good vibe was coming from him and Gordon. They helped us a lot. It was very logical and sensible, we had meetings and everything. I think we even had our VAT sorted out at one point.'

The modest success of Kilburn and the High Roads during their initial foray into the pubs had taken the group by surprise. After all, their presentation was a shambles and the motley assortment of musicians defied the prevalent trends in music – glam, progressive rock, larger-than-life stadium shows and absurd posturing. Ian's oddball crew subscribed to none of this, but at a time when musical proficiency was a key ingredient, Ian's singing was way off key. According to Paul Tonkin, 'Ian was practising his scales in a Kentish country lane one dark night, and a farmer's wife emerged from her cottage asking, "Is there a pig out?"'

'I used to apologize for singing out of tune,' said Ian. 'I'd say, "Sorry about that, I'll try harder on the next one, ladies and gentlemen." Charlie Hart used to get the hump with me for apologizing. He said, "Don't apologize, the only people who know you're out of tune are other musicians, and they don't even pay to get in." But I apologized anyway because it was making *me* wince. It was pretty far off the mark occasionally. Charlie Hart thought it all came out of the heart, which is probably true. He'd say, "If your heart's in tune, you'll be in tune."'

Charlie Hart was actually becoming exasperated with Ian's refusal to acquire some musical skills, telling Ian: 'Look, you're trying to be a singer. Do you want to be a singer or don't you? Sit down at a keyboard and learn the notes of the fucking scale.' Ian told Hart that he didn't want to learn any notes. 'He really didn't want to know about it,' says Hart. 'Why? Well, there's a lot of mystique around what makes a great musician. People think it's not something you can learn, like carpentry. That's a myth, and Ian was heavily affected by it. He had his gods like Little Richard or the Rolling Stones and he thought it was an insult to them to start unravelling it, to see how it worked.'

Knowing he would never be a great vocalist in the traditional sense, Ian compensated with his commanding physical presence. It was a trick he had developed at art school, hyper-aware of the magic he could generate with a limp and a glower. Charlie Gillett remembers, 'It was a slouch and a glare and a stare, and it did look as if he might be angry about something. He would scowl at the musicians, and the whole place would be under a certain amount of tension. The musicians really didn't know if he was suddenly going to throw a wobbler.'

Confident that he could hold an audience's attention, Ian avoided eye contact and exaggerated his condition whenever the need arose. It worked! Nothing compared with the high drama of his stage entrance. The band members would saunter on and commence a slow-burning riff, then Ian would cut a mysterious figure in the full thirty seconds it took him to reach the microphone. An audience would gather in front of the stage, its curiosity aroused. Then, rooted to the spot, Ian would hold the crowd's attention with smaller gestures such as a contorted facial expression or the deployment of some bizarre prop. Still hungry for attention and without uttering a word, Ian would exploit the more sinister aspects of his appearance, cleverly converting his disability into a solid gold asset.

Ian certainly enjoyed his heightened status on the pub rock scene and now felt that stardom was within reach. And anyway, as a disabled former grammar school boy with modest qualifications, whose teaching post at Canterbury was about to be terminated due to frequent absence, he had little choice but to try and mould the Kilburns into a working unit that would generate some income and fulfil his unique rock 'n' roll vision.

'I got the sack from Canterbury, where I was supposed to be teaching two days a week,' said Ian. 'That was where the old wedge was coming from. It was quite well paid, teaching in art school, but it all sort of exploded.'

In March 1973, the Kilburns 'came off the road' and went into Jackson's Studio in Rickmansworth for 'a day's banging'. The demos they recorded that day with engineer Vic Maile are reckoned to be among the best tracks the group ever achieved, but the tapes are lost. Another session, at Island Studios in Basing Street with producer Muff Winwood, was less successful, but the group was slowly gathering material with which to approach the record labels. Charlie and Gordon started shopping around and also encouraged Ian and Russell to come up with more original material. 'Ian would type up the words and come out with ideas about how the song should go, suggesting the meter,' recalls Russell. 'I tailor-made my tunes in order that Ian could put them over vocally. That's how I had to learn to write songs. I could play piano and knock up a tune, but I told Ian I thought I was a shit piano player. He replied, "It doesn't matter!"'

Ian's next priority was the all-important group publicity shot. He orchestrated the 'bus stop' pose for the photographs taken in the garden at Gordon Nelki's house in Stockwell, in front of a large white sheet draped against the rear wall. Mick Hill, who was behind the lens, recalls that the bus stop idea originated from Charlie Gillett saying on the radio: 'If you go to the Tally Ho and see some people hanging about as if they're waiting for a bus, that'll be the Kilburns.' The same gag would be rolled out a number of times in the coming years to help emphasize the group's extraordinary physical characteristics.

Ian would tinker with the line-up to maximize its visual appeal but, more importantly, to remain in control. As unchallenged leader, he was the conduit to the group's management and therefore in a position to influence business decisions, although he claimed he wasn't interested in record deals. He told me: 'I wasn't that ambitious beyond doing it properly within itself. I would have liked to have done the Albert Hall but I knew I wasn't that good. What first made me really wanna do it was seeing bands at the Royal College of Art. I saw the Pretty Things a lot in 1963, it was all right, but I thought I could do it better.'

Equipped with Ian's 'WEM Vendetta' p.a. system, the Kilburns returned to the live circuit, but there were rumblings in the ranks. Ian already felt threatened by Keith Lucas, the only other Kilburn with front man potential, who was given to unexpectedly thrusting forward during one of his manic guitar solos, momentarily stealing the limelight from Ian. 'We were well aware we had a couple of good-looking boys in the band,' said Ian, 'but Keith Lucas? I never let him anywhere near a microphone!' Although Lucas had to be reined in, he was a relatively minor High Road, happy to defer to Ian on most group matters. Ian was never quite sure where he stood with Davey, the wayward sax man, whose menacing presence rendered him immune from bullying. Conversely, Russell was a poodle whom Ian could easily dominate: shy and unsure, yet bursting with composing talent and practical skills. Russell mildly accepted his role as the group's dogsbody and everyone was grateful.

But bass player Charlie Hart was showing too much muscle. He had his own ideas about where the Kilburns might be going, and even if it was precisely the same destination that Ian had in mind, Ian could not possibly share the glory with a mere bass player, lest anyone should perceive the vision to be less than 100 per cent Dury. 'Me and Charlie Hart had a parting of the ways,' said Ian. 'It was a kind of leadership struggle. I just knew that I wanted to do it a certain way. It wasn't musical differences or anything because it was really early days. We didn't have any musical differences.'

As the Kilburns' musical arranger and owner of the ex-post office van that was used to cart the group's equipment, Charlie Hart was a one-man power base who would confidently challenge Ian on various issues, unaware of the singer's true agenda. Ian's priorities didn't encompass musical arrangements and mundane matters such as transport, providing of course that his own personal ride was assured. He was more interested in cultivating the look of his group. Consequently, he was secretly hankering after the return of Humphrey Ocean to the ranks of Kilburn and the High Roads.

Although still at Canterbury studying art, Humphrey was desperately trying to improve his bass playing and constantly kept in touch with Ian. 'He came down to Whitstable and took me for a walk along the beach,' recalls Humphrey. 'By this time, the Kilburns were becoming a bit of an item. Ian told me: "Charlie Hart is ambitious and so am I . . . but it's not the same . . . I want you to be in the band." The Kilburns were something of a state of mind. I didn't want to be a musician but I didn't mind being on stage and dressing up. I loved that part of it, the artiness of it. I said yes.'

With Humphrey onside, Ian plotted his next move. Ian's problem was his insecurity among 'musos', as he referred to them. Musicians, he believed, were insiders with whom he was unable to communicate. Beginners like Humphrey were impressionable enough, subservient even, but the experienced players had their own language and in-jokes – a different kind of power. Power-sharing was not on Ian's agenda, and so he decided that Charlie Hart had to be fired in as public a manner as possible.

The Kilburns had spent the afternoon rehearsing in the crypt at St Matthew's Church in Brixton, after which they returned to the Nelkis' house in Groveway and convened in the kitchen. As Andra Nelki quietly prepared supper, Ian suddenly exclaimed: 'Charlie, you're out of the band.' It was crude, yet unequivocal. In one dramatic moment, Ian had asserted his authority and sent a shiver through the ranks. It came as a shock to everyone, especially Gordon Nelki and Charlie Gillett, who thought they were managing something that was fixed but now discovered just how fragile groups could be. 'I never knew Ian's logic in choosing musicians,' says Gillett. 'He definitely went for the look as well as for the competence. If musicians were not prepared to kow-tow to Ian, he would rather not have them around. He needed to be the boss and he needed to take arbitrary decisions and not have people argue with him.'

'Ian kicked me out,' confirms Charlie Hart. 'It was his group, but if I work with somebody and put a lot into it, I want that to be acknowledged. Maybe my price was too high in terms of what I wanted Ian to acknowledge, but it was more like a strategic move on his part. Humphrey looked great dressed up in all that stuff that I wouldn't go near. Ian's attitude was: "The band is a tableau." He'd had a very profound involvement in the Mick Hill photo shoots and was always on to me about my hair, which he thought was too long. I didn't have the look he wanted and I wasn't prepared to let him mould me.'

Following Hart's dismissal, Davey Payne walked out in sympathy. For a moment it looked as if others might follow. Threatened with mutiny, Ian announced that the Kilburns would be put on ice for the foreseeable future, or at least until Humphrey had finished his studies at Canterbury. 'Charlie and Davey pulled away,' said Ian. 'I was quite pleased because I'd sooner work with Humphrey than Charlie at that point, and Humphrey was coming to the end of his final year, I think, and he was free to be in the band. Humphrey really wanted to join. He had been in an early line-up with a green Gretsch guitar, a boiler suit with nothing on underneath and his hair in pigtails. His guitar wasn't plugged in, but he looked so great on stage. And I definitely wanted the group to look sprauncey, giving it a bit.'

The Kilburns reconvened with Humphrey on bass, but Davey Payne had gone missing. With live dates fast approaching and no sax player, Gordon Nelki sent out a search party. 'Had anyone seen him on the Underground . . . or in the pubs?' wondered Gordon. 'For a couple of weeks we went out looking for Davey Payne like people today look for teenagers who have left home. It took a while to find him, but when he rejoined and Humphrey was in it became the spectacular visual band.'

But first Davey had to be convinced that returning to what was now clearly Ian's band was the right move. A discussion took place, again in the kitchen at Groveway. Ian summoned all of his persuasive powers to assure Davey that the Kilburns would soon be recording and securing a contract with a major label. Davey consented.

'This was the final piece in the jigsaw,' says Humphrey. 'I was walking past the door when Davey said, "Yeah, I'll give it another try." I came into the kitchen and said, "Yeah! We've got a band!" and I could see Ian going, "Ssh . . ." in case it frightened Davey off. We now had the new line-up, ready to go, and we started rehearsing.'

As those who have tasted a modicum of success in the precarious world of pop will attest, to keep your feet on the lowest, yet crucially important rungs of the ladder, it helps to be close to the action. For Ian, this meant 'the smoke' and the dim lights and grubby venues of the capital's pub rock circuit. By 1973, he knew London like the back of his permanently gloved left hand. He loved the city and was thrilled when the city reciprocated. He found celebrity intoxicating. 'Every night, you'd always meet somebody who knew what you were trying to achieve,' said Ian. 'That encouraged me. It was like sharing a secret. We used to go down all right, but you do in a real good atmosphere. When people discover you they sometimes think they own you and they get quite defensive. I remember getting out of the motor at Scratchwood one night and being recognized. Thank you, London!'

In July, after a three-month hiatus, Kilburn and the High Roads returned to the boards with dates at the Kensington and, on 2 August, their debut at Dingwalls Dancehall. Dingwalls had recently opened in Camden Town, offering extended drinking hours and bistro dining. Canoodlers and surreptitious drug users could take advantage of the club's countless nooks and crannies, and everyone enjoyed its continental canteen atmosphere. Although not a typical pub rock venue, it booked many of the up-and-coming groups and quickly became the haunt of the in-crowd.

'After playing about nine months in London there were about five pubs you could go in and get a free drink,' recalled Ian. 'Dingwalls was like that. I'd go there when I was off-duty and it was nice. The other really good thing is you change back into your civvies and you can go back into the audience, you don't hang about round the back. Not only do you meet a lot of nice people that way, you get a lot of feedback, it's shared. You're not elevated in any way. All those aspects were good. At thirty-one, I was quite fond of myself, with what I looked like. I was quite confident about the glamour quotient.'

Unlike the pubs, Dingwalls was a hunting ground of the seasoned 'rock chick' – typically a summer-of-love survivor in her mid-twenties, a veteran of many a drug-crazed night in the Speakeasy carousing with superstars of the Keith Moon variety. This epitome of groupie sophistication was now turning her attention to more humble prey. 'Ian said they were always fascinated by his disability,' says Russell Hardy. 'He used to work on that angle and it always paid off.' Keith Lucas adds, 'These girls were groupies and Ian wanted to be popular. He thought of himself as incredibly handsome and was quite a vain person. He used to keep himself clean and would never be seen in public looking rough. I can remember being on a train with him once and he told me: "Sit up, the girls like it if you sit up with your back straight."'

Ian had grown accustomed to the odd night away, but as the pressure increased he spent less time with his family. After a sweaty gig in London, he would invariably camp at Keith Lucas's flat or Gordon Nelki's house, which now served as the group's HQ. The basement kitchen was its nerve centre and roadies Mick Hill and Paul Tonkin slept in the roof space of the attached garage, keeping an eye on the blue Commer van, its registration plate bearing the letters KUW. This, declared Ian, stood for 'Kilburns Under Way'!

Back in Wingrave, Betty's life was getting harder. She and Ian had always lived hand-to-mouth, relying on little more than his sporadic teaching income and disability benefit. Now, his absence added to the strain. Occasionally, he would return home, explaining to Betty his need to be in London, where the Kilburns were 'happening'. Betty understood why the group was important to Ian, but she was becoming increasingly suspicious of his motives. She knew only too well that most rock musicians behaved like animals and that many of them – even those at the bottom of the food chain – were at their wildest when casual sex was on the menu.

The wave of female attention in the clubs posed no problem to Ian, the incorrigible ladies' man. As a child he had been surrounded by fussing, caring aunties and had become instinctively sympathetic towards the opposite sex and generally keen to please. He was especially fond of girls who were amused by his latest rhyming couplet and he sought their approval. But none of them measured up to Betty, the artist and hardworking homemaker of whom he was still in awe. She was not one to stand in the way of 'progress' and allowed him to indulge his musical whims, but while Betty was in Buckinghamshire, immersed in her paintings and running the home on a shoestring, Ian was in London, making the scene. Highly susceptible to female flattery and driven by the prospect of fulfilling some long-held erotic fantasies, he exploited every opportunity and slammed his marriage into reverse.

8

No Hand Signals

North London, 6 August 1973. At the Lord Nelson, a Victorian pub in the Holloway Road, music lovers could drink at the bar yet keep one eye on the band via the venue's closed-circuit TV system. A single camera was trained on the stage, where Kilburn and the High Roads were unveiling their new song, 'You're More Than Fair'. A lilting saxophone hook punctuated the arrangement as the singer told us that his girlfriend had 'a gorgeous bum' and 'titties' that were 'nice and small'. As he delivered his saucy story, he was unaware that he was about to meet his dream date/soulmate.

Amongst those digging the Kilburns that night was Denise Roudette, a nineteen-year-old goddess of Anglo-Trinidadian extraction. 'I hadn't heard of Kilburn and the High Roads,' recalls Denise. 'I'd always been in tune with music and wondered where the sound was coming from. I looked up at the TV monitor. The singer had this huge head – he looked triangular in shape, but the visuals didn't match the music. I left my friends at the bar and went to investigate.'

Ian was certainly smitten with Denise when she approached him in the break. He admired her exotic skin tone and quick, sparkling eyes. She was physically more striking than anyone he had ever met and hip to music too, having been raised in South Africa, where, as a child, she witnessed concerts by visiting jazz stars like Ray Charles and Louis Armstrong. At the age of thirteen, while living in Blackpool, she had attended a

Jimi Hendrix concert and briefly met the famed guitarist at the stage door. It had left an indelible impression on her, besotted as she now was with music and music makers.

Denise, who was at college studying dentistry, was spending the summer holidays with friends in London when she wandered into the Lord Nelson with no knowledge of the music on offer. 'I thought the Kilburns were great, but what really got me was that they weren't pretending, or putting on an act. They weren't trying to look odd; they were authentic. They were living their music and they owned their look. I was attracted to Ian, I guess, but it was not a physical attraction. I was attracted to the vibe, how free he was. He wasn't pretentious; he was simply himself. I don't know if that was because he'd had to cope with his physical disabilities. I had this feeling that the Kilburns were his students, which in a sense they were.'

The group returned to the stage and performed 'The Roadette Song', a staple of their repertoire for a year or more. When Denise heard Ian sing 'She's a very high Roadette' in a cod Jamaican accent, it was no surprise that she thought she had heard her own family name – 'Roudette'. It would be the perfect conversation piece. 'We were all around Ian because he took it on himself to be a teacher,' says the eloquent Denise, but in a rock 'n' roll twist on George Bernard Shaw's *Pygmalion* – the play in which an ageing professor coaches a young cockney lass on the finer points of spoken English – Ian would be teaching Denise the language of the gutter.

Since the Kilburns' early days, Ian had been slowly establishing his public persona through the seemingly autobiographical nature of his lyrics. To the outside world, he was one of us, 'a geezer', a streetwise barrow boy, a walking encyclopaedia of East End humour and cockney rhyming slang. To those who knew him well, it was something of an act. 'I was a bit cynical when he later became the thinking man's cockney,' says grammar school contemporary Warwick Prior. '"Mr Apples and Pears" is bollocks.' Ian's cousin, Margaret Webb, agrees that his cockney persona was just that. 'His mum was what my mother always called "a lady" and she spoke very nicely, as did her sisters. Ian did not grow up in the East End. He was born in Harrow, he lived in Upminster and he went to school in High Wycombe. There was no reason that he spoke the way he did. It was put on as part of the image, I think.' Childhood friend Barry Anderson adds: 'I could never understand where he acquired his unbelievable cockney accent, because when I was with him, he spoke like me, fairly well in fact. Maybe a little bit "London", but nothing like the accent he acquired in later years.'

Although Ian hadn't yet crafted his adaptation of Lonnie Donegan's 'My Old Man's a Dustman', he did speak reverentially of his dad Bill, his working-class hero who had pulled himself up by his boot straps. Ian remained less forthcoming about his mother's side of the family as he romanced his London background, but the audience was prepared to believe him because of his arch delivery and the wealth of detail that peppered his lyrics. 'I'm cocky-dick about my words,' boasted Ian some twenty years later. 'I always thought that I didn't have any competition. I'm the best in the world by a hundred miles. In a nutshell, I think I'm shit hot.'

Ian was indeed a gifted 'wordsmith', who had tasted enough of London life to inform his image. He cleverly honed his portrait of a rock 'n' roll street urchin, living by his wits, ducking and diving to stay one step ahead of the law, having nicked everything from racy magazines to flash cars. With the Kilburns as an outlet, his writing had turned the corner, progressing from his slightly derivative early efforts to reporting his own experiences and aspirations, as in 'The Upminster Kid', in which 'Gene Vincent Craddock remembered the love of an Upminster rock 'n' roll kid':

> When I was fifteen I had a black drape jacket and
>   sideboards to my chin,

*I used to go around in a two-tone Zephyr with a mean
    and nasty grin,
Twelve-inch bottoms on my stardust flecks and socks
    of dazzling green . . .*

The truth is, when Ian was fifteen, he *wanted* a black drape jacket, but he had to make do with a mail order 'denim rock suit'. Even though he had sported the classic Teddy Boy hairstyle, the Ford Zephyr with its gleaming chrome and *faux* Detroit fins was pure fantasy. But never mind; didn't the great Chuck Berry once write about 'working on a T-bone steak a la carte, flying over to the golden state' while he was incarcerated in prison? Like Berry, Ian injected his songs with dense lyrical colour. 'The Upminster Kid' was poetic fiction, but if his fans wanted to believe it was for real, Ian wasn't inclined to shatter their illusions.

*My good friend Fryer wore a powder-blue suit,
    a criss-cross lurex thread,
He turned seventeen, bought a big motor-sickle,
    he started wearing leather instead,
I could not afford a ruby snaffle tie or the black suede
    Clubman shoes . . .*

In the changing musical climate of the mid-1970s it became de rigueur for emerging rock musicians to claim working-class roots, bending the truth about their family and social backgrounds and glossing over any whiff of education or privilege. They often came from middle- or even upper-class homes, but in the interests of authenticity the impression of more humble origins was preferable. The rock 'n' roll pose was often effective, with many music journalists going along for the ride in search of ever more colourful copy.

In September 1973, ace reporter Nick Kent profiled Kilburn and the High Roads in *New Musical Express* under the memorable headline: 'Hardened Criminals Plan Big Break-Out'. It was a compelling image, especially when accompanied by a grainy shot of the Kilburns in bus stop pose. At once, Ian and his ruffian band were seen as tough outsiders, railing against authority and struggling for survival on the fringes of Tin Pan Alley. Ian was quick to uphold the image.

Describing the Kilburns' 21 August visit to the 100 Club, primarily a jazz stronghold, Nick Kent set the scene:

> Tonight the duffel coats and beards have been temporarily substituted . . . tonight, you see, is rock 'n' roll night . . . the poster on display shows a particularly squalid photograph of what looks like six hardened criminals lined up in full profile. The stage starts to fill out with a motley assortment of individuals. The drummer, a Negro named David, lifts himself on stage by means of two crutches . . . the pianist, Russell, who looks like an original beatnik, takes his place . . . then some character one presumes to be the singer finally appears; he looks like a greased-back, squat Lou Reed – but even Reed never looked quite as oppressive and sinister as this ... he is simply the most charismatic figure I've ever seen on a small British stage.

Ian was tickled pink. He loved the knowledgeable journalist's description of the Kilburns' musical eclecticism and the way he dropped some impressive names into his text, such as American musicians Meade Lux Lewis and Professor Longhair, both of whom rang a bell with pianist Russell. Ian was amused by Kent's reference to 'a character in a motorcycle jacket dancing with a Bianca Jagger lookalike', this being Denise Roudette dancing with Kilburns roadie Paul Tonkin, who made it his job to try and motivate a listless audience. Even more, Ian loved the 'hardened criminals' tag and the fact that Kent's sign-off credited the Kilburns as 'God's own gift to Shepherds Bush Market threads specialists'. Ian couldn't have put it any better himself.

Through his many *NME* features, possibly with the Kilburns in mind, Nick Kent was instrumental in helping to shape the immediate future of rock 'n' roll. Maybe only a thousand read-ers were paying attention, but they were the influential few who would sway their friends and help to spread the gospel, just as Dave Robinson predicted would happen.

On 18 September 1973, shortly after Denise Roudette had returned to college in Bristol, the Kilburns played the City of London Polytechnic in Whitechapel. It was there that Ian met Roberta Bayley, a twenty-two-year-old American who was stay-ing in London. As a rock 'n' roll fan, Roberta had gravitated towards the Kilburns through the snippets she'd heard on Charlie Gillett's radio show. She had worked part-time at Let It Rock – the Vivienne Westwood/Malcolm McLaren boutique in the Kings Road – and had already attended an earlier Kilburns show with McLaren who, she remembers, was something of a fan. 'I was living in a huge flat in Albert Hall Mansions which belonged to a friend,' recalls Roberta. 'It had wall-to-wall car-pets, a TV and a phone and it overlooked the Albert Memorial. Ian and I ended up hitch-hiking back there from Whitechapel. He was probably supposed to get a ride with the band, but he was like, "Let's go!" Sparks were flying, so to speak.'

'We got a ride in a big lorry and went back to this spacious flat. We had a night of romance. I fell madly in love with him. I'm not trying to make myself seem like I'm oblivious to defor-mity, but I didn't give a thought to the fact that he was crippled. Obviously, it was a big issue for him. It might have been part of the reason I was attracted to him. You go home with this person for the first time and they have this leg they have to unstrap and I was like: "OK, get on with it." It wasn't like Jane Fonda and John Voigt in *Coming Home*; we had great sex and everything was fine.'

The following day, Ian and Roberta went to the cinema to see *Scarecrow*, the road movie starring Al Pacino and Gene Hackman, and had as much fun as possible in the few days they had together. 'The fact I was due to go back to America added the extra-romantic element that I think Ian thrived on,' continues Roberta. 'Peter Blake had an American wife, and I think Ian saw me as his American rose. I was a well-scrubbed, WASPy looking girl, smart but unformed. Ian was very much trying to form me and educate me. He called me his "Breck girl".'*

After their whirlwind romance, Roberta Bayley gifted Ian her gold scarab ring and flew home to San Francisco, wondering if she would ever see him, or the ring, again. Before the month was out, she received a rather coy letter containing some mildly flirtatious suggestions and the news that the Kilburns were about to give an interview to Steven Fuller, an American writer from *Penthouse* magazine. 'How many wankers will buy our wares?' Ian wondered.

Riding high on press coverage, the Kilburns were invited at short notice to support the Who – often described as 'the greatest rock 'n' roll band in the world' – on a short UK tour. Keith Lucas broke the news to Ian on 29 October: 'Guess where we're playing on Thursday night! Belle Vue Stadium, Manchester!' Panic set in; overnight the Kilburns would have to progress from playing to a few dozen fans in tiny pubs to performing in front of thousands. '[The Who] were going to do it on their own,' said Ian, 'but I guess their material wouldn't stretch to two hours without recourse to the dreaded *Tommy*.'

Just before the tour got underway, Ian was hoping to 'secure quarters in Whitechapel', courtesy of his co-manager, Gordon Nelki. Ian had just had a terrible row with Betty, one of their last before he left home for good. Ever loyal, she had ironed Ian's stage outfit for the opening show with the Who, but took modest revenge by pressing his trousers along the side seam, so that when he went on stage, his legs looked flat and wide.

* Breck was a make of shampoo.

Nobody quite knew why the Who had requested the presence of the Kilburns on their 'Quadrophenia' tour, but Ian hung on to the theory that Pete Townshend had seen the group at the Speakeasy in November of the previous year. 'Pete knew what we were about,' said Ian. 'We did eight gigs with the Who . . . I think they wanted us to be on their record label . . . it was a hectic fortnight. I saw what could be done with extreme volume. At the Lyceum, the flunky came down with the plates of gear and Keith Moon smashed the lot – same the next night. The third night they came down with paper plates and he tore them all up. He lived by his convictions, that man.'

The tour played to sell-out crowds in Manchester, Newcastle and London, which sold out so quickly that Ian was unable to get a ticket for Peggy. But the trek did little for the popularity of the Kilburns, or their morale. They were unable to project their visual or musical subtleties in such large venues, and most of the audience had no interest in 'the support act'. The road antics of the Who had an overwhelming effect on Humphrey Ocean, who was about to quit the group. 'Humphrey witnessed a load of dodgy reporters telling Roger Daltrey and Keith Moon to throw things and kick the walls down,' said Ian. 'The reporters were winding them up so they could get some shots. Plus Humphrey had done the best part of a bottle of Pernod. He had to be laid on his left side, in this hotel in Manchester, so he didn't choke on his vomit.'

At one point during the tour, Ian and Pete Townshend became engaged in a long, alcohol-fuelled yak, in which the megastar magnanimously offered the Kilburns a support slot on his group's upcoming American tour. Although this was little more than inebriated banter, in Ian's mind it was a reality, and he excitedly announced that the group would soon be California-bound. Gillett and Nelki were sceptical, but decided that passport arrangements should be made, just in case.

As none of the group had work permits, Gordon's wife, Andra, called the US Embassy to request visas. Kilburns roadie

Paul Tonkin was sent home to Southampton to get his passport and instructed to come straight back to London. Upon his return, Tonkin met the group in the US Embassy in Grosvenor Square, to be greeted by Ian, exclaiming: 'I don't know why you're getting a visa, you're not even coming to America! You dropped an amp the other day. You're out!' All of the tellers looked up from their desks, listening to Ian's rant, while the rest of the Kilburns sat nearby, absolutely mute. It was Tonkin's first brush with Ian's 'bad side'. 'I can date his megalomania from that time,' says Tonkin. 'He'd been treating me like a dogsbody. "Get my suit!" His head was getting big.'

The Kilburns didn't go to America. 'The whole thing was a fabrication between Ian and Pete Townshend,' says Gordon Nelki. 'The Who had already hired Lynyrd Skynyrd!' Ian was naturally disappointed that the US trip had fallen through. He had dreamed of the Kilburns opening for the Who in California and was also looking forward to reuniting with Roberta Bayley, who had flown home to San Francisco just a few weeks earlier. But instead of appearing in front of a 12,000-strong crowd at the Cow Palace, the scene of the Beatles' final US concert appearance of 1965, the Kilburns were booked to play a three-night stint at the Zero 6, a discotheque in Southend-on-Sea.

Following the Who tour, Humphrey Ocean decided to leave the Kilburns. 'I'd had enough,' he says. 'I realized that it was not for me. I wanted to be a painter, and all of the hardships that one had to endure I would endure for painting, but not for music. My heart wasn't in it. I knew very well that I didn't want to be a bass player, having tried it and been quite good at it. It wasn't really what I wanted to make of my life.' Ian recalled: 'When Humphrey decided to leave the Kilburns, I remember Peter Blake outside Dingwalls, more than a bit pissed, trying to persuade him not to leave. Peter was sitting on a Porsche and he kept being sick, then he had to go and sit on another bit of the Porsche! "Tell Humphrey not to leave the band, anyone can be a fucking painter!" But it wasn't true, so he left.'

In December, the Kilburns hired a new bass player, Jerome Lucas (no relation to either Keith or Chris Lucas). Jerome had formerly been in Kripple Vision with David Rohoman, but his tenure in the Kilburns would be short-lived. For a mad moment, the group considered asking Paul McCartney to join. 'Andra worked with Linda McCartney on photography projects, so there was a connection,' says Gordon Nelki. 'We were quite serious about it. We thought Paul would enjoy it.' When it became clear that the McCartney was not about to soil his hands on the pub rock circuit, the Kilburns advertised for a new bassist.

Amongst those who auditioned for the job was Charlie Sinclair, formerly of the band Phoenix. Sinclair, who hailed from the Shetland Islands, was a great musician, and his diminutive stature would enhance the group's unconventional appearance. At a little under five feet in height – a vital statistic not lost on Ian – Sinclair would frequently be described in the music press as either a 'dwarf' or a 'midget'. Ian would affectionately nickname him 'Iron Man'. Charlie Gillett was suspicious about Ian's motives for selecting Sinclair, 'but it kept the look of the circus about it all, a band in which Ian wasn't the only weird one'.

Choosing my words carefully, I remarked upon Sinclair's height to Ian. 'There are people who might say . . . [Ian laughs] that the Kilburns were sort of . . . [Ian laughs again] somewhat visually . . . visually impaired,' said Ian with a smile. 'The day we auditioned little Charlie, at a church in Brixton, we'd had 'em all in, six foot two, banging their basses. Charlie was easily the best. We were rehearsing in the vicar's office, and Charlie was waiting in a pew while we had our group discussion. I was sent out to talk to him. I said, "Well, Charlie, you're the best bass player we've had, but you can't join the band." He asked, "Why?" I said, "Because you're too small." He exploded with rage and said, "That's no fucking reason." I said, "I'm pleading with you, Charlie, three out of six [unusual looking people]?" He said, "No, I'm joining." We went, "Oh, all right then."'

Ian knew that with the wee one on board, the Kilburns

would look more bizarre then ever. Humphrey had observed that people found it hard to walk past the Kilburns without wanting to come back for a second look. Peter Blake agrees: 'The eccentricity of the group was more important than the music. Humphrey couldn't play! But he looked wonderful, a tall gangling figure in a white zoot suit with the crotch at the knees. And Rohoman! When Ian saw him leave his drum kit and walk away on crutches, he had to have him! So when a very short bass player walked through the door, Ian would have chosen him above any normal-size person. I recall they played a gig in Bath and stayed in one of the cheap hotels close to the station. When Ian called to make the reservation, he said, "I want to book some rooms. We're a band. There are six of us, one's a midget, two of us are cripples and one of the cripples is black."'

Although the recent tour with the Who had not won the Kilburns a vast army of new fans, it had lifted the group's profile just enough to attract attention from the major record labels. CBS talent scout Dan Loggins was leading the pack. To investigate the Kilburns' recording potential, Loggins paired them with former Velvet Underground producer Geoffrey Haslam and arranged some pre-production sessions at Majestic Studios in Clapham. Haslam was slightly underwhelmed by the Kilburns' musicality but invested a lot of hours in dissecting 'Rough Kids' and rearranging it as a potential hit single. Ian was extremely excited by Haslam's work and the prospect of signing to a major label. He boasted to friends that the deal would provide the group with 'an equipment van and a nice medium p.a.', the dream acquisitions of every unsigned band.

That Christmas, Ian visited Peggy and his aunties in Devon and had plenty of time to reflect on his musical career. He believed that the CBS deal was in the bag and that the label would be sending the Kilburns into the recording studio with producer Tony Ashton, of 'Resurrection Shuffle' hit-makers Ashton, Gardner and Dyke. Ian had also decided that the Kilburns would be coming off the road for the foreseeable future in order to work up some new songs for their album, but he'd failed to tell David Rohoman and Jerome Lucas. The ill-fated pair heard the news at a New Year's Eve gig in Southend-on-Sea. It didn't bode well for the show, which was also marred by an onstage punch-up between Davey Payne and roadie 'Zeus', in which, according to Ian, 'Davey went berserk because of the awful sound and leapt on Zeus, sax in one hand, mic stand held aloft like an insane Zulu.'

Ian's habit of taking the band off the road in order to pre-pare new material also allowed him to put some distance between himself and musicians he was seeking to replace. It was usually the drummer and frequently David Rohoman. He later told a reporter that the Kilburns had 'been through thirty-six drummers', which was only a slight exaggeration. Ian felt particularly guilty about sacking Rohoman and for a moment considered accommodating him on percussion and backing vocals in an expanded line-up with drummer Barry Ford from Clancy, but the idea was scrapped for financial reasons. Other drummers would come and go, including Louis Larose, who fell out of favour because he had negotiated a healthy session fee, whereas the rest of the group had to make do on a paltry wage.

On 1 January 1974, Ian finalized his next letter to Roberta, con-fessing: 'I've done up a lot of bullshit with girlfriends, getting too far inside defences, building unreal reliance frameworks, needing to be little Mr Terrific to all and sundry.' With Roberta things would be different, he suggested, pleading with her to come back to London to be his live-in lover. 'I'll have a room by 10 Jan and I earn ten quid a week,' he told her. 'Lots of rice . . . hardly any ice cream or movies . . . come to England, as quick as a shiny airplane and a slimy shuddering taxi . . . there is a shocking Roberta shortage in England.'

Hopeful that Roberta would return to London, Ian redou-bled his efforts to find somewhere for them to live. For many months he'd been sleeping in the front parlour of Gordon Nelki's house in Stockwell but craved a personal space where he could set up his desk and write, his current work-in-progress being an early draft of 'Plaistow Patricia'. '[It's] about old East End girlfriend 1960 mingled with dead health service heroin child called Jenny Wren who died in 1962,' Ian would tell his transatlantic muse. By now, Gordon and Charlie had helped Ian find inexpensive lodgings at 26 Stockwell Park Crescent, where he slept on a mattress under a bare light bulb and dreamed of Roberta Bayley returning to the UK.

Another letter and several long-distance phone calls later, the love-struck Ms Bayley was on her way back to London. 'We had no money and it was bleak,' recalls Roberta. 'I didn't know much about Ian, but somehow we'd hit it off. After a couple of months and going to a few shows, Ian introduced me to people like Peter Blake and Chris Killip. He may have been giving money to Betty, but there was no salary, and he wasn't in a position to woo me. His personality was strong, although he had a big chip on his shoulder. He didn't ever speak about it, but I feel he just wanted to be tall and handsome, a matinee idol, like a seventies Tony Curtis.'

The CBS deal was vetoed by the company's business affairs department, but Charlie and Gordon were able to capitalize on the Tony Ashton connection and secure a recording contract for the Kilburns with Raft Records, a subsidiary label of Warner Brothers run by former Soft Machine manager Sean Murphy. Ashton was hired as producer, and recording sessions were booked to take place at Apple Studios in Savile Row during February and March. It was the era of the 'three-day week', and Britain was enduring a period of political crises, miners' strikes and power cuts, from which recording studios were not immune. Many hours were lost at Apple, but the Kilburns and Tony Ashton were happy to repair to the Thistle public house and drink Pils lager under candlelight until electricity was restored. Roberta Bayley notes that Ian had never really been in a big studio before and recalls, 'When he was singing one of his love songs, he wanted me to be in the booth with him so he could look down at me and get that emotion.'

Denise Roudette had returned to college shortly after meeting Ian the previous autumn, but she saw him whenever the Kilburns played in the Bristol area, much to the annoyance of Roberta: 'I found out about it and I wasn't happy about him going back with Denise because I was nuts about him. I went back to America and settled in New York. Then the letters really started.'

Over the next five years, Ian would correspond with Roberta, telling her his frustrations, confessing his innermost worries and sharing his dreams. His letters were often long and rambling, but always fastidiously written, rapidograph on foolscap, or occasionally typed with use of the red ribbon for emphasis. The more vulnerable Ian felt, the smaller his handwriting would become, but if he was on a winning streak, his writing would get bigger as the word count decreased. Throughout the entire period he would fantasize about relocating to America (while making clear his reservations about the country) and sharing Roberta's Manhattan apartment. As an alternative, he pleaded with her to return to London but he knew it was impossible, not least for financial reasons. 'His modus operandi,' says Roberta, 'was that mad passionate thing that can never happen.'

Ian's mail to Roberta was often posted in secret. If she wished to reply, she was instructed by Ian to mail her correspondence to an appointed member of the Kilburns' entourage who would then discreetly pass the letters to him, usually in the group van on the way to gigs. It's probable that Ian's subterfuge was designed to avoid bringing his intimate writings to the attention of Denise, who in the spring of 1974 quit college and headed back to London. When she arrived, Ian had his head in *Penthouse* magazine, which in its April 1974 edition published Steven Fuller's article under the title: 'You Don't Have to Have a Leg Iron but It Helps'. Fuller's piece contained a profile of the Kilburns and an in-depth interview with Ian. It was his first major outpouring in the media and in many ways his most honest, confessing that he'd been 'a right little cunt' at grammar school.

The Kilburns' album for Raft was now completed and much to Ian's delight, the legendary Nesuhi Ertegun, president of Warners International, would be flying in from New York, but not, it transpired, to toast Kilburn and the High Roads. Within days of Ertegun's visit, the Raft label was unceremoniously closed down. At the end of March, a press release stated that all Raft artists would be invited to join another label in their group. For the ailing Kilburns, this would require the approval of Warners' US label chief, Joe Smith. On 16 April, a jet-lagged Smith popped into the 100 Club to check the group out, but was not impressed. After the show, the Kilburns were taken out to dinner by Warners and apparently invited to attend 'an orgy' at the Swiss Cottage Holiday Inn with 'twenty hookers'. Ian feigned disgust, saying he did not wish to partake of such 'Hefneresque pleasures'.

Joe Smith returned to Los Angeles, recommending that Kilburn and the High Roads be dropped, but the company exercised its option for another album, and the group remained contractually tied to Warners, even though there was little prospect of going back into the studio. Ian wrote to Roberta, observing that his bitter missives were 'beginning to look like Robinson Crusoe's diary during the pirate season . . . record company creeps are so fucking stupid and loud and used to their own shit-arseing that they fail to notice when others are not convinced,' he complained. The situation was dire, but Ian was not going to give up yet and there would soon be cause to celebrate.

PART THREE

ACCLAIM

9

Rough Kids

South London, 1974. After many years of wishing to depart the capital, journalist Clive Davies was preparing to quit his lodgings at Oval Mansions on the Kennington Park Estate. Via mutual friend Geoff Rigden, he knew that Ian was in the market for accommodation. Davies was urbane, eloquent and more than a match for Ian when it came to philosophical debate. Rigden had been wary about introducing them to each other as long ago as 1963. 'You know that old cliché,' says Rigden, 'never introduce your best friend to your new best friend? You hope they'll like each other, but usually it doesn't work. When they first met, Ian was unusually reticent. He would always go a bit quiet when Clive was around. Clive was a proper writer, which Ian respected, so he wouldn't try it on.'

The tenancy of number 40 Oval Mansions was transferred to Ian, and on 22 April he and Denise Roudette moved into the tiny flat. It had limited plumbing and was dominated by the nearby gasworks, but it overlooked the Oval cricket ground and for three pounds a week was a steal. The building itself was part of the estate of the Duchy of Cornwall, who employed two ageing spinsters, Miss Piall and Miss Utin, to collect the rent. Three flights of stairs – fifty-one steps in total – were no problem for Ian, who had become fit and lean through tireless gigging with the Kilburns.

Ian told friends that he now lived at 'Catshit Mansions', lest anyone should presume his new address was some grand dwelling. Shortly after taking up residency he encountered one Fred Rowe, who lived on the first floor at number 37 and worked as a glazier for the council. Fred, who was in his late thirties, was balding, wiry and muscular and insisted on giving Ian a hand with carrying various items upstairs. He struck Ian as the sort of man one shouldn't argue with, and Ian's instincts were quickly proven sound. 'Ian wasn't keen on him initially,' says Denise. 'All he could hear from their flat were endless arguments between Fred and his girlfriend, Val. Sometimes Fred would open his window and shout: "Sorry neighbours!" One day I struck up a conversation with him and he said, "Oh, do you live upstairs with the little guy? You must come down for a chat."'

Over cups of tea, Ian sat in rapt attention as Rowe related details of his criminal past. As a child in wartime Battersea, he'd been forced to steal food from bombed-out shops to keep his family alive and, from there, he drifted into crime. He had been in and out of prison throughout his adult life for his involvement with south London's most notorious safe-cracking gang, under the stewardship of the infamous Johnny Pyatt. Fred's party trick, Ian learnt, was shinning up a drainpipe to enter a warehouse building through a top-floor window, earning him the nickname 'Spider'. He would then disable the alarm, allowing the rest of the gang to break in. On his last fateful job, Fred slipped on a drainpipe collar and fell three storeys, only to be discovered by police the next morning, unconscious with multiple fractures.

Fred still dabbled in crime, but he was at a crossroads; either he had to go straight or face the prospect of interminable porridge. A ten-year stretch in Parkhurst had gone some way to curtailing his love of heights, but meeting Ian was Fred's true 'road to Damascus'. 'I'll never forget the day Fred got some legitimate money,' recalls Denise. He felt really strange about it. He and Val needed a fridge, and he talked to Ian about it. Fred said, "I've got a mate who can get me a fridge," and Ian said,

"Why don't you go and buy a fridge, Fred?" Fred said, "What do you mean, buy a fridge?" We'd bought a cooker on hire purchase and suggested this method to him. When Fred bought his fridge he had tears in his eyes. Going straight was a real struggle because he had to re-educate himself. He was suffering from withdrawal symptoms, but Ian was amazing support.'

Ian was gripped by Fred's underworld tales, and Fred was equally taken with Ian's artistic talents. 'Artists have always been a source of amazement to me,' says Fred. 'Ian could get a bit of paper and out of it an image would appear. Amazing, isn't it? He told me he had a band called Kilburn and the High Roads and the oddments he had, the dwarf and the crippled drummer. I was amazed, because he didn't look like a band bloke. He invited me to some of his gigs, but I never got round to it until the day he knocked on my door and said, "Our van's broken down, can you take us to Peckham?"'

Ensconced in his third-floor flat, Ian bolstered his spirits by confiding in Roberta Bayley. Just three days after moving in he wrote: 'My love is warm in my skinny chest and your little tits will find it just the same. I've dropped half a stone and am decorating this joint when I get time . . . my new leg came and it lies there and waits to be walked about with, but the suede bootees are not ready. I've seen the half-finished items and they look horribly surgical . . . I wish I could afford a gold tooth and a warm swimming pool.' As he wrote the lengthy, detailed missive, he dined on low-fat fare, terrified of gaining weight, although each mouthful of Ryvita and soft brown egg and apple was washed down with alcohol. 'Oh God!' he wrote, 'one egg gone, degeneration of handwriting apparent ... the drunkenness is the same as when you were here and I'm not with another person. Not in love. No parties no cocaine no no no . . .'

Ian's depression was accelerated by the failures of the Kilburns and what he saw as a deterioration in his professional relationship with Charlie Gillett and Gordon Nelki, who were now busy submitting the group's tapes to various record companies. The first glimmer of hope came from Richard Branson's Virgin Records, whose A&R man, Jumbo Vanrenen, was enthusiastic, but Ian told his managers he was not going with a 'hippie company'. Charlie Gillett says, 'It's very difficult for the manager who is trying to weave his way through the thicket of the music industry if the artiste keeps changing the target. Ian was an absolute prototype of that destructive sort of person you find in groups.'

Gordon Nelki felt that managing Ian was like climbing a ladder, only to have Ian pull the ladder away and everyone would go back three spaces. 'He didn't like anybody else knowing the plot,' says Gordon, 'and retained his power by keeping everybody apart. If anybody thought they had a handle on where this thing was supposed to be going, Ian would throw a spanner in the works and disrupt it. He told me that one of his principles was to "make sure that you're always in debt to the people around you, then you've got them". He gave us all hell. You could put it down to the school he went to and the ego a front man needs in order to show off, but with his so-called disadvantages, for Ian to become a pop musician was an outrageous idea. He could hardly walk down the street, but the vision he put together was amazing, brilliant. It attracted spectacular attention from the start.'

Whatever Ian's talents, Nelki and Gillett both feel that Russell Hardy's musical contribution should not be over-looked. 'They were equal in my mind,' says Gordon. In 'Crippled with Nerves', a tender soul ballad enhanced by a sublime Davey Payne saxophone solo, one might imagine that Ian was making a play on his own disability, as he told us he couldn't 'give the girl the respect she deserves' because he was 'shaking with fright', but he'd actually written the words with co-writer Russell in mind.

Russell had been shaking with fright ever since he met Ian

in 1965. He was still lacking in confidence nine years later, but confesses to developing 'a slight swagger' as the songs they had written together looked like they might see the light of vinyl. But Russell too was tiring of the Kilburns' desperate situation and having to play the same arrangements every night just because Ian depended on it. When he received a call from Charlie Hart, inviting him to join a new band, he was tempted by the opportunity to stretch his musical skills.

Whispers of a possible betrayal reached Ian, who realized he was about to lose his songwriting partner and ad hoc chauffeur. An eruption was inevitable. It happened on 4 May, ten minutes before show time at Clarence's in Halifax, when Ian casually commented to Russell: 'I've heard you're doing this thing with Charlie Hart, we need to talk about it.' Russell told Ian he didn't want to discuss it and walked away. 'Ian started going mental, stamping his feet and yelling,' recalls Russell. 'He started shouting, "You fucking nobody! I don't need you!" I walked out of the building and kept on walking. My girlfriend Angela got a phone call in the middle of the night from somewhere on the M1, and her dad had to come and get me.'

Guitarist Ed Speight covered for the departed Russell Hardy when the Kilburns played Biba's Rainbow Room on 19 May, atop the old Derry and Toms department store in Kensington High Street. Pub rock veteran George Butler played drums. The venue was celebrating the opening of its roof garden restaurant, and complimentary drinks were served to the invitees. Denise and Betty attended separately, and Ian flitted between them, consuming twelve measures of crème de menthe, followed by several brandies at the Speakeasy later that evening and a sore head the following morning. During the weeks that followed, he grew more dissatisfied as gigs were cancelled at short notice and record company interest started to wane.

As the Kilburns tottered on the brink of disaster, Ian pestered Charlie Gillett for answers, but none were forthcoming. There was the prospect of a pay-off from Warners, not that this would necessarily improve Ian's personal finances. He yearned to have a telephone installed at Oval Mansions but couldn't afford the connection fee. He occupied his time by decorating the flat, with a red and brown colour scheme in the bedroom, and fixing the shower. 'I've put plain grainy wooden shutters up for beauty and quiet, and it has a 6'6" mirror and a heated wall,' he wrote Roberta Bayley, his pen in danger of catching fire as he let his imagination run riot, telling her of all the things they could get up to if only she would come to London.

Within days of his discussions with Ian, Charlie Gillett received a visit from a large, jovial man named Tommy Roberts, purporting to be 'helping Ian'. It became obvious that Roberts was assuming the role of manager. This disappointed Gillett, who, with Gordon Nelki, had put in a lot of hours on the Kilburns, but acknowledges that Ian may have been restless and in need of a change. 'We were very low key in terms of chutzpah,' says Gillett, 'and I think Ian wanted somebody who was more likely to scam.'

The group's booking agent, Paul Conroy of Charisma Artists, had suggested to Ian he should think about Tommy Roberts. Ian said, 'I knew Tommy vaguely. He was a mate of Peter Blake's. He was more like Flash Harry, and he knew about clothes.' Roberts, however, was not the only prospective manager in the frame. 'By this time I suppose I had started getting more ambitious than formerly,' Ian continued, possibly referring to his secret meetings with Justin de Villeneuve, then husband and manager of the model Twiggy. Discussions were going well until de Villeneuve confessed he could not promise to be at Ian's beck and call twenty-four hours a day. 'Ian wanted 100 per cent, he wanted your blood,' says Keith Lucas. 'You had to give your life to Ian, that's the way it was. He blew Justin out.'

So it fell to Tommy Roberts to take over management of the Kilburns. Roberts had studied art and design at Goldsmiths College in the late 1950s. He had been the proprietor of

Kleptomania, a boutique near Carnaby Street that once supplied Jimi Hendrix with his crushed velvet hipsters. Later, Roberts became 'Mr Freedom', with a thriving clothes and furniture business in the Kings Road, with celebrity customers including the Rolling Stones and Pablo Picasso. He employed as assistants Malcolm McLaren and Bernie Rhodes, future managers of the Sex Pistols and the Clash respectively. McLaren remembers Roberts as 'a character out of an Ealing comedy, a jovial, lovable creature, a really brilliant icon of London.'

Roberts also opened a basement restaurant called 'Mr Feed'em', which offered brightly coloured cuisine. Over the next thirty years, he could be found lurking behind the cash register in a succession of London stores selling everything from retro fashion to cutting-edge home-ware. In Ian's eyes, he had other important credentials, such as a thorough appreciation of jazz and pop style, a terrific sense of humour and a genuine cockney accent. He also had a partner named Willie Daly, who was business cool personified. 'Tommy had that kind of verbal,' said Ian. 'He had it down, he had the humour. "I got the instant hippie kit here . . . go to Pontins, get the Indian bedspread, cut it in half, get the bell, today's the first day of the rest of your life . . . instant hippie kit! Forty-two bob!"'

'He was a bit of a mouth,' says Denise Roudette. 'He was Mr Showbiz. I think Ian felt that this was the missing element – someone who could wave the flag for the band. Things started getting more energetic, the Kings Road, Vivienne Westwood's shop, clothes for the boys. We had a bit of money in the bank and it had been very carefully handled up until that point. Within three days, Tommy had blown the lot.'

Other than a brief period managing 'Fire' hit-maker Arthur Brown, Roberts had no track record in the music business. Nevertheless, he had a pretty dim view of it. 'I didn't really like the music business,' says Roberts. 'The artistes think you're screwing them and successful managers treat their artistes like a sack of potatoes. There are some terrible people around. One famous music publisher – plays polo and all that – said to me, "I buy them a curry and they sign up." I never understood why the artistes signed those contracts. It's money for old rope . . . a thieves' charter.' With this in mind, Roberts set about promoting the Kilburns. First, he had to clear the air with Ian's former managers. 'I went to see Charlie Gillett. He was very pleasant at first, but then he turned nasty. I don't know why. I was only helping Ian. He was annoyed, I suppose.

'Ian still had a contract with Warners,' continues Roberts. 'It wasn't going anywhere, and they were certainly not interested in doing anything. I told Ian I'd try to get him out of the contract. I said to Warners – the chap was in a wheelchair – "I'm the new manager, when shall we come in and start recording? Can you book some nice studio time so we can make a start? We'll need a studio with a nice ramp because, like you, the drummer's in a wheelchair. We'll need a few hours, about three weeks actually, because they're not experienced musicians, plus their meals, because they've got no money." Their faces went grey. I said, "You'd prefer to drop the group really, wouldn't you?"'

With one bound, the Kilburns were free. They retained the van and the p.a. system that had been purchased with Warner money and commenced the search for a new label. 'I went to Pye Records,' says Roberts. 'Charlie Gillett had been to all of the others, he'd done the lot, but he hadn't done Pye. Ian said he would be flattered to be 'on the same label as Max Bygraves', but when the deal was finalized, Pye placed the Kilburns on their 'progressive' imprint, Dawn Records. 'They'd had a hit with Mungo Jerry,' adds Roberts. 'The A&R guy wore cowboy boots, feet up on the table, and his briefcase was covered in stickers.'

David Rohoman had returned to the drum chair after a break of six months. After several unsuccessful drummers, Ian had relented and invited him back into the fold just in time for the group's sessions for Dawn. It was decided that the Kilburns would re-record most of the songs from their unreleased album for Raft, including 'Crippled with Nerves' and 'Rough Kids', which had been earmarked as the first single. With music by the recently departed Russell Hardy, 'Rough Kids' was a Dury masterpiece that conjured up the image of a tearaway street gang terrorizing the neighbourhood. An excellent finished product, it anticipated the onset of punk by several years and put Chris Thomas on course to produce the Sex Pistols.

'It was "Rough Kids" that swung it for me,' says future Pistols bassist and songwriter Glen Matlock. 'I loved the staccato guitar at the beginning. The Kilburns were an important step on the road to punk rock . . . it was the way they presented themselves. A lot of bands around that time were very polite, but Ian was a stroppy bugger. I liked the fact that the Kilburns were confrontational.'

As the needle located the 'Rough Kids' groove, one heard the strained voice of Tommy Roberts. 'Oi, Ian, what's going on over there?' he enquired in a delicious Bethnal Green rasp. 'I dunno,' replied Ian in an equally gravel tone, 'I think there's a bit of trouble . . .'

> Rough Kids play rough games and kick tin cans . . .
> Leave their feet out in the aisle!

Ian was bang on target. In 1950s cinemas across the land, the defiant Teddy Boys he once idolized did indeed leave their feet out in the aisle, to prescribe their territory and intimidate the locals. The image was lodged in his brain from the first time he visited the Ritz, Romford as a teenager and was just one of many crucial observations that characterized his writing down the years.

> Rough Kids move supreme and disobey,
> Trouble comes when times are tough,
> Rough Kids move in teams, don't play away,
> They go round knocking off some stuff!

To fill the void left by Russell's departure, session pianist Roderick Melvin was drafted in. Tommy Roberts had bumped into Melvin at the Last Resort, a cocktail bar frequented by the Chelsea set. He had been in a group called the Moodies, whose party piece was 'Thank Heavens for Little Girls'. Ian described it to me thus: 'There were four girls and Rod, as camp as anything. The first girl would come out and go, "Un," and the second girl would go, "Deux," then, "Trois, quatre," and Rod would come out dressed like a fairy in a tutu and wings and go, "Cinq . . . heavens for little girls . . ."'

For the b-side of 'Rough Kids', Ian selected a song he had co-written with former Kilburns bassist Charlie Hart. 'Billy Bentley (Promenades Himself in London)' opens with another spoken introduction. ''Ello playmates,' intones Ian, 'here's a little London song.' There follows a barrage of cockney phrases, such as 'half a quid, mate' and 'stand to reason'. An instrumental break, not dissimilar to the theme from TV's *Steptoe and Son*, was followed by a roll call of London omnibus destinations – Dalston Junction . . . Clapham Common . . . Ealing Broadway – half sung by Ian, no doubt with his late father in mind.

Sadly, Ian's vinyl debut, released in November 1974, failed to chart, as did the follow up, 'Crippled with Nerves'.

Although Ian had been industriously writing lyrics, no new songs had been completed since Russell's dramatic exit. Rod Melvin, who had accepted Ian's invitation to join the Kilburns after playing piano on the recent sessions, would become Ian's new songwriting partner. 'He had a huge pile of lyrics,' recalls Rod, 'and because he wrote rhythmically, it was easy. Sometimes he would use combinations of words where the meaning wasn't obvious, but you could hear the rhythm he had in mind for the song. I had a few of my own songs, but because Ian's lyrics were so good, I felt embarrassed about showing him any of mine.'

Ian and Rod collaborated on a number of compositions, including 'Broken Skin' and 'Thank You Mum', but when it came to recording these and other titles for the album, producer Chris Thomas was unavailable. To help the Kilburns realize their varied and ambitious range of material, the task passed to Hugh Murphy. In the exacting atmosphere of the recording studio, the Kilburns' musicianship went under the microscope. Murphy identified David Rohoman as a weak link, and session drummer Dave Mattacks was brought in. Mattacks has little recollection of his contribution to the recordings, but his sound is unmistakeable, laying down the groove on tracks like 'The Roadette Song' and 'The Mumble Rumble and the Cocktail Rock'.

'Rohoman's legs didn't function,' explained Ian. 'He had to swivel from the hips. We all knew he wasn't Al Jackson and yet the equation felt right. Plus he was such a wonderful geezer, we never thought about his disability. A lot of producers had told us he didn't lay it down too well, but we knew that.' Rohoman wasn't the only Kilburn to be replaced on the recording; Keith Lucas was also a casualty. 'It was a shame that Ian allowed Keith's guitar and Rohoman's drums to be taken off,' says Davey Payne. 'The whole band lifted when Rohoman joined – OK, he may have sped up a bit, but maybe the band sped up naturally with the excitement of the music. That's how we were live, and, in retrospect, it may have been better if we had been recorded live. But Ian had delusions of grandeur in the studio, he got carried away. All the time we were recording he was saying, "This is going to be the best fucking album since *Sergeant Pepper*!"'

When not in the recording studio, Ian settled into a domestic routine at Oval Mansions, usually rising around noon to plot the day. Creativity was top of the list, but first he would make his phone calls to various Kilburns or their agent Paul Conroy, who would get an ear-bashing if the Kilburns were being sent to too many 'khazis'.* As the afternoon unfolded Ian would

---

* Outside lavatories (venues that were no better than).

listen to Capital Radio or read a Chester Himes detective story. Then his thoughts would turn to new songs, which often started with a rhyming couplet or a title such as 'What a Waste'.

Money was tight, but if there was a good gig at Ronnie Scott's jazz club, it would be prioritized, even if it meant living on biscuits for the rest of the week. Ian's philosophy towards money was that it was there to be used. Spare change or 'shrapnel', however, would be chucked on the floor. If cash for sundries was needed, a quick trawl of the carpet would yield sufficient coins for a pint of milk or a newspaper. 'Ian was extremely cautious about the group's finances, as opposed to his own,' says Tommy Roberts. 'He was a bit of an old woman, more worried about doing kind of clerical work, writing down how many studio hours they'd used. There were lots of notes and bookkeeping. He was always a bit like that. I told him to go in there and sing. Never mind how many hours we were using. If it came to it, I could go in and stretch it, but for fuck's sake, "Don't write it down!"'

'Ian always had his lists,' confirms Denise. 'He did a going-away list, right down to the detail of pencil . . . rubber . . . and it would all be packed. He liked to have his bag packed and sorted, and then he wouldn't have to think about it. Then there would also be the monthly gig list. Where it warranted it, he would organize things. I think that's the way he wrote songs as well. Attention to detail. In the studio he would always talk about "building up a picture".'

While their album for Dawn awaited release, the Kilburns were forced to schlep up and down the motorway, now with Denise at the wheel. Having her drive served two purposes; it relieved Tommy Roberts of the task and provided Ian with company on the road. 'Ian wanted her along on the gigs,' says Roberts. 'It caused problems because the others didn't like it. Ian could be a swine, he was an expert at winding people up, and he and Davey were always fighting. If the gig had been fantastic, Ian would go mad. I once threatened to leave him on the motorway. I couldn't drive the van with him ranting. The others would say, "Go on, Tom, fling the cunt out!" It was that sort of group.'

By this stage, the Kilburns looked more bizarre than ever, particularly the night they raided the fancy dress cupboard at a provincial college gig. On the way home, Rod Melvin led the group into Scratchwood service station, wearing his pink ballet tutu. The tea-swilling lorry drivers couldn't believe their eyes when they glimpsed the procession: Ian limping purposefully; Davey wild-eyed; Rohoman on crutches; Keith in his Liquorice Allsort suit; and the diminutive Charlie Sinclair bringing up the rear. With Denise in a white lab coat, it really did look like 'care in the community', especially when Rod sat down and pulled out his knitting.

'What I tried to put into the Kilburns was the secretive aspect of sartorial elegance,' said Ian. 'If you talk about it, you spoil it. As Oscar Wilde said, "The greatest stylist is the one that remains the most obscure." Once it's public knowledge, it's not stylish any more. I knew the New York Dolls a little bit. We'd been to their gigs at Bibas. I read somewhere that their audience used to wear safety pins through their nipples. I thought, "Lighten Up!" So I unwound the safety pin and put it through my lughole. Sartorially, I'm not a claimer, but I would say that I must have worn the first razor blade.'

The razor blade earring was designed by Martin Cole, aka 'Smart Mart', whom Tommy Roberts had brought in to relieve Denise of driving duties. Cole immediately recognized Ian as 'Toulouse', the crippled Bohemian he had last seen digging Roland Kirk at Ronnie Scott's 'old place' in 1964. Another sartorial gem was 'the Billy Bentley dressing gown', a satin boxer's robe worn on stage by Ian. Tommy Roberts had arranged for this and other outfits to be made by Malcolm McLaren and Vivienne Westwood at Let It Rock. 'McLaren and I were always doing things together,' says Roberts. 'Just before punk, the kids all wanted to be glam, like Bowie. I did bits of

Bowie's clothes. I got Vivienne to make a suit for Ian but he didn't like it – "too baggy".'

It was Let It Rock's Saturday boy, Glen Matlock, who was charged with measuring up the Kilburns for their suits. Matlock recalls, 'Malcolm had a tailor in the East End who I never met, but I had to call him up and give him the measurements. I was the bloke with the tape measure – the John Inman of the punk generation. I measured Davey up for the shiny black suit – outside sleeve, inside leg . . . When I measured Ian up, I got to the shoulders and one side was narrower than the other because of the polio. My granddad had polio. When I realized how withered Ian was down one side, I felt a little bit more of a connection than if I'd only seen him on stage. It made him a bigger bloke in my eyes . . . what he had to put up with.'

Denise Roudette would contribute to the look of the Kilburns by finding unusual items of clothing at charity shops and market stalls. She ran her own stall at Club Row market in Shoreditch, selling pre-war bric-à-brac and Bakelite antiques. The meagre takings would help to keep Ian and Denise fed and watered during the increasingly thin patches in the Kilburns' schedule. On 11 March, the group came off the road. 'After about the third time our bubble had gone up and burst again we were still doing Cleopatra's Club in Derby,' said Ian. 'It was a step up from the pubs, but one you'd rather not take.'

The success of Dr Feelgood had become a major thorn in Ian's side. Although he acknowledged that their singer, Lee Brilleaux, was 'a bit of a number,' he was envious of the Feelgoods' status in the music press and any thunder they had stolen from the Kilburns. 'I'd seen them go screaming past us like a rocket ship,' said Ian. 'I started worrying that we were doing it wrong. You blame your agent, but he wasn't neglecting us, it was just their vibes were happening for the Feelgoods, and they went roaring into the mystic.'

The Kilburns' final show, supporting Dr Hook at Hammersmith Odeon on 4 May 1975, saw Ian, Keith and Davey from the original group with bassist Charlie Sinclair and new drummer Malcolm Mortimore. Backing vocals were provided by 'the Blister Sisters', comprising Celia Collin (later to record as Celia and the Mutations) and Denise Roudette. Few people had turned out to see the group in its death throes, despite Tommy Roberts' injection of theatrical excess. 'I tried to glamorize the Kilburns a bit,' understates Roberts. 'I put a show on at the Chelsea Cinema and built a stage set like Tower Bridge, slightly out of perspective. We half filled the venue. I wanted to get Ian a great big shepherd's crook and for him to lean on it, in a pseudo-religious way, for a biblical kind of vibe. Ian wouldn't have it.'

'Ian wanted the glamour,' continues Roberts. 'He wasn't worried about *Top of the Pops*, but he was very hungry. He wanted to be a celebrity. He was a bit older than the others. He had a wife and two children so there was always a pressure to find him some money. He was a married man, thirty odd. I resented it a bit. I told him he ought to consider doing music part-time and get a job. We gigged hard but we didn't make enough, although we eked out a living with the little bit I got from Pye. It came to the end of the road, and I was broke. I'd devoted myself to Ian for a year trying to break it, but the group had to disband. They'd done the circuit.'

It was now unlikely that the Kilburns would reconvene. Ian was troubled by the constant challenge of juggling musicians and had wanted to evict Keith Lucas from the group for some time, but hadn't been able to fire his longest-serving Kilburn. Instead he'd contrived to make life difficult for Keith, hoping perhaps that he would leave. 'Ian and Keith used to argue a lot,' says Denise. 'Ian told him, "I haven't promised you anything. You're along for your own ride." It's tough to take that when you're around someone like Ian, when he's the lyric writer, the singer, the star, and you're doing your bit, whatever that is. You become insecure when you realize someone else could do your job. "You could be replaced!" Ian would joke. "You saw what happened to the drummers!"'

'I'd started to write with Ian, round at his place,' recalls Keith Lucas. 'We'd written this song, "A Band Called the Tights". Ian wrote the words, and I wrote the music, but Ian tried to tell me he had written it all and it was his song. He wanted sole credit. He knew that songwriting was where the money was; he was no fool when it came to things like that. I said, "Fuck it, Ian, I helped you write it," but he started getting a bit funny. He actually said, "I'm the singer so therefore I should have the lion's share of the money." I reminded him that we were in it together and had agreed to split the money equally. He said, "That's no longer the case, I want the money." I told him that wasn't the way I saw it and that we should stick to the verbal agreement we made. But it was all falling apart, so it was a good time for me to go.'

Kilburn and the High Roads were now effectively finished, although their album was awaiting manufacture, and there was the distant hope that its release might reignite interest. But with no further dates in the diary, the last remaining veterans of the Kilburns, Keith Lucas and Davey Payne, felt justified in claiming some of the group's equipment for themselves. On 30 May, they sold the p.a. system to singer Lene Lovich for £3,000. 'Keith and I needed to earn some money,' says Davey. 'Ian had the two Bedford vans, which were worth more than the p.a. It had been purchased with the Warner Brothers money and we sold it.' This simple transaction sparked an incident that would haunt Ian's conscience for decades to come.

In early June, Ian paid Keith Lucas a visit at his Thurlow Hill flat, accompanied by Spider. Having heard that the p.a. system had been sold following the group's acrimonious split, Ian wanted a word. 'Where's the money?' he demanded. 'Ian threatened to break my legs,' says Keith. 'I told him to fuck off or I'd call the police. I reminded Ian that my uncle was the assistant commissioner of the Metropolitan Police. I also reminded Ian that everything was equal, but he said he was the singer and wanted all the money and I shouldn't have taken any of it. They were still threatening to break my legs if I didn't hand the money over. Maggie, my girlfriend, had gone downstairs and called the police. Ian started saying, "So we can expect a visit from the police then, can we?" I said, "Of course you fucking can, get the fuck out of it."'

Ian's menacing behaviour towards Keith was one part theatrics, two parts desperation. His beloved Kilburns had crumbled, and he was in deep despair, burdened by guilt because his family were living in poverty and there was little he could do about it. He was broke too, having to spend 'three days living on a quid' and unable to afford the stamps to mail an advance copy of the Kilburns' album to his New York muse.

10

England's Glory

Puttenham, Buckinghamshire, 1975. Betty and the children were now destitute and had left the Wingrave vicarage to live in an isolated cottage in a muddy field at nearby Long Marston. Peggy would often step in to help, somewhat embarrassed by her son's inability to contribute to the family. There would also be visits from Aunt Molly and the concerned wives and girl-friends of various ex-Kilburns. Angela Hardy recalls: 'We went to see Betty when she and the two kids were living in that dead and alive hole with hardly any furniture. She had no money but insisted on making us tea and scraped together a tin of tuna and made sandwiches. She didn't complain, but Ian left her with nothing. It really got to me.'

Jemima Dury was now six and attending primary school, a two-mile walk every day. She recalls 'lots of arguments and screaming' between her parents and felt obliged to apologize on their behalf to visitors. 'Mum would occasionally smash a whole load of china, and I remember once she cut herself when she went crazy with the washing-up. It was the worst time for mum as a single parent. Somebody tried to attack her – a mad farmer maybe and there was an incident where a man cornered her in a room.' Looking back on her childhood, it is Jemima's belief that her mother 'released Ian to his career' when he left home in 1973. But it's debatable whether Betty could have lived with a budding rock star any more than Ian could have played second fiddle to a potentially successful painter. Much like his parents' break-up, it appeared to be a separation of convenience.

Funds permitting, Betty would make trips to the nearby cash and carry store to buy food in giant catering packs to save money. For eighteen months, she had been claiming social security payments for herself and the children on the basis that Ian had deserted them. As an absent father, he had been ordered to pay maintenance for his two children, but found it difficult to come up with the money. Although he would visit his family at the cottage and sometimes stay for a few days – on one occasion cutting three-year-old Baxter's hair and perceiving him to be 'male and rugged' – Ian usually came and went under the cover of darkness. If it were discovered that he and Betty were in contact, Betty's social security payments would have stopped, and Ian lived in fear of being prosecuted for fraud. 'Betty can't get welfare if I'm traceable,' he wrote Roberta Bayley. 'The authorities wish to put me away for non upkeep,' he added, only slightly exaggerating the situation.

Back at Oval Mansions, Ian's relationship with Denise was rocky, and from time to time she would return home to Blackpool. Ian admired her 'spirit' and the fact that she could 'fight like a man' and was not afraid to retaliate if he started dishing out the verbal, but behind the knockabout there were deeper emotions at work. Denise may have been ready for slightly more commitment from Ian, but the thought of a second marriage or fathering more children, especially in such straitened circumstances, were anathema to him. He was professionally and personally at his lowest ebb. He sold the Kilburns' Bedford van for £850 but saw none of the cash himself as it was required to pay off group debts.

To his credit, Ian was not deterred by failure, frequently shoring up his confidence by recounting an incident that occurred when he was living in Upminster with his mum; Aunt Molly's guru, Basanta Kumar Mallik, had foretold Ian's life and predicted great fame and fortune. More recently, a horoscope had surfaced, obtained by Molly in Lucknow, India in 1950, while Ian was in Black Notley Hospital, his twisted torso en-cased in plaster. Its predictions were inconclusive, but Ian chose to believe success and happiness were imminent. 'He set great store by that sort of thing if he trusted the source,' says Humphrey Ocean. 'Via his aunts, the guru was to be trusted. I remember after a very late Kilburns gig Ian met a German woman who mesmerized him with her Viennese intelligence and knowledge of Freud and Schoenberg. Or perhaps it was the size of her tits, who knows. But Ian told me, in genuine wonder and belief, that she too predicted he would be famous, and soon! Ian had a way of being right slightly more often than the national average.'

Following the departure of Tommy Roberts, a number of management types were hovering. Dave Robinson reappeared, suggesting that Ian and Rod Melvin ought to relocate to the USA, where they might emulate the recent success of pub rockers Ace. Malcolm McLaren, recently back from New York, was also making noises, but Ian was concerned he might end up little more than a clothes horse for Malcolm's fancy threads. 'There was a point where the subject of management may have passed both of our lips,' says McLaren. 'I was selling music and the look of music. I was interested in the sound of fashion, and at that time in London the sound of fashion was represented by Kilburn and the High Roads.'

Like many of Ian's friends who found it hard to abandon him despite his erratic ways, Charlie Gillett kept in touch while continuing to plug the Kilburns' music on *Honky Tonk*, but there was little prospect of Ian making any real money. He was still tied to his recording and publishing contracts, but his advances were heavily unrecouped, and he calculated that he needed to sell a quarter-of-a-million albums to start earning royalties. He was still writing songs with Rod Melvin, but Russell Hardy had reappeared on the scene, wishing to renew collaboration. Torn between two writing partners, Ian drew a fantasy sketch of an interior with three interconnecting rooms; Rod and Russell were in the east and west wings respectively, each with a grand piano. Ian occupied the middle room, in which he would write lyrics and distribute them to his two co-writers in equal shares. His tiny drawing serves to illustrate his analytical thought and sense of loyalty towards Melvin and Hardy at a low point in his career.

The Kilburns' debut album, entitled *Handsome*, was eventually released in June 1975, but ironically the group had disbanded. Ian didn't much care for the record but loved its packaging. The front cover featured Betty's painting of 'The Kilburns Near Tower Bridge' and on the back was a photograph of former roadie Paul Tonkin, credited to Ian's *nom de camera* 'Poundcake', with the amusing caption: 'Paul Hangs Loose'. The picture had been taken at Wingrave two years earlier. 'Ian was an excellent amateur photographer,' says Tonkin. 'He set up a tripod and lights, put a Chuck Berry record on and every so often said "Freeze!" Lo and behold it turned up on the album cover.'

Handsome received some good reviews from caring journalists who recognized Ian's unique qualities, but the LP failed to sell. Having worked his arse off for five years, during which time the music press had proclaimed him 'a genius', why wasn't it paying off? Perhaps Ian was trying too hard. In retrospect, one can see that his timing was abysmal. Beyond a small number of *NME*-reading devotees, the public were not ready for the musical eclecticism or outré appearance of the Kilburns, easily the most musically adventurous and stylish group on the pub rock scene, but for those seeking a sneak preview of the impending punk phenomenon, Kilburn and the High Roads were a revelation.

Although the Kilburns were no more, there was still some television work in the pipeline. On 25 June, a scratch line-up recorded 'Upminster Kid' and 'Billy Bentley' for ITV's *The*

London Weekend Show, hosted by Janet Street-Porter. Ian, Rod Melvin, Charlie Sinclair and Malcolm Mortimore were augmented by saxophonist George Khan and, on guitar, Oval Music protégé 'Jimme Shelter' (real name Jimmie O'Neill, later to form Fingerprintz). Ian looked sharp with a safety pin earring hanging from his left ear lobe, but his performance was restrained. He had a lot on his mind, balancing a television appearance with the need to maintain a low profile so that Betty would continue to receive social security payments.

On 8 October, the surrogate Kilburns pre-recorded their second appearance for *The London Weekend Show*, performing 'Vidiot' and 'Tell Your Daddy I'm Not a Baddie'. Bassist Charlie Sinclair was replaced by George Dionisiev, whom Ian christened 'George Dinner Suit'. Ian's hair was now greying around the edges, but in his herringbone suit and trilby he once again looked the business. Fred Rowe accompanied the group to the TV studios, giving them a ride in 'the donkey', his maroon van with 'a piece of string on the throttle', registration number UVF 917H (that week). Rowe had never stepped foot in a television studio before and was impressed by the sight of well-known TV newscasters strolling around the building. 'They're just like us,' Ian assured Fred, as were the cameramen and lighting technicians with whom Ian enjoyed a laugh. Rod Melvin cracked up when he heard Ian warning a studio electrician to 'mind those Finsburys [Finsbury Park(s) = arc (lights)], darling.'

Later that month Ian renewed contact with Dave Robinson, who was just six months away from co-founding the independent record label that would give Ian his big break. Ian always had a sneaking admiration for Robinson. 'He was a hustler, and we liked him accordingly. His coat was still hanging in my wardrobe a year later, and he kipped on my floor more times than I've had hot dinners. I've seen him loading boxes in the back of a van and getting sweaty. For all of his verbal, he still gets down there on the concrete, rolls his sleeves up and gets stuck in. But I didn't feel for one minute that I never saw him coming. I could see him coming a mile away.'

Dave Robinson suggested a revised billing to push Ian's name to the fore and build his reputation as a performer. Ian had been thinking along similar lines, telling Roberta, 'If the money arrives I'm going to give the road another go. The band will be me and Rod and four or five other people. I hope I get to like them, but if they play good I don't care. I've been out of circulation long enough to either be written off or loudly welcomed. This one is the last try . . . if this fucks up I won't have the lungs or guts for another go. If one person of wealth or control recognized my attempts and decided to remove the burden vis-à-vis wages and rehearsal place and equipment and allowed me thus to have full control over the qualitatives, I would cool right out and be happy to plough on . . . we're an inch away from making some music of a kind I've always dreamed about.'

Ian also poured out his emotions to Roberta, reporting that he was sick of dossing in other peoples' flats, during periods when he had fled Oval Mansions because of rising tension between himself and Denise, who would now disappear with regularity and one night left her keys on the pavement, to be later found by Fred Rowe. Ian described himself as looking 'very thin and haggard, in need of sun and exersise [sic] and spelling lessons'. He also reported risking trips to Long Marston to see Betty and 'the offspring' in secret. Meanwhile, he continued to fantasize about Roberta coming over to the UK, 'but at this juncture I cannot promise freedom from molestation'.

Towards the end of October 1975, Ian re-emerged with his new band and began playing the London pubs as 'Ian Dury and The Kilburns', mixing old favourites and new songs including 'Back To Blighty' and 'Nervous Piss', in which Ian sung of being caught short just as he was about to have 'a little cuddle and a kiss'. Rod Melvin was retained from the previous line-up and old friend Ed Speight was recruited to play guitar. The group was completed by Malcolm Mortimore, George Dionisiev and saxophonist John 'Irish' Earle, who sported a distinctive Zapata moustache. Robinson agreed to manage the combo, exclaiming to Ian: 'I'm a loser, you're a loser, let's get together.'

Spider Rowe was also on the firm. At the Newlands Tavern in Peckham he learnt that his job entailed a little more than driving. 'When we got to the gig Ian said to me, "Right, you can put the drums up." I carried them over and put them on the stage. The drummer said, "I want them set up." He showed me and said, "That's how I want it done every time." I said, "What do you mean every time? I'm only here to deliver the gear." But Rowe warmed to the idea of working with the Kilburns. Future Dury-aid Kosmo Vinyl remembers seeing Spider in Ian's retinue during this period. 'The first time I saw Fred, he was in the toilet at the Hope and Anchor, on his own, practising introducing the Kilburns! I also remember seeing Ian and Fred outside the Victoria Palace. I said, "Wotcha, Ian," and Fred said, "Fuck off!" He had the vibe.'

Ian paid Fred 'petrol money' and hoped to deter him away from crime. 'I'm busy trying to prevent a bank robbery,' Ian cryptically told friends, adding, 'Spider is a very pleasant fellow and, if you know his boiling point, most useful.' Ian enjoyed having Fred around, but needed to get one thing straight. 'Fred said he wanted to help out,' said Ian, 'but added, "I must tell you, Ian, I've been a very violent man." I said, "Well, I don't mind you being frightening, Fred, because in my game you do get a few nutters. Usually, in my case, they want to love me to death, but if you ever fucking hit anybody on my account, you'll be defenestrating my bollocks. I can look after myself with the mind and the verbal, plus I'm not frightened, but if you ever hit anyone, we stop working together." And we shook hands on that. He never hit anyone, but he did intimidate people.'

Spider's notoriety was to become evident. A popular diversion for many of the groups on the pub rock circuit was to play a Sunday-afternoon concert for the inmates of Wandsworth Prison in South London, organized by promoter John Curd.

The fee was a statutory £2, but for Ian the thrill of playing to a room full of jailbirds compensated for any financial short-coming. On 7 December, when the new Kilburns paid a visit to the prison, Ian's confidence was bolstered by Fred's presence. He was absolutely sure he had the right man on his team the minute he heard one of the prison warders exclaim: 'Spider Rowe! To what do we owe the pleasure?'

'I did "I Made Mary Cry" in Wandsworth,' recalled Ian. 'I felt real shy, looking at the floor. The second time I felt more brazen, fixing the inmates with a stare. They all looked away.' Or, as Ian wrote to Roberta that December, 'The prison gig was very rewarding, but I think the cons were a bit shattered even though I toned my outlaw shit down . . . I've been looking at audiences and give eyeball stick these days, but the prisoners (all ages and proclivities) seemed to be embarrassed at too intimate a relationship . . . [the warders] were quietly peeved at seeing Fred driving his van in and out of the main gates.'

Ian Dury and the Kilburns were musically more accom-plished than the High Roads, but a new era was dawning in which image would become more important than musicianship for musicianship's sake. This could be summed up by Kosmo Vinyl's succinct theory: 'You can look good and play good; you can look good and play crap, but you can't play good and look crap!' In order not to 'look crap', Ian would give his band haircuts and suggest various outfits, but sadly the new Kilburns were far less visual than their predecessors, even though Ian convinced himself that Ed and Irish were 'pushing forward' at a packed Dingwalls gig. 'We got a really good buzz going,' said Ian, 'doing new stuff and old Kilburns gear. I had brilliant musicians, but they weren't stylish like the original Kilburns, and I felt a bit sad because I knew we weren't going to be stars. By that time I was looking at my watch, thinking I wouldn't mind a little result now.'

In his frustration, Ian was becoming a less than satisfac-tory performer. Where his vocal once contained some relatively subtle inflections, it now ranted, and his all-important words were lost in a torrent of anger. 'I Made Mary Cry' had become a particularly gruesome spectacle, with Ian brandishing a Solingen Steel bone-handled switchblade, 'with a spring so strong it nearly leaves the gloved hand'. Ian's bitterness was starting to show. Reporting on a Hope and Anchor gig in the *New Musical Express*, journalist Chas de Whalley identified the problem:

> Among certain circles, Ian Dury has gained the reputation as one of rock 'n' roll's losers. It's not hard to see why . . . think back over the versions of Kilburn and the High Roads . . . the musical content has always been low . . . up until now Dury has consistently failed to locate musicians skilful and imaginative enough to breathe real life into his ideas . . . [but] the music is now potentially as sharp as the songs themselves are interesting . . . but then Dury isn't the guy for a slick back-up band . . . which means ultimately, he can't be groomed for stardom, and is destined to remain a cult. It must be sad to be a loser when you're really that good.

On his nights off Ian would still visit London pubs and clubs in his 'civvies', both for social relaxation and in the hope of making a connection that would rescue his career. Spider was his constant companion. Freshly scrubbed and besuited, the odd duo paraded themselves all over town. Ian particularly enjoyed visiting some of Fred's South London haunts such as Crusaders Steak House at the Elephant and Castle, or the Prince of Wales in Cleaver Square, Kennington, where small-time villains could be observed at close range. 'Who you working with now, Freddy?' asked a local burglar, as Ian basked in the possibility of being mistaken for Spider's bag man.

However, it was at the familiar music venues in which Ian had cut his teeth that he and Fred were all too visible. Whereas Ian was once welcomed by his music biz acquaintances, he was now an outcast. 'I used to see Ian out and about,' recalls publicist Glen Colson. 'After being his biggest fan, I started avoiding him because he looked like he was doomed, scowling around. I thought, "Nothing's going to happen for this poor fellow." You'd avoid him like the plague.' At Dingwalls Dancehall in Camden Town, the patrons found Ian's and Fred's combined presence somewhat unnerving, as did eight-piece soul band Kokomo, who were so intimidated by Ian and Fred lurking menacingly in front of the stage that they suspended their set until security staff arrived to remove the pair.

Dave Robinson could only run so far with Ian, citing other commitments, chiefly his management of Graham Parker, now recording his debut album with producer Nick Lowe. Ian was irritated by Parker's rapid success and ribbed Robinson repeatedly. Graham Parker remembers, 'I was playing Dingwalls with the Rumour, our first big headline pub gig in London, and I distinctly remember that for much of the show Ian and Fred Rowe were standing at the lip of the stage, both wearing shades, presumably attempting to put the frighteners on me.'

Robinson knew that, ultimately, Ian was unmanageable. There were, however, other managers who fancied their luck with the troubled genius, little realizing the aggravation that lay ahead. Three years earlier, Robinson had referred Ian to Messrs Gillett and Nelki, but Ian had ruthlessly fired them in favour of Tommy Roberts. Now, he would offer Ian to Peter Jenner and Andrew King, proprietors of Blackhill Music Publishing, whose premises at 32 Alexander Street would imminently house the nascent Stiff Records. 'They won't screw you,' Dave Robinson told Ian, 'they're vicars' sons.'

Jenner and King were Oxbridge graduates with rock sensibility. They had been the instigators of the famous Hyde Park free concerts and managers of Pink Floyd, but the psychedelic superstars had moved on, leaving a void in the roster. Initially, it was Ian's writing that impressed Peter and Andrew. 'He had these lyrics, typed up, and I remember reading "Nervous Piss",' recalls Andrew. 'We realized that they were incredible words and offered him a deal. We were going to pay him £25 a week, which was what he would have got on the dole.' Peter Jenner adds, 'I suspect Ian thought we were suckers, but we weren't your standard music biz schmucks. We recognized that Ian was an extraordinary person.'

Despite this breakthrough, Ian was still in the doldrums and continued to lurk around Dingwalls in heavy dude mode. There was talk of live work in Europe, but the dates fell through when early in 1976 Rod Melvin fled to Sussex to become a Scientologist. Ian came close to calling it a day, but there was always a ray of hope. 'I have decided to become a famous person this year and told my mum at Christmas,' Ian wrote to Roberta Bayley as soon as he heard that the Kilburns had just been booked for yet another session – their third – on *The London Weekend Show*. At the tele-recording on 7 January Ian looked superb with his crimson blue-beat trilby and safety-pin earring. The group performed a storming version of 'Rough Kids' and a new number entitled 'England's Glory', co-written with Melvin.

'England's Glory' was essentially a list of British entertainers, eccentrics and popular products of the post-war era that were 'jewels in the crown of England's Glory'. These included: Walnut Whips (a chocolate confection); Stafford Cripps (the Christian socialist politician); Vera Lynn (the popular wartime singer); and Mr Pastry (a children's entertainer). The song, as performed by Ian in 1976, pulling faces like an exasperated Alastair Sim, offered a glimmer of what might have been if he had chosen to become a mainstream entertainer. 1970s television might have welcomed a modern-day Harry Champion or Sir George Robey, music-hall maestros of the double entendre, but there was nothing remotely showbiz about Ian's routines. He confessed to Roberta Bayley that he had been 'nicking a lot of strokes from Max Miller and Max Wall', whom he saw as great English comics, Miller being particularly strong with words and Wall 'a master of lewd visuals and physical innuendo'. But Ian refused to record his own version of 'England's Glory'. Dave Robinson thought Max Wall would make a cracking cover and kept the idea up his sleeve.

On 9 February 1976 Ian signed his contract with Blackhill Music, who would publish his new songs and manage his career. Suddenly, Ian was happy; he now had the beginnings of an infrastructure, including a band, a small road crew and personal minder Spider Rowe. '[Blackhill] were investing in my potential as a writer and performer,' said Ian of his new managers. 'My tab at the bar was running up. I wasn't getting motor car money, it was about £25 a week, but they were getting us a nice Elsie and Doris [Kelsey Morris, a renowned speaker manufacturer] p.a. system and a nice van to go around in.'

Following Rod Melvin's departure, the Kilburns hung on minus a pianist. Guitarist Ed Speight thought that the band needed a keyboard player and took the initiative to seek out Rod's replacement. 'We don't need a piano player,' Ian told Ed, 'they're all poofs.' But Speight disagreed and persisted in his quest. Via a musical instrument shop in the Goldhawk Road, he tracked down one Chaz Jankel, who was summoned to an interview at the Nashville in April 1976, where the Kilburns were playing one of their regular dates. Ian recalled being slightly nervous about meeting the young musician: 'I was in the dressing room, a bit disgruntled, when Jankel walked in with his big white teeth. I said, "Do I know you?" He said, "No." So I said, "Well do us a favour and fuck off then!"'

Ed Speight confirms the brief encounter. 'It's true. Ian was so rude to Chaz that I had to be the diplomat. I was sent out to apologize to him. He was wearing his nice suit. I don't know if Chaz knew what he was letting himself in for, but I told Ian to stick with him. He had that broad musicality, that attention to detail. It was just what Ian needed.' Chaz Jankel, from Stanmore, Middlesex, was 'a nice, middle-class, Jewish, suburban boy,' according to Ian's co-manager, Peter Jenner. He joined the group in its dying days and played a handful of dates, including the

Kilburns' last ever show on 17 June at Walthamstow Assembly Hall.

Also on the bill were the Stranglers and the Sex Pistols, whose manager, Malcolm McLaren, had instructed his raging young protégé, John Lydon, to study the Dury stage persona 'and learn'. Ian was accompanied that night by his new publicist, B. P. Fallon, a quick-thinking and creative Irishman who had a good relationship with the music press due to his PR work for Led Zeppelin. 'Ian made a great show of being furious with Malcolm for Rotten nicking his poses,' recalls Fallon. 'He and Spider stood each side of Malcolm till they got the haberdasher twitching.'

Lydon, now known as 'Johnny Rotten', would soon be hanging onto his microphone stand for grim death, just like Ian and Gene Vincent before him. 'Ian, like me, was part of an older generation, but he passed the baton on,' says McLaren. 'He was influential in the whole advent of punk. He was a mirror to the crowd, as huge as the crowd and had this immense reservoir of electricity that would ultimately spark and give birth to something else that the new generation was going to feel was their own. Punk, really, was born out of that, the anger all us disenfranchised art students at the end of the sixties felt.'

But Ian had no desire to align himself with the oncoming punk movement, although he frequently complained that Johnny Rotten had stolen his shtick. 'John did borrow a little from Ian,' says Glen Matlock. 'Some of his stance, the razor blade, an homage to small elements.' Peter Jenner recalls, 'Ian would say, "Rotten ripped me off. I showed him the razor blade. That was me." He always said that.' Following his encounter with the Sex Pistols, Ian wrote an article for *Melody Maker* in which he described his preparation for the performance that McLaren and Lydon had witnessed:

I prepare myself properly for my beloved Walthamstow. Black embroidered lace widow's scarf and Pikey satin shirt.

I polish the razor-blade ear-piece, oil the knife, primp the barnet, dip the gloves in water to make them wearable and spray and splash until I smell like a moose. Green eye-shadow and Argyle socks from Burlington Arcade. The Brixton tuxedo is still wet from the previous engagement. I would love to become Gene Hackman's wardrobe mistress. We were magnificent and the Sex Pistols are smashing.

Ian also revealed in the article that he had recently seen a doctor – 'a pricey-looking geezer with a miner's lamp on his head' – who had diagnosed a weak heart due to 'giving it too much stick on the boards'. A break from live performance was recommended, but Ian protested: 'I'm not nearly famous yet so I can't stop now, you bastard!' Ian closed his *Melody Maker* piece with: 'I'm a performer and people like me don't operate too well in cupboards. It isn't applause that gets me at it. It's knowing that somebody is really there.'

The health scare was something of a fabrication. B. P. Fallon, whose job it was to help Ian reinvent himself, or at least amplify his existing charisma, says, 'It was madness, the idea of making this Ian Dury fellow into a mega rock star. That was part of the catalyst for me, that and his wordsmith talent and embryonic visual charisma, not only on stage but as the geezer walking down the street. From the get-go the man had a magnetic visual but it had to be honed, because at the beginning it was a front, a shield. Ian was putting it on, but it had to become like a flag, with the cat truly believing it, rather than acting it out.'

The one grain of truth in the 'weak heart' story, however, was that Ian really did crave the affection and approval that only a live audience could provide. But it would be another fifteen months before he would enjoy the warm glow of the spotlight. Tired of running his band on a shoestring, Ian made half-a-dozen telephone calls and despatched the Kilburns into the pages of rock 'n' roll history.

11

A Mouth What Never Closes

South London, 1976. 'This is you, Mr Dury, isn't it?' asked the government VAT inspector, pulling a sheaf of *Melody Maker* cuttings from his drawer. Ian had been summoned to the Kennington Customs and Excise office to substantiate his tax returns. Imagining that he was in the presence of a pop star, the civil servant was fascinated as Ian pulled out his little black book. It was finally going to come in handy as it contained written evidence that the Kilburns had performed exactly 365 shows in just over forty-two months and that their average nightly fee was £75. Ian explained that the expenses of running a group were considerable, and his tax bill was reduced accordingly.

His indebtedness to Blackhill, however, had now reached £7,000, and there was no sign of a record deal. Since his realization that the cost of running a group was prohibitive, Ian decided he would remain a solo act until such time as he had a great band, a great album and a recording contract. Songs were the priority, and Chaz Jankel was to be his new co-writer. Retreating to Oval Mansions, Ian spent countless hours at his desk assiduously writing lyrics with a giant cardboard cut-out of Gene Vincent watching over him. Hungry for inspiration, his antennae were constantly receptive to any phrase or newspaper headline he thought might make a good song title. When he found one, he'd confer with Denise. 'I've got it, I've got it . . . listen to this! "Sink My Boats" – brilliant! Does it work for you?

This is great – "I've Got A Lump In My Jeans For You". What do you think?'

Denise was always amused by Ian's wordplay and offered encouragement. She was also optimistic about the Dury/Jankel songwriting partnership, knowing that Ian had been waiting for a collaborator who spoke the same language . . . well, almost. Unlike many of the musicians who had passed through Ian's 'academy of Jack-the-lademy', Chaz was not exactly 'street', but his instrumental skills would introduce a welcome degree of musical sophistication. He had tasted modest success with the rock group Byzantium and more recently formed a 'dubious cabaret duo', Pure Gold.

Ian learnt that Chaz's cousin Robert was married to Jennifer Loss, daughter of the famous bandleader, Joe Loss. This excited Ian. He told friends, 'I've met this young bloke, he's terribly talented . . . you know his uncle is Joe Loss!' Although Joe Loss was the epitome of square and symbolized the old showbiz establishment, he was – crucially for Ian – a household name. 'Ian was very impressed by Chaz Jankel's musicianship,' says Peter Jenner. 'He told everyone that Chaz was "a fucking genius". In Ian's eyes, everyone was either a complete genius or a total wanker. You were either a diamond geezer or a tosspot.'

Chaz started to visit daily with his guitar and Wurlitzer piano and would occasionally bring his toothbrush and stay over for days at a stretch. Ian had reams of new lyrics and used his miniature drum kit to convey the rhythmic feel he envisaged for each song, much to the annoyance of Mrs Cave, who lived in the flat below. All she could hear was the thump of Ian's bass drum, not the intricate words and cool, jazzy melodies that Ian and Chaz were now producing. She also had to contend with other disturbances in Oval Mansions, namely the odd 'domestic'. On the first floor, Fred and Val argued noisily, and there was always the possibility of Fred receiving a visit from some gangland overlord offering him 'work'. Ian told Fred that, if he had to revert to crime, why not make it 'a retirement job, like a good £200,000 airport raid?' But Fred was trying to go straight. Mindful of his criminal connections he'd installed bullet-proof glass in his windows, boasting to Ian, 'You can hit those with a fourteen-pound sledge hammer, mate – they won't fucking break!'

Upstairs, Ian and Denise's interminable rows heightened the pandemonium. The sound of flying crockery could be heard by passers-by, who were constantly in danger of being struck by flowerpots falling from Ian's third-storey window ledge. The mansion block was a war zone, but it was in this atmosphere that Dury and Jankel produced a body of work that would become the cornerstone of Ian's career as the rock 'n' roll poet laureate.

Unsure of his future with Denise, Ian flitted backwards and forwards between Oval Mansions and Betty and the kids, who in July 1976 moved into their new home in Mount Pleasant, Aylesbury, a street Baxter remembers as 'impoverished, multi-racial; we were one of the wealthier families'. The house had been purchased with financial help from Aunt Molly, which aggravated Ian's guilt further, but music remained his focus. On 27 July, he and Chaz went into Livingstone Studios and recorded five tracks with Pete van Hook and Kuma Harada on drums and bass respectively, with Geoff Castle adding synthesizer. Songs included 'Wake Up and Make Love with Me' and 'Sink My Boats'. Ian was excited, but his new demos would simply gather dust in the A&R offices of the half-dozen major record labels propositioned by Andrew King.

Elsewhere, the long hot summer of 1976 was proving to be a musical turning point. If punk wasn't yet making the headlines, the signs of a revolution were in the air. Fired up by the then influential British music press and, specifically, hip writers like Nick Kent and Giovanni Dadomo, adventurous young music fans began checking out the sounds that had in recent years been emanating from New York and Detroit – the New York Dolls, the MC5, the Stooges and now the Ramones and Patti Smith. In the UK, it was the incendiary live performances of Dr Feelgood that had inspired those same kids to buy guitars and drums, cut their hair and play fast. One Mark Perry, a young bank clerk from Deptford, crucially started the short-lived fanzine *Sniffin' Glue*, which covered the Buzzcocks, the Sex Pistols and the Clash and would probably have found space for Ian Dury.

Another significant event that summer was the launch of Stiff Records. Ian's former manager, Dave Robinson, had been plotting for some time to start a record label, primarily as an outlet for his pub rock casualties. When he hooked up with human dynamo and former Dr Feelgood tour manager Jake Riviera in July 1976, the label was born. Stiff was a shoestring operation that nevertheless had the wit and imagination to forge would-be hits from its roster of musical underdogs, most of whom were too unconventional for the major labels. Ian was a perfect contender. Riviera tried to persuade him to let Stiff release some of his demos and unissued recordings, but Ian was intent on keeping his head down until he was ready to re-emerge. 'I'm going to be a rock 'n 'roll star one day,' he wrote to Roberta, 'in case you hadn't noticed.'

It was an exciting time and Ian understood only too well what was happening. In February, at the behest of Malcolm McLaren, he had seen the Sex Pistols at the Marquee and later at Walthamstow. He thought they were 'dire', but saw the funny side of it. He had investigated the Ramones' debut album, which he liked. He had also dragged Ed Speight to see the Feelgoods, but Speight was 'worried' by their 'hi-octane aggression'. Ian decided that the omens were good, noting that in recent weeks his name had featured as a music press crossword clue on no less than three occasions!

In August, Denise left Oval Mansions once again, leaving Ian and Chaz to get on with their music. An early gem was

'Hit Me with Your Rhythm Stick', although it would not be fully realized for another two years. Also hot off the press was 'Razzle in My Pocket', a semi-autobiographical account of a thieving expedition, Ian's quarry a copy of the ultra-sleazy *Razzle* pin-up magazine. He'd gone out in his 'yellow jersey' to South Street Romford Shopping Arcade. Much detail was contained in the three-minute opus. With keen perception Ian captured the shopkeeper's coy reference to the merchandise: 'I think you've taken one of my books.' The observation was spot on; 'one of my books' was exactly how the purveyor of 'top-shelf' titles such as *Razzle* would refer to his titillating merchandise, glossing over the true content. 'It's not a maga-zine, for God's sake, it's a book!' As in 'The Upminster Kid', the imagery of 'Razzle in My Pocket' placed Ian in a geographical and social context his fans would come to appreciate. He was *from* the street and *of* the street. He was single-handedly invent-ing British 'street credibility'.

'Razzle in My Pocket' would later appear as the b-side of Ian's first solo record, the seminal 'Sex and Drugs and Rock and Roll'. Its groove had been hatched at a late Kilburns practice session. 'Jenner had sent us to Headley Grange for a week's rehearsal,' Ian recalled. 'We went there, Irish, Malcolm, Ted, Chaz and myself. We wrote a few songs. I went down early one morning and started playing Malcolm's drums, a straight-down-the-line groove. Behind me, I heard Chaz on the piano, playing the "Sex and Drugs" riff. I heard what I wanted to hear, what I'd been waiting to hear for years – "Superstition", that area of groove.'

Chaz tells it differently: 'Ian presented his lyrics to me on foolscap paper. Quite regularly I'd see "Sex and Drugs and Rock and Roll" appear at the top of the pile. I'd heard the expression before, but I couldn't get a handle on it as a song. One day Ian said, "how about [hums the riff]" – I thought it was very good – he didn't generally come up with musical ideas – but I later discovered the tune was a Charlie Haden bass solo from Ornette

Coleman's "Change of the Century"!' Davey Payne adds, 'It's "Old Joe Clark", an old-time Virginian folk song. In America, kids are taught it in school. Charlie Haden would have played it on the fiddle as a child.'

> *Sex and drugs and rock and roll*
> *Are all my brain and body need,*
> *Sex and drugs and rock and roll*
> *Are very good indeed . . .*

Like a number of Ian's titles, 'Sex and Drugs and Rock and Roll' would work its way into the English language and appear in *The Oxford Dictionary of Quotations*. Variations of the phrase had shown up in the counterculture press of the early 1970s (see John Sinclair's 'Rock 'n' Roll, Dope and Fucking in the Streets'), and in 1972, Australian band Daddy Cool had released an album entitled *Sex, Dope, Rock and Roll: Teenage Heaven*, but it was Ian who seized on the words to create a song. The middle eight was particularly insightful:

> *Keep your silly ways; throw them out the window,*
> *The wisdom of your ways; I've been there and I know,*
> *Lots of other ways; what a jolly bad show*
> *If all you ever do . . . is business you don't like*

Ian's spirits picked up in the autumn of 1976, despite his first quarrel with Chaz over collaboration on an advertising jingle, which, although it was potentially lucrative, Ian saw as a distraction – 'business you don't like' perhaps. But after a blazing row in which Chaz accused Ian of being a 'shitty singer' and Ian told Chaz he wouldn't recognize a good lyric if it bit him on the arse, they made up and commenced work on 'a song for Gene Vincent'.

•

'Is this the place where any old cunt can bring a tape and get a record deal?' asked Eric Goulden, a twenty-two-year-old singer/ songwriter who showed up at Stiff Records in September 1976, brandishing a demo cassette. Goulden, who had catchy songs and youth on his side, was perfect. He was quickly signed up and told that he would be known professionally as 'Wreckless Eric'. Within days, Goulden was despatched to Pathway Studios to cut his song 'Go the Whole Wide World' with producer Nick Lowe, who was also busy producing Stiff act the Damned, the first UK 'punk' group to appear on vinyl.

Slightly bemused by the speed at which his career was gaining pace, Goulden found himself thrown into the gigging-and-ligging world of all things Stiff. On 26 October, he attended a concert by Graham Parker and the Rumour at the Victoria Palace and later that evening met Ian. 'Nick introduced us,' recalls Eric. 'It was at some hideous after-show party. Ian was at quite a low point then, but he was there with Denise, who was beautiful, with gold chains on her leather mini skirt. Ian was wearing an old raincoat. I was a big Kilburns fan, and I told Ian I thought he was great. He thought I was taking the piss and started calling for Fred, but Denise told Ian, "He's serious, he means it."'

Ian recognized in Eric Goulden a kindred spirit and took him under his wing, but despite Goulden's talent, Ian was clutching at straws. He was desperate for anything that might sway his fortunes in the music business, including mentoring Eric, whom he summoned to Oval Mansions. Eric arrived on 1 December to find Ian and Chaz finishing up a new song entitled 'Sweet Gene Vincent', with its reference to 'Thunderbird wine', a drink Ian had first encountered when he met two black GIs on a Cambridge-bound train back in 1963.

'Ian and I became friends,' says Eric. 'We'd both been to art school and we talked about rock 'n' roll, but there was something a bit sad about him. He was looking for something, playing the waiting game. He had to keep reminding everyone that he was the greatest lyric writer in the country to shore up his confidence. He used to say to me, "Eric, you should never forget that you are the second-greatest lyric writer in the country." So I would ask him, "OK Ian, who do you reckon then is the number one lyric writer?" He would get really cross.'

Expecting that his first single would soon be released by Stiff, Wreckless Eric looked around for musicians for his backing group, to be known as the New Rockets. Knowing that Denise was learning to play bass, he asked Ian about her. 'Oh, she won't want to play with you,' said Ian. By the end of the year, however, Denise had become Eric's lodger after Ian had suddenly declared, 'Me and Denise are having a difficult time at the moment, would you mind if she came and stayed at your place for a while?' Ian wondered if Eric had a spare room he could put Denise in. The next day, she turned up on his doorstep with a bag of clothes and a bass guitar. 'I still had a job and I'd come home from work and she would have been playing the bass all day,' says Eric. 'We were both very shy, but I said to her, "We could play together if you like," so we started playing my songs. It was like a secret society, a lot of nervous giggling. Eventually she went back to Ian but she carried on coming over to go through songs.'

At Humphrey Ocean's behest, Eric and Denise were joined by Davey Payne on sax. Davey was amused to discover that Eric lived at 'number one Melody Road'. 'When I told the musician's union my address,' says Eric, 'they thought I was taking the piss. Anyway, Ian decided he was coming over to hear what Denise and I were doing. I think he thought we were having an affair. We started to play the songs and he said, "What you need is a drummer." He went out in the back yard, got an old enamel bowl and started hitting it with a couple of pens. Suddenly I had a band, but Ian was in charge. He had a fire-damaged Olympic drum kit, which was delivered to my house by Spider Rowe whilst I was out. I don't know how he got in, but I came home one evening and there was Ian's drum kit, set up, with a note from Fred that read: "You can never keep the spider out."'

In his next letter to Roberta, Ian once again begged her to come to London and laid his soul bare. 'I want to join a swimming club. Get a new leg. Get even more beautiful. My next band and my next songs are going to allow me to build the castle. I only have one ambition and that is to work without hindrance till I die . . . my time will come.' Despite his confident prediction, Ian was still pondering the advice of Tommy Roberts, who two years earlier had suggested that Ian might consider getting 'a real job'. Maybe it really was time to retract his bid for stardom and seek gainful employment, or what musicians apologetically refer to as a 'day job'. Any kind of backroom occupation was out of the question for Ian. His ideal role would be in the public eye, yet menial in nature. When he saw a newspaper advertisement for a 'lift attendant' at Harrods, he imagined a uniform with red velvet trim, brass buttons and a pillbox hat. He was seriously tempted and on 6 December attended an interview at the Knightsbridge department store, but the job had been taken.

Instead of charming or possibly horrifying customers at Harrods, Ian spent much of the early months of 1977 in Aylesbury with Betty and the children, commuting into London to visit Blackhill or write and record with Chaz. Jemima remembers, 'It was a big deal when dad came home. He was developing his fame persona, his mystique. He became "Ian Dury" a bit more and started to believe in himself.' Occasionally Jemima and Baxter would stay at Oval Mansions. Jemima remembers that her 'official job' was sorting out her father's records and putting them back in their sleeves. 'He wasn't a dad that came and did things with you,' remembers Baxter. 'You did things with dad, whatever he was doing, which was more or less how it always was.'

In January, Ian heard that sixty-eight-year-old music hall veteran Max Wall was about to record a version of 'England's Glory' for Stiff, with Dave Edmunds producing and Humphrey

Ocean drawing the picture sleeve. Things were looking up. In his spare time, Ian grilled Fred Rowe about his prison experiences and recorded three hours of Fred's stories on cassette. He also taped discussions with roadie Pete Rush, who would provide him with tales for a proposed 'roadies musical'. Ian fantasized about ways in which he would present his new songs, envisaging 'a one-off violent gig at the Roundhouse with a tough band of slick pros . . . fifteen heavy-duty songs written in two weeks, played by Alan Spenner on bass, Bryan Spring on drums, both from Hackney and Pete Townshend on "gtr chunks" and Davey Payne on sax. Maybe call it "The Hard 10 Men", roadies recruited by Fred.'

Ian needn't have worried. With a batch of great new songs to demo, he and Chaz booked a month of Tuesdays in February at Alvic Studios in Wimbledon. After four weeks they emerged with eight promising demos. There was also an unexpected bonus. Alvic studio was owned by Al James, a bass player at the Talk of the Town and Vic Sweeney, a drummer at the Park Lane Hilton. Actually, Al and Vic had played slightly hipper gigs in their time but were too modest to put themselves forward when Ian mentioned that he was looking for a hot rhythm section. But Al and Vic did know just the guys – Norman and Charley, who 'played so loud they broke all the VU meters'. Ian had to have them in his band.

Bassist Norman Watt-Roy was born in Bombay, India in 1951 and had come to England at the age of four. The veteran of numerous UK bands, including 'The Greatest Show on Earth', Norman was blessed with that rock 'n' roll 'just-got-out-of-bed' look and authentic dark circles under his eyes. An extremely physical bass player, he neatly dovetailed with Guyana-born drummer Hugh 'Charley' Charles, who could lay down a groove like no other percussionist in London. They had played together in the Radio Caroline-sponsored group Loving Awareness and were the UK's greatest undiscovered rhythm section. Making contact with them was Ian's next piece of good fortune and the turning point in his quest for musical perfection. 'It took off like a rocket,' remembers Peter Jenner. 'As soon as he found Norman and Charley, Ian went up five gears.' Excited by his discovery, Ian wrote Roberta on 28 March: 'I'm tooled-up to steam into any one of a lot of record companies. I'm the best wordsmith and performer and I'm learning how to sing. I'll be on the road by the autumn with a hand-picked band and nothing is going to top it.' It was a bold claim given past disappointments but, amazingly, it would all come true.

As well as his collaborations with Chaz, Ian was also writing a number of songs with Stephen Nugent, the American anthropologist and writer who had been responsible for one of the earliest press articles about the Kilburns. Upon returning from a two-year trip to Brazil, Nugent was asked by Ian to provide music for what Ian described as 'the heavy duty songs'. Denise would give Ian a lift over to Nugent's home in Highgate, or Ian would sometimes take a bus. 'The bus was a bit of a struggle for Ian,' recalls Nugent. 'He came with the lyrics, and I would work out a tune. He would sometimes stay over, or I would put him on a bus and send him back south. Some people say that it was odd that he was working with an American, but it turned out that the ones I wrote were the more Englishy songs whilst Chaz was more fixated on American funk.'

The Dury/Nugent compositions included: 'My Old Man', 'Billericay Dickie', 'Blackmail Man' and 'Plaistow Patricia'. When combined with the Jankel co-writes, Ian had the basis of a winning album with which to relaunch his career, but he was still worried about the amount of debt he was incurring through the Blackhill arrangement. Writing to solicitor David Gentle on 4 May, he expressed concern that he was 'labouring under the weight of his advance', which now stood at 'fourteen Gs'. He was also anxious about his impending birthday. 'By this time I was nearly thirty-five,' recalled Ian. 'I remembered reading that Bruce Forsyth was at the end of Woolacombe Pier a week before getting *Sunday Night at the London Palladium*. Arse pretty much hanging out, about thirty-odd when he got the call. He said the reason it went well for him was because he wasn't bitter. I always rated Bruce Forsyth. He was still in love with his craft. I've been at the end of the pier a few times since then.'

On 20 May, Ian found himself back at Alvic Studios, overseeing the recording of 'Semaphore Signals' for Wreckless Eric. It was to be the b-side of 'Go the Whole Wide World', which had been recorded six months earlier, but kept on the back burner while Stiff sought a distribution outlet. Ian also produced Eric's four-song EP entitled *The Swan and Edgar Suite*,* named after the Piccadilly department store where Eric had worked. 'We recorded it in Pathway Studio,' recalls Eric, 'but Ian couldn't get on with the place. I didn't want to put it out. Ian's attitude was, "We are making art," but his strength was not the recording studio – I think he'd had too many bad experiences.'

But Ian was about to have a good experience when he entered the Workhouse studio in the Old Kent Road in July 1977. Co-owned by Blackhill and pop pragmatist Manfred Mann, the twenty-four-track facility was ideal for Ian in all but one respect – its steep and narrow staircase leading up to the control room. Under the watchful eye of Peter Jenner, in his role as producer or, to quote Chaz, 'spliff-maker, adjudicator and foil for Ian', and engineer Laurie Latham, Ian kept a chart that plotted out the songs and who would play the various solos. The band consisted of Chaz (keyboards and guitar) and Norman and Charley (bass and drums), augmented by Ed Speight (guitar) and Geoff Castle (Moog synthesizer). Former Kilburn Davey Payne was called in to overdub sax. Before each song was recorded, Ian would play the musicians the demo version and urge them to replicate their parts with only minor adjustments to the arrangement.

---

* *The Swan and Edgar Suite*, which was never released and the tapes of which are lost, consisted of four songs: 'Excuse Me', 'Personal Hygiene', 'Rags And Tatters' and 'The Piccadilly Menial'.

With a limited budget and no firm outlet for the record it was crucial that the recording schedule was adhered to. The album was completed in just three weeks, but once again there was no major record company interest. There was, however, one obvious solution. 'Andrew had taken it to every record company in the country and got a blank,' said Ian. 'We spoke to Jake and we couldn't lose by putting it out on Stiff, because, if they'd have gone up the wall, ownership would have reverted to us. It was a lease deal. Blackhill didn't really want Stiff to have it. I didn't care. I thought we'd have more chance with Stiff. Jake and Dave together were hot property.'

Thirty-two Alexander Street was the right place and the right time for all concerned. Blackhill owned the building and managed Ian's career from their offices on the first floor. They rented the ground floor and basement to Stiff Records, the perfect refuge for left-of-centre artistes like Ian. Everyone was within shouting distance of each other. On 12 July 1977, Blackhill licensed Ian's album to Stiff, who were enjoying unprecedented publicity for their then humble status. Ian was a journalist's dream – a human quote machine whose image neatly complemented Stiff's marketing flair, then the province of Jake Riviera. To make matters even more exciting, Jake and Dave Robinson were planning a UK tour for their leading 'stars', Elvis Costello, Nick Lowe, Larry Wallis and Wreckless Eric. Ian slotted in nicely. 'Yeah, I'll 'ave some of that,' he said.

At the end of August, Stiff released Ian's first solo single, 'Sex and Drugs and Rock and Roll'. Not surprisingly, it received scant radio play and failed to sell in great quantity, but in the eyes of the music press it was an instant classic, signalling Ian's long overdue change of fortune. Amongst ear-to-the-ground music writers, he enjoyed a groundswell of support going all the way back to the Kilburns. Less enlightened journalists were having their ears bent by Stiff's latest staffer, Kosmo Vinyl, serving under the label's publicity guru, Glen Colson. 'I had been retained to hype "Sex and Drugs",' says Kosmo, who had originally joined Stiff as an office boy and general factotum. Twenty-year-old carrot-haired Kosmo Vinyl (born Mark Charles Dunk) had ingratiated himself at Stiff simply by hanging around Alexander Street and turning up at Graham Parker shows, offering to help the roadies. 'I pestered Dave Robinson for a job although I didn't know what the jobs were,' he says. 'The first thing I had to do at Stiff was fix a door. Then Dave and Jake had me fly-posting. You'd just turn up and be told what to do. It evolved. My big mouth put me in a certain direction.' Within twelve months Vinyl's big mouth would earn him a place as Ian's press officer and media consultant.

For the cover shot of his debut LP, Ian called upon the services of photographer Chris Gabrin, whom he knew from his pub rock days. 'Ian already had a title in mind,' says Gabrin. 'I think he'd seen the outfitter's shop in Victoria* when he was waiting for a bus, and it had given him the trigger. He specifically wanted to do the shot there and have his son, Baxter, with him. The shopkeeper was delighted; he let us get on with it and when the album came out, he stuck a sign in the window saying: "We sell to the stars". In the reflection in the shop window you can actually see my old mini van, but I managed to position Ian and Baxter so as to obscure my own reflection. Baxter was shy, and I remember Ian trying to encourage him.'

'I don't think I was there on the premise that I might be featured,' says Baxter Dury. 'I was six years old and I think I was just hanging out with dad because I was staying with him for the week. Dad always romantically maintained that I just strolled into the shot, which I don't think was quite right, I think it was slightly more orchestrated than that, but I'm wearing a pair of football boots, so I must have been just mucking about. I don't really think dad thought I was going to be in it.'

Chris Gabrin took twenty-four shots of Ian that afternoon. Immediately after the session, he rushed off to get the film

* Axfords at 306 Vauxhall Bridge Road.

processed so he could show them to him without delay. 'He came up to my darkroom to look at the results,' recalls Gabrin. 'We both instantly went for the same shot, but I remember Ian bollocking me because my darkroom was on the fifth floor and he didn't like the stairs. The banisters were against the wall, and he couldn't grip the handrail properly. I got paid a very small amount for my work, but Ian did my telephone answering machine message as part payment. It got ridiculous; people would call just to hear Ian's voice. They'd phone and tell me not to answer their next call so they could listen to it.'

With recording and photography complete, Jake Riviera asked Ian to come up with a shortlist of ten possible titles for the album. Ian had been playing around with various ideas, including *4,000 Weeks' Holiday* (which he would use for a later album), *His Hundred Best Tunes*, *No Hand Signals*, *Live at Lourdes* and *The Mad Spastic*. 'I said to Jake, "Stop me when you hear the one you like,"' recalled Ian. 'It takes more than one brain to work these things out.' Riviera gave the thumbs-up when he heard Ian utter the immortal phrase 'New Boots and Panties'. It was vaguely erotic and neatly complemented Chris Gabrin's cover shot of Ian and Baxter outside a shop that offered that winning combination of footwear and knickers. It also echoed Ian's earlier remark that he only ever bought his clothes from second-hand shops, with the exception of his underwear and Dr Marten boots, which, 'for reasons of hygiene, had to be pristine!'

Barney Bubbles, Stiff's in-house graphics genius, designed the packaging. 'I think Barney had more of a dialogue with Ian,' says Gabrin. 'That brush stroke lettering came about after their discussions. They'd both been art students and they could communicate on those levels.' Ian was in awe of Barney's creative ability: 'Speaking as someone who's spent half his life at art colleges, Barney was easily the most incredible designer I'd ever come across, speaking as a sophisticated or as an unsophisticated observer of these things. His vision was fantastic. It really did impress me. He scared the shit out of me. He was righteous.'

Released at the end of September 1977 to great critical acclaim, *New Boots and Panties!!* was a songwriting master class, from the smooth, measured funk of 'Wake Up and Make Love with Me' to the frenzied, venomous rock 'n' roll of 'Blackmail Man'. Ian had spent many hours honing the words and finding the right 'voice' for 'Wake Up', a song that would open his concerts for years to come. On the demo he had tried for a soulful and sexy performance with an American accent until former co-manager Gordon Nelki asked, 'What's with the Barry White impersonation, Ian?' Ian reconsidered his approach. 'That's when I started singing with an English accent,' he said. 'I stripped it down and tried to be funny.'

Ian poured it all out in 'My Old Man', the song that made Elvis Costello's jaw drop when he heard an advance tape in Blackhill's listening room. It was a ghostly pen portrait of his late father, of whom he saw little in the latter years. Care had been taken to write the words in a way that would not upset Peggy, but the finished song was tinged with regret. It failed to mask a decade's worth of guilt, but succinctly captured the drudgery of a chauffeur's lot as he 'did the crossword in the *Standard*, at the airport in the rain'.

The post-modern music hall of 'Billericay Dickie' neatly anticipated the emergence of 'Essex Man', a social phenomenon of the 1980s that Ian unwittingly helped to shape. The song's character, loosely based on art school chum Terry Day, whose pulling power Ian envied, boasted of a string of sexual conquests twixt the Isle of Thanet and Shoeburyness, where he met a 'lovely old toe rag, obliging and noblesse'. But Dickie was proud; he wanted you to know he 'ain't a flaming thicky', who ever 'shaped up tricky!'

'Clevor Trever', by contrast, was a less confident, stammering fellow, who 'ain't never had no nothing worth having never ever never, ever . . .' The song was originally written for Wreckless Eric, whom Ian confessed was the inspiration for 'Trever' and 'would be able to express what it was about', but he later decided to keep it for himself, because performing it was enjoyable, 'a bit like playing the bongos'.

'Plaistow Patricia' was a song Ian had been working on since 1973. Today it would guarantee *New Boots* a 'Parental Advisory Explicit Content' sticker, not only for its coarse opening line, but also its drug-related theme. From here, the record got even darker. 'Blackmail Man', with its litany of rhyming slang, some of which appears to have been created by Ian especially for the song, took a dig at racism and prejudice, with its roll call of minority groups and social outcasts, including a 'paraffin lamp' (tramp); a 'buckle my shoe' (Jew) and, taking a pop at himself, a 'raspberry ripple' (cripple).

'Blockheads' was Ian's brutal observation of the cricket fans he glimpsed from his window at Oval Mansions, whose 'shapeless haircuts' failed to enhance their 'ghastly patterned shirts'. He later recalled them pouring out of the Cricketers pub, 'with freckled shoulders and ginger hair, wallowing in lager.' 'They've got womanly breasts under pale mauve vests,' Ian observed, and 'shoes like dead pigs' noses'.

New Boots and Panties!! remains Ian's strongest collection of songs, owing much of its success to extensive preparation and an artistic hunger born out of rejection, failure and a desperate desire to prove himself. All of the songs were first demoed by Ian and Chaz, and then redemoed with engineer Philip Bagenel in a Bermondsey basement with Charley and Norman adding their considerable funk. When it came to cutting time, the pre-production paid huge dividends. Ian always maintained that a surfeit of material was crucial in order to enjoy choice and leeway. For *New Boots*, only the best songs were selected.

For the Stiff tour, Ian and Chaz needed to expand the nucleus of musicians that had recorded *New Boots*. Ian was disinclined to retain Geoff Castle and Ed Speight, neither of whom he felt were suitable for prolonged road work. When he made this known, Norman and Charley were quick to recommend their former Loving Awareness colleagues, keyboardist Mickey

Gallagher and guitarist Johnny Turnbull, two cheery Geordies each with over a decade on the clock as stalwart players in bands that had been tipped for success but never made it beyond the second division. Saxophonist Davey Payne would complete this dream team, his inclusion helping to maintain the Kilburns connection. All they needed was a name. 'Charley Charles had a T-shirt,' recalled Ian, 'purple with "Lois" on it and the trousers with the patches that weren't really patches, sewn-in squares, DPNs – shoes with a big cluster of dead pigs' noses. He read the lyric to "Blockheads", checking out where he was gonna come in, and he said, "Ian – he's dressed just like me!" I said, "You must be a Blockhead, then, Charley!" Norman had the green crushed velvet. We didn't know what to call the band until Norman said, "I know . . . we're Blockheads, aren't we?" I said, "Of course we are."'

Many 'blockheads', Ian observed, 'sported the mullet, the Mel Gibson look, the worst haircut you've ever seen in your life'. Ian would one day sport a mullet of his own, an unavoidable consequence of his constantly evolving coiffure that changed with the seasons, never dwelling on one look for long. If Ian celebrated spring with a 'number one' (severe skinhead cut), he would greet winter with a full head of curls. There would occasionally be visits to fashionable salons such as Smile in Chelsea's Kings Road, but often Ian would hold do-it-yourself hairdressing sessions at home, creatively snipping the locks of various band members.

Oozing style, Ian consolidated his image by scouring thrift shops for outfits to match his many moods. Styles varied wildly, from the Edwardian smoking jacket with satin reveres to a labourer's donkey jacket with imitation leather yoke. Kohl black mascara was applied for special occasions. It was the sartorial style he had been honing for five years. It was now time to take it to the nation.

12

Oi Oi!

'The great advantage of a hotel is that it's a refuge from home life.'
G. B. Shaw, *You Never Can Tell*, Act 2

High Wycombe, October 1977. It was the opening night of the 'Stiff's Greatest Stiffs' tour, featuring quick-fire sets from Elvis Costello, Nick Lowe, Wreckless Eric, Larry Wallis and Ian Dury, on what was intended to be a revolving bill as the tour progressed. Every act, claimed Stiff, was a potential headliner. Ian was firing up the audience at the Town Hall with his tales from the modern music hall. 'I'm from Essex in case you couldn't tell . . . my given name is Dickie, I come from Billericay and I'm doing . . . very well!' The fans winked and nudged as he regaled them with his tales of a 'love affair with Nina', in the back of his Cortina. They gazed in awe at this East End geezer who had sprung from nowhere to sing about sex and drugs and rock and roll and they scrambled on the floor in an attempt to collect the song's button badges that publicist B. P. Fallon threw from the stage 'like heavy confetti'.

Actually, Ian had two audiences that night – the paying customers out front and his own band on stage. It was the first time that the Blockheads, other then Davey and Chaz, had witnessed him working a crowd. 'I wasn't ready for his performance,' says Mickey Gallagher. 'It was phenomenal. He couldn't really sing, but he had the chocolate tones and the great verbal. He put a lot of work into his performance with the coat over the Hawaiian shirt and the striped vest underneath that. We'd never experienced that kind of theatricality before. In an early interview I said, "Ian's the perfect front man," thinking I was praising him, but he gave me shit. "How dare you call me a front man!" He was really offended by it.'

The High Wycombe crowd wasn't to know that their town was such a resonant setting for Ian; eighteen years earlier he had concluded his secondary education at the nearby Royal Grammar School, where he was repeatedly beaten by prefects and was once knocked out by his headmaster. Now he was back, co-headlining a national rock tour with Stiff's other not-so-young hopefuls. Elvis Costello, yet to break through on the pop charts, adopted a confrontational stance from the get-go, alienating the audience by refusing to perform his better-known songs. Ian, in contrast, formed an immediate bond with the crowd. A useful sprinkling of original Kilburns fans 'down the front' acted as his trusted rabble-rousers. 'Oi Oi!'* he rasped, reaching for the microphone. 'OI OI!' the Buckinghamshire crowd responded. Two simple syllables, one united room. 'Dury just slayed 'em,' recalls Kosmo Vinyl. 'Wallop! He couldn't put a foot wrong. It was obvious on the first night that Ian was a force to be reckoned with.'

Behind the scenes, Ian came up against several strong personalities, notably the powerful alliance of Elvis Costello, Nick Lowe and their manager, Jake Riviera. All three were verbally adept, but Riviera was a motor-mouth of staggering oral agility. Not only would he yell fearlessly at security men twice his size, he would also incorporate a slick joke for the benefit of onlookers. One night, while haranguing a bearded and blundering student's union secretary, Riviera let fly with the cruel jibe: 'Just

---

* Ian later remarked that 'Oi Oi' was a pre-war chant at West Ham football ground, although he may have taken the catchphrase from veteran music hall and TV comedian Jimmy Wheeler, whose parting shot to audiences was: 'Aye aye! That's your lot!'

because you've got hair all over your face, it doesn't give you the right to speak to me like a cunt!'

At once, Ian recognized that he was not the only wheel on the bus, although *New Boots* had started to pick up sales. Reluctant to be drawn into backstage rows, he adopted a low profile and conserved his energies for the nightly performance. Carefully avoiding the Costello/Riviera axis, he would spend time with Denise Roudette or, if their relationship was going through a rocky patch, the Blockheads. With their confidence growing, Ian and his band took advantage of any downtime to analyse the previous evening's set and make small improvements, thus honing their show night by night. At the start of each performance Ian would urge the Blockheads to hit the stage running. 'Don't walk – run!' he would shout from the wing before making his own slow and purposeful entrance. 'He had the band decked out in football shirts,' recalls Eric Goulden. 'I always wanted to get him a referee's whistle. I thought he'd like that.'

The Stiff tour would stretch Ian's manipulative powers to the full. His objective was to emerge as the star, ahead of Costello, which he sought to achieve by contriving to close as many of the shows as possible. This was only possible because Ian was able to exploit a weakness in Stiff's 'revolving bill' concept. Although it was the label's intention for its 'stars' to alternate as headliners, Nick Lowe and Wreckless Eric were reluctant bill-toppers, leaving Costello and Dury to slog it out. Through a succession of shrewd manoeuvres, such as demanding a break after playing the drums in Wreckless Eric's band – thus pushing his own set later into the running order – Ian would win on points.

A key incident occurred two weeks into the tour, at the University of East Anglia. 'Elvis was perturbed,' recalls Ian's minder, Fred Rowe. 'Ian was going down better than him, and Dave Robinson wanted Ian to close the shows. Jake Riviera, who was Elvis's manager, started on Ian, threatening him with the verbal, but you can't do that with Ian, he will slaughter you.

Jake's good . . . but Ian! This was winding Jake up even more. I said, "Hold on Jake, leave it out, what you getting all excited about?" Jake says to Ian, "I see, you're all right ranting when you've got your monkey with you," referring to me. I was getting wound up, so I backed off before it got nasty.'

Ian later gave me his side of the story. 'It got really sticky. Jake was screaming at hall porters, bullying people and being obnoxious. I said, "Jake, come outside for a minute, I want a word with you." And Fred said, "Yeah, come on, Jake." And Jake started yelling and protesting vehemently. Costello got up and said, "Look out, Jake's in trouble." Kosmo said, "Sit down, Elvis! There's nothing you can do about it if he is!" We went outside, and Jake said, "I know, Ian, you're gonna fuck my mind with the verbals, then Spider's gonna beat me up." I said, "No, Jake, all we were gonna say was that we want to keep it all smashing."'

Rowe and Riviera never came to blows, but their showdown was a turning point for Ian, establishing him as a powerful force on the tour and emboldening him for future outings. He could now get away with murder because Fred Rowe would always be there to protect him. 'He knew he could go a bit further than he normally went,' says Fred. 'Ian was a pacifist, but he wanted to be a tough guy, a gangster. He told me, "If I hadn't have been the way I am, I would have become a hard nut." I said, "Yes, I suppose you would, Ian."'

As the Stiff trek continued, Ian inched his way towards headline status. When 'Sex and Drugs and Rock and Roll' was adopted as the tour's anthem and nightly closing routine, his aims were achieved. Although Costello put up a fight with incendiary performances of new songs such as 'Watching the Detectives' and 'Lipstick Vogue', it was Ian who emerged as the people's hero. 'He was very competitive,' confirms co-manager Andrew King. 'He went to endless lengths to ensure that he did better than Elvis and calculated that, if Elvis agreed to alternate the headline, it would be Ian's turn when the tour hit London! He had it in the bag.'

The Stiff tour ended at Lancaster University on 5 November 1977, the day on which Stiff released Ian's next 45, 'Sweet Gene Vincent', an up-tempo lament for his late rock 'n' roll hero. Stiff had every reason to expect a strong chart placing, but sales were sluggish, despite a growing fan base and the song's pure abstract poetry:

> Black gloves, white frost, black crêpe, white lead,
> White sheet, black knight, jet black, dead white . . .
> Sweet Gene Vincent!

The single bombed, but Ian's career had achieved lift-off, with *New Boots and Panties!!* nestled comfortably in the Top 10, destined to remain there for months to come. Exhausted by the six-week Stiff slog, Ian and Denise were in need of a break. Nothing less than a three-week sojourn in Barbados would suffice. 'It was my first visit to the West Indies and it was amazing,' recalls Denise, but she was beginning to sense that after four years her time with Ian was ticking away. 'It felt like the end of an era. It was hard to take because our emotions were involved, but the work was done, and it was clear in my mind that Ian had to do what he had to do. He simply told me: "Denise, you've got to do it on your own." This was hard to take, but at the same time there was no arguing. I knew that's how Ian was with people.'

Returning from Barbados, Ian threw himself into a quick UK tour to capitalize on recent progress, largely at the behest of Kosmo Vinyl. 'Ian was hot,' says Kosmo, 'and people wanted to see him, although his managers took some convincing. We were all in a twelve-seater van, with Fred driving, when he wasn't punching people out.' Davey Payne, now an official Block-head, was at first reluctant to join the tour, but was 'kidnapped' by Fred Rowe and driven to Leeds. The 'Dirty Dozen' tour returned Ian to some of the towns he had conquered on the Stiff outing. The venues were packed, and it was no surprise to see entire audiences singing along to the words from *New Boots*.

In the early hours of 17 December, following a show at Bath Pavilion, Charley Charles' car was stopped by police in Pulteney Street. Ian was in the passenger seat. Upon attempting to breathalyse Charley, police constable Graham McQuillan was allegedly kicked in the leg by Ian. Ian's solicitor claimed that, due to Ian's disability, it would not have been possible for him to kick the officer, but Ian was found guilty and fined £50 at Bath Magistrates Court for 'obstructing the police'. 'PC: Punk rock star kicked me,' screamed the headline. 'My earrings might have frightened the policeman,' explained Ian.

When the Dirty Dozen tour climaxed at London's Round-house on 18 December, hundreds without tickets were turned away. Writing in the *NME*, Monty Smith described Ian as 'a ragged-arse Robert Newton, festooned with gaudy garters and handkerchiefs and a pair of crotchless unmentionables worn over his trousers . . . his Chaplinesque gesture at the end of the opening number marks him as a man intimate with the intricacies of stage acting and immediately endears him to the audience . . . rock 'n' roll needs Ian Dury.'

Heavy touring in the UK had brought Ian to a new record-buying audience and established a dependable fan base, but it nearly bankrupted Stiff. With the departure of Elvis Costello and Nick Lowe from the label, Dave Robinson needed to recoup fast and decided to blow his entire marketing budget on a full-out Dury campaign. The odds were favourable; sales of *New Boots* showed no sign of abating as it became the perfect lewd dinner-party album of the pre-Derek and Clive era.* It certainly caused embarrassment at family gatherings, where much loud

---

* In 1980, popular comedians Peter Cook and Dudley Moore, as their alter egos Derek and Clive, would release an entire LP of conversational profanities, but back in 1977 it was hard to find a hit record containing the F-word. John Lennon's song 'Working Class Hero' (1971) is the only other example that readily springs to mind. *New Boots and Panties!!* went several stages further.

coughing would herald the entry of 'Plaistow Patricia'. In sitting rooms across the land, parents fumbled with the volume control to mute Ian at his most toxic: 'Arseholes, bastards, fucking cunts and pricks, / Aerosol . . . the bricks!'

The record's notoriety helped to expand its appeal. 'Kids all love swearing,' said Ian. 'I'm only swearing for the kids, I'm not swearing for the oldsters! But I'm very careful about swearing on record, just enough. You're allowed one "fuck" and two "bloodies" on BBC2 after 11 o'clock. If you see a film like *Serpico* and every other word is "fuck", it's horrible. In real life I swear as much as possible, but when I wrote "Plaistow Patricia", it seemed the only way to do it was to get rid of it in one line. I think that's all the swearing there is on *New Boots and Panties!!*' Ian was thrilled when he learnt that architects and lawyers were buying the album, knowing that he also appealed to middle-class professionals.

Swearing notwithstanding, Ian was poised for national stardom. A television documentary profiled the rising star in a twenty-minute romp around Oval Mansions and Walthamstow Market. 'He looks and dresses like a totter,' ran Yvonne Roberts' commentary, 'but at thirty-five, this could be his year.' Ian took the opportunity to further muddy his background. 'The name is Dury,' he told the camera, 'and I come from Upminster and 'ornchurch and Romford and Walthamstow and 'arrow and other places.' He also made a return appearance on TV's *The London Weekend Show* in which an excerpt from his 1976 performance of 'England's Glory' was screened. Presenter Janet Street-Porter declared: 'Ian Dury believes that the way forward lies in taking punk out of exclusively teenage venues into a new, much wider sphere.' In the interview that followed, Ian responded: 'There's something there for all of us. Music hall was a family outing. Your little brother can go and bang his head against the wall, if he wants. I'd like to see everybody there, having a picnic, dogs running about, I wouldn't like to say that nobody can come.'

Ian's invitation to a raucous evening's entertainment was not restricted to Britain. Stiff had now licensed *New Boots* in various overseas territories where Euro-interest was starting to build. Ian and the Blockheads set off on a quick round of live dates and TV appearances, with brief trips to Germany, France, Sweden and Holland. In the UK, the Stiff publicity machine continued to milk the Dury phenomenon, sending Ian to dozens of interviews with a newly inquisitive media. 'The main target was the provincial press,' says aide-de-camp Kosmo Vinyl. 'Those local newspapers like the *Newham Recorder* would hang around the house for a week. They far outsold the *Record Mirror*.' Vinyl would always be present at press interviews to help deflect awkward questions. If Ian was unsure of a response, Kosmo would be either nodding or shaking his head. But although Ian was rarely lost for words, his sound bites were becoming repetitive. Only an American tour would save him from over-exposure.

Ian wasn't keen on the idea of taking his music to the USA. 'You'll never find me in Malibu, darling, because I don't like America, I think it's a pig sty,' he announced in a TV interview. This was followed by the show's presenter, Godfrey Hodgson, cryptically describing Ian as: 'London's latest temporary export'. But Stiff Records had bigger ideas. In its second year of existence, though it was still a tiny operation, label boss Dave Robinson was typically upbeat about cementing a US licensing deal with the mighty Arista Records. 'I foresee no problem,' Robinson would frequently announce. In *his* mind, Ian was the crucial piece in the jigsaw and would be nominated to spearhead Stiff's campaign in America.

When an opportunity arose for Ian to appear on a coast-to-coast tour with Lou Reed, himself an Arista artiste, it seemed too good to be true. Kosmo Vinyl had to persuade a reluctant Ian that it would work. 'My point of view was that the Lou Reed audience would have been closer to what Ian was all about than some other American acts,' says Kosmo. 'I thought that if people liked Lou Reed, they could like Ian Dury.' Ian put forward a number of reasons for not wanting to tour the States, including the state of his teeth. In typical style, Dave Robinson offered to pay for cosmetic dentistry if Ian would agree to the trip.

At a surgery in Harley Street, Ian was measured for new crowns and fitted with a temporary veneer on his lower incisors. 'Can you paint on the veneer?' he enquired of the dentist, knowing it would soon be time to fly the flag. An hour later, he strode out into the spring sunshine, flashing a Union Jack grin. When Kosmo heard about the teeth he was on the phone to the press. Photographs of Ian's patriotic smile appeared everywhere. It was now the eve of his first trip to America and other than two brief visits in later years it would be his one and only US tour. 'He got off the plane,' recalls Kosmo, 'and said, "I hate America," and he got back on the plane six weeks later and said, "I told you so."'

Despite his protestations, Ian had been privately savouring a reunion with his former lover, Roberta Bayley, whom he hadn't seen since she was in London four years earlier. As soon as the tour was confirmed, Ian made some frantic phone calls and persuaded Roberta to fly from New York to San Francisco, where the tour with Lou Reed was due to kick off on 22 March. 'Several years had gone by,' recalls Roberta, 'and even though we had been having correspondence, I'd gotten a whole life, taking photographs and doing well. I was willing to go see him, but – this would always be his thing – he said, "It is definitely platonic, nothing has to happen, I just need your support, I really want you to come out." I went to the first gig, and Ian wanted me to stay with him. I really didn't want to, and we had a huge row at the hotel, so I just left and called my friends. As much as you say to the person, "I don't have those feelings any more, and we're not going to sleep together," and they say, "Absolutely yes," they think that when you see them everything will change. It's a big challenge.'

•

Headliner Lou Reed was not unlike Ian: 'squat', chip on shoulder, lethal with words. Proud of his New York street savvy and exalted status as founder of the Velvet Underground, he was in combative mood when paired with 'the limey upstart'. Peter Jenner's opinion of Lou Reed was unequivocal. 'He was just awful. It was all Arista; we were the hot new signing from England, so they put us on a tour with Lou. It seemed like a good thing. In San Francisco all the Arista people were there . . . lots of attention, lots of interviews. Second night, no sign of anyone from Arista . . . we learnt that they'd all been called to Los Angeles because Clive Davis was launching his book. He pulled all his PR people out to promote it. That really upset us. Also, Lou Reed never spoke to us. His crew were nice, but Lou gave us the classic example of how to treat a support band badly. He made us feel very unwelcome.'

Reed's ego was about to be deflated. On 26 March, the tour played the first of four consecutive nights at the Roxy in Los Angeles. Expatriate superstars Ron Wood and Rod Stewart turned up to cheer Ian and the Blockheads and, in a gesture of solidarity, set about detuning all of Lou Reed's guitars in the backstage area, effectively wrecking his performance. Reed would get his own back. The Blockheads had already befriended members of Lou's band and invited them to sit in on 'Sex and Drugs', but Reed instructed his musicians not to fraternize with the opening act. He also made sure that his sound engineer put minimal effort into mixing Ian and the Blockheads. Convinced that Reed was intent on sabotaging the show, Ian sent for Ian Horne, formerly Paul McCartney's live sound engineer. Horne turned up in Phoenix, Arizona, ready to mix Ian's set and stayed for the rest of the tour and many years thereafter.

Chaz Jankel hadn't participated in the American tour. 'Every now and again I had to get some breathing space,' says Chaz. 'Ian was pretty intense.' Of Jankel's defection, Ian told the *NME*'s Paul Morley, 'I went on the road without Chaz. He wanted to stay at home and write, and that nearly broke my heart, 'cos I really love him.' Working two sets a night across the United States, the five-piece Blockheads perfected their musical arrangements to the point where they and Ian could work with or without Chaz. 'They valued his creative input in the studio,' says Kosmo, 'and they liked him, but they became so tight on stage that Chaz Jankel was now superfluous to a great Ian Dury and the Blockheads concert.'

The US tour ended with a two-night stand at New York's Bottom Line on 2 and 3 May. Although his love affair with Denise had effectively ended, Ian flew her over for the final dates, greeting her with two brightly coloured Afro wigs he'd bought in a 42nd Street novelty store. Later that night, Ian's career in America came to an abrupt end, thanks to the over-zealous actions of his roadie and minder-in-waiting, Pete Rush, aka 'The Sulphate Strangler'. Rush was a man-mountain, pock-marked and heavily pierced, whose devotion to Ian knew no bounds. His misguided loyalty extended to 'warning off' the president of Arista Records when he attempted to visit Ian in his dressing room. 'Roadies were part of the act back then,' quips Kosmo Vinyl.

Clive Davis had guided the stratospheric careers of Janis Joplin, Barbra Streisand and Bob Dylan and was accustomed to strolling backstage at any venue in the world where one of his protégés was appearing. He might have helped Ian too, but for Rush's actions. The Strangler had received no express instructions to bar Davis from the backstage area, but he knew that, earlier in the week, Ian and Kosmo had visited the record company boss at his New York office, armed with a test pressing of Ian's next 45, 'What a Waste'. He had also heard that Davis was uninterested in the record and removed it from his turntable the moment he heard Ian's voice. Rush had picked up on Ian's displeasure and, aware that Davis might be *persona non grata*, advised the legendary music biz mogul to 'keep walking [away from the dressing room]'. When Davis did eventually get backstage, Kosmo Vinyl made some remarks about Davis's 'nice Pringle sweater'. 'That was it,' says Peter Jenner, 'the end of Ian's career in America.'

The US tour did earn Ian some good reviews during its six-week trek, but he lost interest by the halfway point. Twenty years earlier, his obsession with all things American had helped to shape his teenage tastes, but once on US soil, the reality was different. His romance with the USA blew hot and cold: one minute he was dazzled by the neon, but if the landscape was bland he would find fault. In a press interview he disapprovingly described the town of Utica, New York State, as 'Romford at right angles'. Ian put forward countless excuses for not pursuing success in the USA. 'All the girls have fat bums,' he flippantly observed, but kept the truth to himself. Deep down, he was worried about being upstaged by his own band. It wouldn't have happened in the UK, of course, where audiences lapped up his quirky stories about 'Clevor Trever' and 'Billericay Dickie', but Ian's alien songbook would never be widely appreciated by 'the septics' [the septic tanks = yanks). The faultless musicianship of the Blockheads, on the other hand, was a revelation in music-obsessed America. Ian's worst fears were confirmed during a performance in Los Angeles when he heard a heckler shout: 'Hey Ian! Shut up and let's hear the sax player!'

Returning to Britain in May 1978, Ian received a hero's welcome. 'What a Waste' had entered the charts and reached number nine, guaranteeing him a spot on BBC TV's *Top of the Pops*. It was an important milestone for cult followers who had been monitoring his progress since he emerged with Kilburn and the High Roads five years earlier, but for most of the show's twelve million viewers, Ian Dury had simply appeared from nowhere. No one was more excited than his old record label, Warner Brothers. They were quick to exploit his success by issuing their previously discarded Kilburn and the High Roads album under the title *Wotabunch!* – 'featuring Ian Dury'.

Written in 1976 with Rod Melvin, 'What a Waste' found Ian slightly tongue-in-cheek, musing on life's lost opportunities:

I could be a teacher in a classroom full of scholars,
I could be the sergeant in a squadron full of wallahs,
I could be a writer with a growing reputation,
I could be the ticket man at Fulham Broadway station,
What a waste!
I could be the catalyst that sparks the revolution,
I could be an inmate in a long-term institution . . .

Ian permitted himself a knowing little laugh delivering the 'institution' line, as if reminded of his time at Chailey Heritage Craft School for disabled children. After such a harrowing start in life, to have achieved a hit record with one of his own songs was little short of a miracle, a testament to his dogged determination. Coming on top of *New Boot and Panties!!*, the success of 'What a Waste' assured Ian that Aunt Molly's guru had been right all along – he had always been destined for fame.

It was inevitable that, after years of public indifference, stardom would provide Ian with a licence to go bonkers. Dave Robinson notes: 'He always wanted to have girls and when he had hits there were lots of girls, and that was one of his fantasies, world domination. He was a very good-looking guy and knew the power he had.' Denise Roudette noticed a change in his personality. 'Up until then he was quite open and trusting, but when he became famous, it was a scary business. His eyes went black and he lost it.' Denise had prepared herself for the emotional fallout, and, although she and Ian were no longer together, their lives were still intertwined.

While Ian had been on the road for several months, living out of a suitcase, Denise had stayed on at Oval Mansions, but Ian was now packing his bags for good. Homeless but cash-rich, he checked into London's Montcalm Hotel near Marble Arch, planning an indefinite stay. The appeal of the Montcalm was its excellent location; its elevators and twenty-four-hour room-service. Anyone requiring an audience with Britain's hot new star would be summoned to the hotel, where Spider was on hand to keep order. Ian's managers tried to dissuade him from indulging in such extravagance, but Ian was determined to apply his 'if you've got it, spend it' philosophy.

Now footloose and free, he opened the window of his suite and surveyed the 180-degree view. On a clear night he could see the lights of Edgware Road, running north to his Middlesex birthplace; Kensington in the west, where he'd studied at the Royal College of Art; Victoria to the south, reminding him of his dad's undignified death from cancer. Silently reflecting on his childhood at Chailey, coming to terms with polio and his beatings at the hands of the Royal Grammar School prefects, he also remembered those who had mocked his attempts to get a foothold in the music business. But they would not laugh now. It was time to get even.

PART FOUR

REVENGE

13

Up Like a Rocket

England, 1978. Punk rock, the strident voice of disaffected youth, had by now mutated into 'new wave', spearheaded by the likes of Blondie and Elvis Costello. Ian wished to align himself with neither musical movement, but it did him no harm to be described as the UK's 'godfather of punk'. Although Ian's music with the Blockheads was more sophisticated than the primeval wail of the Sex Pistols, his street poetry and uncompromising attitude gave him godlike status in the eyes of his fans. Elsewhere in 1978 Britain, cricketer Ian Botham became the first player in Test Match history to score a century and take eight wickets in one innings, although since leaving Oval Mansions Ian Dury would no longer hear the distant sound of leather on willow. In politics, Margaret Thatcher's Tory party was biting at the heels of the minority Labour government as the country headed for the 'winter of discontent'. In September, Prime Minister James Callaghan was under pressure to call an early election. Thatcher's election victory the following year would not best please Ian – a committed socialist – but he would eventually come to appreciate the value of property acquisition.

Externally, Ian was a man of the people, a role he played to great effect on his national tour, supported by UK reggae outfit Matumbi and rockabilly boys Whirlwind. Opening in Birmingham on 11 May, he made a point of boning up on some local trivia so that, in the time-honoured showbiz tradition, he could make amusing references to the town's landmarks. It was a trick he would employ on every one of the tour's twenty-six dates. Local audiences were delighted, of course, and gazed in awe at the ever-changing wardrobe of their lovable cockney rascal, part pearly king, part pantomime villain. Ian's career as the diamond geezer was gaining momentum.

Music-hall legend Max Wall, whose version of Ian's 'England's Glory' had recently been released on Stiff, was given the thankless task of warming up the audience at Hammersmith Odeon on 13 and 14 May. Unfortunately, the London crowd were in no mood for Wall's slapstick antics and heckled him into submission. 'They only want the walk,' he sadly remarked as he shuffled off into the wings. Ian was furious and berated the crowd for giving Wall a hard time.

Kosmo Vinyl, in his role as Ian's press officer, persuaded the *NME* to run a competition to find the country's 'Champion Blockhead' – first prize 'a pair of new boots and panties and a night out with Ian Dury'. It was won by young Clive Pain of Hampshire, who popped into a Woolworths photo booth and tried to make himself look as numb-skulled as possible. Pain, aka 'Slim', later took up the accordion and became a popular musician on the live circuit. 'It can all be traced back to winning that Blockheads competition,' says Pain. Another fan who came to see Ian on the 1978 tour was Jock Scot, a twenty-five-year-old building worker who would eventually be employed by Stiff Records and the Dury operation.

Scot turned up at Edinburgh Odeon on 1 June wearing full highland regalia. 'I was wearing this Scottish hat,' recalls Jock, 'a sort of navy-blue beret with a red pompom and little tails and an army badge, a Glengarry. I was in the foyer before the gig and I saw one of the road crew with an "Access All Areas" badge and I asked him if he would give my hat to Ian as a present. The guy looked at me and said, "Well, come with me and give it to Ian yourself."' Jock nervously entered the backstage area, where he was vetted by Spider. Ian was sitting in the corner of his dressing room, applying stage make-up and arranging his props, including a number of plastic fried eggs he would hang from his shirt. The Union Jack still adorned his teeth. Ian acknowledged Jock, who cautiously proffered his Glengarry. 'It's just a present from your Scottish fans,' he said. 'We hope you'll support Scotland during the World Cup.' Ian graciously accepted the gift, and Jock made his way to his seat in the stalls.

Ten minutes later, as the Blockheads commenced the opening chords of 'Wake Up and Make Love with Me', Ian made his entrance, wearing Scot's headgear. 'With his limp, he looked like one of those war veterans, an old soldier!' recalls Jock. 'I was completely knocked out, screaming, "He's wearing my hat!"' After the show, Jock returned backstage, where he was introduced to the Blockheads. It was quite normal for Ian to allow fans into his dressing room so he could meet 'his people'. 'It was exciting for a country boy like me,' continues Jock. 'We drank all the beer and Ian said, "Come back to the hotel and have a drink." We stayed up all night, and Ian invited me to the next gig, which was in Glasgow. Again we sat up all night, this time drinking whisky with Peter Blake. The next day I hitched a lift to Newcastle City Hall, went straight to the stage door and was greeted by Spider. I was on the whole tour after that.'

Ian invited Jock to join his crew, but the kilted Scot was not sure if he should leave the relative security of the building trade. To help sway matters, Ian deployed his notorious money-burning routine. 'So, Jock, how much money do you make on the building site?' Ian asked. 'Thirty-six pounds a week,' replied Jock. Ian summoned one of his road crew, 'Roadent! Come 'ere! Have you got thirty-six quid?' 'Roadent' (born Steve Connelly) pulled out a wad of bank notes and handed it over. 'Watch this,' said Ian, producing a box of matches. 'He set fire to the money!' recalls Jock. 'He said, "The money's got fuck all to do with it! You're wasting your time digging that hole. Come with us, we'll find you something to do."'

Ian's offer to Jock typified his attitude towards those he considered uniquely talented, but who were, in his opinion, wasting their life. It frustrated Ian if able-bodied men were 'copping out' when he had worked so hard to overcome his own adversity. In much the same way as he operated in his teaching career, he would often provoke such individuals into 'owning up' while remarking: 'It's good for people to have at least one nervous breakdown.' He had no time for tiresome bores, but those he liked he goaded until they showed their true selves or, as he put it, their 'spirit', whereas, if you cowered in fear, you were 'asking for it'!

Ian had by now moved from the Montcalm to the Dorchester. When staying on Park Lane started to decimate his finances, he announced that he was tired of hotel life and began a search of the surrounding area for a suitable apartment. He found the ideal place over an antiques shop in Mount Street, Mayfair. 'Come and see what a hundred grand gets you,' Kosmo Vinyl exclaimed to Jock Scot, now on the road crew. Not that Ian was buying – Mount Street was the first of several West End service flats he would rent at the height of his fame, but none of them was conducive to songwriting. Seeking a little solitude, he searched for a home in the countryside, ideally one with a swimming pool so that he could enjoy his favourite form of exercise. In July 1978 he moved into the curiously named Toad Hall in Sandhurst Lane, Rolvenden, Kent, a luxurious property with endless rooms and grounds. The Blockheads were invited down to work on songs, including 'Hit Me with Your Rhythm Stick', the words of which Ian had been honing for two years.

Chaz Jankel was quite pleased with the little accented piano riff he had created for 'Wake Up and Make Love with Me' and sought to emulate the effect for 'Rhythm Stick', toiling for hours over his keyboard set-up in the garage at Toad Hall. Ian, meanwhile, was in the house, supposedly working on the words. 'I had "Rhythm Stick" for about three years on a bit of paper,' said Ian. 'I did a little demo of it with a drum machine and I gave it to Chaz.' The Blockheads remember walking along with Ian chanting 'Hit Me' in the States, noting that it came from James Brown.* When the song was finished, Chaz phoned his mother and excitedly announced he had just composed his 'first number one'.

> *In the deserts, of Sudan*
> *And the gardens, of Japan,*
> *From Milan, to Yucatan,*
> *Every woman's every man,*
> *Hit me with your rhythm stick*
> *Hit me! Hit me!*
> *Je t'adore, ich liebe dich*
> *Hit me! Hit me! Hit me!*
> *Hit me with your rhythm stick*
> *Hit me slowly, hit me quick*
> *Hit me! Hit me! Hit me*

Ian knew that the b-side of 'Rhythm Stick' would generate cash for its writers and music publishers, as each side of a single earned an equal royalty from record sales (although the a-side made additional royalties from radio play, television and live performance). With this in mind, Ian chose 'There Ain't Half Been Some Clever Bastards', a song that he'd co-written with Russell Hardy, his songwriting partner from Kilburn and the High Roads, that was part published by his former managers, Charlie Gillett and Gordon Nelki, through their company, Oval Music. It was Ian's way of recognizing the crucial part they had all played in the early days.

'Clever Bastards' was one of Ian's sharpest lyrics, extolling the virtues of a handful of history's great geniuses, his East End

---

* James Brown shouts 'Hit me!' in his song 'Ain't That a Groove', among others.

rasp making the song's irreverent observations all the more poignant. 'Yeah, that was a good one,' Ian conceded.

> *Noël Coward was a charmer,*
> *As a writer he was Brahma,*
> *Velvet jacket and pyjamas,*
> *The Gay Divorce and other dramas . . .*

'*The Gay Divorce* was a Fred Astaire movie!' admitted Ian, as he recited the words to me in his work den two decades later. 'It had nothing to do with Noël Coward! Plus, I did:

> *Van Gogh was an eyeball pleaser,*
> *He must have been a pencil squeezer,*
> *He didn't do the Mona Lisa,*
> *That was an Italian geezer!*

'I'd already used that [Mona Lisa line] in a song I did with Rod Melvin, called "I've Left the Rag Trade to Join the Drag Trade", but I didn't let that stop me, I carried on. You can eat your own foot if you want, can't you?' Rod Melvin recalls, 'The origins of "Rag Trade" came about because we were looking out of Ian's window at Oval Mansions and there was a guy getting out of a car. Ian said, "That's my neighbour, he's been in the rag trade but now he's a drag artiste".'

'As a wordsmith, I felt I was in a unique position really,' Ian told me. 'Noël Coward's all right, Cole Porter's all right. OK, he wrote four good songs. He did his best work when he was very rich, swanning around Venice, cocaine and champagne to order and a bloke sharpening his pencils for him. Then he fell off his horse and never wrote another decent song. You'd think it would be the other way round, wouldn't you? I think I've written maybe three good songs. A good song will get off the table and go out in the street and get a minicab down to Tin Pan Alley. It'll look after you.'

Listening to Ian comparing himself with Coward and Porter, I felt compelled to ask him what his 'three good songs' were. 'Sweet Gene Vincent' was at the top of his list. 'It's a bit ponderous,' he said, 'a bit poetic, but I quite like it . . . it's well written, although the genre isn't exactly where I'd want to hang my hat. Rock 'n' roll is great, but it's slightly predict- able. I'd much rather be noted for something like "Wake Up and Make Love with Me" or "Sex and Drugs", something more interesting rhythmically. I get a real buzz knowing that Bootsy Collins has sampled one of our tracks. Chaz and the Blockheads are top-quality musicians. As soon as I heard Chaz play, I wanted to work with him because he's a funky musician. That's what I always wanted to do – all through the Kilburns – music that had that dancing element, but still be English, not just slavishly American stuff. So if it's a rock 'n' roll track like "Sweet Gene Vincent" or "Blockheads", it's got the "Nutbush" element.'

Although Ian was undoubtedly a great lyricist and received plaudits in the press, he often sought approval from friends. 'Wreckless' Eric Goulden recalls him taking his lyrics into Blackhill Music in a shopping bag and asking his managers if his work was good enough. Charlie Gillett remembers, 'He was full of self-doubt, more insecure than most people ever under- stood. I told him that he was a songwriter in the calibre of Cole Porter or Leiber and Stoller, but he had very little confidence in his own ability to deliver what he knew were pretty clever words.'

Whatever Ian's insecurities, his lyrics were frequently bril- liant and kept him aloft in the eyes of the Blockheads, who were still in awe of his genius. Released by Stiff in November 1978, 'Hit Me with Your Rhythm Stick' was an unstoppable hit. Returning from a three-week European tour on 7 December, Ian learnt that it had entered the UK charts. On *Top of the Pops* he was resplendent in black tie and shades, fronting his tuxedoed Blockheads with innate cool and concealing his disability well. Seven weeks later 'Rhythm Stick' would be at number one, having sold nearly a million copies. This would be the priceless moment; a number one record was the reward he had been dreaming about since he had first heard Elvis Presley's echo-laden voice ring out from the end of lonely street.

The final show of 1978 was a landmark event for Ian's fans on the Essex/East London border. Few major artistes had bothered to play on their doorstep, but earlier in the year Kosmo Vinyl had become convinced that, if a suitable auditorium could be found, the show would sell out immediately. The 1,700-capacity Gants Hill Odeon near Ilford was identified as being 'on Ian's manor'. He had appeared there in the summer in what was billed as 'the first rock show ever' at the venue and returned on 23 December for a historic concert. The theatre had not been designed for rock 'n' roll and the organ pit, which was immediately in front of the stage, had been boarded over and carpeted for the evening. During a souped-up 'Billericay Dickie', the floor gave way beneath the weight of a hundred pogoing fans. 'It looked like the whole audience had dropped about eighteen inches,' recalls Kosmo. 'It was one of Ian's proudest moments.'

Stiff Records, delighted with Ian's richly deserved number one hit, had high hopes of his next album repeating the success of *New Boots*, but the label had not heard much new material, partly because Ian had found touring to be less than conducive to his writing. The previous autumn the band had repaired to Toad Hall, where Ian put each Blockhead in a different room and gave him a lyric to set music to. 'Ian walked round like a school teacher,' recalls Mickey, who received a draft of 'This Is What We Find', the funniest of Ian's new lyrics.

> *Home improvement expert Harold Hill of Harold Hill*
> *Of do-it-yourself dexterity and double-glazing skill*
> *Came home to find another gentleman's kippers in the grill*
> *So he sanded off his winkle with his Black and Decker drill*

'It's the only good verse though,' said Ian. 'I had a problem because I couldn't do a funnier one than that. It's the only funny verse. Did I put it first to grab the attention or third to provide a climax? I put it first, it had to be.' (It is actually the third verse on the record.) Guitarist Johnny Turnbull was asked to put music to 'Uneasy Sunny Day Hotsy Totsy', a lyric that contained some vague political sloganeering and an assortment of vulgar phrases, causing Johnny to caustically comment, 'I knew I wouldn't get double-glazing out of that one.' There were 'swear words galore' in the lyrics Ian gave Mickey and Johnny, whereas Chaz appeared to get all the clean ones. 'I mentioned this to Chaz,' says Mickey, 'and he said, "I just told Ian to take the swear words out." I never fucking thought of that!'

Ian and the Blockheads were due to enter the Workhouse studio in February 1979, but there was barely enough material for a forty-minute disc. 'After *New Boots*, there wasn't a lot more left in the cupboard,' confesses Chaz Jankel, who was tasked with eking more songs out of Ian. The duo had recently flown out to Barbados with the aim of writing songs at Bluff Cottage, but they returned with little. As well as co-writing, Chaz was also charged with producing the record. For this he would earn the cryptic credit: 'Chaz Jankel is musically direct.' This was easier than announcing to the other Blockheads that Chaz was, in fact, their producer.

Another difficulty that had to be overcome before recording could start was reaching an agreement on the division of artiste royalties. Up until that point, the Blockheads had been on a wage of £75 a week, largely sustained by interminable touring. Ian and Chaz additionally enjoyed writer's royalties. A meeting was held, with Ian's accountant, Ronnie Harris, in attendance, at which the Blockheads put forward their case for a share of the recording cake. Ian opened the proceedings by announcing: 'I want two and a half points [per cent],' to which Chaz responded, 'Well I'm not taking less than Ian.' Blackhill, as managers, also considered themselves to be worthy of the same. 'After seven-and-a-half points, there wasn't much left,' says Mickey Gallagher. 'It left us with a point each. We were happy with that, but then Ian announced that he wanted to give points to the roadies!'

Peter Jenner confirms Ian's support for the road crew: 'He liked to line up with them. They were the "working classes", not poncey musicians.' The Blockheads were left with a tiny royalty, and Mickey Gallagher, who called Ian's bluff by offering to take nothing if it meant the other Blockheads could each have one per cent, walked out in disgust. 'Then Ian said he wouldn't sign anything,' says Davey Payne, who was becoming angered by the situation. 'He wanted to do a handshake agreement, "like the Red Indians do!" Chaz Jankel didn't do handshake deals – he'd come in with a lawyer – but the rest of us shook on it and got a really bad deal.'

With the royalties issue more or less resolved, the recording of the masterwork commenced. On their first long-play outing with Ian, the Blockheads were eager to demonstrate their musical prowess. The lack of ideas emanating from their leader allowed the various group members to submit pieces of music that might have lyrics added later. What largely emerged was a work in which the songs' words – that is to say Ian's *raison d'être* – were subservient to the musical settings, many of which bordered on gratuitous 'jazz-funk'. Interestingly, Ian would never allow his lyrics to be reproduced on the record sleeves, saying: 'My words have got to be audible. People have got to be able to hear them, that's what it's about.'

After the album's backing tracks had been captured and lyrics found, the Blockheads stayed away from the studio until called in to record their various overdubs, a process that ate up a good deal of the budget. Ian would usually stick around, until the day Chaz sent him home for being disruptive. 'It was getting so protracted,' says Chaz. 'The music was taking second place to whatever Ian wanted to chat about. He loved to have an audience. If he were here now with us, we would both be listening to Ian. When I told him to go home, there was the longest pause in the history of recording. He said, "I don't fucking believe it! I've just been asked to stay away from my own album!"'

In the spring of 1979, Ian was at the top of his game. With *Do It Yourself* complete and a big promotional tour booked for the summer, he was planning on taking a break, but on 16 April – Easter Monday – he received some sad news from Peggy. His aunt, Elisabeth Walker, had died. Ian was devastated by the death of his 'auntie nice' and asked Martin Cole if he would drive Betty and himself to Barnstaple for the funeral. Following the loss of her sister, Peggy decided to vacate the National Trust cottage they had shared and talked about moving back to London. Ian was quick to assist with her relocation, paying £48,000 in cash for a flat in Fitzjohn's Avenue, Hampstead, an area Peggy loved and knew well.

Returning from Devon, Ian was focused on the sleeve concept for *Do It Yourself*. Attempting to repeat the shop-front gag of *New Boots and Panties!!* he found a wig shop near Baker Street, with pictures in the window of six unhappy-looking bald men and, below, pictures of the same models wearing toupees and looking cheerful. Along with photographer Chris Gabrin, Ian and the Blockheads crept up to the shop at 3 a.m. after an intense mixing session at Workhouse Studios. Ian lined the Blockheads up, all wearing sailors' hats and placed Fred Rowe, who was bald, at the end of the queue, face on, smiling. The resulting photo appeared on the back of some early pressings of *Do It Yourself*, but Ian received an injunction from the wig shop, and Gabrin had to give a written undertaking to destroy the negatives.

Expanding on the 'home improvement' theme of the album's title, Blockheads logo designer Barney Bubbles ordered a selection of Crown wallpaper samples from which he chose twelve different patterns for the front sleeve. This would result in at least a dozen variations hitting the shops simultaneously, thus creating instant collectors' items. To help promote the album, Stiff Records rolled out one of its most inspired campaigns, despatching record company minions to provincial record shops with point-of-sale material and buckets of emulsion paint, offering to 'tosh up' the premises.

Despite the odd filler track, such as 'Waiting for Your Taxi', *Do It Yourself* was a fairly listenable record, with 'Don't Ask Me' and 'Lullaby for Frances' being standouts, but it was nowhere near as entertaining as its predecessor. *New Boots and Panties!!* contained a wealth of tales of Essex boys and East End girls, whereas the new subject matter was less direct and, in truth, a disappointment. But it was unfair to expect Ian to dream up another 'Billericay Dickie' simply to repeat a successful formula. *Do It Yourself* at least kept the cash flowing for Stiff Records, but ultimately sold far less than *New Boots*. Another factor in the album's under-achievement was Ian's refusal to include one or two of his recent hit singles. Had *Do It Yourself* kicked off with 'What a Waste' or 'Rhythm Stick', another 100,000 or so sales might easily have been achieved, but Ian refused to compromise. 'He would not put his singles on albums,' says Mickey Gallagher, 'and it would cost him dearly. He would always argue that it was his artistic licence.'

Behind Ian's stance was the influence of Kosmo Vinyl. 'Kosmo would tip Ian off on what was hip,' says Glen Colson, 'a bit of obscure reggae, then some Max Miller.' Managers Jenner and King welcomed Vinyl's youthful input but didn't necessarily agree with his strategy. 'It was Kosmo who stopped us putting the singles on the albums,' says Andrew King, 'because the Small Faces never did it.' In Kosmo's mind, the Small Faces' *Ogdens' Nut Gone Flake* was the model album, a prime example of how to make a record (although, ironically, *Ogdens'* did contain the Small Faces' then hit single, 'Lazy Sunday'). 'We never put our singles on albums,' said Ian. 'I had a vision that one day we could put out a singles album. Asking people to buy something twice was not on, in my opinion. In those days me and Kosmo were trying to . . . he had a thing . . . if I got asked to go on the *Wogan* show, Kosmo would say, "Would Johnny Rotten do it? No, so we ain't doing it." That was one of our yardsticks.'

Ian didn't need any advice when it came to his image, but the rather less sartorially inclined Blockheads definitely benefited from having Vinyl on hand as their informal stylist. 'On the Stiff tour they were wearing snakeskin boots and cowboy jackets,' recalls Davey Payne. 'They were vegetarians, into the Loving Awareness thing, that pseudo cosmic vibe. When they met Ian they changed overnight . . . they started wearing Dr Martens and eating sausages. Norman shrunk about a foot when he stopped wearing the cowboy boots.' Mickey Gallagher admits, 'We had long hair and beards at the start. Kosmo took us all out, one a time, and got us togged up, haircuts, the lot. He was invaluable. He created the look of the band.' Chaz Jankel adds, 'Kosmo was Ian's ear on the street. He was a sharp, Clash-loving, soul-loving wide boy – very lippy and hugely entertaining. Ian found him irritating, but fun. He wore loud zoot suits and dyed his hair – like an East End Elvis. He would wind up the press and get Ian noticed.' Vinyl's promotional stunts included walking into the offices of *Sounds* with a chainsaw and threatening to cut the desk in half if they didn't listen to *Do It Yourself*. At *Record Mirror* he'd ripped a Jimi Hendrix poster off the wall, shouting, 'Never mind about dead people! What about *New Boots and Panties!!!*'

Just as Ian refused to put his hit singles on *Do It Yourself*, he also forbade singles to be sourced from it. 'We didn't particularly have a problem with this, although it did affect sales,' says Stiff's Dave Robinson. 'But Ian wanted to be a legendary artiste, and in Ian's mind, legendary artistes like the Beatles and the Stones usually kept their singles off albums.' Stiff 'did what they were told,' says Andrew King. 'I came across some of the letters we wrote to Stiff and they are fucking ferocious: "Dear Paul, unless by five o'clock tomorrow afternoon we receive x thousand pounds, we will have no option but to . . ." No one writes a letter like that nowadays.'

Professionally, Ian was surrounded by the finest team he could wish for: the Blockheads, quite simply one of the world's greatest musical units, with the considerable funk of Charley and Norman underpinning every groove; Chaz Jankel, back on board and ready to set Ian's lyrical gems to music; a loyal and hard-working crew, with Ian Horne at the helm balancing front-of-house sound; Stiff Records, now in essence the fearless Dave Robinson, ready to throw money in any direction that would further Ian's career and general manager Paul Conroy, already a marketing wizard; Andrew King and Peter Jenner of Blackhill, a solid, honest management team; graphics genius Barney Bubbles, packaging Ian's records as works of art; right-hand-man and bodyguard Fred 'Spider' Rowe, who loved and protected Ian like a brother, and media consultant Kosmo Vinyl, whose energy would help propel the Clash to world domination. It was an unbeatable team, but Ian would systematically piss them all off, or as Dave Robinson quips, 'Ian burnt his bridges whilst we were all standing on them.'

14

Reasons to Be Cheerful (Part 1)

Zurich, Switzerland, 1979. Barry Anderson hadn't seen his childhood chum for sixteen years. As he drove through town on a warm spring day he turned on his radio and heard the strains of 'Rhythm Stick' and the deejay back-announce 'the latest hit from Ian Dury!' Barry was stunned. He had no idea that the crippled art student he had last seen at South West Essex College during the height of Beatlemania was now an international hit recording artiste. When he reached his office, where he worked as a marketing consultant, he mentioned that the pop star Ian Dury was 'an old mate'. Quick to pounce on an opportunity, Barry's colleagues immediately suggested that Ian should be involved in their next advertising campaign for Swiss Air!

Barry was asked to make contact with Ian and persuade him to endorse Switzerland's national airline. It would be a worthwhile exercise. Ian asked Barry to meet him at his hotel in Paris, where he would put him up. Barry took the train from Bern and when he arrived was amazed by the number of photographers present, all waiting for his old pal. Journalists were asking Ian about music, and Barry was surprised when he heard him say, 'Jazz is my real true love. You can ask me any question about jazz you like and I'll answer it.' 'I thought, "You conceited bastard!"' says Barry. 'In the old days it was all Chris Barber and Terry Lightfoot. Later, I asked Ian if he was really up on the jazz business. He said, "I love it." I went to the concert that evening and was backstage before the show. What surprised me was how seriously Ian was taking the whole thing.'

The Blockheads liked to have a drink and a smoke, but Barry noticed that Ian was forbidding it, telling his musicians, 'We're going on in a minute; we've got to concentrate.' Barry loved the show and remembers, 'When Ian came out of the theatre, there was a row of girls lined up. He picked out the three prettiest ones by pointing at them and saying, "You, you and you." He took them to the restaurant, then back to the hotel. I was in an adjoining room, drinking, and they were all next door. Fucking hell! When we were having dinner Ian said, "We'd better have our chat now because we're all going to be pissed in an hour's time." We got talking, and I raised the subject of the Swiss Air promotion, and Ian said, "Barry, I'm not going to endorse any commercial enterprises." I said, "All you've got to do is let them take a picture of you coming down the stairs. It's all lined up, the money's there." Ian said, "No, I'm a socialist." It was bloody news to me. He never used to be. I saw a total change in him. I couldn't persuade him, so we got pissed and had a chat about the old days.'

Ian might have insisted on abstention before show time, but he found other ways to pump up the adrenalin during the long hours of travel between venues. An element of drama often surrounds the touring rock 'n' roll musician, be he a Rolling Stone, armed to the teeth and carrying Class A drugs across international borders, or one of the Clash, arrested for shooting pigeons with an air pistol. Ian was somewhere in the middle and always made sure there were a few petty criminals on the team to keep everyone 'on the edge'. He considered it fatal if a colleague slipped into his comfort zone. Tension was the order of the day. He was also something of an *agent provocateur* who liked to light the blue touch paper then stand well clear when things started to kick off. Although he didn't condone violence, 'Knock him out, Fred' was an oft-heard command. His son Baxter, who was taken on tour at an early age, recalls, 'Dad was brilliant at

creating a dramatic environment that you suddenly found yourself in. He completely and utterly thrived on it. He thought that,
by surrounding himself with people like Spider and Strangler,
he had found real people who could fill it out. You gotta meet
Little Chris, a lively spiv character from Brixton who liked
fighting. He was about sixteen and worked as Spider's junior
security assistant.'

I bumped into 'Little' Chris Brown in Hoxton. A former child
boxer, he was a film company runner when he happened upon
Ian and the Blockheads on the 1977 Stiff tour. Although Brown
was asked to join the road crew, he didn't much care
for Ian at first. 'When Ian asked me if I would work for him,
I said, "I don't wanna work for you, you one-legged cunt,
you're fuckin' 'orrible." I thought he was a genius, but I didn't
agree with the way he behaved towards people. He was
knocked back by my remark and fell in love with me. If you
stood up to him, he would respect you, but if you buckled under
the pressure, he would rip you to pieces. It was like a machine
gun – his tongue lashings sounded like an Uzi going off.'

The European tour of May 1979 was a non-stop rock 'n' roll
riot, visiting eight countries in five weeks. 'The workload was
heavy,' recalls Brown. 'A different country every day, bed at
four, up at seven to get on the coach to the next town . . . sound-
check, hotel, bath, back to the gig, show, party . . . if there were
drugs on top of that, it would take its toll. They did burn the
candle.'

As the tour crossed various borders, with Ian picking up
gold and silver discs for sales of *New Boots*, Fred Rowe became
impressed by Ian's ability to communicate in the local language.
'He'd hardly been out of the country until he became a singer
but he could speak French, German, Italian . . . I asked a cab
driver in Rome if Ian was really speaking Italian. The cabbie
said, "He's very good, not in complete command of the language, but he's saying the right words in the right order." I was
amazed. He'd only been over there a few days, first time in Italy.

Same in Germany, same in France . . . I asked Ian how he did it, and he said, "All you've got to do is listen to them and you can pick it up." He had such an incredible brain.'

Do It Yourself reached number two on the UK album chart in June 1979 and remained a bestseller for several months, sustained by the success of Ian's next single, which was written and recorded on tour when an electrical fault at a venue resulted in cancelled shows and unexpected time off in Rome. Chaz Jankel was in his hotel room, bashing out a rhythm on the back of the sofa, when he called Ian and told him he had a great idea for a song. The next day Ian showed Chaz a lyric he'd written called 'Reasons to Be Cheerful (Part Three)'. 'I'd never seen it before,' says Chaz. 'I started playing a little guitar motif and the song came together.' With the song finished, Ian summoned the Blockheads to a local recording studio.

> *Some of Buddy Holly, the working folly,*
> *Good Golly Miss Molly and boats,*
> *Hammersmith Palais, the Bolshoi Ballet,*
> *Jump back in the alley, add nanny goats*

Praise and admiration for such a wide array of things: buildings, animals, a ballet company and old rock 'n' roll, saw Ian at his most charitable, but Davey Payne had for some time been extremely critical of the financial disparity between songwriters Ian and Chaz on the one hand and the rest of the Blockheads on the other. 'I wanna make enough money so I can give up rock 'n' roll,' Davey told the *NME*'s Declan Lynch. 'It's horrible. I think it stinks.' Davey would frequently mention 'money' until one day Ian got the message. In order to placate Davey, he would give him a lucrative share of his next record by manipulating the songwriting credits. He instructed Chaz to incorporate a 'pretty bit' in the middle of 'Reasons', over which Davey could improvise a sax solo and thus earn a share in the song. But as

Ian always insisted on a 50 per cent cut, on the basis that he had written all of the words, the remaining half had to be split between Chaz and Davey.

'He wanted to give Davey a squirt – a piece of the action,' says Chaz, 'so what had started out with me going to Ian with this idea for a song, ended up as just a 25 per cent share. Ian would never compromise on his 50 per cent for the lyric. I can understand why he wanted to put Davey in the frame, because he'd been with Ian for a long time and wasn't getting money for writing. The Blockheads' income came from touring, and maybe that was part of Ian's reason for wanting to keep the band together and play gigs, because that was how they made their money. But expenses were high. We would hire limos, anything excessive. It was a way of letting off steam.'

> *Health service glasses, gigolos and brasses,*
> *Round or skinny bottoms,*
> *Taking Mum to Paris, lighting up the chalice,*
> *Wee Willie Harris*

On 24 June, Ian commenced a six-week UK tour. He was at the height of his fame, yet still found time for his fans. A post-show dressing room party would occur every night, occasionally spilling out into the front row of the stalls, where Ian would hold court as the equipment was being packed away. Spider was always around to ensure that fans formed an orderly queue, but if anyone outstayed their welcome Ian would summon his minder with a coded message. A seemingly innocent remark from Ian such as 'Spider, do you have a cigarette?' translated into a request to eject a particularly irksome person.

'We had other code words,' says Fred. 'Ian might say the word "Rhinoceros", which meant "This bloke is asking me questions I don't want to answer." So I would say, "Ian we've got to leave now, you've got another appointment to go to." It was designed to make Ian look like a reasonable guy and I was the baddie who made sure he kept to his schedule.' Spider's

usual technique, so as not to offend, was to put his arm around
the interloper, start a conversation – which might have been
interpreted as an affectionate gesture – then slowly walk him
towards the exit, and he would be on the street before he realized what had happened.

Ian's meet and greet sessions were not always peaceful
affairs. On one occasion, in a dressing room packed with fans,
Davey Payne switched all the lights off 'for a laugh'. When
the lights came back on, everyone could see him attempting to
grope a female fan. 'Ian was fucking furious,' says Jock Scot,
'because he felt it reflected on him. Ian made a comment, and
Davey retaliated.' Payne was the fiery Blockhead, whose behaviour was sometimes unpredictable. Wreckless Eric, who once
roomed with Davey on tour, recalls him placing the ubiquitous
glass ashtray within arm's reach on his bedside table and in the
morning, at the sound of the alarm clock, blindly reaching for
the receptacle and hurling it at the opposite wall, showering the
room with glass shards.

Payne's relationship with Ian was equally strange and quite
unique within the group. Davey was no stooge; as Ian's longest-
standing sideman he would frequently challenge his authority
without fear of intimidation. Consequently, Ian was wary of
Davey and knew better than to tangle with him if he wanted to
avoid trouble. Ian had once confided in Denise, telling her that
Davey was the only person he'd ever been afraid of. 'Having
survived the Kilburns, it surprised me that Davey lived to see
another day,' says Denise. 'They had a love/hate relationship.
They very rarely had altercations, but when they did, it was
serious, so they left each other alone. You got the impression
they'd made a pact. It wasn't very cosy.'

'We let Ian throw his moodies,' says Davey, 'we were all a
bit mumsy with him, apart from me, who would snap every
now and then and smack him. I didn't do it because I couldn't
verbalize with him, I simply couldn't be bothered to verbalize
with him. It was better to give him a smack, but he had his good

points. He had a lot of compassion. He was intelligent and he could talk about a lot of things. When we were on tour we used to walk around second-hand shops and discuss paintings. He was one of the nicest people to be with, but he could also be annoying.'

Fred Rowe, who saw his job as 'trying to guide Ian through the shark-infested seas of rock 'n' roll', also remembers the two sides of his personality: 'Overall he was quite a nice bloke, complex but all right and then, like a schizophrenic, he'd go off on one. We had these enormous rows where he would say, "I'm a pop star," and I would say, "No you ain't, you're fuck-all, and you should keep your feet on the ground." He would start shouting and screaming at me like a maniac, then he would go on stage and do the best gig ever. All that energy and rage came out in the performance. Peter Jenner used to say to me, "Fred, you've got to upset him more."'

As 'Reasons to Be Cheerful' entered the singles chart, where it would reach number three, Ian played an astonishing seven-night stand at Hammersmith Odeon. A number of celebrities came to pay their respects, and each night promoter John Curd would knock on Ian's dressing room door to announce a surprise visitor. 'Guess who's outside *now*?' asked Curd one night, exasperated by the constant stream of well-wishers. It was none other than the flamboyant Wee Willie Harris, accompanied by his wife, Sheila. Ian insisted a path be cleared for the pioneering British rocker, one of the first to write his own songs. Ian first saw him perform in 1958. 'I thought he was a brilliant singer,' said Ian. 'I had "Rocking at the 2 I's". Wee Willie Harrris could imitate Johnnie Ray. At the Ritz Romford they said: "Ladies and gentlemen, we've got a surprise item on the menu for you tonight . . . Johnnie Ray!" In the wings was Wee Willie . . . "When your sweetheart . . ." We all went, "Johnnie!" Then Wee Willie came on in his drape – brilliant!'

As Wee Willie Harris sat down and poured himself a light ale, Ian began to croon the words that were etched on his memory. On hearing Ian's heartfelt rendition of 'Rocking at the 2 I's', the ageing star shed a tear and confessed, 'I've been in the business for thirty-five years and it's the first time anyone's sung one of my songs,' to which Ian replied, 'You're in my song, son, for a reason.'

'Reasons to Be Cheerful' was another of Ian's song titles that would appear as a newspaper headline on a daily basis. Ian noted: 'The two songs they use are "Sex and Drugs and Rock and Roll" – it's part of the language now, and I don't get any credit for it, which pisses me right off – and "Reasons to Be Cheerful" – they use it as a phrase like "Seasons to Be Cheerful", which I love. "Part Three" means there's loads of reasons to be cheerful. I can never remember the words when we do a gig, I have a cheat sheet. It's like a Peter Blake painting, lots of detail, a huge load of gear.'

Buried in the list of things that made Ian's life worth living was the Italian pop singer Adrian Celentano. Ian had never actually heard of him, but a Swiss-Italian girl named Zegnia, whom Ian was dating that summer, proposed Celentano for inclusion. The lyricist was happy to oblige.

> *Saying okey dokey, sing-a-long-a-Smokey,*
> *Coming out of chokey,*
> *John Coltrane's soprano, Ade Celentano,*
> *Bonar Colleano*

Ian was most flattered when he heard the oft-expressed theory that 'Reasons to Be Cheerful' was one of the first rap records, even though it came from the wrong side of the Atlantic. His rhythmic phrasing was certainly in the style of the then emerging black music genre, although instrumentally the track owed much of its appeal to the immaculate disco styling of Chic as it did the street poetry of the early rappers. 'It was three months before "Rapper's Delight" by the Sugar Hill

Gang,' said Ian. 'I thought they'd been listening to my song but then I realized we'd gone to the same source – the Last Poets, James Brown.'

Copies of 'Reasons' were exported to the USA and were to be found on display in New York's hip hop record stores, alongside early rap hits by Grandmaster Flash and Kurtis Blow. By coincidence, Kurtis Blow's UK agent, Ian Flooks of Wasted Talent, was also Ian Dury's concert booker. When Blow turned up at Flooks' London office, Ian happened to be present and was the first person Blow encountered. 'Hi Ian, I'm Kurtis Blow,' said the US rapper. 'And these are the Breaks!' replied Ian, referring to Blow's recent hit record. 'Ian Flooks?' asked Blow. 'No, Ian Dury,' came the reply. 'He'd never fucking heard of me!' said Ian. 'I was gutted. I thought, "You should study up, mate, I was there first."'

By the middle of August, Ian had been on the road for three months straight. Exhausted, he turned down an offer of £100,000 to open for Led Zeppelin at Knebworth. 'I don't want to work in front of 90,000 people,' he told James Henke in *Rolling Stone*. 'That many people just can't relate to seven musicians onstage.' Spider was miffed because he and each of the Blockheads could have pocketed 'five grand', telling Ian, 'You're depriving our children of an education.' But Kosmo was adamant that Ian should not appear at 'a hippie festival'. It would not be the first time that Ian would turn down lucrative work, much to the frustration of the Blockheads, who depended on touring for an income whilst Ian and Chaz were earning songwriting royalties while they slept.

Tired but triumphant, Ian luxuriated in his new-found wealth and was not slow to repay Betty for the years of uncertainty he'd put her through. Firstly, he provided his family with a holiday in Barbados, a place he now knew well. Betty, Jemima and Baxter went ahead as 'the advance party', and Ian flew out to join them, following his string of sold-out London dates. Betty was reunited with her college friend (and Ian's former 'human crutch' at art college), Alison Armstrong, now living in the Caribbean. Peter Blake also showed up for several weeks of fun and frolics, and Ian was quick to invite members of the Blockheads and their families to join them. 'He bought them air tickets in the hurricane season,' says Baxter Dury. Alison Armstrong adds: 'They rented two villas on the west coast and for what they paid for them I could have bought a house.'

Ian's next stroke of generosity was designed to improve his family's quality of life. The house in Aylesbury they had occupied for three years was more comfortable than either Wingrave or Long Marston, but nowhere near as nice as Orchard Cottage in Tring, which Betty found after Ian had given her the nod. Conveniently located for Jemima to attend her private dancing lessons, it was 'the big leap forward', according to Baxter. 'Tring was the real sign of wealth,' adds Jemima. 'Stirling Moss had a house opposite. I was just thinking how quickly you get used to it, but we were still pretty frugal. We didn't have the monogrammed gates, but when the money started rolling in, mum and us had some huge spend-ups. There were a few trips to Hamleys toy shop for gratuitous purple aluminium skateboards.'

When Andrew King and Peter Jenner took over management of the Clash in late 1979, the famed punk rock trailblazers were at their commercial peak and set to become Blackhill's priority act, much to Ian's annoyance. To exacerbate matters, Blockhead Mickey Gallagher, who had played piano on the Clash's *London Calling* LP, joined the group as an auxiliary keyboardist for live shows. Ian hated the Clash and resented their presence on the Blackhill roster. There was no trace of irony in his voice when he accused them of being 'public school rebels'. Referring to singer Joe Strummer, Ian asked, 'Why would anyone want to change their name from Mellor [Strummer's real name]? "Mellors" is the gamekeeper in *Lady Chatterley's Lover*. Joe must be barmy!'

Ian and Joe Strummer were about to share the same stage in a series of charity concerts in aid of emergency relief for the people of Kampuchea, held over four nights at London's Hammersmith Odeon. The line-up included the Clash, the Who, Elvis Costello, the Pretenders, Robert Plant, Paul McCartney's Wings and, headlining over all these legendary rock names on 27 December, Ian Dury and the Blockheads. As Ian hobnobbed with the superstars backstage, the thrill in his bones was palpable.

It had been a fabulous year, but Chaz Jankel was once again becoming restless. In the early days of their partnership, Ian had surrendered much of the musical decision-making to him but now, having tasted success, Ian wanted to reclaim some of that territory. Although he wrote his lyrics rhythmically, often with a groove or tempo in mind, Ian had no musical know-how. 'He didn't want to be arguing with Chaz about whether it was an F7 instead of an F major,' says Charlie Hart, who had written with Ian in the Kilburns. 'He preferred to communicate in riddles and do it all through emotional games and psychological symbols. By not getting involved in the mechanics of the music, he could keep himself in a different realm.'

It was debatable whether Ian's inability to read or compose music was a pro or a con. History was littered with successful songwriters of limited musical skill, for example Lionel Bart, who played one-finger piano yet composed hit musicals such as *Oliver*. Even the great Irving Berlin, who wrote 'White Christmas', hummed his tunes to an arranger and later wrote on a mechanical piano that allowed him to transpose the key with the aid of a lever. Ian didn't often come up with a tune, hummed or otherwise, although Baxter says of his father, 'He had an incredible perspective in his head about how it would work. He considered the rhythm and thought much more melodically then anyone ever gives him credit for.'

Ian loved Chaz Jankel's contribution to the songwriting process, but even though Chaz had supplied the tunes for their two biggest hits, he was not immune from Ian's taunts. Chaz, one of the more sensitive Blockheads, was also embarrassed by Ian's cruel remarks to other members of the band, along the lines of: 'Your wife is a fucking maggot – I don't know what you see in her.' 'It was classic bully behaviour,' says close observer Stephen Nugent, 'provoking someone to the point where they were forced to respond, then telling them: "Now I can see what you're really made of."'

Rather than jump through hoops to please his master, Chaz Jankel once again jumped ship. 'I tried to keep my distance so that Ian didn't feel like he owned me,' says Jankel, referring to his departure at the end of 1979. 'I had to let him know where I stood or he would have taken advantage. When you're writing with somebody, it isn't just the business of sitting down and writing songs, it's an intimate scenario. Your whole life is caught up with that other person and the songs are only one part of the picture. Ian was a perfectionist but he also liked to relax. His idea of a perfect evening would be a bottle of Moët, champagne cocktails and to have Ed Speight sitting next to him, rolling spliffs and telling jokes.'

With 'Rhythm Stick' and 'Reasons' under his belt, Ian was confident of being able to find a replacement for Chaz to help him create his next album, but those in the immediate vicinity could not compose at Jankel's level. Ian would have to cross his fingers and hope for the best. Anyway, fame was not all it was cracked up to be. He enjoyed hearing the occasional 'Hey, Ian!' from passing cabbies, but hated being stared at in public, even though it was nothing new. Passers-by had been staring at Ian since he first limped out of hospital in 1951, but now many more were gawping. 'People would come up to me wherever I went because I was so recognizable,' said Ian, 'but I got paranoid about being disabled.'

Ian's adverse reaction to celebrity can be charted from this point. He used fame as an excuse for not going out alone because, he said, 'People stop me in the street.' The situation was exacerbated by his addiction to sleeping pills. He had started taking Mogadon tablets nine years earlier when he was teaching art and was told they were 'not addictive', but his dependence had recently come to an abrupt end when a hotel chambermaid in Amsterdam threw his tablets away with the rubbish. Paranoia set in. 'I had it shocking,' said Ian, 'self-loathing . . . it coincided with me giving up Mogadon. I slept all right, but I had these strange symptoms. Then I read that withdrawal from that drug has side-effects. I associated the paranoia with being a pop star, not the withdrawal.'

To make matters worse, celebrity had deprived Ian of one of his greatest pleasures – that of being able to confound those who didn't know who he was by unexpectedly switching persona mid-conversation. As an unknown, he could toggle between the East End rascal and the connoisseur of arts by dispensing an expletive or a few lines of poetry. Initially, new acquaintances were impressed, but now that Ian's biographical details were in the public domain, the Dury enigma was threatened with extinction. The shock tactics would no longer work – everybody knew about Ian and his rhythm stick. The game was up.

15

Oh Lonesome Me

'Before seeking revenge, first dig two graves.'
Confucius

London, 1980. At the start of the new decade, it began to dawn on the Blockheads that there was no pot of gold at the end of their rainbow. All of their touring income had been absorbed by heavy expenses. Recording royalties were paltry after studio costs had been deducted, and the lion's share of songwriting royalties had gone to Ian and Chaz, creators of the hits. The Blockheads may have stayed in some fancy hotels and been allowed to overdub *Do It Yourself* to death, but there would be little reward for those musicians unable to muscle in on the songwriting action. Unsure of Ian's plans, the group set up camp at Milner Sound Studios in Fulham that February, with the intention of working up some original material. To get the ball rolling, Davey Payne cut a roaring version of the Duane Eddy instrumental 'Peter Gunn', but the twenty or so group compositions that followed had only shorthand titles such as: 'Chicken', 'Fatback' and 'CC's Rock'. As songs, they were largely unfinished.

Ian, meanwhile, was on another extended holiday in Barbados, a place he had come to love. 'Dad liked the laid-back black culture,' says Jemima Dury, 'its history, safety and privacy. He hated being famous, but he could be anonymous in Barbados. It was quite exclusive.' Coming home via the United States on 6 March, he dropped in at the Tower Theatre, Philadelphia,

where the Clash were appearing, augmented by Mickey Gallagher. Ian was keen to see New Orleans legend Lee Dorsey,
who was also on the bill. After two years of accompanying
Ian on tour, Blackhill's style guru Kosmo Vinyl had more or
less defected to the Clash camp, but as a loyal friend Kosmo
continued to look out for Ian. When the Clash's rousing set
climaxed with 'Janie Jones', Ian was hauled up on stage. Introduced by Joe Strummer as 'a special guest from England', Ian
sang along with the chorus, making whooping noises and intermittently shouting, 'Fill 'er up, Jacko!'

The next day, Ian accompanied the Clash to New York,
where the stunt was repeated at the Palladium. For the first time
in two years, Ian ran into his former lover Roberta Bayley, now
resident in Manhattan's East Village. 'I didn't have any idea he
was coming,' recalls Roberta. 'He hadn't said anything to me,
but I went backstage, and we hung out a little bit, then we had
another huge fight in the hotel lobby, right across the street from
Madison Square Garden. He tried to pull the same shit. He'd
lock me in the room, and say, "What's wrong, why don't you
want to have sex with me?"'

On his return to the UK, Ian paid the Blockheads a visit at
Milner. Mickey Gallagher recalls, 'Ian came down to our studio
and thought, "Oh this is all right, I'll make my album here." We
said, "Hang on!" But he offered to pay the studio costs for three
months and said, "We'll make an album."' Ian also announced
that Wilko Johnson, the former Dr Feelgood guitarist, would be
making a single with the group and suggested a cover of the Don
Gibson song 'Oh Lonesome Me'. Ian had recently encountered
Wilko at the Rainbow theatre, during a benefit concert for Hugh
Cornwell of the Stranglers, who had just been imprisoned for
drug offences. Before long, Ian invited Wilko to become a Blockhead, much to the surprise of the others. 'Ian didn't consult us
at all,' says Mickey. 'He just casually said, "Wilko's joining the
band." We all got on well, but everything now had to accommodate that choppy guitar sound.'

Ian may have had more than instrumental accompaniment in mind. Although the Blockheads' visuals had suffered little from Chaz's departure, Ian was never averse to enhancing his tableau. Wilko, whose trademark skittering movements would enliven any stage, was also a known quantity as a songwriter, having composed much of the Feelgoods' early repertoire. With his own solo career in the doldrums, Wilko grabbed the opportunity to become a Blockhead. Although he was a great fan of the group's superlative rhythm section, he was less familiar with its *modus operandi*. Curious about Ian's future plans, Wilko decided to call on him at his flat in Little Portland Street, the latest in a succession of rented West End bolt holes.

Wilko quickly discovered that the Blockheads had been out of action for several months and faced an uncertain future. As the meeting continued, Ian sat nervously scribbling diagrams on sheets of A3, supposedly mapping out the next six months, but feeling 'a little adrift musically, getting depressed'. Detecting Ian's insecurity, Wilko bravely remarked, 'You're fucking shitting yourself, aren't you?' Ian confessed that he was unsure of his next move and terrified of returning to live work. For the moment, however, recording was the priority.

During the new album's tricky gestation period, tensions between Ian and the group began to develop. Ian cleverly defused the situation by asking the Blockheads to make a heavy metal album with guitarist Ed Speight, his former school friend and occasional member of the Kilburns. Ian would fund the recordings and buy Ed a new Gibson Les Paul guitar to achieve a suitably 'heavy' sound. Speight dutifully laid down a number of hard rock classics, including Cream's 'Sunshine of Your Love' and Black Sabbath's 'Paranoid', with Norman and Charley completing the basic trio and various Blockheads providing the vocals. Ian then wrote a story that he would narrate between the songs. It was entitled *The Master*. With the deepest, most sinister voice he could summon, Ian announced:

This is the story of the master versus the human condition. It happened that a dread plague came upon the land and the audience dropped like flies. 'Let the master out of his cage,' cried the anguished peoples. 'He will save us!' But the powers that be were sorely afraid of the master's strength and from their lofty citadel high above the sufferings of the throng . . .

And so on. *The Master* was a tedious work, never to see commercial release. When it was completed, Ian and the Blockheads started to prepare songs for the album proper. New material was once again in short supply, but Ian thought he had the answer. He would collaborate with individual members of the Blockheads, his theory being that it would help to dispel any dissent and potentially up their earnings. The Blockheads were certainly excited by the possibility of earning songwriting royalties; provided that Ian retained control over the words, it would be a win-win situation. Consequently, some of the tracks the Blockheads had recorded at Milner would find their way onto Ian's next album. 'Chicken' became '(Take Your Elbow out of the Soup) You're Sitting on the Chicken'; 'Public Party' was transformed into 'Dance of the Crackpots' and 'Pardon', written with Norman Watt-Roy, echoed the cool funk of 'Rhythm Stick'. 'Black and White' emerged as 'Yes and No (Paula)', a sketch rather than a song, rescued by some great improvisation from Davey Payne on wailing tenor sax and jazz legend Don Cherry, who would later tour with the group, on pocket cornet.

During the sessions, Ian unexpectedly revealed the new album's title – *Laughter* – but the songs were far from funny. 'I had it as a working title to cheer myself up,' said Ian. 'Well-written misery . . . I was getting depressed. I thought I'd shot my bolt.' Distanced from real life and 'the street', which had provided Ian with so much of his earlier material, he had to get his inspiration from somewhere. He decided to reflect on his early experiences at Chailey. The autobiographical slant resulted in a torrent of harrowing lyrics. 'They were all about

institutionalization,' says Mickey Gallagher, 'and people born
with their legs back to front and all that. Ian had an indomitable
spirit. Nobody with a weak spirit could have survived it.'

The first new product to hit the shops, in August 1980, was
the single, 'I Want to Be Straight', a lolloping shuffle in which
Ian announced that he was 'sick of taking drugs and staying
up late'. Instead, he declared, 'I want to confirm, I want to
conform.' This pedestrian yet amusing ditty made a minor dent
on the hit parade, as did its follow-up, 'Sueperman's Big Sister'
('his superior skin and blister'). Co-written with Wilko, and
added to *Laughter* at the eleventh hour, 'Sueperman's' – inten-
tionally misspelt to avoid copyright infringement – featured
MOR-style strings scored by the legendary Ivor Raymonde,
co-writer of Dusty Springfield's early hits. Ivor was also asked
to provide orchestration for the glorious 'Fucking Ada', but
couldn't believe his ears when he heard Ian and a massed
chorus of Blockheads indulge themselves in the art of gratuitous
swearing, football terrace style. You could hear the joy in Ian's
voice as he wrapped his larynx around the offending phrase,
but radio play was non-existent, and co-writer Johnny Turnbull
still had to make do without double-glazing.

One of the best recordings from the *Laughter* sessions – 'Duff
'em Up and Do 'em Over Boogie' – was omitted from the album
because Kosmo Vinyl, still orchestrating Ian's press campaigns,
thought it might encourage football hooliganism, then rampant.
'It was very reactionary on the street,' says Kosmo. 'The skinhead thing had come back with none of the style but all of the
violence. I was living in Bow and getting the tube and dealing
with blokes on glue and swastikas. I didn't expect Ian to be on
the front line – he was riding around in a cab – but I said to him,
"Those guys are gonna end up kicking somebody's head in to
your tune." It was like *Clockwork Orange*, but I think Ian saw it
as b-movie, Teddy Boy fun.' The song was eventually given new
lyrics and emerged on *Laughter* as 'Oh Mr Peanut'.

Not only did Ian tell us on *Laughter* that he wanted 'to be straight', but in the sing-along 'Uncoolohol', he denounced alcohol entirely! Although he had the self-discipline to occasionally abstain, he would consume vast quantities of booze when in the mood. But, as Mickey Gallagher observes, alcohol did not agree with Ian: 'He was such a little guy. One beer made him very happy; two, and he'd start wobbling; three, he turned into a horrible drunk, insulting everyone. He was never hung-over, except for one occasion after a party in Stratford-on-Avon, when we had to get back to London, and he sat in the back of the car and put a bag over his head.'

It was the idea of being drunk that Ian liked, but he was what is often referred to as a 'lightweight'. He only had to hear the sound of a beer can being cracked open and he was gone, causing friends to wonder if he was allergic to alcohol. He preferred to sup on an empty stomach as food would tend to make him too bloated to drink beer, his usual tipple. Some days he didn't much care for eating at all. He favoured a meal he could eat with his hands, often standing up. This led to much fast food such as kebabs in pitta bread or pie and chips. It was a poor diet that did not bode well for his health, but it dispensed with the need for cutlery, the manipulation of which Ian sometimes found tedious due to the limitations of his left hand. 'He would put his arm around a bowl of food,' says Davey Payne, 'as if someone was going to steal it.'

At the rehearsals for the *Laughter* promotional tour, which would mark Wilko Johnson's live debut as a Blockhead, Ian suddenly announced: 'We're not doing "Sex and Drugs" any more.' Wilko was gobsmacked. 'Fucking hell! I only joined the band to play "Sex and Drugs",' says Wilko. 'Of course we did do it, but playing the Blockheads stuff with my limited chords was a nightmare! I had to learn the back catalogue. The middle of 'Reasons to Be Cheerful' was particularly difficult. For the first few shows I had a piece of paper in front of me with the chords on it. I'll also admit there were times in the set when I would turn my guitar off and mime. I was lost.'

The tour was marked by a number of tense moments. 'There were many backstage brawls,' recalls Dutch über-fan Kees Bakker, 'but Ian could break up a fight by simply fluttering his eyelashes.' Ian couldn't, however, prevent the inevitable showdown with Davey Payne, who, Wilko Johnson observes, 'was a coiled spring, with eyes like acetylene torches.' The incident occurred in Dublin on 24 November, where the group was staying at the lavish Gresham Hotel. Ian had upgraded to a suite, whereas the rest of the entourage had to contend with single rooms. 'The Blockheads were complaining,' recalls Wilko, 'but I thought, "For fuck's sake, he's the star, let him have a suite!"' Ian justified his extravagance by explaining that he would be using his luxurious accommodation to host a party, following that night's performance at the Olympia Theatre. Plans changed when Ian decided to restrict the festivities to two fans he'd met after the show. For Ian, it was the perfect scenario – a young girl who was in awe of him, and her poor boyfriend, whom Ian would proceed to belittle in front of the girl.

The Blockheads were not amused to be confined to the hotel bar while Ian held court upstairs. Davey was particularly angry, suggesting they should all invade the suite, along with a number of other fans they'd picked up en route. 'We all went up there,' says Wilko. 'It was a good scene with champagne and punters hanging about. Suddenly Davey came in and said, "I've just knocked Ian out." Ray, the minder, was cradling Ian in his arms like a child. "Party's over! Band meeting!"' When Ian regained consciousness he confronted the Blockheads with an ultimatum. 'Right, are we going to carry on without Davey Payne or are we going to blow the tour out?' Wilko, the new boy, made a speech: 'Listen, guys, I bust up with one really great band through total bollocks and personal crap and I'm fucked if I'm going to do it again.' The Blockheads sent for Fred Rowe, who had to come over from England and arbitrate. Fred suggested that Davey should be fined £200.

Wilko Johnson was in his room at Copenhagen's Plaza Hotel

that December when word reached him that Ian was causing a commotion in the bar. He had encountered several well-known musicians and had cornered their American tour manager. Ian's language was so offensive that the American suddenly roared, 'Look, man, I always used to dig you, but if you say one more word to me I'll punch you out.' Wilko, fast becoming the peacemaker, dashed down to the bar and positioned himself between Ian and the American. 'He doesn't mean it,' pleaded Wilko, trying to usher Ian back to his room. At that point, Ian grasped the brass handrail at the edge of the bar with both hands, shouting 'Help me!' 'Ian thought that, because he was a cripple, people wouldn't hit him,' says Wilko, 'so he would go way past the stage where most of us would get a punch on the nose. I got in between him and the American, apologizing for Ian. "He doesn't mean it . . . come on Ian, back to your room." He threatened to sack us all. We put him in the lift, got him up to his room and removed his leg iron.'

The confiscation of Ian's calliper was a tactic invented by Fred Rowe as the safest method of dealing with an out-of-control situation. Whereas bodyguards are traditionally employed to protect their clients from over-zealous fans, Rowe's job was to protect *others from Ian*. So when things got really ugly, Fred would simply 'take off the leg' and stow it in hotel reception. On one tour, Ian sought to confound Fred by ordering a spare calliper to be sent ahead, by post, to his Edinburgh hotel, but Fred intercepted the parcel. He maintained a blank expression when Ian kept asking, 'Is there any mail for me?' 'Hiding the calliper didn't ever stop Ian,' says Andrew King, 'because at three in the morning, there he would be, sitting on his backside in the corridor, lifting himself by his hands, screaming, "You cunts!"'

Laughter entered the UK album chart in December 1980, where it remained for just four weeks, peaking at number forty-eight, its commercial appeal possibly restricted by the challenging subject matter of its songs. Meanwhile the tour continued into Europe, and Ian's drinking gained momentum. There were now effectively 'two Ians' – the relatively charming but manipulative Ian and the monster he would become after the third drink. Fred Rowe referred to the drunken Ian as 'Tom', as in: 'Is this Ian talking, or is it Tom?' As his drunken alter ego, Ian particularly disliked being excluded from the conversation. 'He developed the annoying habit of grabbing at your elbow,' recalls Andrew King, 'and muttering, "D'ya mind? D'ya mind if I say something? Have you got a minute? D'ya mind?" I used to call it "the four-wall thing". He had to have control of all four corners of a room and wasn't very happy if there was something going on in one of the corners that he wasn't in control of. When he came into a room, he dominated it and, if the action wobbled away from him, he'd start getting lairy.'

Unless he was the centre of attention Ian could only keep schtum for so long and belligerently tried to steer the conversation in his direction. If another strong-willed individual managed to interrupt him while he was spouting forth, Ian would slope off or launch some preposterous distraction. There had been many examples of this. Excluded from a technical discussion in the recording studio, he crumbled digestive biscuits into the intricate workings of the mixing desk, effectively bringing the session to a halt. At a rehearsal, while the musicians were practising their parts, he cracked an egg on Ed Speight's head. Realizing Speight's annoyance, Ian then cracked an egg over his own head to compensate for his behaviour – a characteristic gesture when he knew he'd gone too far. In short, Ian couldn't bear to be ignored.

Ian's most outrageous conduct occurred at the Midem music festival in Cannes, where he was guest of honour at a huge dinner party thrown by Eddie Barclay, boss of Barclay Records. Barclay distributed Ian's music in France, and Ian was due to receive a special award. He was seated at the top table, between Barclay and his girlfriend, a young, glamorous actress. 'Ian pulled her,' recalls Andrew King. 'It took him twenty minutes.

He said, "This is a bit boring, shall we go somewhere else?" She said, "Yes," and off they went. Eddie Barclay was very powerful – the kind of guy who had photographs of himself with John F. Kennedy on top of his piano, mates with Chirac and all that – and Ian had stolen his bird. When challenged, Ian said to him, "Eddie Barclay, *tu es merde* [you are shit]," and Eddie coolly replied, "Ian Dury, you will never sell another record in France." That was more or less the case.'

Ian had pushed the self-destruct button one too many times and effectively wrecked his career. His commercial demise coincided with the contractual expiry of his three-album deal with Stiff Records. Finishing with Stiff came as a relief to Ian; ever since his initial success he had felt a sense of obligation to Dave Robinson, Stiff Records and the Blockheads, but he found it hard to conform to a recording schedule that made such demands on his time and creativity. 'I think there's a whole wrong aspect to this game that we play,' Ian told me, 'the follow-up syndrome or the momentum syndrome. If you make a good record I think you should have the right to milk it for thirty-five years. It's not about following it with another one.'

Being out of his recording contract provided Ian with the opportunity to break free from the infrastructure he believed was suffocating his art. 'Money had been fun at first, but it caused an inner conflict,' says Kosmo Vinyl. 'Ian was not materialistic. He was a Bohemian at heart, happy with a few key possessions such as his Bill Haley poster, his Chris Killip photos and his bongos.' Nevertheless, Ian was now without an outlet for his music. As he reflected on his dicey predicament, he took comfort in the pronouncements of Basanta Kumar Mallik, Aunt Molly's guru who had predicted his fame some twenty years earlier. But Ian might also have considered the mountaineer's mantra: 'When you reach the summit, you're only halfway there.' Ian now had to deal with the descent.

16

'Phil, You Don't Know What It Involves'

In the spring of 1981, Ian instructed his managers to seek out a new recording contract with as much up-front money as possible. The hottest companies knew that Ian's career was in meltdown and gave him a wide berth, but there was always Polydor Records. Sustained by the massive international sales of MOR giant James Last, the German-based label had deeper pockets than most and would sign almost anything with a pulse. A&R man Frank Neilson at Polydor's London office knew that adding Ian Dury to their pale roster would give the label a much-needed shot of credibility.

When the Polydor deal was announced, Ian talked it up in the same way that he had tried to glamorize Pye Records – the last refuge of Kilburn and the High Roads – seven years earlier. 'I went in there [Polydor] and there were geezers wearing diamond pullovers with Krugerrands round their necks, talking about "units",' Ian recalled, adding, 'they all read the *Daily Express*.' He quickly discovered that the *Express*-reading geezers in the Argyle sweaters were expecting him to make good their investment by immediately delivering a hit album, but once again new material was non-existent. It was time to reunite with Chaz Jankel, now seemingly refreshed after a spot of solo success, having co-composed 'Ai No Corrida', a hit for Quincy Jones.

Chaz was watching *Top of the Pops* when a group named Freeez appeared, performing their hit 'Southern Freeez'. On the other side of town, at the Dorset Street flat he now shared with his white Barbadian girlfriend Ashley and her two Burmese cats, Ian was similarly glued to his TV set. Chaz and Ian were both taken aback by the quiet power of Freeez vocalist Ingrid Mansfield-Allman, who was the main topic of conversation when Ian called Chaz. Ingrid would become the catalyst in their reunion as songwriters. 'Chaz phoned me,' recalls Ingrid. 'He asked me to come down to his studio to do some work with him and Ian. It was the first time they had spoken in eighteen months. We did "Stop Wasting Your Time" and "Sister Slow", the words of which went: "I was bored with my Ford, the Wolseley is coolsey, but a Lancia is fancier . . ."'

Ian quickly persuaded Ingrid to sign to Polydor and arranged for the Blockheads to provide accompaniment. He also promoted himself as Ingrid's executive producer, a role for which he was ill-equipped. 'We used to have to arrange decoy studios to prevent Ian turning up,' says Ingrid. 'He would sabotage the sessions, and it would waste hours and hours of studio time. Because it wasn't really his thing, he would try to take over.' As Andrew King notes, 'Ian wanted to be a great record producer, but he wasn't. It's a knack, but Ian didn't have that knack.'

In addition to concocting material for Ingrid, Chaz helped Ian come up with a batch of songs for his Polydor debut, the first of which would derive its inspiration from an unexpected quarter. 1981 had been designated the 'International Year of the Disabled'. Obviously, this got right up Ian's nose. The campaign was undoubtedly well intentioned – to give disabled people a voice. Predictably, the loudest voice of all was Ian's. 'Oh, I see . . .' he pontificated, 'so in 1982 we'll all be all right!'

Ian had a point. As possibly Britain's most famous disabled celebrity, he was called upon to take part in various media events. He had already appeared on the BBC television programme *Scene*, in an episode entitled 'To Be a Lunatic' in which he expounded on the subject of madness. Visiting mentally disturbed teenagers at the Cassell Hospital in Richmond, he commented: 'The only medicine at this hospital is "talk".' For once, Ian let others do the talking and he proved to be a skilled listener, coaxing out of the young patients their various experiences of depression and schizophrenia.

'I got asked to do so many things in the year of the disabled,' said Ian. 'We had the "polio folio", which was this great big folder . . . "Lesbians in Wheelchairs"! I can't tell you what we didn't get asked to do. I got a cassette from a guy called Kelly who was in a sheltered home for the disabled and he wrote me a letter saying: "This place is all right during the week, but the weekends are murder 'cos all the staff go home. They have the weekend off, it's bloody lonely." Kelly wrote a song called "This Is the International Year of the Disabled". If a do-gooder heard it, they'd say, "Oh, you little ingrate." But it's murder having organized sports if you're all of differing abilities. You can't handicap the handicapped!'

Ian had become something of a poster boy to the differently abled community, but he quickly tired of the endless requests for his involvement in charitable causes. Instead, he responded with his best song in years. Written from the heart, for handicapped people everywhere, it was the mighty 'Spasticus Autisticus'.

> *I'm Spasticus! I'm Spasticus!*
> *I'm Spasticus Autisticus!!*
> *I widdle when I piddle*
> *'Cos my middle is a riddle*

'I wrote "Spasticus Autisticus" to be a completely anti-charity song,' said Ian. 'I've written seven good songs, that's one of them. Live, it requires an incredible amount of energy. When we came to do it with the Blockheads, I told Charley, "You gotta play the bass drum and imagine you're nutting somebody." He said, "Can do, I. D." Charley was a foot-fighting champion with the old Thai boxing.'

So place your hard-earned peanuts in my tin,
And thank the Creator you're not in the state I'm in,
So long have I been languished on the shelf
I must give all proceedings to myself

A secondary source of inspiration for 'Spasticus' was the 1981 television screening of *Spartacus*, starring Kirk Douglas. Ian saw it on a rare visit to Tring, to look after the children while Betty was in hospital recovering from an injury sustained in a nasty car accident. 'I'm Spartacus!' yelled the slaves of ancient Rome. It was one of Ian's favourite films, having first seen it at the cinema in Romford in 1960. Viewing it over twenty years later, he made the connection. The following day he was still thinking about *Spartacus* when Ed Speight visited. 'I thought about going on tour as 'Spasticus and The Autistics',' recalled Ian, 'but Speight said, "No, it should be Spasticus Autisticus – he's the freed slave of the disabled."'

Ed Speight recalls, 'We kicked a few phrases around, drinking more dandelion and burdock. "I wobble when I hobble," was one of them. We knocked out the hooks, then Ian did the real artwork: "So place your hard-earned peanuts in my tin, and thank the Creator you're not in the state I'm in." Some of it was influenced by Lenny Bruce – the "half-man/half-woman" routine. Ian said he wanted a record that would be banned. It certainly did the trick.'

Predictably, the irony of 'Spasticus' was lost on the media when it was released as a single. Radio producers didn't seem to 'get it', although sections of the community it discussed were quietly amused. 'It's been banned by the BBC,' Ian protested almost boastfully, but in fact the disc had been barely promoted. Like many a controversial song, it had been buried by the record pluggers, who found it too much like hard work to promote, while its failure could always be turned on its head in a stab at notoriety. '"Spasticus Autisticus" was misunderstood by everybody except spastic people,' said Ian, 'and a lot of them hated it as well. But a few really understood it. By the people, for the people . . . it's a war cry!'

Ian and Chaz flew to Nassau in the Bahamas to record at Compass Point studio with famed reggae musicians Sly Dunbar and Robbie Shakespeare. Some of the songs were patched together at the last minute, and Chaz recalls Ian finishing lyrics on the plane. Crossing the Atlantic for the second time in a year, Ian's thoughts turned once again to his American muse, Roberta Bayley. He flew her down to Nassau from New York but the reunion was short-lived.

The Compass Point album, entitled *Lord Upminster*, was a lacklustre work, rescued only by 'Spasticus Autisticus' and a startling cover photograph of Ian wearing a white cardigan 'that belonged to an Italian grandmother', its sleeves now meticulously frayed. Managers Jenner and King were unable to summon up the courage to tell Ian it was a weak album and persuaded publicist Glen Colson to pay him a visit. 'I was naive enough to think I could tell Ian it would make a good four-track EP,' recalls Colson. 'He responded by throwing an ashtray at me.'

Despite everybody's disappointment, Ian managed to stay afloat by securing a publishing contract with Warners Music in which he signed over much of his songwriting catalogue via his agreement with Blackhill. Andrew King recalls Warners managing director Rob Dickins being very keen to sign Ian. 'He was hopping up and down like a dog on heat. He was frothing for it. He gave us a fantastically good deal, a huge lump of cash.' The advance of £80,000 – colossal for the time – enabled Ian to invest in more property. Having already bought a flat in Hampstead for Peggy and a house in Tring for Betty, it was time for Ian to look for a place for himself. He had been living in a succession of hotels and service apartments for three years and needed a permanent home, even if it meant he could no longer romantically claim to be 'homeless'. 'Ian was going round the bend, living in rented,' says Humphrey Ocean. 'What had appeared to be quite glamorous was really very unsettling. He didn't have an HQ, a secure base. He needed a gaff.'

Through Humphrey, Ian met Monica Kinley, a collector of 'Outsider Art', who was looking to sell her flat in Digby Mansions, Hammersmith. When Ian viewed his prospective pad, Monica assumed he was 'some thick rock 'n' roller', but was shocked and surprised when he started to recognize some of the paintings on her walls. Ian later boasted, 'For every picture I named, Monica knocked a thousand pounds off the price of the apartment!' The second-floor flat overlooked the Thames by Hammersmith Bridge. It didn't have an elevator, but Ian was OK with the stairs and he would find the balcony ideal for viewing the annual Oxford and Cambridge boat race and throwing cans of beer to the fans that would congregate on the riverbank.

Two months elapsed before Ian could move into his new apartment. He stayed with manager Andrew King and his wife Wendy for several weeks. 'I remember going out for a Chinese in Richmond with Ian,' recalls Andrew. 'There was a couple at the next table, nudging each other . . . "Isn't that, er, Ian Dury?" One of them came over and said, "Ian, your music has given me so much pleasure, may I have your autograph?" and he said, "Why don't you fuck off and leave me alone?"'

As the weeks dragged on, Ian complained that his managers were taking an unduly long time to complete on the purchase of the property and returned briefly to the Montcalm Hotel, the scene of a drunken encounter with Ingrid Mansfield-Allman, whom he affectionately nicknamed 'Big Ings'. Ingrid had intrigued him ever since they met in the recording studio earlier that year. 'Ian's minder, Ray Jordan, lumbered me with Ian,' recalls Ingrid. 'We were in the pub, and Ray was trying to get off with Janice from accounts. So he told me, "Take the raspberry [ripple = cripple] back to the Montcalm and here's twenty quid to get home." At the hotel, I foolishly went up to the room with Ian. He promptly picked up the phone and ordered club sandwiches and champagne. He was drunk. He said, "Do you know how much a club sandwich costs in 'ere?" He told me, "Ring up Carruthers [Andrew King]." I phoned Andrew and said, "Ian wants to talk to you." Ian grabbed the phone from me and roared, "I didn't tell you to fucking talk to him, I just told you to ring him up!"

'I thought, "Fucking hell, who am I locked in a room with here?" I went to get my bag to leave and Ian suddenly became psychotic. He tried to prevent me from getting it and he chucked the bag across the room, then he emptied the contents out of the second-floor window. Everything except my purse and my sunglasses went, then he ground them into the carpet. I locked myself in the bathroom, where there was a phone. I didn't know who I was going to call, but I picked up the receiver. Ian grabbed the extension phone by the bed, so I thought, if he's over there he can't be outside the bathroom door, so maybe I could make a run for it, but he was whizzing about everywhere. The room-service geezer arrived, and I thought Ian was not going to hit me in front of him, but the geezer left, and I was alone with Ian again. He got hold of me and started spitting, so I pushed him and he went over. I got my purse and ran all the way home. I phoned Chaz and said, "You're not going to believe what's just happened." Chaz was like, "Oh yeah?" It was normal. The next day Ian phoned me to say sorry. He was crying. I told him I wished I'd never met him, only heard his records. I never spoke to him again for eighteen months. I used to see him up at Blackhill, but I would look through him like he was a pane of glass.'

Ian appeared at the Pinkpop festival in Holland that June and came face-to-face with the massively popular Madness, who had drawn much of their early inspiration from Ian during the Kilburns era of the mid-1970s. Madness's three founder members, Chris Foreman, Lee Thompson and Mike Barson, all saw

Kilburn and the High Roads on the pub rock circuit, initially attracted by their unusual name on a poster. Foreman recalls seeing Ian in the car park at the Tally Ho, but was unaware of who he was. 'A guy with a bow tie came limping along, and I thought he worked at the pub. I asked him what time the band was on and he replied, "No idea mate." I later realized it was Ian. We started following the Kilburns around and thought they were brilliant, visually and musically.'

'Madness were on Stiff, and Ian had been on Stiff,' continues Foreman, 'but we never really met him until that day. Lee Thompson and I had decided not to fly, so we got the ferry and Ian was on the coach. I was sitting next to him, he was my hero but he was threatening me all the way. "You young pups are trying to steal my thunder!" He was going to get Spider to dust us up, but he was just mucking about. When we got to know him better, he became "Uncle Ian", like a relative of us all.'

Ian had now moved into Digby Mansions. A string of girls, most of whom he met on the road, waltzed in and out of his life. Friends and colleagues observed that they often had curiously similar physical attributes and were boyish in appearance. 'They were usually short skinny women with small tits,' says Fred Rowe. 'He would put them all in the same gear – black jeans and DMs, short-cropped hair. He used to make them look like boys. I thought he was "the other way", not that there's anything wrong with a bit of AC/DC, but he wasn't ["the other way"], he just liked that look on girls.'

Ian viewed the girls he met as either a challenge or a pushover, preferring a challenge to an easy conquest. 'He thought he had to try and get off with women, just to prove to himself that he wasn't hideous,' says Ingrid Mansfield-Allman. 'But I wouldn't say he was a womanizer. I think he had to reassure himself he was handsome. I think "If I Was with a Woman" is the most honest song Ian ever wrote. "Little things would slowly go askew . . . I'd make quite sure she never understood." That's what he was like. If you weren't on your toes, he would fuck

your head, but behind it all there was this really nice guy struggling to get out. He was very good at listening. One time I went
round to see him, and he'd run a bath for me, put aromatherapy
stuff in it and taught me deep-breathing exercises and I thought,
"Wow! Is this the same person who was chucking my stuff out
the window a few months earlier?"'

Despite Fred Rowe's acceptance of Ian's foibles during his
five-year tenure as his minder, things were about to come to an
abrupt end. On a hot and sticky evening in August 1981, Ian
found himself at a party in Oxford Street, where he'd been
invited to cut the cake to celebrate the sixtieth anniversary of
the HMV record store. It was a tedious event for Ian, but a
networking opportunity nevertheless. He was accompanied, as
ever, by Fred, who had brought along Karen, his new girlfriend
of just six weeks. Wearing darkened goggles and a crushed
bowler hat, Ian circulated. He was on his best behaviour until
he bumped into Thin Lizzy main man Phil Lynott, who persuaded Ian to switch from Perrier water to vodka because he
should be having 'a proper drink'. Fred intervened, telling
Lynott, 'Phil, you don't know what it involves.'

A couple of fans asked Ian for his autograph, but he told
them to 'fuck off'. Fred stepped in, offering profuse apologies
for Ian's behaviour. 'Is this Tom coming onto the scene now?'
asked Fred, referring to Ian's drunken state. 'Allow me to apologize for this pig, he *will* sign that for you,' Fred told the
autograph hunters. The room was crawling with journalists and
photographers, and Fred decided he had to get Ian out before
it became sticky. 'We got to the car,' recalls Rowe, 'and, as Karen
went to sit in the front seat, Ian shouted at her, "Get out of there
you fucking slag! Get in the back where you belong!" I was
about to blow. I told Ian to apologize to Karen, but he said, "I
ain't apologizing to nobody!" I drove off and left him standing
on the pavement.'

Ian woke up the next morning with deep regrets for having insulted Karen. He thought that Fred would call round as usual but he would have to wait eight years for that privilege. Losing Fred wasn't the only setback he had to deal with that year. Things became even bleaker when *Lord Upminster* stalled at number fifty-three on the UK album chart. Ian now had to face up to the reality that he was no longer the pop star of his dreams. A headline appearance on Michael Parkinson's TV chat show in November did little to boost sales, but Ian appeared chipper, proud of his billing above the actress Diana Dors and trades union leader Arthur Scargill. In a moment of hilarity, Ian pondered the National Health Service. 'It didn't begin until about . . . [Ian looked in Scargill's direction] . . . 1948, wasn't it, Arf'?' Scargill smiled benignly, and Parkinson chuckled.

Lord Upminster may have flopped, but Ian was still a face on the London music scene. At the press launch for a comeback single by legendary British rocker Billy Fury, Ian worked the room. A photographer named Andy Philips persuaded Ian to pose with Fury. Published in the *NME*, the Dury/Fury picture showed a bemused Billy, but the look of adulation on Ian's face left one in no doubt that he was still a fan, drooling in the presence of near-greatness. But he knew that for faded stars like Fury, the chance of an eleventh-hour hit was remote. His time had been and gone.

With his record sales dwindling, there was no option for Ian but to continue touring. The Blockheads had unofficially disbanded following a ten-day tour of Spain in September and no more work in the pipeline, but an Australian promoter had submitted an astonishing offer. Ian did his sums and quickly calculated he could net £50,000 for a month's work down under. He immediately signed the contract and made the travel arrangements. Then, almost as an afterthought, he summoned the Blockheads, but hadn't reckoned on them demanding near parity to partake in the trip. A meeting took place at Blackhill at which Ian was inebriated. Mickey Gallagher spoke on behalf of the group and demanded £5,000 per man for the tour, a not unreasonable fee in the circumstances, but Ian told the Blockheads they could all 'fuck off', and they did . . . for a while. As the tour loomed, a settlement was reached, and Ian resigned himself to earning rather less than he had originally anticipated.

On 14 November, Ian and the advance party, which included his cousin, Martin Walker, gathered at Heathrow to board a British Airways flight to Sydney, via Muscat and Singapore. The tour got off to a shaky start as soon as Ian's plane touched down at Sydney Airport in the early morning of 16 November. The promoter's tour itinerary advised: 'Proceed through routine Customs and Immigration check', but for Ian it was not that easy; imagine his anger when greeted with the command: 'OK, you! Polio! Over there!' It may have been the International Year of the Disabled, but, separated from his colleagues and forced to join a special queue (of one), Ian felt as if he had stepped back into the dark ages.

He was in a black mood when he checked in at Sydney's elegant Sebel Town House, but was pleased to discover a number of celebrities in residence, including Johnny Mathis, Freddie Starr and Bucks Fizz. Also staying at the hotel was the actor Warren Mitchell, with whom Ian enjoyed a spot of lunch. But he was still fuming when he encountered the microphones and flashbulbs of the Australian press the following day. Patti Mostyn, the promoter's PR, advised Ian not to overreact, but it was too late. The unfortunate episode at the airport had set the tone for the whole tour.

Following a sell-out show at the Capitol Theatre later that week, Ian returned to the hotel and, still jet-lagged, headed for the bar. 'He'd got it into his head how badly the Australians had treated the Aborigines,' recalls co-manager Andrew King. 'It was getting late, and there was a group of businessmen in the corner. Ian ranted at them, "You killed the fucking Abbos, you cunts!" and started lobbing gob at them, little realizing that this was a harmless group of Swedish mining experts.' Jenny

Cotton of Blackhill recalls tour manager Ray Jordan getting hold of Ian and putting him in the elevator to take him up to his room. 'Ian got hold of Ray's dreadlocks and started pulling them out. The next morning, there were dreadlocks all over the floor. The hotel banned us for life.'

Ian's behaviour at the Sebel Town House was so outrageous that the hotel had to placate other guests by offering them a free night's accommodation. But despite the dramas one had come to expect, the tour of Australia and New Zealand was a hit with audiences. On the flight home, co-manager Peter Jenner started to talk excitedly about the group touring 'six months out of every year for the next ten years'. It was an idea that, financially, appealed to the Blockheads, but Ian slept throughout the flight, oblivious to Jenner's optimistic plan. On returning to London, Ian and the Blockheads delivered an inspired performance at London's Lyceum, but beneath the surface group morale was at an all-time low. The Blockheads no longer trusted Ian as he continued to pick them up and put them down, purely to satisfy his intermittent touring requirements. There would be a few scattered dates in the coming year, but the damage had been done.

17

I Want You to Hurt Like I Do

Hammersmith, London, 1982. Ensconced in Digby Mansions and fast approaching forty, Ian glanced around his L-shaped flat with its panoramic views of the Thames and close proximity to some fine riverside walks, but he felt strangely despondent. The year got off to a bad start when he was diagnosed with hepatitis, thought to have been contracted in Australia. His doctor advised him to lie low and stay off drugs and alcohol, but this was a tall order. He was able to quit drinking, but made up for it with copious amounts of hashish. Unlike some of his associates, he shied away from the harder drugs. Fred Rowe confessed to trying heroin 'just the once' and had taken great pride in walking away from what he described to Ian as 'the greatest feeling in the world', but Ian was unimpressed by Fred's dabbling. As for cocaine, a popular drug in music circles, Ian professed complete distaste for 'nose candy', claiming that it was 'elitist'. The main issue, possibly, was its exorbitant cost. 'When coke's the same price as sugar, I'll 'ave it,' Ian announced.

On the business front, Blackhill Enterprises was sinking fast and forced to sell its music publishing interests, including much of Ian's catalogue. He was no longer selling records in quantity, and Polydor was in no hurry to record a follow-up to 1981's disappointing *Lord Upminster*, although Ian was already working on his next batch of words. He was also starting to think of the Blockheads as a financial liability he could do without, especially since they had recently asked for £2,000 per man per show. 'It wasn't that unrealistic,' says Andrew King, 'we were going out for twenty grand a night.'

The Blockheads may have been under the impression that they would be hired, on royalties, to play on the next album – this was certainly what everyone else would have liked – but Ian felt it was time to establish his own identity and he began to distance himself from the band. One wondered if he fully appreciated that the Blockheads were integral to his success, or if they truly understood that Ian's genius as a writer and enter-tainer was essential to their commercial viability. 'Ian and his management didn't quite understand how fucking great the Blockheads were,' says Wilko Johnson. 'By the same token, the Blockheads didn't always appreciate that, in Ian, they had this absolutely unique character. Neither side quite understood what they owed to each other.' Baxter Dury adds: 'You take dad away from the Blockheads, and they are a funk band. You take the Blockheads away from dad, and he could have been a monotonous punk poet. Together they were motivated by des-peration and need, the very things that make people brilliant.'

But Ian was now considering recruiting unknown musicians to help him realize his new songs. There was no shortage of young players who held Ian and the Blockheads in high esteem, and, when word got out that he was in the market for a new band, several eager hopefuls materialized. Two such candidates had already worked with Blockhead Davey Payne, who had recently been sent to New York by Stiff Records boss Dave Robinson to record an album of instrumentals. Former Kilburns drummer Terry Day accompanied Davey as 'chaperone', and the pair spent their evenings jamming with the locals in the jazz clubs of Greenwich Village.

Overseeing Davey's New York sessions were producer Adam Kidron and, playing bass, one Mike McEvoy, an Ameri-can multi-instrumentalist barely out of his teens. Davey saw Ian on 11 May and enthused about the 'child prodigy' McEvoy.

Perhaps this young instrumentalist could be the new Chaz Jankel, thought Ian, having also heard good things about McEvoy from Adam Kidron. Mike McEvoy was a 'musical guy' who could write charts and hire horn players. He had never been part of the punk scene, preferring jazz-funk, jazz fusion and Weather Report. He knew music theory and always wanted to challenge his musical chops. 'Ian was always talking about rock 'n' roll in the fifties, especially Gene Vincent,' says McEvoy, 'but a lot of the Blockheads stuff had an incredible underbelly of funk. There was Ian's edginess, but the riffs were funk.'

McEvoy, who lived with his parents in London, was summoned to Digby Mansions, where he found Ian surrounded by sheets of A3 covered in meticulously handwritten song fragments. Ian wasn't giving much away at their initial meeting, but McEvoy presumed his task would be to turn Ian's lyrical sketches into cohesive, recordable gold. 'I used to go round and wake him up,' recalls McEvoy. 'He told me where I'd find the key, and he'd be in bed with some girl. I'd make them coffee and bring it in. He was having fun. An hour later we were writing, jamming, I was just hanging out.' Over the next few weeks, the prodigiously talented McEvoy dazzled Ian with his musical skills, to the point where Ian began to refer to his new songwriting partner as 'Magic Mike McEvoy'. In this upbeat atmosphere, the duo started to write the songs that would fill one half of Ian's next album. For the remainder, Ian reunited with his former writing partner Russell Hardy, with whom he sought to concoct a more quirky selection. Ian was effectively hedging his bets by imagining an album that would combine a neo-Blockhead jazz-funk groove with an endearing Englishness, more akin to the late Kilburns era. Russell, now a carpenter by trade, was coincidentally building Ian some shelves.

As well as writing with Ian, Mike McEvoy also got a taste of life on the road. In August 1982, Ian was offered a short tour of Greece and reluctantly called on the services of the banished Blockheads, now lured only by money. McEvoy, who was taken along to deputize for the ever-absent Chaz Jankel, recalls, 'I was a twenty-one-year-old who had never toured, put together with these old road dogs who'd cut their teeth, paid their dues and then some. You had all the interpersonal politics going on, and they might have perceived me as a threat, but the real conflict was between the Blockheads and Ian. Without their vocalist they couldn't work, thus he was integral to them being able to pay their bills. The vibes weren't good.'

Blackhill, meanwhile, had gone into receivership. After nearly two decades working together, Peter Jenner and Andrew King were on the verge of parting company, but their dissolution provided a fortuitous outcome for Ian. Blackhill's contract with Stiff had recently expired, and ownership of Ian's first three albums had reverted to the doomed company. The official receiver, whose task it was to salvage as much as possible from the situation, recognized that the Dury master tapes were one of Blackhill's few tangible assets and was prepared to let them go to the highest bidder. Ian got wind of the once-in-a-lifetime opportunity to own his own recordings and put in a bid. For just £5,000 he acquired the copyright to all of his hit records, allowing him to negotiate record distribution deals around the world and enjoy improved royalties for decades to come.

Despite the comings and goings of a few casual girlfriends and the occasional presence of Mike McEvoy, Ian found Digby Mansions cold and unforgiving. Since the sudden departure of his most loyal minder, Fred Rowe, he'd been reluctant to venture out alone for fear of falling over in Hammersmith Broadway, or being recognized and cornered by fans and unable to escape. Imprisoned in the apartment, he yearned for a new driver to ferry him around and a permanent girlfriend who might take on domestic duties. Perhaps he could find someone who was a combination of the two. Ian's best opportunity of meeting new faces was on promotional outings or at media interviews. He was still considered to be a worthy voice on matters of coping with disability, and this took him to television and radio stations around the country. 'He would sit next to a girl in the canteen and she'd be on the train with him back to London that evening,' recalls Andrew King. 'He could fucking well pull if he put his mind to it.'

One girl whom Ian 'pulled' in such circumstances was quickly enrolled as his new live-in assistant in the autumn of 1982, following a discussion about the long, camel-coloured overcoat she was wearing at a provincial TV studio. Ian told her he wanted the coat and repeatedly phoned her on the pretext of seeing if she would part with it, while pleading with her to come to London. The young girl, who has since established a notable career in media and wishes to remain anonymous, became known to Ian's friends as 'The Overcoat'. Arriving at Digby Mansions, she was given the keys to his customized blue delivery van to run him to appointments and recording sessions.

'He was quite a powerful and persuasive person,' she says. 'He talked very warmly and respectfully about his ex-wife and children but he didn't make any effort to contact them at that time. He saw his mum quite a bit and seemed very proud of the fact that she was fairly posh. He would often mention it. Even though I really liked him, he was a sadistic person in terms of mental cruelty. Initially he liked the fact that I was a university-educated person, but it was as if he had to take that on and expose what I didn't know. He enjoyed making people feel uncomfortable, there's no doubt about it. His idea of a "nice evening in" was to make you sit in a room and listen to jazz albums while complaining about how crap modern music was. He would drum along to the jazz for hour after hour and, if you tried to leave the room, he would force you to stay. It was like being held hostage.

'He was also extremely controlling about what I wore. He had an eye for style, but he would say, "You'd look much better if you lost weight or dressed like that person over there." One night he said we were going out to dinner. I asked what kind of place it would be – girls need to know how to dress – and he said, "It's just a little caff." When we got there it was Le Caprice, recently opened, the hottest spot in town. We met Tommy Roberts – Mr Freedom – and I was in Doc Martens and jeans. Why not just say, "We're going somewhere nice"? It was his idea of fun, to deliberately piss you off. There was a slight element of contempt.'

Throughout the winter Ian persevered with his keep-fit regime and continued to write and record new material. When he and the Blockheads played London's Lyceum just before Christmas 1982, Chaz Jankel put in a fleeting appearance, having been out of the group for two years. Although the Lyceum was 'a triumph', Chaz chose not to join the group on the return trip to Greece that immediately followed, and Mike McEvoy was again called upon to deputize at the two shows in Athens. It was in Greece that Ian and 'The Overcoat' parted company. 'Living with Ian had been a bleak experience from my point of view,' she says. 'It ended with a physical fight, which was pretty horrible. I don't think he knew that I had been injured. I didn't tell anyone, I was ashamed of the whole business.'

Ian had agreed to take part in a television documentary to be directed by Franco Rosso for Channel 4, then in its infancy. For six weeks, Rosso's camera crew filmed Ian in various locations, including Digby Mansions, Island Studios at Basing Street and a hydrotherapy pool in Putney, where he exercised his 'little arm' under the watchful eye of Doctor Kate Forrest, known to her clients as 'Dr Kit'. Ian was becoming suspicious of Rosso's motives and started objecting to various crew members and generally prevaricating. Rosso responded by calling Ian's bluff. 'I told him if he didn't want to do it, that was OK, we would all go home. Then I'd get a phone call and we'd start again. He was very suspicious. I think he thought we were going to stitch him up. He had a naughty streak in him that was great, but you had to front him off the whole time. You also had to be prepared to indulge him, then you'd get something out of it.'

The project picked up when Rosso recruited cameraman Chris Morphet, who had worked on various film projects for Stiff Records. But then Ian wanted to know what Rosso was aiming for . . . what kind of film would it be? How would it be edited? The truth was, the director didn't know. He was embarking on a journey into the unknown, over which Ian would have equal control. The finished work would be a true reflection of its subject in that period. As soon as the cameras started to roll, Rosso realized that Ian was playing a clever game. Ian seemed to know exactly how much film there was in the camera and how much time remained and measured out his performances accordingly. Even when Rosso covered over the red light that signified recording was in progress Ian was able to sense with some degree of accuracy whether or not the film was rolling. 'He had a knack for reaching the climax of a scene just as the tape was about to run out,' remembers Rosso. 'He held back on the big interview – the one he knew we wanted. He left it until midnight on the last day of filming.'

'He insisted Jenny Cotton was with him,' continues Rosso, 'to hold his hand if you like, then he started, and we let it roll. It was hysterical when he was reading the lyrics, Ian at his naughty best. Before we did the scene, he said, "I've got to talk to you." He took me into the music room, and there was a large box in the corner. He said, "I'm a bit worried . . . do you want me to get the callipers out?" I didn't know what the hell he was going on about, then he opened the box, and it was full of his old, worn-out leg irons. I think he was trying to embarrass me. "Here they are, is this what you want?" he shouted, waving them around. Then he sat on my knee and put his arm round me and said, "It's going to be all right, isn't it?" I think he thought it might have bothered me. It was an odd moment. Then he started to talk. We started rolling, and he was off. It was just what we'd been waiting for – Ian relaxed, talking about his lyrics.'

Just before midnight on 3 November 1983, Franco Rosso's fifty-minute documentary was screened on Channel 4. Peggy tuned in to watch the director's totally disarming portrait of her son and was justly proud. She and thousands of viewers saw various aspects of Ian's life: the diligent songwriter, thumbing his thesaurus for inspiration; the skilled swimmer, pushing himself to the limit in a hydrotherapy pool; the fitness fanatic, sweating on his exercise bike; and the compassionate role model, demonstrating the joys of percussion to children with special needs at Brookfield House School in Waltham Forest. Most touchingly, viewers saw an ancient photograph of Ian at Chailey, in cape and calliper, the little crippled boy who had gone on to conquer adversity.

But had Ian overcome his childhood tragedy? 'The Overcoat', his former live-in lover, thinks not. 'He was a very angry person, possibly because of the hand he'd been dealt. He was also bitter about having to scrabble around.' Ian was certainly forced to come to terms with the fact that his hit-making days were over, but his anger was always bubbling below the surface. During one interview in Franco Rosso's film, he talked about the high incidence of cruelty to children in society – some of whom, he said, were 'put in spin dryers'. As his story continued he was clearly trying hard to suppress his rage. It was an understandable emotion, but as his nostrils started to flare and the pitch of his voice rose, one could see how easily he might have lost control in private.

Friends remember how he would explode with rage at the slightest irritation. Chaz Jankel: 'There were many incidents after gigs where what could have been a beautiful evening would change suddenly with Ian screaming at somebody in the dressing room. A nice after-gig atmosphere would turn into hell, everyone scattering to get away from Ian's mania, his anger.' Future collaborator Max Stafford-Clark says, 'His disability did make him angry. I remember him getting drunk one night and saying, "Every morning I wake up and have to put this thing on my leg. You don't have to fucking do that, but I have to, every morning." It defined him.'

Others talk of Ian's tears welling up at the mention of his dad's death or recalling his nightmare time in Chailey where he was made to masturbate bullies. 'I wondered if he was acting when he cried,' says Ingrid Mansfield-Allman. 'It seemed very clever – the "look at poor me, I'm hideous" routine when he'd done something really awful that he wanted to get away with. If he realized he was bang-to-rights it was one of his strategies, to use this thing that you haven't got.'

Polio was Ian's 'get out of jail free' card. He was certainly mentally scarred by the experience, but he would turn on the waterworks for dramatic effect. Furthermore, behind the mainly tranquil television image, his life was in turmoil. It had been that way ever since his dream of success had become reality and had got worse since success had deserted him. His sudden outbursts were often attributed to the drink, but when Rosso's cameras first entered Ian's life he was still recovering from hepatitis and had hardly touched a drop in months.

Although his recording career was in cruise mode, Ian was still in demand. Recruited by the media as a cultural commentator, he appeared on BBC2 television to review the Royal Academy's Summer Exhibition, where he picked out a couple of figurative paintings that caught his eye. On ITV's *A Better Read* he recited poetry from *Hard Lines – New Poetry and Prose* – and then produced a pile of books to illustrate his love of words. These included *The Oxford Dictionary of English Proverbs* and his well-thumbed copy of *The Lawless Decade*, *New York Post* journalist Paul Sann's account of the American prohibition era of the 1920s that had fired Ian's imagination and formed the basis of his thesis at the Royal College of Art in 1966.

Although Ian struggled to articulate his love of art and literature, he was very much the verbal gymnast when it came to discussing music. This was especially true in radio interviews, where, relieved of visual concerns, his mind would race faster than a Charlie Parker sax solo, occasionally throwing in some unexpected phrase or cultural reference. When he talked himself into a blind alley, he could improvise his way out. If he tripped over his tongue as some mild untruth was delivered, he would just keep on blowing. If his interrogator was female, he could be quite flirtatious, as was the case in his conversation with Anne Nightingale for Radio 1's *Mailbag* in August 1983. Anne, by the way, was a fan, and her admiration became clear.

> *Anne* – Do you need good musical knowledge to write
>   good song lyrics?
> *Ian* – The most important thing is the rhythm of it, not the
>   chords. I don't know a thing about chords. I don't
>   know my brass from my oboe!
> *Anne* – How do you set about writing lyrics? Do you
>   think, 'Right, scribble scribble' immediately, or do you
>   let it go round your head a bit first?
> *Ian* – I whack it down immediately but I don't make it into
>   a finished article . . . I started writing a lyric to come
>   and talk to you about. The first thing I wrote is called
>   'The Day We Changed the World'. I write the title
>   down first, 'cos that hopefully will get me at it.
>   Therefore I've got to describe the horribleness of
>   before this happened. All I've got is: 'I grew more
>   cynical and jaded, expecting nothing but the worst,
>   and my bright potential faded, and my bubble slowly
>   burst.'
> *Anne [excited]* – Oh! I think that's marvellous!

Polydor had declined to release Ian's new album, *4,000 Weeks' Holiday* – a reference to the average person's lifespan – due to the inclusion of a song entitled 'Noddy Harris' (aka 'Fuck Off

Noddy'). It wasn't the offensive language that perturbed the label so much as the threat of an injunction from the Enid Blyton estate. The late children's authoress would have been horrified by the thought of Noddy – her innocent little creation – associating with Winnie the Pooh, who was 'having a wank', watched by 'Thomas the Tank'. When Ian refused to delete the offending track, the album was taken off the release schedule.

As Ian was squaring up to Polydor, holding out for his artistic credibility as he saw it, his old pal Barney Bubbles, who had been working on the *4,000 Weeks* sleeve design, was in a battle of his own. In the depths of depression and aggravated by a crippling tax demand and the mainstream record industry's crass demands on his talent, Barney committed suicide on 14 November 1983 at his Islington home. Ian was stunned. Barney's pre-eminent sponsor, Jake Riviera, remarked to me in Dingwalls later that night: 'It's amazing what some people will do to get out of designing a Nick Lowe sleeve!' On the surface, this seemed to be a callous comment on such a tragic death, but, like many of Riviera's throwaway lines, it was bang on the money; Bubbles was indeed tired of serving an industry that in the main failed to appreciate or reward his genius. Ian, though, assumed a kinship with the artist, telling me, 'Barney didn't have the faults or the ego. He made me feel second class. I wanted his approval in a strange kind of way. I wanted the acceptance. Towards the end of his life he told me a few straighteners. He told me I'd been a horrible piece of work.'

Throughout the prolonged recording sessions for his new album Ian had met and worked with a number of young musicians introduced to him by Mike McEvoy and producer Adam Kidron. He was more than happy with the musicianship of his new line-up, which included Merlin Rhys-Jones (guitar), Tag Lamche (drums), Steve Sidwell (trumpet) and Jamie Talbot (sax). When the dependable Mickey Gallagher was added on keyboards, Ian believed he had come as close as possible to replicating the power of the Blockheads. However, to defuse comparison and pre-empt criticism, he cleverly christened his new combo 'the Music Students'.

The younger musicians in the band were somewhat in awe of Ian, having been inspired by the funk of 'Rhythm Stick', a hit at the time they were learning their craft. They were also enchanted by Ian's charisma and were prepared to compete for his attention in the general throng. 'Ian was usually surrounded by an entourage of management types or sycophants,' says Merlin Rhys-Jones. 'He once said to me: "You can always judge a man by the quality of his sycophants." We used to go and see the boat race from his balcony at Hammersmith, and there would always be people around he half knew, all trying to ingratiate themselves with him.'

On 9 December, Ian and the Music Students appeared along-side Simple Minds on Channel 4's *The Tube*, performing three songs from the imminent album, from which 'Noddy Harris' had been deleted following Ian's capitulation. Co-presenter of *The Tube* Jools Holland managed to displease Ian in some small way, and a lively altercation took place off screen, reportedly placing Holland in Ian's 'bad books' for some years.

The music press was still generally supportive of Ian, but were less than kind about *4,000 Weeks' Holiday* in the advance reviews. Ian had told the *NME*'s Gavin Martin that *4,000 Weeks* was the only LP he'd made that he was happy with and that he no longer liked *New Boots and Panties!!*. Unfortunately, the record-buying public begged to differ. Only one track, 'Peter the Painter' (a tribute to Peter Blake), was really up to par, containing the inspired lyric: 'It's not a fake it's a Peter Blake, it takes the cake make no mistake!'

Compared with *New Boots*, the new album was a lifeless platter, destined to gather dust on even the most ardent fan's shelf. Mike McEvoy took much of the stick. 'When we were recording, it was all hopeful,' he says. 'There were going to be hits. There was never any talk of Ian's sound being worn away by this American influence, but when *4,000 Weeks* wasn't successful, it was down to this American who didn't get it, right? Who's gonna carry the can? The one you can pass it to who's not gonna be able to get rid of it. Ian didn't want to take responsibility because ultimately he had a career. I wasn't the one making the decisions, I was just jamming along, but to this day, it's all *my* fault.'

When Chaz Jankel played London's Electric Ballroom in support of his *Chazablanca* album Ian made a brief appearance on stage as Chaz's 'special guest'. After the show he met a girl named Belinda Leith, whom he invited to sit on his knee when she came into the dressing room. Ian was immediately attracted to the twenty-one-year-old Belinda, a fashion designer who specialized in machine knitwear and marketed her designs around London. Within days they were living together at Digby Mansions, where Belinda installed her knitting machine in the now infrequently used music room.

Belinda was taken with Ian's cheeky grin and boyish charm and he no doubt fell for her big eyes and hourglass figure. Her striking appearance turned heads and it would certainly help to deflect attention away from Ian when they were out, which was a welcome side benefit. They had both been art students and despite the twenty-year age gap had much in common including a love of clothes and design. 'Ian was quite intellectual,' says Belinda. 'Rock 'n' roll was his true love, but he had another side to him and a unique character and voice. He was able to draw you in.'

But Ian was now besieged by writer's block. He was back on the booze and every morning, after a champagne breakfast and a little spliff, he would sit down at his desk with a blank sheet of paper that remained blank all day. Thankfully, the road beckoned, but Ian's musical director, Mike McEvoy, was fretting about deserting his own band, the relatively unknown MP Giants. McEvoy thought that a solution might be to get the

Giants some work as Ian's support group. On 16 February 1984, when Ian and the Music Students commenced a series of four warm-up gigs at the Hope and Anchor, billed as 'Wanker and Son', the MP Giants opened the show, with McEvoy and drummer Tag Lamche appearing in both bands.

The following week Ian and his group, now augmented by guitarist Ed Speight, departed for Israel, where they would play a short season at the Kolnoa Dan, a converted cinema in Tel Aviv. Jenny Cotton, now co-managing Ian with Andrew King and trading as Cotton and Carruthers following the dissolution of Blackhill, went along as tour manager. On the opening night, Jenny was stationed at the back of the venue, preparing to operate the spotlight, when word reached her that Ian was refusing to go on stage until somebody produced a pair of gloves. 'Can you imagine the difficulty in obtaining gloves in Israel in the middle of the night?' asks Jenny. 'The poor promoter's girlfriend said she had a pair at home, and the show was delayed for ages whilst they were located. When Ian got the gloves, he went on stage. I just wanted to kill him.'

'The whole concept of "F Troop" was born in Israel,' says Ed Speight. 'If there was one lady in the place, who you or I wouldn't even contemplate chatting to – the big girl with the chain round her neck, who's a sergeant major in the reserve army, been married, a couple of kids, works behind the bar – "Eva" – you know her . . . Ian would be there in a big way! One night he went off with just such a woman in a cab, to the suburbs of Tel Aviv, the equivalent of Northolt or Perivale. We got the anguished phone call from someone. They were saying: "He's outside the house now, she's throwing things at him, his trousers are down round his ankles and he's mouthing off. You've got to come and get him." Mickey, Merlin and myself – F Troop – jumped in a cab at half four in the morning. Ian's standing in the middle of the road as the milk float comes round the corner and the neighbours are saying, "This is a quiet neighbourhood, can't you please do something?" She'd kicked him out, but she was too much of a challenge for Ian to turn down.'

Returning to the UK at the end of February 1984, Ian and the Music Students readied themselves for 'The Lecture Tour', in support of *4,000 Weeks' Holiday*. The new young band provided Ian with a fresh audience for his golden verbal. Merlin Rhys-Jones remembers: 'There was a blokeish, almost militaristic atmosphere backstage, with lots of rhyming slang, prison stories and minicab scenarios. Second World War army phrases were regular features of Ian's high-volume exchanges. I was "cashiered" one evening for failing in my new duties as his "libations officer". It was all very amusing, but Ian hated it if wives and girlfriends stopped mates from hanging out. Ian's attitude towards women was extreme in both his contempt and his adoration.'

For one of the Music Students, the tour would end in tears. Mike McEvoy had been Ian's musical collaborator for nearly two years, but his job was hanging in the balance. The seed of the problem – and a key factor in McEvoy's eventual nervous breakdown – was the responsibility he felt towards his fellow musicians from the MP Giants. Even though some of them had been hired to play on Ian's album, McEvoy shouldered a massive burden of guilt. 'I made a selfish decision to go with Ian,' he says, 'and I left behind people who had been loyal to me. I tried to make amends by getting them involved in the tour. Ian was concerned that maybe I didn't have the energy and that it would detract from him. I was his boy, and he wanted me to be fully focused on his set, but there I was saying I also wanted to open the show with my band. Not many gigs into the tour I was getting really tired, trying to manage relationships with the Giants and keep everyone, including Ian, happy.'

McEvoy's time with Ian ended on a tour bus as it raced down the M1 in the early hours of 4 March. That evening Ian and the Music Students had played to a half-full house at Manchester Polytechnic, where McEvoy had walked on stage draped in a large overcoat and scarf and intermittently placed his head inside the bass drum. Halfway through the set, he started shouting abuse at Ian, then walked off stage, leaving the MP Giants' Joe Cang to take over on bass. The minute the show finished, McEvoy was grabbed by Ian's minder, 'The Sulphate Strangler', and marched to the back of the hall, where he was taken into a quiet corridor. 'You don't ever talk to Ian in that way!' roared the Strangler. Mercifully, McEvoy's dressing-down stopped at a verbal warning, but once on the bus he flew into a rage, shouting and screaming at Ian, who was sat up front with the Strangler. 'You wanker!' shouted McEvoy. 'You need that big ugly cunt to protect you, you cowardly little shit!'

When the bus reached London, McEvoy was dropped off in the Finchley Road. It would be another five years before he heard from Ian again. 'People like to remember Ian as a cultural icon,' says McEvoy, 'but he was also a clever and talented businessman and very good at manipulating people. He knew how to wind you up. If you are being wound up by someone with a disability, what are you going to do? Punch him? He knew that. If you couldn't match his verbal – and he was an expert – he had you. I wasn't that articulate, and he was winding me up in subtle ways. A year down the line, I was not the favoured son. Things were going on with the record company, tracks were being pulled, the album wasn't getting any promotion. Ian was under a lot of pressure, maybe he was questioning all of his decisions, who knows? But I do know that I felt psychologically bullied.'

Mike McEvoy had come into Ian's life at a time when his musical talent was sorely needed, but he became the classic victim. For a while, he'd been the blue-eyed boy, but his 'mistake' was to not retaliate when Ian started dishing it out, if indeed Mike's personality would have allowed it. 'Ian knew he could push people with the verbal,' says Jock Scot. 'If something annoyed him, he could destroy you. He could be quite cruel.' Merlin Rhys-Jones adds, 'Some people stood up to Ian, some didn't. Others just kept quiet. Joe Cang got the "you middle-class cunt" thing from Ian out of the hotel window on a few occasions. I didn't want to appear obsequious. I thought I would just do the gig and see how it evolved. Ian came up to me halfway through the tour and said, "We never talk – do you know why that is? It's because we don't have to." It was a warm, reassuring remark. Other people approached Ian in an obsequious way and got the full cockney geezer in return.'

'The Lecture Tour' continued without McEvoy and on 19 March 1984 arrived in the Wiltshire town of Chippenham. At Gold Diggers night club – about a mile-and-a-half from Rowden Hill, where in 1960 Gene Vincent survived the auto wreck that killed his pal and fellow legend Eddie Cochran as they headed back to London from Bristol – Ian would meet his wife-to-be.

PART FIVE

REDEMPTION

18

Equity

Chippenham, Wiltshire, March 1984. The Strangler was guarding the dressing room door at Gold Diggers when the young woman from the nearby village of Christian Malford explained her credentials. 'My dad taught Ian at art school,' she said, hoping it would passport her to the inner sanctum. The Strangler was unsure but thought it best to relay the message to his boss, just in case. The girl was then ushered into the dressing room, where the star was holding court. Within moments, they were face to face. 'Your dad never taught me,' growled Ian. 'Peter Blake taught me.'

Dark-haired Sophy Tilson was a nineteen-year-old art student, the daughter of fêted painter Joe Tilson. She'd been a huge fan of Ian's since the age of twelve, when she made a cassette copy of *New Boots and Panties!!* from her older sister's LP. A live appearance by Ian Dury at Gold Diggers was a big local event, and she had edged her way towards the backstage area in the hope of meeting him. Later that evening, she found herself hanging out with Ian and the Music Students at the nearby Bear Hotel, where the tour party feasted on a supper of egg and onion sandwiches. 'I told Ian I thought he was brilliant,' recalls Sophy. 'He replied, "You're not too bad yourself!"'

Ian tried to persuade Sophy to join him on the rest of the tour, but she knew her college studies had to come first. Some weeks later, however, Sophy caught up with her idol at a gig in Bristol. 'Ian got a bit fruity, but he was really sweet,' says Sophy.

'We obviously really liked each other, but I was aware of his girlfriend, Belinda, and I didn't want to cause trouble.' Instead, Sophy kept in touch with the Strangler and occasionally contacted Ian throughout her time at college in Swindon and, later, the Chelsea School of Art. 'Ian was totally in my heart,' she says, 'but I really wanted to get on with my work, even though we were deeply attracted to each other.'

Weariness with Ian's outrageous behaviour had set in long ago amongst those he needed to be onside, and his musical career was now precarious. It was four years since he'd enjoyed the sniff of a hit, and it was unlikely that Polydor would exercise its option for a third album. Forced to tour, Ian and the Music Students undertook a series of European dates. One of co-manager Jenny Cotton's abiding memories of the jaunt was Ian's request one afternoon for a bowl of soup, something he insisted upon having before giving an interview that had been set up. The hotel kitchen was closed, but, after a lot of fuss, a huge tureen of delicious soup arrived. Ian then did the interview, but didn't touch the soup! His prima donna behaviour was wearing thin, and the Music Students, who a year earlier had had nothing but admiration for Ian, were displaying signs of unrest. Mike McEvoy had already quit, and now, as with the Blockheads, money had become an issue.

Between the various members of the Music Students there was the usual financial disparity. Bassist Joe Cang, one of the more poorly paid, asked for a raise halfway through the French leg of the tour. 'I was sharing a hotel room with the drummer,' recalls Cang. 'We had retired for the night when there was a knock on the door. It was Ian, really hammered on brandy and accompanied by the Strangler. Ian sat on the end of my bed – I was in it – and he started on me, saying, "You don't fucking deserve any money." After a while, I told him to fuck off, and he said, "You're sacked!" He would do this thing where he would keep riling you, then challenge you. "What you gonna do? Hit me? Knock me out?" I told him I was going to leave the tour – they had a live TV show in Spain the next day. Ian said, "I'll fly Norman [Watt-Roy] in . . ." It escalated. He got Strangler, who threatened to beat me up. Then he started following me around the hotel at 4 a.m., but my bags were packed. I said, "If you think I'm being paid too much and you can do without me, I'm off." Andrew and Jenny ironed it out, but Ian was never the same with me after that. He was a bit embarrassed.'

Despite a well-received set at Glastonbury that June and an appearance at the Edinburgh Festival in August, touring to make ends meet was no longer viable, as the Music Students were disintegrating, and all contact with the Blockheads had ceased. Royalties continued to dribble in, but songwriting was no longer a pleasure. At forty-two, Ian was disillusioned with the music business. Seeking a new creative outlet and an alternative source of income, he decided he would reinvent himself – as an actor.

'I think I'm probably better in films than I've appeared to be because I've never really been given a chance to act,' Ian told me. 'The only film I've played a big part in was *Burning Beds*. I played the lead, a bit of German, a bit of English. That was a worthwhile project. I earned a lot of money and when I got back I had a tax bill that gobbled up the whole lot. I enjoy acting, but not to the exclusion of rock 'n' roll.'

Ian had hankered after an acting career ever since the night in 1981 when he rubbed shoulders with theatrical aristocracy. Landing a part in a London charity production of Tom Stoppard's *Dogg's Troupe 15-Minute Hamlet*, at Stockwell Manor School, he shared the stage with Vanessa Redgrave and Derek Jacobi. After the performance, he wangled a lift home from Dame Vanessa and, true to form, couldn't resist flirting with the legendary actress. 'How do you do this acting lark, then, Vanessa?' he enquired in his finest cockney accent, hoping his wry humour would break the ice. 'Doing a spot of mini-cabbing on the side, are we?' Ian's chat-up lines may have amused an impressionable fan, but not the redoubtable Ms Redgrave. As she drove on in silence, Ian began to cringe at his own gauche remarks, but he would drop the actress's name at every opportunity in the coming weeks.

The following year, Ian was put forward for a part in *And the Ship Sails On*, a film to be directed by the great Federico Fellini. Ian failed the audition, but years later, in an interview with the *Daily Telegraph*, he proudly recalled, 'Fellini had a great pile of photographs in front of him and said, "Mr Dury, you have a beard." I stammered that it was no problem to shave it off immediately. He said, "Film to me is faces, and I like your face." I didn't get the part, but it was a great moment.'

Although he was not an outstanding thespian, Ian was well equipped for character roles and cameos on the strength of his quirky appearance and undoubted charisma. His 'dark brown voice' was also an asset, which he put to good effect in a voice-over job as 'The Fertilizer' on the audio cassette accompanying an early computer game, *Deus Ex Machina*. The fact that he'd been a successful pop singer didn't hurt either: many a luvvie would claim to be an 'Ian Dury fan'.

Pippa Markham, the theatrical agent who would become a key factor in Ian's acting career, had first witnessed the individuality of his live performance when she'd worked as an usherette at the Victoria Palace in 1974. Ten years later, Ian sprang into Pippa's mind as she took a call from Mary Selway, the eminent casting director who was working on Roman Polanski's *Pirates*, a film starring Walter Matthau. 'Mary was having trouble finding someone to play a sort of hunchback, gnome-like character,' recalls Pippa. 'I didn't have anybody on my books who was right, but as I always like to suggest ideas, I said, "The person who seems obvious to me is Ian Dury." Mary thought it was brilliant idea. I knew Ian's manager, Andrew King, because he was the manager of Alberto y Lost Trios Paranoias, who once did a show at the Royal Court with one of my actors [Gorden Kaye]. Polanski always casts on tape as he can't come into the country, so Ian went over to Twickenham to record his audition. He got it, his first real acting job.'

A list of some of the offbeat characters Ian would go on to portray in various film and stage productions illustrates Markham's adroit marketing of her client, not to mention Ian's image in the eyes of various directors. At the risk of becoming typecast, Ian accepted roles such as: 'The Devil', 'Bones', 'Weazel', 'The Plughole Man', 'The Boot Black' and 'Rat's Dad'. When given the part of a named character, it would be of the 'Terry Fitch' variety. 'Ian never hassled me for work,' adds Pippa. 'He always responded to messages, and we'd discuss stuff, but he didn't view it in the same way as somebody who was exclusively an actor would. It was just one part of his life.'

When Ian signed his contract for the part of 'Meat Hook' in *Pirates* it was the start of his modest, yet eventful movie career. Filming was delayed while Roman Polanski's team built the galleon *Neptune*, which, at over 60 metres in length, would be the most expensive prop in movie history. While he was waiting for Polanski's call, a number of agreeable roles began to materialize. In the film *Number One*, in which a small-time snooker hustler, played by Bob Geldof, is encouraged by a crooked promoter to go for bigger stakes in a national contest, Ian would play 'Teddy Bryant'. Despite an able cast including Mel Smith, Ray Winstone, Alfred Molina and Alison Steadman, it would make little impression at the box office. The sub-*Minder* script included over thirty instances of 'you know worrimean?' and Ian's first words on the big screen were 'Oi! 'Arry!'

Slightly more satisfactory would be *King of the Ghetto*, a four-part TV serial that placed Ian alongside Tim Roth, also a client of Cotton and Carruthers. *Ghetto* received good reviews, with Herbert Kretzmer of the *Daily Mail* describing Ian as 'a natural actor', but the renowned critic reserved his greatest praise for Roth, who 'towered over it all'. Ian was not pleased by Tim Roth's runaway success, or the fact they shared the same management team. Andrew King recalls Ian bullying Roth at a party: 'You'd think Tim Roth was tough, but Ian must have found some weakness in his armour and turned on him. He was in like Slim, destroying Tim with the verbal. "D'ya mind? D'ya mind if I say something, you useless cunt!"'

In the spring of 1985, Ian flew to Tunisia to film his modest part in *Pirates*, a job that continued for 'eight fun-packed weeks'. Ian's girlfriend, Belinda Leith, joined him for ten days in Tunisia and remembers them having a pleasant dinner with Walter Matthau and his wife. But most of the time boredom got the better of Ian. He was often seen chatting up the ladies in the company and on one occasion he unwisely insulted a Polish stuntman, who responded by picking him up under one arm and throwing him into the swimming pool. Protracted shooting by Polanski, combined with lucrative overtime rates, earned Ian nearly £60,000 in fees – good money indeed – but what made film work doubly attractive to Ian was his realization that actors, unlike musicians, shoulder little responsibility for the finished product.

Ian hadn't completely given up on music, however. Following a two-and-a-half year break he reunited with the Blockheads. The band were sceptical but knew it was their musicianship that gave Ian his confidence on stage and were keen to prove themselves following the Music Students debacle. 'If Ian made a mistake by coming in early on the chorus, the Blockheads would go with him,' says Mickey Gallagher. 'He didn't even know he'd made a mistake!' That summer they headlined the pyramid stage at Glastonbury. Mid-way through the set, a reveller in the audience started throwing mud, and Ian stormed off, only returning for 'Sex and Drugs' after a lengthy interval.

Ian also played Hammersmith Odeon with a set that included 'We Want the Gold', a jolly, nautical number said to have been inspired by Ian's involvement in *Pirates*. Ian and Chaz were soon writing together again and created the theme song for the TV production of Sue Townsend's *The Secret Diary of Adrian Mole*. 'Profoundly in Love with Pandora' would be released as a single and make a modest chart showing that October. Some years later, the 'Adrian Mole' connection would lead to Ian and Mickey Gallagher providing music for Sue Townsend's stage play *The Queen and I*.

Following Glastonbury and Hammersmith, there was much pressure for a permanent reunion with the Blockheads, but Ian was reluctant to commit. In a Capital Radio interview that September, he told deejay Roger Scott: 'Randy Newman stated that he'd only go out with a band when he's in the top five. Once you've got a band and a road crew together, a system whereby you've got your gear and your trucks are all ready to go, when you come off the road, then what do you do? If you're not going to go back on the road until you've got a good album together, you get a situation where, by doing nothing, it's costing you such a lot of bread . . . to keep it going is literally an impossibility.'

Although Ian had identified the financial and logistical pressures of maintaining a working band, the truth was that he no longer needed to perform live. A few thousand pounds for a mini-tour and all the stress it entailed did not compare with trousering a similar amount for a few hours' voice-over work in Soho. 'He wouldn't leave the house for less than five grand,' says Mickey Gallagher. 'He wouldn't get up for a test for less than £500. If it were a toss-up between a voice-over and a gig, the voice-over would win every time. That's what the Blockheads were up against.'

Ian had already adapted 'Reasons to Be Cheerful' for a Thomson Holidays ad. A better-known TV commercial – for which he asked to be paid 'in used five pound notes' – would quickly follow. An advertising agency had dreamed up a campaign in which a humanoid would expound on the virtues of Toshiba television sets, mouthing the immortal words: 'Hello Tosh, got a Toshiba?' The jingle was unashamedly based on Alexei Sayle's 1984 novelty hit, 'Hello John, Got a New Motor?' The public's flirtation with all things cockney (see *Minder*) had already peaked, but Ian's East End tones were a shot-in-the-arm for the Toshiba brand and its 'flattest, squarest tube'. 'They ain't 'alf built well,' Ian reliably informed viewers.

Meanwhile, Ian and Betty had quietly agreed that it was time to get divorced. On 21 October 1985, their marriage formally ended in a thirty-second hearing at the London Divorce Court. Betty attended, Ian did not. Two years earlier, Betty had met a fellow artist named Clive Richards in summer school at Falmouth College of Art. Having lived for several years at Orchard Cottage in Tring, Betty, Jemima and Baxter moved to a flat at Sutton Court Mansions in Chiswick. They were joined there by Clive, with whom Ian struck up a cautious friendship. Ian had remained close to Betty during their decade of separation and would often visit his family in their new home, just a mile or so from Digby Mansions, where he was living with Belinda Leith.

Belinda had been Ian's partner for two years, but their time together was coming to an end. Belinda felt that she had to 'get out', in order to pursue her own goals and escape Ian's controlling and jealous ways. She reports a generally harmonious time, with only the occasional turbulence. 'He wanted me to be this person he owned,' says Belinda. 'I could see that I wasn't going to have any freedom. Ian was romantic and very gentle, combined with the ability to be more aggressive. It would be completely out of the blue, and he would just go mad, but only when he was intoxicated by alcohol and, on a couple of occasions, cocaine. Moments later he would be calm, as if nothing had happened. Nine tines out of ten he wouldn't remember anything. It was almost as if it was another person.'

Pirates would not see a theatrical release until the summer of 1986, but Ian wasted no time in furthering his acting career.

Another, slightly more obscure film made in 1985 was *Rocinante*, starring John Hurt, in which Ian played 'The Jester'. *Time Out* would later describe *Rocinante* as 'appalling'. To progress into live drama, Ian needed to join the actors' union Equity. To demonstrate his commitment to the profession, he went into repertory theatre in February 1986 at the Palace Theatre, Watford, where he played the part of 'The Devil' in Mary O'Malley's *Talk of the Devil*, alongside T. P. McKenna and Annette Crosbie. The *Watford Observer* called it 'an inspired stroke of casting', adding '[Dury] exudes just the right air of gleeful menace.' Peggy proudly watched Ian from the stalls on opening night alongside his agent, Pippa Markham, and the actress Frances Tomelty.

To be accepted into the acting community appealed to the middle-class, conservative side of Ian's personality that lurked beneath his otherwise rebellious exterior. He especially enjoyed the backstage banter and camp conceits of 'the luvvie brigade', as he later confessed in the BBC documentary *On My Life*: 'I remember that we came out into the green room, as we call the bar, after a matinee in Watford and Caroline Langrishe says, "Well I'm afraid I rather busked it this afternoon," and T. P. McKenna, the voice, says, [adopts Irish accent] "I have never busked a performance in my life!" I went, "Oh, you fibber!" Things like that . . . afterwards, a bloke in a green velvet suit and a cravat comes up and says, "My darling, I laughed 'til I cried," and I went, "On your bike, mate, you never," and he was a crestfallen person. I like the congratulation aspect of acting. I like the fact they really do stroke each other's ego or massage the old neck muscles and there's all that old caper going on all the time. I love all that. It's all bollo, but I love it.'

Ian's new career was gradually gaining traction. More movie roles were in the pipeline, as he proudly told Terry Wogan in a television interview in May 1986. 'I always wanted to be an actor,' he exclaimed, bouncing with life on Wogan's sofa, fluttering his eyelashes and grinning coyly. To the TV viewers, Ian appeared modest and polite, but away from the camera's glare he was less humble. Backstage, he bumped into his former girlfriend known as 'The Overcoat', now working at Television Centre. Ian proudly introduced her to his latest flame, Delphi Newman, whom he suddenly berated for not wearing the clothes that would, in his opinion, suit her best. 'Look, you see, that's the sort of thing you should be wearing,' he told Delphi, holding up his 'ex' as a paragon of style (whereas three years earlier she had been harassed by Ian for failing to please in the punk couture area).

Delphi Newman was a fan who had come into Ian's life some months earlier when she turned up one night at Digby Mansions. 'Delphi found Ian,' says Ingrid Mansfield-Allman. 'She freeze-framed the Rosso film and worked out where he lived. She rang his doorbell and threatened to walk into the River Thames if he didn't let her in. Ian rang Jenny Cotton, saying, "There's this mad bird outside!"' Jenny and her friend Cheryl Madley arrived on the scene and escorted Delphi out of the water. Delphi would later return, but the only evidence of her presence that night was a trail of wet footprints leading to the Underground station.

For Mickey Gallagher, new musical adventures beckoned, having been hired to produce an album by Kiyoshiro Imawano, 'the Japanese Cliff Richard'. Imawano, a confirmed anglophile, came to London in 1986, craving the involvement of some British 'new wave' musicians. Mickey dutifully rounded up the troops and delighted Imawano with a band consisting of various members of the Clash and the Blockheads. A tour followed that September, with Gallagher, Johnny Turnbull, Charley Charles and Davey Payne jetting out to Japan, along with trumpet player Geoff Miller and Mark Bedford of Madness deputizing for Norman on bass. Returning from the tour, Mickey paid Ian a visit, raving about the joys of working with Imawano, suggesting that Ian might like to tour Japan. Ian responded by revealing that he had just signed a contract to appear in a film with Bob Dylan.

Dylan had first become aware of Ian's work and that of a number of upcoming British artistes in 1978, when he was in London for a series of concerts at Earls Court. The CBS press office had supplied Dylan with a welcome pack of recent UK albums on various labels, including *The Clash*, Elvis Costello's *This Year's Model* and *New Boots and Panties!!*. In the ensuing years Dylan had familiarized himself with *New Boots* and, during filming, greeted Ian in his trailer with: 'Hi! Sweet Gene Vincent!' 'The very same,' Ian replied. *Hearts of Fire*, in which Ian had a small part as 'Bones', was filmed in the autumn of 1986 and released the following year. It told the story of a reclusive rock star, played by Dylan, on the comeback trail. The movie's director, Richard Marquand, was to die, aged forty-nine, shortly after filming was completed and just before the diabolical reviews appeared. Channel 4 described the film as 'a blunt instrument of eighties vacuity'.

Following *Hearts of Fire* Ian flew to Greece for his part as 'The Acrobat' in *Red Ants* (also known as *Paradise Unlocked*). He would humorously recall the part some years later in a Radio 4 interview with Peter White: 'I got a call from a Greek man called Vassilis Boudouris, who wanted to know if I could ride a horse, and I said, "There's no way I'm getting on a horse, mate, forget it." Then I got another phone call saying, "Can you ride a motorbike?" My answer came in the negative again: "Not even if it's got a sidecar on it." Then the third phone call, he wants to know if I've still got a face . . . so I went to see him. I said, "Well, Mr Boudouris, here I am, there's me face, what's the part?"And he said, "Tightrope walker!" I did it. I had somebody on a horse, filling in for me, somebody went up in a balloon for me, somebody rode a motorbike and somebody did the tightrope. He wanted my face to look like I was on a tightrope . . . there was a box about eight feet high on top of which was another box about five feet high on top of which they put me, with an umbrella, shooting it against the sky ... it looked as if I was eighty feet up in the air . . . I was really scared. Then he said, "Can you go down on one knee?"'

In November, Ian returned to London and commenced a three-month run at London's Royal Court Theatre in *Road*, a play by Jim Cartwright. 'It's about a road, innit?' Ian remarked, explaining his move from music to theatre to Adam Sweeting of *Q*. 'All the gigs I've done in the last two years have been the kind of gigs that you can't avoid, either financially or because somebody's being really nice. I wouldn't do that for a living, know worrimean?' In *Road*, Ian played 'Scullery', a central narrator who takes the audience through an evening in a northern town, from the point where the characters are getting ready to go out to pubs and clubs to the moment where they become drunk and despondent. Also in the cast of *Road* was twenty-two-year-old Jane Horrocks, later to become the star of the movie *Little Voice* and a revered actress. Ian and Jane hit it off, and she moved into Digby Mansions, staying for twelve months. 'Jane and Ian had some incredible outings,' recalls Andrew King. 'The holiday in Greece – they went to Hydra together – phwoar!' Interviewed in *The Observer*, Jane Horrocks recalled: 'I was in my twenties when I went out with Ian. I have always chosen men who apart from being very bright were also untameable. There's something a bit wild and unpredictable about them. Ian Dury was the most incredibly unpredictable of them all and that's why the relationship didn't last. But it keeps you on your toes. It was a long time after the golden years of "Rhythm Stick", so it wasn't like going out with Robbie Williams.'

A more lasting and satisfactory outcome of *Road* was that Ian established a working relationship with its producer, Max Stafford-Clark. 'Ian was really a musicologist,' says Stafford-Clark. 'He came from the music-hall tradition too. All of those elements were part of his armoury, what he had to offer. The theatre took advantage of those. He was a wonderful presence but he was quite high-maintenance. One evening, when he was quite drunk, he was very bitter about the whole business . . . the music business. He needed to diversify.'

Max Stafford-Clark was due to direct *Serious Money*, a play by Caryl Churchill. '*Serious Money* was about the City,' says Stafford-Clark, who had asked Ian to come up with some songs. 'It dramatized an area that hadn't previously been seen on stage. As the play was being written, Ian was part of the research. We went down to the Futures Exchange,* which was very much where the action was, and people were signalling each other the whole time – mostly Essex boys and girls making lots of money. Ian was a God to those people. We had guest passes and we went down onto the trading floor. They were so intrigued by Ian that they stopped dealing all together, and he was banned from appearing on the floor.'

The two songs for *Serious Money*, written with Mickey Gallagher, enlivened the production and contained Ian's sharpest words for years, sadly never recorded. 'Futures Song' was particularly apposite:

> *I've dealt the gelt below the belt and I'm jacking up*
> *   the ackers,*
> *My front's gone short, fuck off old sport, you're standing*
> *   on my knackers,*
> *I've spilt my guts, long gilt's gone nuts, and I think*
> *   I'm going crackers,*
> *So full of poo, I couldn't screw, I fucked it with my*
> *   backers.*
> *Out! Buy, buy, buy! Leave it!*
> *No! Yes! Cunt!*
> *Four! Five! Sell!*
> *Quick! Prick! Yes! No! Cunt!*

* London International Financial Futures Exchange (LIFFE, pronounced 'life').

> *How hard I dredge to earn my wedge, I'm sharper than*
>   *a knife,*
> *Don't fucking cry, get and buy, Chicago's going rife,*
> *You're back to front, come on you cunt, don't give me*
>   *any strife,*
> *You in or out? Don't hang about, you're on the floor of*
>   *LIFFE!*

Serious Money was a big hit at the Royal Court in March 1987 and won the *Evening Standard* award for best comedy of the year, although it did little to prevent the imminent stock market crash known as 'Black Monday'. When the play later opened off Broadway at the Public Theater in New York, it received a positive review from Frank Rich, the legendary critic of the *New York Times*, who wrote: 'The traders on the floor of LIFFE transform their hand signals and brokerage jargon into a rap number (with lyrics by Ian Dury) that really makes their business seem, as one character describes it, "a cross between roulette and Space Invaders".'

But when *Serious Money* transferred to Broadway's Royale Theater the following year, the show closed after only fifteen performances, due in part to a language barrier that Ian had experienced some years earlier when he toured the USA with Lou Reed. There was also much use of the dreaded 'C-word'. Max Stafford-Clark recalls, 'I heard a woman in the audience say, "Margaret, I couldn't understand one word of that whole half, and the one word I could understand I couldn't possibly repeat to you." And the other song Ian wrote to end the show was not quite as good. The producer, Joe Papp, said to me, "The problem with this show, Max, is you got the eleven o'clock song at nine o'clock – what you gonna do about that?" He was right.'

Despite the Broadway debacle, Ian had secured a modest foothold as a writer of libretto, with Stafford-Clark at least. Years earlier, at the height of his fame, Ian had apparently turned down an opportunity to work with Andrew Lloyd-

Webber on the musical *Cats*. 'I said no straight off,' he would tell Deborah Ross of the *Independent*. 'I hate Andrew Lloyd Webber. He's a wanker, isn't he? Every time I hear "Don't Cry for Me Argentina" I feel sick, it's so bad. He got Richard Stilgoe to do the lyrics in the end, who's not as good as me. He made millions out of it. He's crap, but he did ask the top man first!'

Lloyd Webber notwithstanding, Ian and Mickey Gallagher were now an established songwriting team. Mickey was quite happy to drive to Digby Mansions from his home in Essex to work with Ian. He was also willing to accompany him on his daily walks or run the odd errand. It was the start of a long, close working relationship in which Gallagher would be forced to witness the best and worst of his writing partner. 'Contrary to the way I sometimes come across when I talk about Ian – like I'm "Mr Angry" – we were good mates,' says Mickey. 'This was because he allowed me to hate him.'

Ian and Mickey became mentors to each other and would enjoy walking in Richmond Park so that Ian could get his much-needed physical exercise. The arrangement would continue from Monday to Friday for the next eight years, sometimes taking in visits to Roehampton Hospital, where Ian would get his callipers made. He no longer tended to wear a lisle stocking under the support to prevent chaffing because technology had moved on. 'But the leg irons had a life,' says Mickey. 'It used to take ages, shaving bits off the calliper to make it comfortable. When we were out we never talked music, we talked about nature and what was happening in the world, it was lovely. Ian used to like me driving him through Buckinghamshire at 30 miles an hour. People would be tooting us from behind, and Ian would say, "Don't go any faster!"'

Although Mickey enjoyed working with Ian, it was not always easy to get away at the end of a long day. Sometimes he could escape before 'the night shift' – usually meaning when Ian's other co-writer of the period – Merlin Rhys-Jones – arrived. 'At 6 p.m. Ian would say, "You couldn't get me a few beers, could you?" I'd get him the beers, and then he would say, "Give us half an hour." His biggest indulgence was your time. He would want to keep you sitting there as long as possible, even when you'd been with him all day. Then it would be, "Can't you stay here until Merlin gets here?" I'd meet Merlin on the stairs. Phew!'

Despite Ian's initial reluctance to play Japan, he and the Blockheads visited the country in June 1987, giving concerts in Osaka and Tokyo. As usual, there was tension between Ian and Davey. When Ian was shown a video from the previous year of the Blockheads playing behind Kiyoshiro Imawano, he spotted Davey in the brass section and muttered under his breath: 'Fucking Davey Payne . . .'As Ian continued to make snide remarks, Davey reached boiling point, suddenly smashing a beer bottle and pointing it in Ian's direction. 'We jumped in,' remembers Mickey Gallagher. 'The Japanese were loving it: "Lock 'n' loll!"!'

Davey Payne had known Ian longer than anyone else in the inner circle and had a most perceptive insight into Ian's psyche. 'He may have been seen as the leader of the group, but inside he was still like the Plato guy in *Rebel Without a Cause*, tagging along and looking up to everybody. His dream was to be the leader of a gang, and the only way he could do it was with his mind. He knew that, and that's what made him aggressive.' But Davey still loved to see Ian enjoying himself at Digby Mansions, playing tapes for mates during the mainly friendly drinking sessions. Davey remembers that Ian would keep going when everyone else was passing out and would 'put you to bed like an old mum and place a bucket nearby in case you felt sick'.

Ian would be on his best behaviour when Peggy or Betty and the kids visited, and there would be expensive cake from Fortnum and Mason with Earl Grey tea, but as soon as they left, it was: 'OK, Davey, let's get drunk on Jack Daniel's!' Sometimes it would 'go off'. Davey, who at that point had not been drinking for fifteen years, remembers a session when the Strangler turned up. 'I said something to Ian, maybe about his mum, and suddenly he turned. He was winding me up, knowing that the Strangler was there. I slammed my glass down on the table, and the whiskey went shooting over everything. Ian said, "Right Strangler, get him!" Strangler grabbed me round the throat, and his black painted finger nails were piercing my neck. Then Ian shouted, "Off him, Strangler!" Ian staggered out into the hallway, then suddenly his legs were in the air, and he was lying on the stone floor with a broken tooth. The Strangler was crawling around, looking for pieces of tooth.'

19

'Ian Wrecks Bash in Rhythm Stick Row'

The Czech Republic, August 1987. The bar of Prague's Hotel Panorama was packed with East Germans, whose custom it was to cross the border on the weekends to drink cheap beer. Today they found themselves rubbing shoulders with a vast film crew under the direction of Bob Hoskins, in town to film his new movie, *The Raggedy Rawney*. Glancing across the bar, Jenny Cotton noticed that Ian was ordering drinks. He had decided they were going to have champagne because he was due to meet some important people to discuss his next film. He turned to Jenny and asked her to carry the champagne to the table, leaving him free to walk through the packed bar and goose-step past all the Germans. 'That is the kind of nerve he had,' says Jenny, 'he was lucky not to have been beaten up.'

The Raggedy Rawney tells the story of a young army deserter who joins a gypsy caravan and evades capture by dressing as a girl and being adopted by the travellers as a 'Rawney' – in gypsy culture a half-mad woman with psychic powers. Ian had a small part as 'Weazel'. Filming often involved long hours of inactivity, and, when boredom set in, Ian's thoughts turned to the bottle, although he disciplined himself during most of his time in Prague. 'If I drink I'm out of the game,' Ian told me. 'It's boring, locations . . . sixty noisome mates of Hoskins, that's a lot of cockneys.' There were frequent disturbances at the Hotel Panorama caused by the tension between the British film crew and the German contingent singing, 'Happy

Birthday, dear Heinzig'. 'Amazingly, it never went off,' said Ian.

On Saturday nights the caterers would throw a party, usually with a theme. 'We had a Roman party,' recalled Ian. 'Hoskins would come down with the laurel leaves on his head. Then we had a beach party – snorkels, flippers and all that caper. I was so bored I started a newspaper called *The Pikey Bugle*. Early mornings were a doddle. There were three yobbos doing the catering. They had half an hour's kip a night. You'd see 'em on the roll run . . . when you go round at three in the morning in the hotel corridor looking for discarded food on trays, 'cos you're hungry – something to soak the alcohol up with. At half-five we'd be off on location, asking catering for an egg and bacon sandwich – Vince the Mince – "Quick Vince, I'm dying!" You get locked into this mad world. Zoë Wannamaker, brilliant actress. "Where's the Jack Daniel's?" I did have a drink one night. I was off-duty watching the explosions. Me Doc Martens were in the camp fire, "Oi, mate, your boots are on fire!"'

Ian enjoyed back-to-back film roles throughout the late 1980s, usually playing minor characters. In *Burning Beds*, however, he would have a starring role as 'Harry Winfield', a kettle drummer who travels to Germany to play with a symphony orchestra. While there, he shacks up with 'Gina', played by Pia Frankenberg, who also wrote and directed the 'comedy'. Filming took place in Germany in the autumn of 1988. While in Hamburg, Ian called his old friend Humphrey Ocean and flew him over from London. 'He needed some support,' says Humphrey. 'Me and Strangler stayed in a hotel on the Reeperbahn, but Ian was at the Four Seasons. We were sitting in a club, and Ian had the Strangler "parked up". There was a German bloke bothering Ian, but Ian was ignoring him. Then suddenly Ian turned to this German and said, "Weren't you the people responsible for Auschwitz?" The German lunged towards him . . . Strangler sees it, jumps over the table. Next thing there's a brawl. Ian was sitting there amongst it all, but nobody was touching him. He didn't spill a drop of his drink.'

Pippa Markham remembers: 'At the end of a day's filming in Hamburg, Ian would get on the tables and do the entire Third Reich. Referring to the Strangler, the club owner said, "Mr Animal can come in any time he wants, but not Mr Dury."' While Pippa was telling me this story, she phoned Frances Tomelty for her recollections of working on *Burning Beds*. Frances recalled: 'Oh God, yes! The female director was trying to get Ian to improvise. He planted both of his feet very firmly on the ground and said, "Sorry love, you're asking me to do jazz. I only do rock 'n' roll."'

Other late-1980s movies included *Die Stimme*, aka *The Voice*, in which Ian played 'Kowalsky', and *Bearskin – An Urban Fairy-tale*, with Ian cast in a minor role as 'Charlie'. *Bearskin* starred Tom Waits. 'He talks like that when he's off-duty as well, I couldn't believe it,' said Ian of Waits' guttural drawl. Ian also appeared in *The Cook, the Thief, His Wife and Her Lover*, written and directed by Peter Greenaway, a contemporary of Ian's at Walthamstow School of Art. In the 1989 movie, Ian plays 'Terry Fitch', a low-life villain. Michael Gambon plays 'Albert Spica', the drunken, bullying proprietor of a gourmet restaurant, who terrorizes his customers. He also taunts his wife, the apparently infertile 'Georgina', played by Helen Mirren. In order to exact revenge on her oafish husband, 'Georgina' enjoys spontaneous sex with 'Michael' (Alan Howard) in the restaurant's various cubby holes.

Helen Mirren has since stated that she 'quite fancied' Ian during his hit-making years but was 'far too intimidated by his image' to ever get in touch, but *The Cook, the Thief* eventually brought them together. Despite minimal onscreen interaction, Ian and Helen formed a brief friendship and attended a Royal Academy of Arts dinner together. Mirren reportedly visited Digby Mansions on several occasions and once accompanied Ian to Dr Kit's house in Putney, where she enjoyed a late-night dip in the hydrotherapy pool. Close observers note that Ian was somewhat intimidated by Mirren, who could match him verbally to the point where his only recourse was to 'pour scorn' on her.

Also appearing in *The Cook, the Thief*, as an extra, was Ian's minder, the Strangler. Ian had sacked the Strangler on a number of occasions, but in 1985 invited him back into the fold to keep an eye on fourteen-year-old Baxter, then staying with his father at Digby Mansions. 'Me and this guy [Rush] bonded,' Baxter would tell the *Independent*'s Glyn Brown in 2002. 'He was six foot eight, covered in tattoos. He'd drive me to tutorial college every day, then cook me pie and chips when I got back. I was invited into his world and I saw a few weird sights at a young age. He became my best mate.'

Friends expressed concern that Ian had entrusted the care of his teenage son to the wayward Strangler, but Ian considered him to be a loyal and dependable aide. With his typically lateral logic, Ian figured that, actually, *Baxter was looking after the Strangler*! 'It was the same with Spider Rowe,' says Ed Speight. 'Ian always considered himself to be minding his minders and he'd go into that convoluted logic. He had that attachment to criminal matters and glorifying the underworld, it always intrigued him. He used to say that if he hadn't got the polio then he would have probably been a bank robber. I said, "Don't talk rubbish," and he would quote George Bernard Shaw* at me.'

Pete 'Strangler' Rush was asthmatic and would apparently get through four Ventolin inhalers a day plus a bottle of Scotch. In 1989, his lifestyle caught up with him, and he died from a heart attack while in police custody in his home town

---

* Ian's favourite quote about criminality was, in fact: 'The criminal is the creative artist; the detective only the critic' (G. K. Chesterton). He also liked: 'A neurotic is a man who builds a castle in the air. A psychotic is the man who lives in it. A psychiatrist is the man who collects the rent' (Jerome Lawrence).

of Bournemouth. Baxter and Ian attended Rush's funeral on 17 September. Ian kept in touch with Rush's mother, Marge, for many years thereafter and generously continued to pay her telephone bill.

Any spare time that Ian had during the late 1980s was spent developing *Apples*, set to become his lone foray into the world of writing stage musicals. It was Royal Court Theatre director Max Stafford-Clark who suggested to Ian that he should try his hand at the notoriously challenging medium. Encouraged by Stafford-Clark, Ian took a batch of songs he had been writing with Mickey Gallagher and attempted to build a story around them. Ian would play the central character, 'Byline Brown', a tabloid journalist on the hunt for sex scandals, bent coppers and dodgy MPs, notably 'Hugo Sinister'. 'Ian arranged the songs into a sequence,' says Mickey, 'but there was no real storyline. The producers gave him carte blanche, but Ian had no idea how to write a play or a musical. The director, Simon Curtis, was so awestruck by Ian that he didn't question anything.'

Advance publicity for *Apples* included an interview on BBC Radio 4's *Loose Ends*, chaired by Ned Sherrin, in which it sounded as if the musical might be a shot in the arm for West End theatre. Auditions and rehearsals began in the spring of 1989 and continued for some months in the gaps in Ian's schedule. Jemima, who was then living at Digby Mansions, remembers Ian talking about the audition process 'day in, day out' and going 'misty-eyed' about actress Frances Ruffelle, who would be playing the part of 'Delilah'. Jemima felt that her father had been taken in by the world of theatrical performers who were going to bring his show to life. 'He was somewhat naive,' says Jemima, 'but charming.'

Ian had always been green about certain aspects of the entertainment business, but such naivety was crucial to the creative process. If he had known then what he knew now, 'Spasticus

Autisticus' would never have left the drawing board, but he was even less clued up about musical theatre.

The soundtrack recording of *Apples* took place at Liquidator Studios in July, for which Ian recruited his former songwriting partner, Mike McEvoy, to play bass. It was the first time they'd met since their bust-up in 1984. The mood was tentative as Ian and Mike got reacquainted, but the old animosity was quickly forgotten as the music took shape. 'Ian liked working with me,' says Mike. 'I was quick and good-natured. He paid me good money.'

In August Ian signed his contract for the show's three-month run at the Royal Court Theatre. *Apples* opened on 4 September, but ticket sales were patchy and reviews poor. Jack Tinker of the *Daily Mail* referred to 'the barrow-load of dispiriting mush to be found in Ian Dury's half-baked musical'. The *Financial Times* called it 'a feeble night out'. Ian was devastated by its failure at the box office and felt even more let down by critics who panned what was the culmination of many years' work.

Jemima was working at the Royal Court as an usher and witnessed countless performances of her father's show. 'Some nights I would be sitting in the stalls, hoping the audience would laugh at the jokes, but it was a painful experience all round. There was a lack of control over the end product, and dad didn't know how to write a script. People didn't step in early enough to tell him about the weak parts. I'd seen about 200 plays and I knew *Apples* was on a very simplistic level. The characters were two-dimensional, archetypal. He sent me a postcard saying: "To my daughter, the greatest critic." It was slightly sarcastic, but a bit of a nod from him realizing how much I was noticing about what he did. There would be about twenty-five people in a matinee, it was excruciating.'

Apples had been funded and produced by Royal Court patron Diana Bliss, who put a tab on the bar at a pub near the Royal Court for the cast and friends to get 'bladdered' every night after the show, which presumably helped to keep up morale. Meanwhile, the Royal Court was coping with the worst financial situation they had ever experienced as Ian's musical failed to attract customers in sufficient number.

Back in 1976, when he was considering writing 'a musical about prison' in conjunction with Fred Rowe, Ian confidently wrote to Roberta Bayley: 'The basic essentials for musicals are fairly straightforward. I can write to themes very easily. The difficulty will be in making sure that the music is good and proper, and not some clanky old pit orchestra reading boring dots. The only way to do it is to star in it as well, so I'll have to always do musicals that limp.' *Apples* did indeed limp, but the show completed its three-month run. Many old friends showed up to see it, including Fred Rowe, who hadn't spoken to Ian for eight years following 'the HMV incident' of 1981. Another friend, Sophy Tilson, reappeared during the *Apples* run. In the five years since meeting Ian at Gold Diggers in Chippenham, Sophy had studied sculpture at the Chelsea School of Art, where she attained a BA, and the Accademia di Belle Arti in Florence. After the show she went backstage and said to Ian, 'You don't remember me, do you?' Ian took her to one side and said, 'Go on, give me your number, Soph.'

Ian and Sophy started courting and they fell in love. Sophy, who then lived in south London, recalls: 'I had this crazy old boyfriend from Italy who kept threatening me with physical violence. It was over, but he kept turning up on my doorstep. I told Ian about it, and he said, "What you need is a Rottweiler, a minder, or . . . you can come and live with me."' Sophy moved into Digby Mansions with her sculpture materials and met Jemima, who was still staying with Ian and working at the Royal Court.

The aura of *Apples* hung around Digby Mansions long after its demise, with posters from the stage show adorning the walls and lyric sheets littering the floor, artefacts that served to remind Ian that he was not the invincible wordsmith – 'the top man in his field' – he'd once considered himself to be. Mortified

LIMOUSINE INTERIOR, NEW YORK CITY, 1978:
(L–R) DENISE ROUDETTE, IAN, KOSMO VINYL, PEARL HARBOUR

QUIET REFLECTION: SITTARD,
NETHERLANDS, 1978

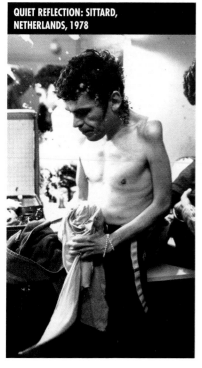

'A LITTLE BIT OF TOMMY COOPER', 1978

IAN WITH HIS *NEW BOOTS AND PANTIES!!* CO-WRITERS, STEPHEN NUGENT (LEFT) AND CHAZ JANKEL (RIGHT)

'MINDING HIS MINDER': IAN WITH FRED 'SPIDER' ROWE

KEEPING THE BLOCKHEADS IN LINE, 1978: (L–R) IAN, JOHNNY TURNBULL, MICKEY GALLAGHER, CHARLEY CHARLES, DAVEY PAYNE, NORMAN WATT-ROY, CHAZ JANKEL

TONIGHT'S PROP – THE INDOOR
PLANT SPRAY: DUBLIN, 1979

PART PEARLY KING,
PART PANTOMIME VILLAIN:
IAN AT THE HEIGHT OF
HIS FAME, DUBLIN, 1979

HE AIN'T HEAVY: SPIDER CARRIES IAN
ONTO THE STAGE, DENMARK, 1981

WITH 'MAGIC' MIKE MCEVOY: IAN DRESSED UP
FOR A ROYAL ACADEMY DINNER, 1983

'BARNEY TOLD ME I'D BEEN A HORRIBLE PIECE OF WORK':
IAN WITH GRAPHICS GENIUS BARNEY BUBBLES, 1983

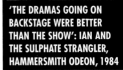

'THE DRAMAS GOING ON
BACKSTAGE WERE BETTER
THAN THE SHOW': IAN AND
THE SULPHATE STRANGLER,
HAMMERSMITH ODEON, 1984

'A WELCOME DEFLECTION OF ATTENTION': BELINDA LEITH RUBS SHOULDERS WITH IAN, 1984

'THEY WANT ME TO HAVE A CIGAR': IAN'S MOVIE DEBUT, ALONGSIDE WALTER MATTHAU IN *PIRATES*, 1986

PEGGY, SO PROUD OF IAN: AT AN *APPLES* AFTER-SHOW PARTY, 1989

BAXTER, JEMIMA AND IAN, HAMPSTEAD, 1994

DOMESTIC BLISS: BILL, ALBERT, IAN, HAMPSTEAD, 1997

UNICEF SPECIAL REPRESENTATIVES, 1998: (L–R) DAME VANESSA REDGRAVE, ALBERT, SOPHY, BILL, LORD BILL DEEDES, IAN

JEMIMA AND IAN, SHEPHERDS BUSH EMPIRE, 1999

MAGNIFICENT TO THE END: LONDON PALLADIUM, 6 FEBRUARY 2000

'WE'RE GONNA HAVE IT PROPER': IAN'S FUNERAL CORTÈGE IN HAMPSTEAD, 5 APRIL 2000

'YOU'RE THE WHY': THE BLOCKHEADS PAY AN EMOTIONAL TRIBUTE TO IAN AT GOLDERS GREEN CREMATORIUM

THE AUTHOR INTERROGATES MOLLY WALKER: IAN'S 'AUNT MOLL' – OVING, 2001

by the bad reviews, he started drinking heavily and didn't stop for nine months He was embittered by the whole experience and went into another deep depression, severing connections with friends and associates. Personal assistant John Wynne, whom Ian nicknamed 'Grey Wolf', was one of the first to walk out, unable to take the verbal lashings any longer. Even friends such as Jock Scot and Smart Mart were not spared in the trail of devastation. Shocked and upset over the failure of his musical, he was on a mission of destruction, systematically cutting himself away from his past. 'It was critical death,' says Sophy, of the response to *Apples*. 'He absolutely couldn't believe it. He couldn't control the depression, it was bigger than him. There was heavy drinking every day. It was too destructive, so we decided to part. He told me and Jemima we should go. He was hurting us with his anger.'

Sophy didn't leave Ian – yet – and there were periods of work to take his mind off the pain. In February 1990, he returned to Japan as 'Ian Dury and the Apple Blossom Orchestra', largely driven by his desire to show his daughter Jemima 'the beautiful Japanese countryside'. A little film work dribbled in, including the part of a bartender in *The Rainbow Thief*, which ironically put Ian back in the company of Omar Sharif, with whom he now shared a drink and a laugh. A few years earlier Omar had whacked Ian in a restaurant punch-up.

It happened in 1985. After years of pushing people too far, someone – and not just anyone – had given Ian a black eye. It happened at the chic Mayfair eatery Le Caprice. Ian and Norman Watt-Roy had gone for dinner with Peter Blake and his wife Chrissie. Ian had consumed a few drinks beforehand. From the corner of his eye, he spotted Sharif at a nearby table, accompanied by a young girl (whom he thought he recognized) and two burly minders. Emboldened by alcohol, Ian couldn't resist going over to Sharif's table and telling him that all of the films he'd made since *Lawrence of Arabia* were 'rubbish'. Sharif remained calm at first, but when Ian continued ribbing him, the movie star leapt up from the table and landed his bronzed fist in Ian's face. In the taxi home, Ian proudly told the driver he'd just been 'punched in the teef by Omar Sharif', upon which the cabbie replied, 'That's the most expensive fist you'll ever have in *your* mouth.'

Ian's attitude towards Omar Sharif typified his opinion of any famous person with whom he had briefly come into contact, but not fully endorsed. 'Omar Sharif?' he would say. 'What a cunt!' But, of course, once he'd worked with Sharif, it was: 'My old mate Omar!' Other celebrities received similar treatment. 'Nigel Kennedy? What a wanker!' Until, that is, Kennedy chose one of Ian's records on *Desert Island Discs* and suddenly it became: 'Nigel, a fucking gem!' 'Jools Holland? Another wanker!' 'Paul McCartney? "Yesterday"? It's the sound of sewage,' said Ian, prior to befriending the legendary Beatle some years later.

There was also some light relief amidst the gloom; Ian had turned on his television one August afternoon and seen an advertisement for Edam cheese. He couldn't believe his ears. The narrator's voice sounded just like 'Ian Dury', but he was sure it was not his own work, no matter how many bottles of Beaujolais he'd been knocking back. He called his agent, Pippa Markham, who in turn sought advice from the actor's union, Equity. There was no option but to send a 'cease and desist' letter to the advertiser's agent. Ian's solicitor, John Kennedy, recruited a voice expert to analyse the TV ad as evidence. In his submission, the expert wrote:

> Having seen and heard the commercial myself and know-ing the style and sound of Mr Dury, I must agree with Miss Shelley [voice-over agent at Markham's] that the out-of-vision performer on this commercial performs and sounds very much like Mr Dury and it is my view that any viewer of the commercial might reasonably believe that the per-former in the commercial is Mr Dury, given that Mr Dury has a very individual sound and performance technique.

Whether or not it was your intention to engage an out-of-vision performer to imitate Mr Dury is I believe arguable, but regardless of your intention, I believe that the performer engaged is or could be said to be copying the style of Mr Dury. It is for this reason therefore that Mr Dury's solicitors wrote to you in an attempt to try and discuss this matter further and this is my reason also. Needless to say, both sides could refer this matter to their solicitors, which would be a costly and time-consuming business.

The Edam ad was quickly taken off the air, and Ian received compensation.

Ian's next film was *After Midnight*, starring Hayley Mills and Saeed Jaffrey, a tragicomic drama set in an old hotel, in which Ian played 'Harry', the crippled telephonist. Filming took place at the Fitzpatrick Castle Hotel in Dublin. 'It was a low-budget job,' recalled Ian, 'Saeed Jaffrey really had a go at me.' According to Mickey Gallagher, Jaffrey had come on the set and performed an ancient Indian ritual. 'He smashed a coconut and gave a piece to everyone involved in the production, as a token of good luck. The idea was, and Saeed kindly explained this to us, you were supposed to keep your piece of coconut until the filming was complete. Ian ate his.'

The film's director, Shani Grewal, asked Ian to contribute some music, but Ian didn't 'do music'. Words were his speciality, but he would insist on the credit: 'Words and music by Ian Dury and Mickey Gallagher', thus blurring the lines between their individual roles and claiming spurious credit for compositional skills he didn't possess. Whereas Gallagher was never asked how he came up with the lyrics, which were of course written by Ian, many of the stage directors and producers assumed that Ian's talents were all-encompassing and might say, 'Oh, Ian, your music, it's wonderful,' when his contribution had extended to playing the bongos. 'They were in awe of him,' says Mickey. 'I had to fight for my position, but it was funny when the stage director would say, "Ian, the musical director wants to talk to you." Ian would try to bluff it out, but invariably I'd jump in and save him.'

Mickey Gallagher helped with the *After Midnight* songs, as did former Music Students guitarist Merlin Rhys-Jones. Two numbers, 'Bye Bye Dublin' and 'Quick Quick Slow', plus some incidental music were recorded at Turbot, Tom Robinson's studio in Shepherds Bush. Further recording took place at Jamestown Studio in Whitechapel, where, on 2 September, an incident occurred that cost Ian several hours in police custody. When a recording engineer by the name of Fraser accidentally wiped one of the tracks (instantly earning him the sobriquet 'Fraser the Eraser'), Ian threatened to set fire to the studio. Before Ian could locate a box of matches, Fraser had phoned the police. By the time the cops showed up, Ian was drunk and started asking the policemen if they were 'homosexuals'. 'They were amused at first,' says Merlin, 'but eventually they dragged Ian out and took him to the station.' Following Ian's arrest and removal to Leman Street police station, Baxter and Sophy were contacted at Digby Mansions. They arrived by taxi to hear Ian's anguished cries from the cells, 'Don't beat me!' 'They've taken my shoelaces!' Ian was released without charge in the early hours of the morning, proudly proclaiming, 'Sophy sprang me!'

Ian hadn't seen much of drummer Charley Charles in recent years. Norman kept in touch with him, but otherwise Charley had been out of the picture. Of all of the Blockheads, he was the most militant, ready to down tools if he felt the band weren't getting a fair shake. Despite being one of the greatest drummers on the planet, Charley had been reduced to driving mini-cabs, just as Norman had been seen standing in the dole queue when the session work dried up. It was a crime that such great musicians were out of work, and Ian knew it. It was made worse by the news that Charley had now been diagnosed with cancer.

Ian and the Blockheads planned a series of benefit shows for Charley, but were overtaken by events. 'I think he'd been very ill for a long time,' said Ian, 'but it was only five weeks from the time they discovered it to him dying. He had colon cancer. They can screen for it, but he wasn't getting any medical attention . . . by the time he went to the hospital it had spread quite a lot.' Stunned by Charley's tragic death on 5 September 1990 – just weeks before the benefit concerts were due to occur – the Blockheads joined Charley's family and friends at his funeral at Lambeth Cemetery on 13 September. The wake took place back at Digby Mansions, and many old friends and colleagues attended, including Fred Rowe and Chaz Jankel, just back from the USA. As the drink flowed and the spliff kicked in, Charley's wake climaxed around midnight, by which time Sophy was getting ready to quit Digby Mansions for the peace and quiet of her flat in Wandsworth. She had already made up her mind to leave Ian to his own devices, hoping that Chaz's return to the UK would help him to concoct some exciting new songs for a Blockheads reunion that now appeared to be unstoppable.

To raise some money for their drummer's grieving family, Ian and the Blockheads played three nights at the Forum in Kentish Town, their first London shows together in nearly five years, with drummer Stephen Monti filling in for the late Charley Charles. As soon as the dates were announced it became the hottest ticket in town. 'We hadn't seen each other for ages,' recalls Wilko Johnson, 'but when we played Charley's benefit, the feeling came back.' Ian was so overjoyed to be working again with Chaz and Davey and company that an additional benefit show was arranged to take place at Brixton Academy on 22 December (recorded and released as *Warts and Audience*). Following a tour of Spain in the New Year it looked like Ian and the Blockheads would be reuniting on a permanent basis.

•

Ian added yet another string to his bow when he was asked by London Weekend Television to introduce *Metro*, a series of thirty-minute arts programmes under the aegis of executive producer Melvyn Bragg. On 18 March 1991, Ian met with Bragg to discuss the appointment and was introduced to the show's editor, Nicola Gooch. She wanted to find a presenter who wasn't highbrow or too arty; someone who could make the arts accessible and bring them to a wider audience. 'We met with Ian, and I thought he'd be very good,' says Nicola. 'He'd been an actor, but he hadn't done presenting before, so it was a bit of a risk.'

Despite a £100-a-week wardrobe allowance to find something fancy for his *Metro* appearances, Ian insisted on dressing in black and donning a Blockheads T-shirt. 'He has taken to wearing black since he put on two stone,' wrote Serena Allott in the *Sunday Telegraph*. 'I've been sitting round on my arse drinking too much,' Ian responded. 'When I've lost weight I'll go back to wearing white.' Ian had been fretting over his weight since 1957 when, as a chubby schoolboy, he sought to emulate his rock 'n' roll hero, Gene Vincent. Unable to shake off the puppy fat, he remained cuddlesome throughout his adolescence, and it was not until his early thirties that he began to slim down, following an arduous string of nightly performances with Kilburn and the High Roads. By 1974 his weight had become an obsession, and he remained trim for a decade or more. By the mid-1980s, however, alcohol and middle age had caught up with him, and he found it impossible to shake off the excess pounds.

The first edition of *Metro* on 12 May saw Ian reading his script from an autocue as he nervously introduced singer Alison Moyet, but he would soon thrive in interview mode. A discussion with the lively Miriam Margolyes went well, largely due to Ian's willingness to listen to the actress's flamboyant stories. 'It was wonderful watching Ian trying to have a conversation with somebody,' says Humphrey Ocean. 'He'd never had a con-

versation with anybody in his life! It was one long monologue!
It was torture for Ian, waiting to speak.'

In a later edition of *Metro*, Ian was perhaps overly relaxed,
greeting veteran actor Anthony Hopkins with an embarrass-
ingly familiar 'nice to meet you, mate'. It had been a scoop for
Metro to get Hopkins on the show the week that his hit movie
Silence of the Lambs was due to open, but Ian talked about himself, even to the extent of comparing notes with the famous
thespian. 'I went for an audition last week for *Dracula* and I had
to play a loony in a cell,' Ian told Hopkins, who was wondering why he wasn't being asked about his new blockbuster. But
Hopkins remained the complete professional, responding with
warm gestures, momentarily bestowing upon Ian his seal of
approval.

Metro kept Ian in the public eye, but he prayed that his off-
screen exploits would escape newspaper coverage for fear of his
mother reading about his occasional bad behaviour. Although
it is doubtful Peggy would have ever bought a copy of *News of
the World*, there was always the chance that she could have
caught sight of its 19 May headline: 'Ian wrecks bash in rhythm
stick row – another belting exclusive'. As part of his *Metro* contract, Ian had been asked to present a feature on the English
National Opera's production of *Timon* at the London Coliseum.
It was an optimistic brief, but LWT had decided Ian was the man
for the job and sent Melvyn Bragg's limo to collect him from
Hammersmith for the opening night. As the curtain rose, Ian
was in the front stalls, accompanied by *Metro* editor Nicola
Gooch. Immediately behind them sat the opera's composer,
Stephen Oliver, whom Ian was due to interview later that week.

Ten minutes into the first act, Ian became exasperated and,
during a particularly quiet passage, exclaimed, 'I'm not fucking
staying for this, it's about fucking cottaging!' His outburst was
causing consternation amongst the audience, who mainly consisted of friends and patrons of the Coliseum who would have
been pleased to see the opera featured on television. Nicola tried

to pacify Ian, but before long he was out of his seat and headed for the bar. By the time that the interval drinks were being served, Ian was stuck into a bottle of champagne. Then he visited the lavatory and was delighted to discover that the attendant, an elderly lady named Ivy, was also a callipered polio victim. He dragged her back to the bar, announcing to Nicola, 'Meet Ivy, she's a raspberry ripple like me! We're having champagne!'

Ian started knocking it back big time. 'I'm not fucking going back in there, I'm staying with Ivy!' he shouted when the bell rang for the second act. Nicola tried to force him back into the auditorium, but Ian refused to budge. She returned to her seat, so she could at least tell him what happened in the next act, but by the end of the performance Ian was rolling drunk, still with Ivy. The opera glitterati looked on as flunkies carried silver trays laden with food for the first-night party in the foyer. A girl came out of the lighting box and recognized Ian. She said, 'You're Ian Dury, you must come and meet my father.' Ian turned round and saw a tall, rather distinguished-looking gentleman who had proudly come to see his daughter operating the lights at the opera. Ian greeted him, saying, 'Tell you what, mate, shall I show you how far I can spit? Let's have a spitting contest!' 'Ian spat across the full length of the room,' recalls Nicola, 'right into the man's face. He was horrified.'

The bar refused to serve Ian any more drinks. At the height of the reception he was swinging his stick around and prodding people in the back, asking for cigarettes. Gradually everybody moved away until he was alone, surrounded by a wide space in the middle of the room. 'I couldn't wait to see what would happen next,' says Nicola. 'The front-of-house people asked us to leave – I think they thought I was Ian's moll, because I was wearing a leather jacket – so I asked them if they could help me get him out, as I couldn't really cope with him. He started being really horrible and abusive to me, swaying and staggering. I said, "Look Ian, on Friday you've got to interview the man who wrote this opera. You must leave now otherwise he is going to back out of the show."'

Security arrived and picked Ian and Nicola up by their armpits and took them into a corridor, as Melvyn Bragg looked on, appalled. Ian, still spitting and cursing, fell over, only to be kicked by a security man, who shouted, 'Get up, you fucking cripple!' Nicola exploded and pushed the man against the wall, yelling, 'Don't you dare talk to him like that!' On the other side of the double doors, the row could be heard by the opera-goers, one of whom called the police. Ian and Nicola were escorted from the Coliseum, out into the pouring rain. Ian leant against a wall and, as he fell onto the pavement, Nicola hailed a taxi. 'I took him back to Digby Mansions and literally put him to bed,' says Nicola. 'I took his calliper off and everything. I was really pissed off with him but, as I tucked him in, feeling slightly maternal – I think Ian had that sort of effect on people – I said, "OK, I'm going now," and as I said it, he took my hand and replied, "Nicola, I just want to say something to you. Don't fall in love with me, will you?"'

20

The Passing Show

The *After Midnight* recordings of 1990 would become the basis
of Ian's next album, *Bus Driver's Prayer*. Ian had no recording
contract at the time, and the tracks were self-funded. Fans had
hoped that it would signal the return of Ian and the Blockheads
as a recording act. Although Messrs Gallagher, Turnbull and
Payne all appeared on the album, they were rarely to be found
in the same studio at the same time. Chaz Jankel had contributed some keyboard and guitar parts, but Ian wouldn't
allow any of the material he'd co-written with Chaz to appear
on the album, favouring songs he'd concocted with Mickey Gallagher. 'Ian omitted the Chaz Jankel songs from *Bus Driver's* on
purpose,' says Mickey, 'to demonstrate that he was in control.'

Ian was far from ready to commit to a full-blown reunion,
explaining that he needed to select musicians according to the
demands of each song. It was a neat way of side-stepping 'the
Blockheads issue' while peppering the credits with their names.
When it came to the drums, Ian insisted on using a machine,
even though a number of hot drummers, including Steve White
from Paul Weller's band, had been involved in the demos. 'Ian
loved that Alesis drum machine,' recalls Merlin Rhys-Jones. 'He
was intrigued by the endless programming possibilities. Being
a percussionist himself, he would always get on drummers'
cases, even Charley Charles had suffered from it.'

Bus Driver's Prayer (which would be released on Jake Riviera's Demon Records in 1992), included the songs: 'That's

Enough of That', written with Mickey and Merlin, which mirrored 'Reasons to Be Cheerful', in that Ian presented a list of the mundane things in life of which he might easily tire: cornflakes, commuting, the office, pub grub; 'Bill Haley's Last Words', a rap based on an obscure reference to Haley's post 'Rock Around the Clock' days in Mexico, interspersed with brief snatches of the Haley hits that Ian knew intimately from his schooldays, and 'Poor Joey' – prime Dury humour, as Ian climbed inside a bird's brain and contemplated the daily routine of the average budgerigar, including 'at least half-an-hour trying to undo my catch'. And how was Joey expected to speak, with 'half a ton of cuttlefish stuck in his beak'?

For 'O'Donegal', Ian returned to the land of his forefathers to sing about his love for the Irish countryside. 'Our families were from neighbouring villages nearby,' says co-writer Gallagher. 'Ian was Protestant, I was Catholic. We felt we had roots there. Ian wanted to put bagpipes on the track. We drove to a hotel and there was a piper doing a wedding, so we thought we'd record him in the woods. We took him up there with a beautiful microphone, but everyone was walking their dogs. They were barking and howling, so we couldn't get a decent recording. When we eventually managed to capture a perfect take, the piper asked, "Was that all right?" over the last dying note!'

Despite a couple of childhood holidays in the Finn Valley, Donegal was a long way from home. Ian was in more familiar territory with 'Poo-Poo in the Prawn', possibly the first rock song to tackle the subject of sewage, in which Ian informed us that he'd been down to the beach and encountered human excrement in the ocean and that, although the 'turds were teeny tiny', they all 'fucked up the briny'! It was definitely a case of 'too much information', but his observations were hilarious.

Ian's coarse poetry was still flowing nicely. The album's title track, 'Bus Driver's Prayer', was an amusing monologue based on the Lord's Prayer, set to musical backing and seemingly genuine studio laughter, similar to the version to be found on the *Apples* soundtrack. Ian had been reciting 'The Prayer' on stage since his Kilburns days, but its origin is uncertain.*

> *Our father who art in Hendon*
> *Harrow be thy name*
> *Thy Kingston come*
> *Thy Wimbledon*
> *In Erith as it is in Hendon*
> *Give us this day our Berkhamsted*
> *And forgive us our Westminsters*
> *As we forgive those who Westminster against us*
> *Lead us not into Temple station*
> *But deliver us from Ealing*
> *For thine is the Kingston*
> *The Purley and the Crawley*
> *For Iver and Iver*
> *Crouch End*

Listening to the songs on *Bus Driver's Prayer* it's easy to see why stage director Max Stafford-Clark recruited Ian and Mickey Gallagher to write songs for his production of *A Joviall Crew* (or *The Merry Beggars*) for the Royal Shakespeare Company. Written c.1641 by the Jacobean dramatist Richard Brome, the play, explained Stafford-Clark, 'was about a group of beggars . . . Ian came up to Stratford and wrote three or four songs for it – cockney rhyming slang comes from thieves' talk and beggars' talk. Ian threw himself into it. He was quite well-read and articulate – the "East End lad" was a cover-up. He came and lived in Stratford, and all these young actors would be hanging out with him. He was the life and soul of the season.'

That February, the *Joviall Crew* rehearsals took place in Clapham. They involved vocal coaching sessions for the cast,

---

* 'The Bus Driver's Prayer' is thought to have been written by the jazz pianist George Shearing, when he lived in London in the 1940s.

with Michael Tubbs, musical director of the Royal Shakespeare Company, taking charge. Ian, Mickey and Max were in the stalls, making notes and commenting on the suitability of the various singers, when Tubbs started having problems with his new electronic keyboard. 'Get your finger out!' shouted Ian. Tubbs was displeased by Ian's heckling and threatened to leave the RSC, having never been so insulted in all his life. Ian was persuaded to apologize so that the rehearsals could continue and *A Joviall Crew* opened at the Swan Theatre, Stratford-upon-Avon, on 13 April.

Ian's fiftieth birthday party at Deals restaurant in the Chelsea Harbour was to be a grand affair. Organized by Baxter, it was a chance for family and friends to toast their beloved Ian. Sound engineer Ian 'Horny' Horne made an impassioned if slightly off-the-wall speech. There was no shortage of girlfriends in Ian's life at the time; he was dating television executive Elaine Gallagher, who was unable to attend the bash due to her commitments at the Cannes film festival, but he was also seeing Delphi Newman, whom he brought to the party. After the dinner, Ian invited a number of the revellers back to Digby Mansions, where Sophy Tilson made a surprise appearance. During a long conversation, Ian convinced Sophy that she should try for a place at the Royal College of Art to pursue sculpture. Sophy enrolled that summer.

Ian had now been living at Digby Mansions for nine years and the flat was sorely in need of redecoration. He had already taken exception to the remarks of a visiting journalist who described the place as 'dingy'. His friend Jenny Forrest, daughter of his hydro-therapist 'Dr Kit', remembers: 'He liked things clean but not in an organized way. The flat deteriorated around him, but it got more and more character. Over the years, the wallpaper started to come loose. The cobwebs had grown across the carpet, it had changed colour.'

Unable to face the inevitable disruption, Ian decided to vacate while the decorating work was carried out. On 18 June 1992, he moved into a bungalow at Strawberry Acre Farm in Charvil, near Reading in Berkshire, for the purpose of writing songs with Chaz. He originally intended to rent the property for seven weeks, but would stay there rather longer, despite the fact that the outdoor pool – its principal attraction – was too cold to use most of the time. 'I'd say, "Take it for a month,"' recalls Ian's accountant Ronnie Harris, 'and he would take it for six months, and before you blink it's a year. Ian always had to have a pool, he felt it was the best thing for his leg, for the polio, but of course it added to the cost. He felt he needed the place to write, but you suddenly find that planes go over it and that's no good. There was outflow and we had to balance the books.'

Despite Ronnie Harris's fiscal concerns, Ian's creative juices started to flow once he was away from the distractions of London. He invited Chaz Jankel out to 'the gravel belt' and they worked on new songs including 'Christopher True', 'Come and Find Me' and 'You Mustn't', the latter being a play on Jenny Cotton's habit of reminding Ian 'you must!' Countless hours were spent trying to perfect 'A Million Grooves in the Naked City', but it never came up to Ian's expectations and, like many of the songs written during this period, would never be recorded beyond the demo stage.

That summer Ian and the Blockheads appeared at 'Madstock', a music festival in London's Finsbury Park headlined by Madness. Also on the bill was the former Smiths star Morrissey. As he walked on stage that afternoon, Morrissey earned a quick 'Good luck, mate' from Ian. 'It was like the curse of doom,' says Ingrid Mansfield-Allman. 'Morrissey was bottled off. What Ian really meant when he said "Good luck, mate", was "See you in hell".'

In September, Chaz and Ian had one of their periodic fallings-out, prompting caustic columnist Julie Burchill to describe them as 'the Burton and Taylor of the pop world'. Chaz quit Charvil, and Ian immediately called Merlin Rhys-Jones, with whom he went on to compose 'Age of Steam', 'You're Nasty', 'The Ghost of Rock 'n' Roll' and the curiously titled 'Dick the Dancing Durex'. 'Ian sometimes referred to himself as "Durex",' says Merlin. 'The song unambiguously promoted contraception, so Ian didn't feel it was right for an album, a view that I think Mariella Frostrup shared when she visited Charvil. Another one we worked on was "Sur le Plage with Marge", inspired by the Strangler's mum, whom Ian would phone from time to time.'

Friends and relatives were summoned out to Charvil, and occasional visitors included Peggy, Smart Mart, Davey Payne and Ian's then girlfriend, Elaine Gallagher. Fred Rowe also turned up. He recalls: 'We spoke for eight hours. It was such an interesting conversation. He said it was a shame we'd wasted all those years. I told him I loved him, and he was my best ever pal. It had nothing to do with his fame. He said, "I look on you as my left leg and left arm; the other parts of my body I can't use."'

One of Chaz Jankel's abiding memories of staying at Charvil was the soup Ian made. 'It was this amazing vegetable soup, six pounds of cheddar . . . cream . . . great soup. It was the only time I ever saw him prepare anything to eat, but it had so many colours it looked like a Rembrandt.' Others have made less than complimentary comments about Ian's culinary skills. 'His tomato soup,' recalls Merlin, 'was so concentrated it stuck your tongue to your uvula. He once told me he tried to roast a smoked chicken for Christmas and was surprised when it tasted horrible. "I even made gravy," he said, still disappointed.'

After nine months at Charvil, Ian returned to his freshly decorated apartment at Digby Mansions. Within five days he was whisked off to Scotland to film his part as 'Dr Reid' in the BBC's production of Boswell and Johnson's *Tour of the Western Isles*. This was swiftly followed by the filming of *Skallagrigg*, directed by Richard Spence for BBC television. The story told of a legendary, mysterious force that promised protection for the disabled. *Skallagrigg* mixed professional actors, including Bernard Hill and Richard Briers, with non-professionals, many of whom were disabled themselves. Ian found himself in the middle of the mix and, although he played the part of 'Rendell', a sadistic bully who terrorized the inmates in a 1930s asylum, he was fêted on set by the disabled cast members. 'Ian was very good with them,' says Mickey, 'but a lot of them were verging on the "touch me/heal me" vibe. Ian would walk amongst them.'

When asked how he got so much film work, Ian would say, 'Because I've got a good agent.' Pippa Markham says, 'I loved having Ian to work with. There was no manifestation of ego; he was always very grateful for everything one did and he had a sense of humour and a healthy cynicism.' To add to Ian's hectic schedule, Max Stafford-Clark had put his name forward to write songs for *The Queen and I*, a stage show to be based on Sue Townsend's story of the same name. On 29 April, Ian and Mickey Gallagher met with the authoress at a Chinese restaurant in Leicester to discuss the proposed work and were given the go-ahead. Stafford-Clark was also about to engage Ian and Mickey to write music for the Royal Shakespeare Company's production of *The Country Wife*, a Restoration comedy written around 1672 by William Wycherley.

With *The Queen and I* and *The Country Wife* in prospect and *A Joviall Crew* due to open in London, Ian and Mickey were becoming deeply entrenched in Stafford-Clark's theatrical world and his quest to bring half-forgotten plays from the seventeenth century to a wider audience. Ian missed the rock 'n' roll life, but in the absence of a proper record deal he would happily settle for hanging out in Stratford-upon-Avon, into which he injected an inevitable craziness. TV and film work continued to pour in, notably the role of De Flores in Marcus Thompson's film version of *Middleton's Changeling*, which started shooting on 7 May. Everything was sailing along nicely, but Ian's boat was about to be rocked.

On 14 May 1993, Peggy Dury suffered a severe stroke at her flat in Fitzjohn's Avenue. Ian was shocked to find her unconscious on the bathroom floor when he called to visit later that day. Peggy was taken to the Royal Free Hospital and then transferred to a post-stroke hospital annex nearby. Within days, her empty flat was badly burgled. Ian decided he had to move in so that he could keep an eye on the place and also be close to the hospital, where he visited her daily. On 20 July, he gathered together some clothes and possessions and moved into her flat, simultaneously swapping Richmond Park for Hampstead Heath for his daily constitutionals. Peggy was later taken into Compton Lodge, a nursing home which was close to the flat where she had lived with Bill nearly sixty years earlier.

Having moved to Fitzjohn's Avenue, Ian met one of Hampstead's more eccentric residents, George Weiss, better known as 'Rainbow George' of the Rainbow Dream Ticket party. Weiss was an anarchic fringe politician and, as 'George from Hampstead', a serial radio phone-in caller who had stood as a parliamentary candidate in countless general elections but had never polled more than a handful of votes. He was a friend and neighbour of the comedian Peter Cook and met Ian at a party to mark the launch of the *Derek and Clive Get the Horn*, a video showcasing Cook's lewd routines with Dudley Moore. Ian was one of dozens of celebrities invited to the high-profile bash, where attendees included Keith Richards, Ronnie Wood and numerous well-known comedians. After chucking-out time, the party continued until dawn at Cook's Hampstead home, just yards from Ian's flat in Fitzjohn's Avenue. Weiss cornered Ian and bent his ear with political theories and his unique vision of Hampstead as 'the magic mountain'. Ian was nonplussed, but he and Weiss became good friends.

Throughout the summer of 1993, Ian and Mickey Gallagher refined their songs for Max Stafford-Clark's production of *The Country Wife* with the Royal Shakespeare Company. As writers they'd been summoned to Stratford-upon-Avon, where the play opened in August, but Ian was naturally consumed with his mother's illness. There were frequent trips back to London to visit Peggy and also visits from Sophy Tilson, who had re-appeared in Ian's life that summer after he had attended her first-year show at the Royal College of Art in June.

As well as being Ian's consistently loyal co-writer, Mickey Gallagher had also been his right-hand man for some eight years. Although he savoured Ian's company, Mickey felt a sense of relief when Derek Hussey appeared on the scene. Known to his friends as 'Derek the Draw', Hussey was a south London R&B musician who met Ian through a mutual friend and had started visiting him socially at Charvil and Digby Mansions earlier that year, often driving him to Hampstead to see Peggy. 'Mickey got busy organizing a few more gigs for the band, so we started sharing the duties,' recalls Derek.

When Ian asked Derek to go on the road with him, Derek insisted that he wasn't to go on the payroll. He was a friend who enjoyed Ian's company and particularly appreciated being included in all of Ian's conversations with others. 'We were mates,' says Derek, 'and, by not taking any pay, I didn't come in for any of the canings that his previous employees came in for. If we were sitting around on a Sunday afternoon listening to jazz, Ian would get a "nifty fifty" out and send me round to Oddbins for a couple of bottles of bubbly.'

Derek would quickly see active service with Ian on sporadic dates with the Blockheads and at Shepperton Studios, where Ian filmed his part as 'Geiger' in the Sylvester Stallone movie *Judge Dredd*. The role, Ian reckoned, was the eighth in which he'd been required to smoke a cigar, unshaven. 'If you're smoking a cigar in a film – twelve hours on *Judge Dredd* – at the end of the day I have thirty-two different cigars going, on a little shelf under the table where I kept them all because they say, "In the next scene it's got to be shorter", to keep the conti-nuity going. Then I get shot, and the geezer takes it out of my mouth, and they might not shoot it chronologically, and you do that stuff yourself if you're a pro. My God . . . they want me to have a cigar!'

Ian's bachelor existence at Fitzjohn's Avenue was brief. In February 1994, Sophy Tilson attended London's Tate Gallery to view the 'Picasso: Sculptor/Painter' exhibition (later to be dubbed 'Sex and Jugs and Pots and Bowls' in Scotland's *Sunday Herald*!). 'I took my sketch book, but one of the attendants told me to stop drawing,' recalls Sophy. 'I couldn't believe it. Students are always allowed to draw in art galleries. He didn't give a reason, he just said, "There's a new rule." It escalated. I was shouting my head off and said, "I'm not leaving until you get [gallery director] Nick Serota. I'm not moving, you cannot say that students can't draw." There were all these attendants, and they got someone down. The *Independent* phoned me and asked me about the incident. It was in the paper the next day, and Ian saw it and got very excited. He called me.'

Thus Ian and Sophy were reunited after a break of over three years and proceeded to live together at Fitzjohn's Avenue. 'I was in love with Ian,' continues Sophy. 'My friends told me, "You want to get married and have kids? He's the last person on earth . . ." I thought, "No, he's a good guy, the way he treats his children and Betty, you can't get better than that." Meeting his mum and seeing what an intelligent base he came from . . . I wanted to rescue him as well. There was a huge physical and mental challenge. He'd had all these dodgy birds, I came back determined.' By the time of her degree show in June 1994, Sophy was pregnant. She was twenty-nine years old, and Ian, a family man at heart, was fifty-two and delighted.

Betty had remained a big part of Ian's life following their separation and eventual divorce in 1985. Of course, as the parents of Jemima and Baxter, they found much to talk about, and there were numerous occasions when Betty and Ian came into contact over practical matters. This would often result in Betty bumping into Ian's latest girlfriend, such as the occasion when he was living at Oval Mansions and Betty dropped by to donate some kitchen utensils. Denise Roudette opened the door, and the two women became friends, empathizing with each other over the ups and downs of living with Ian. Years later, when Betty drove Ian and Jemima to the airport for their trip to Japan, she encountered Sophy Tilson at Digby Mansions and once again struck up a friendship.

There was no jealousy on Betty's part; she still cared about Ian and he had undying love for her. 'Mum was quite an extrovert trapped in an introvert's life,' remembers Jemima. 'She was subsumed by everyone else's larger lives, and I suspect a lot of the time she was quite depressed. She was always trying to better herself, going on little courses to get jobs, but she felt she had learning difficulties. Her whole world was related to painting. She could seem quite downtrodden about things, but at the same time she was so graceful and able to defuse a situation. People adored her.'

No one adored Betty as much as Ian. He was distraught when she died on 2 October 1994, aged fifty-two. She had been feeling unwell for two years, originally suspecting cystitis. A couple of visits to a doctor in Newport, to where Betty had returned following the death of her father, resulted in only the briefest investigation of the problem. It was not in her nature to push for a second opinion, but by early 1994 the pain had spread to her back and she was diagnosed with bladder cancer. Ian and Sophy travelled to Wales to see Betty before she died and found she had not lost her sense of humour; when told that Ian and Sophy were expecting a child, Betty remarked, 'Blimey, he's at it again!'

Following Betty's death and Peggy's worsening condition, Ian tried to distract himself by going on the road, but a number of dates were cancelled because of poor ticket sales. On 17 December, he flew to Bilbao for a show with the Blockheads but when he returned, Peggy's health had deteriorated considerably. She died on 20 December, aged eighty-four. That Christmas would be the first in a very long time without Peggy present at the family get-together. She had lived for Ian and been his biggest fan, collecting newspaper articles and pictures and following his progress. 'He spoke very grandly of his mum,' says Denise Roudette. 'She held that unique position, and Ian was never ambivalent. He thought she was wonderful. Her gift to him was extraordinary.'

1994 had truly been Ian's *annus horribilis*: within three months he had lost his first wife and his mother, two of the most prominent women in his life. Now he had the love and support of Sophy. Friends noticed that his attitudes started to soften during the grieving process, and the New Year would bring joy.

On 2 January 1995, Ian became a father for the third time when Sophy gave birth to her first child at the Royal Free Hospital. Denise Roudette was in attendance, at Ian's request. 'I'd never given birth before, and Denise had just had a baby,' says Sophy. 'I was going upstairs to the labour ward with Denise on one side and Ian on the other. Suddenly the baby started to arrive . . . I was holding onto their hands as I gave birth. Denise helped out a lot in the early days. We named the boy Bill, after Ian's dad. Everything was really lovely, but emotions were mixed. Ian had to do Bill's birth certificate and his mum's death certificate on the same day. Losing Betty and his mum and then Bill coming along really focused him. It was as if he thought, "Oh shit, I've got to get my act together."'

The old Ian was not too far from the surface though. His tour diary with the Blockheads was now a little fuller than in recent years, perhaps due to a downturn in acting and voice-over commitments – Ian had steadfastly turned down a TV commercial for a well-known brand of chocolate biscuits that required him to sing: 'Hit me with your choccy bick!' In January 1995, he undertook a mini tour of Ireland followed by a festival appearance in Las Palmas, Gran Canaria, an engagement instigated by the Blockheads, each of whom stood to earn a rather useful

£600. Ian was reluctant to play 'Atlantica 95', but was persuaded by the group that it would be the perfect opportunity to warm up for their imminent trip to Japan. The concert took place on the beach, which was not ideal terrain for Ian. After the show, he returned to the hotel and commenced a heavy drinking session. By 2 a.m., he was so drunk that the barman refused to serve him. 'We arranged our morning calls and shuffled off to bed,' recalls Derek Hussey. 'Ian pissed in the lift.'

When the hotel concierge discovered the elevator ashtray full of urine, he exacted his revenge by neglecting to arrange the Blockheads' wake-up calls. Mickey Gallagher stirred early, however, and with a 6. 30 a.m. flight to catch, rushed around waking up his colleagues. He remembers Ian 'with his coat on from the night before, completely pissed', claiming he would get a later flight. 'I told him we had to get home, pack and be ready to go to Japan, but he said, "Fuck off! I'm not going to Japan!" We all got on the rickety bus to the airport and left Ian behind. Suddenly, this car whizzed past the bus. It was Ian, with the promoter, in a BMW.'

The car reached the airport ahead of the bus, Ian having persuaded the promoter to 'drive like a maniac'. When the Blockheads disembarked, Ian was shouting, 'You bastards! You left me behind!' At the airline check-in, Ian continued to scream and wave his stick, in full view of security – 'You fucking cunts!' The Blockheads knew that, if any of the officials had attempted to pacify Ian, he would have screamed: 'Oi! Assault!' so Mickey Gallagher stepped in. He laid him down on his back, so he couldn't move, at which point Davey Payne leaned over Ian and whispered, 'The trouble with you, Ian, is too much easy money.' When they boarded the plane, the Blockheads sat some distance from their singer, who had been 'sent to Coventry'. Towards the end of the flight, Ian walked down the aisle to visit the toilet and, as he passed Gallagher's seat, quietly uttered, 'I want me car back.'

21

A Tricky Operation

Hampstead, London, November 1995. He felt the first nagging symptoms on the flight home from Los Angeles, where he'd been filming his part as Noah in *The Crow: City of Angels*, the 'tepid sequel' to the blockbusting scary movie *The Crow*. "Iggy Pop and me . . .' mused Ian, referring to his fellow actor, 'Iggy had this gun, he shoved it right up me nose.' Ian was clearly excited to be back in movies after a lengthy break, but cruising past Hollywood's Capitol Tower – probably reflecting on the songs his idol Gene Vincent once recorded there – he was unaware of the sinister developments taking place in his body.

A couple of days later, while recovering from jet lag, he felt the pains again. He put it all down to air travel and tried to carry on as normal, but over the next few weeks the aches intensified. 'He got progressively worse,' recalls Sophy. 'His digestion was poor; then he started throwing up everything he ate. There were some theories – irritable bowel syndrome was one.'

Ian was never one for consulting the doctor or undergoing any kind of check-up, preferring the do-it-yourself approach. Even toothache he treated with oil of cloves, although this had not been necessary of late; in 1994, he'd acquired a full set of dentures (which he would take out and show to friends as a party piece). Ian rarely bothered the medical profession but held them in high regard, believing passionately in the National Health Service. But he continued to rely on home remedies and

put his trust in fate. By the beginning of 1996, his luck was
running out.

For some months, Ian had been writing again with Chaz
Jankel, following a reconciliation brokered by Derek Hussey.
'I dropped in on Chaz in his studio,' recalls Derek. 'I told him,
"Ian is gutted, you know, he realizes he's dropped a bollock . . .
He told me that, without you, Chaz, it ain't happening. Ian told
me he loved you to death." Ian didn't exactly use those words,
and I may have been telling a few porkies, but I was trying to
make them rub up against each other again. Chaz came round.'

Things between Ian and Chaz were going quite well, so well
in fact that Ian started to talk about the Blockheads going back
on tour, possibly to America. But once again Ian overstepped
the mark, needling Jankel with sarcastic remarks, specifically:
'When we're in America, Chaz, I don't want you sloping off
to see your uncle.' Chaz was puzzled. He didn't even have an
uncle in America but, ever sensitive to Ian's digs, he felt his
only recourse was to instruct his solicitor to write and sever all
ties. Sadly, Ian was in no fit state to consider Chaz's position.
His body was now in turmoil, and he was vomiting endlessly.
He found the pain unbearable, telling Sophy that he felt his 'gut
was about to pop'.

When Mickey Gallagher knocked on Ian's door he was
astonished at how ill Ian looked. 'He was grey,' says Mickey.
'He hadn't even been to see a doctor.' Unable to keep anything
down, Ian relented and allowed Mickey to run him down to
Harley Street for a private consultation with Doctor Adrian
Whiteson. 'You're not thinking of getting on a plane, are you?'
Whiteson asked in all seriousness. 'Because, if you do, you'll
burst.'

The investigation showed a massive build-up of partially
digested food in Ian's large intestine. He was immediately diagnosed with cancer of the colon. On 22 March at the London
Clinic in Devonshire Place, surgeon Charles Akle performed
keyhole surgery to remove the 'doughnut tumour' that had

been constricting Ian's colon. A post-op scan showed that the operation had been 'a success'.

'The procedure,' Mr Akle informed Ian, 'was to reconnect your mouth to your arsehole.' It was a graphic description that very much appealed to Ian, now relieved to learn there was 'a 90 per cent chance of a full recovery'. 'It was an amazing prognosis,' says Sophy. 'If it had ruptured, he would have died from septicaemia within hours. They saved his life. He didn't carry any medical insurance. He was quite socialist about it, but when you're told: "If you don't have the operation NOW, you're going to DIE," you find the money. Ian paid for it all himself.'

Ian's lack of private health cover was often the basis of a lot of laughs, especially when he was presented with an itemized hospital bill, as Derek Hussey recalls: 'Ham sandwich six quid, bandage ten quid . . . he didn't like to shout about the fact he was getting specialist treatment because he realized he was lucky enough to have the cash to do it, but in a way it was embarrassing for him. He felt lucky, but he was busking it a lot of the time. He wasn't always abreast of the costs. His finances would fluctuate from being drastically in the red, then an advertising job would come along and pay enough to dump him back into the black. He didn't use credit cards, but he had a little failsafe that nobody knew about. He always kept a little brown envelope with a monkey [£500] in it. If the shit hit the fan, the bail-out would be there.'

Ronnie Harris suggested that Ian should recuperate by the seaside and recommended Pevensey in East Sussex. With its old-fashioned tea shops and beach huts, where the actor Peter Sellers once spent many happy hours shooting endless home movies – a piece of local trivia that was right up Ian's street – it was the ideal location. With Sophy and fifteen-month-old Bill, Ian took up residence in a rented cottage and begun his convalescence. 'He lost his voice and got very skinny,' recalls Sophy, 'but it was a very special time.'

During his six weeks in Pevensey, various helpers would

take it in turns to drive Ian around local beauty spots like Beachy Head. 'Smart' Martin Cole took him to Eastbourne in his camper van, to find they were the only people on the pier, 'except for a guy painting the railings, who told us that his dad used to go to college with Ian'. Mickey Gallagher hired a car throughout April, the Nissan having been 'confiscated' by Ian after the Las Palmas affair. 'I offered to take him out for lunch, but all he wanted was a fried egg sandwich with a runny yolk. He said, "My doctor told me I can eat anything. " Then he wanted an ice cream. He'd just had the operation and he had a big scar on his body, but he was still chucking the shit down.' Derek, who also ferried Ian around, says, 'His digestive system had accelerated because he'd had a length of pipe out. Once he'd mastered that and got his strength back, his cancer went into remission. He thought, "Well, that's cracked it." He went and had a couple of check-ups and he was all right, so it passed by.'

Mickey brought Ian and his family back to Fitzjohn's Avenue. The summer would be a happy time for them after such a lucky escape. Ian threw himself back into his work with the Blockheads, performing outdoor shows and preparing to record a new album. However his elation was deflated in August when he received the news that his old friend from Dagenham, Alan Ritchie, was dying from cancer. It was an ominous portent: first Charley, then Betty and now Alan. Ian called up his old pal Terry Day, and on 8 August Mickey picked them all up so they could visit Alan and his wife Mary at their house on Eastern Avenue. Within a week, Alan was dead, causing Ian to reflect on his own mortality and write a new song about remembering lost loved ones entitled 'The Passing Show'. In it, he noted: 'When we're torn from this mortal coil, we leave behind a counterfoil . . .'

In September, Ian consolidated material for his first studio album with the Blockheads in sixteen years. It would be called

Mr Love Pants. Ian didn't have a recording contract and decided to pay for the sessions himself, confident that a record company would quickly pick it up. Not since 1977 had he enjoyed a surfeit of songs from which he could choose a hot selection. He'd settled his score with co-writer Chaz, and they now had ample material. 'We wrote forty songs and threw thirty away,' said Ian. 'It's the first time I've taken so much trouble over an album since *New Boots and Panties!!*.' Recording took place at AIR Studios in October, with Davey Payne overdubbing his saxophone parts at Mute Studios some weeks later. Partly to save money and partly to perfect his performance away from the studio glare, Ian chose to record his vocals on home recording equipment. But as he repeatedly listened to the backing tracks, he became convinced that the drums were 'not happening'.

This wasn't the first time that Ian, himself a frustrated drummer, had been dissatisfied with the grooves, although Blockhead Stephen Monti had done a sterling job. There was nothing wrong with Monti's drumming, but Ian had recently befriended the legendary American funk drummer Bernard 'Pretty' Purdey. When Purdey was hired to play on a demo at Chaz's studio, the only other Blockhead Ian invited was Norman. Ian never said a word around Purdey, but got it into his head that the whole album should be re-recorded with Purdey on drums. The Blockheads refused. 'When you get beyond the hero worship, it wouldn't have worked,' says Mickey Gallagher. 'It would have broken the band up. Just sitting in the van with Bernard for a couple of hours, you'd want to commit suicide . . . listening to him telling us about all the Beatle tracks he played on. Bernard played on everything apparently, even "Love Me Do".'

Funding the recording of *Mr Love Pants* would make a big dent in Ian's finances. The album was to be mixed at the high-end AIR studios by *New Boots* veteran Laurie Latham, and leading designer Storm Thorgerson was instructed to execute the artwork. Ian was under some pressure to find an outlet for the soon-to-be-completed album. His able business team, consisting of manager Andrew King, accountant Ronnie Harris and new lawyer Mark Krais, put some feelers out, but there was little interest in the UK. The best that could be achieved was a licensing deal with Arcade Records for mainland Europe. Arcade needed a single to trail the album and suggested remixing one of the tracks. 'They asked my permission if they could Europeanize "Mash It Up Harry",' said Ian. 'Girl backing vocalists . . . I said, "You can have my full permission, cock."' Ian's one proviso was that the remixed version would not be marketed in the UK, containing, as it would, backing vocals of the 'Ooh Harry, you're so sexy' variety. Following the Arcade deal, royalties on Ian's back catalogue were reorganized by his advisers, enabling the Blockheads to share in the proceeds. 'There wasn't much consultation,' says Mickey Gallagher. 'Chaz ended up getting royalties for albums he wasn't even on!'

During a break in recording Ian was a guest 'castaway' on BBC Radio 4's *Desert Island Discs*. 'It was wonderful,' says Sophy. 'He loved Radio 4 with a passion. We got him up really early – the cab was waiting for him. He'd worked on the list for weeks on end, discussing it with his mates.' The show's presenter, Sue Lawley, grilled Ian about his life. A dramatic moment occurred when Ian started talking about Betty, who had died two years previously. There was an audible sob and a pause in Ian's speech as he gathered his composure.

'On reflection I chose a load of really boring tracks,' Ian told me a couple of years later. 'Peter Blake said, "That was a funny selection." I said, "You can talk – you had the Spice Girls!" But that was his second go at it. [When] Hugh Laurie did *Desert Island Discs* he chose what he said was "the second-best pop song ever written" – "Hit Me with Your Rhythm Stick". I took that as a real compliment.'*

•

* Other 'castaways' who have chosen records by Ian Dury on *Desert Island Discs* include: Sir Christopher Frayling, chairman of the Arts Council ('Reasons to be Cheerful');

For years Ian had been bombarded with invitations to take part in charity work, many of which he accepted, but it was impossible to entertain them all. Most proposals were filed away in the 'polio folio'. In February 1997, however, he received a letter that truly aroused his curiosity. It was written by two young colleagues at UNICEF (the United Nations Children's Fund), Claire Williams and Jo Bexley. Claire's work involved raising money and looking after UNICEF's corporate partners, such as the Sheraton Hotel Group, who were at that time funding polio vaccination programmes in various parts of the world. Her friend, Jo Bexley, worked in the press office, helping to generally raise the profile of UNICEF. They were both 'Ian Dury fans' and thought that it would be wonderful if they could get him involved. Together, Claire and Jo wrote:

> Dear Ian, you gave our generation reasons to be cheerful. Now we'd like to give you one! UNICEF is on target to reach its goal of a completely polio-free world by the year 2000. You made us feel whole as kids. You expressed what we felt but could never say. We want to give you the chance to feel that vital and that alive. We want you to help us kick polio off the planet. We guarantee your part in this will be an experience of a lifetime.

Looking back on the letter, Jo Bexley feels that it was a little naive. 'It was almost like fan mail. I saw Ian on *Top of the Pops* when I was thirteen and I remember reading something about him having polio. He hadn't been on the scene for a decade or more, and some people might have thought he was washed up, but in our eyes there was a lingering legacy of great records. He was a bit of a hero. I had this image of him as a good person, but on the edge, very un-UNICEF. Writing to him was a bit of a risk.'

But the letter paid off. Ten days later Claire Williams

Sir Peter Blake ('Don't Ask Me'); Nick Danziger, photo-journalist ('Hit Me with Your Rhythm Stick'); Suggs from Madness ('Sex and Drugs and Rock and Roll').

received a call from Sophy, asking what UNICEF wanted Ian to do. Sophy was told that they wanted to take him on a field trip to Africa, to witness a national immunization day when all children under five would be given a vaccine to fight the five major diseases, including polio. Ian was thrilled to have been asked, knowing that Danny Kaye had been UNICEF's first 'goodwill ambassador'. Ian had carried Kaye's autograph in his wallet for years after his dad had chauffeured the famous entertainer back in 1958. 'Then Audrey Hepburn did it,' Ian told me, 'Peter Ustinov . . . I thought these people were pretty good. They had skill and a kind of a vibe. The photographs of them in the situation with kids all around them are breathtaking. When they asked me, it all linked up with my old man. If only he'd known I was working for UNICEF, he would have been well pleased . . . and my mum, but especially my dad!'

Now that Ian had agreed to help, the next step was for Jo and Claire to sell the idea to UNICEF executive director Robert Smith. At this point, Jo started to get a little nervous and wondered if Ian would be considered an appropriate person to represent the organization. Robert Smith asked her to brief him. 'I dug out some press cuttings, but of course everything was sex, drugs, rock 'n' roll and a lot of swearing, with Ian sounding off about spastics,' says Jo. 'Robert was basically asking: "Are you sure this guy is an appropriate ambassador for UNICEF?" Then Robert asked to see lyrics from Ian's songs! I got round it by saying: "Let's meet him." We invited Ian to UNICEF's office in Lincoln's Inn Fields to meet with Robert.'

'It was like getting the Victoria Cross, being asked,' Ian told me. 'I had to go down there and meet this geezer. "Here comes Mr Sex and Drugs and Rock and Roll. Look out!" The press officer was there, and I was trying not to eff and blind and so forth. I asked my mate Steve Nugent, who's an anthropologist and knows about these things, to give me the low-down on UNICEF. Steve said, "If you've got 'UN' on the side of your truck, it's sanctioned."'

When Ian met with UNICEF's Robert Smith it was probably the first time in years he'd been in the company of an eminent person who knew absolutely nothing about him. It was a rare opportunity for Ian to shock and surprise. Accompanied by Derek Hussey, Ian turned up at UNICEF with 'a rag tied round his neck and wearing a crumpled jacket'. Jo Bexley nervously showed the ominous-looking duo into the meeting room, its walls festooned with insignia, its atmosphere formal and businesslike. 'Ian immediately engaged with Robert,' remembers Jo. 'He looked like the most unlikely ragbag character, but as soon as they shook hands, Robert was charmed. Ian was a total contradiction. He was totally up for it and humble about himself. He was probably checking us out too. Robert warmed to him. Ian dropped loads of theatrical references and talked about the London Palladium. He blew us all away.'

Ian blew away a different but equally challenging audience that April when he was asked to open an art exhibition at Riverside Studios, Hammersmith, organized by Roy Marsden, an old friend from the Royal College of Art. Roy was teaching painting at H. M. Prison, Wormwood Scrubs, and the exhibition featured works by the inmates, most of them serving life sentences. Ian told the organizers, 'I can't possibly open a show without the artists present, they have to be there.' As this was clearly impossible, it was arranged for Ian to go to Wormwood Scrubs to meet them. He was accompanied by Humphrey Ocean, who recalls, 'We visited the "middle-class wing", so named because the prisoners are "just murderers": they've only done one crime – the big one – but they're "not criminals". They made a mistake. We spent two hours there. There was one growler who wasn't very good with members of the public, but really it was just like art school, except you couldn't go home at four o'clock in the afternoon.' Roy Marsden recalls Ian being slightly nervous at the prison. 'He spent a morning there, talking to the lads, looking at their stuff. They loved it. He also popped into the music wing and gave them a little show on the drums. They went mad, he was a hero.'

1997 was proving to be quite a mellow year, punctuated by periodic check-ups at the London Clinic, all of which confirmed that Ian's cancer had gone into remission. Young Bill Dury was now two years old, and Ian and Sophy were expecting their second child any minute. On 9 May, three days before Ian's fifty-fifth birthday, baby Albert arrived. 'It was a special time,' says Sophy, who recalled Ian's domestic lifestyle at Fitzjohn's Avenue after his two sons were born. 'He read constantly: he would get all the papers on a Sunday and the *Evening Standard* every day. He would have the radio on non-stop – the World Service or Radio 4, news, sports, he was interested in everything. He didn't go out much, but had contact with the world. He was always reading – biography, travel books, Graham Greene, he always had a book on the go.'

At Fitzjohn's Avenue, old friends continued to visit on a regular basis. No matter how often they might have witnessed one of Ian's tirades, the inner circle stayed loyal: Humphrey, Denise, Merlin, Smart Mart, Ed Speight, Norman – some of whom Derek the Draw would refer to as Ian's 'moths'. Mickey Gallagher remembers the period as the best time he'd had working with Ian. 'The illness had taken the edge off his bitterness. It was a bigger thing. He was through with picking up on people's weaknesses. It mellowed him out on all fronts. He was relaxing, singing well and easy to work with. We also spent some time putting finishing touches to Digby Mansions, so that it could be rented out. There were lots of visits to the shops to buy door handles, all the proper stuff.'

It was a time for enjoying life and having a laugh with chums. Ian was at his most content on Sunday afternoons, when he usually declared 'open house'. 'He was a brilliant deejay,' recalls Jock Scot. 'After he'd got the kids to bed, he'd get the weed out, and we'd have a dozen cans, and he'd play records all night – everything: jazz, songs from the shows, Noël Coward. He would mix tapes on his beat box: he'd have sounds of the jungle, rainstorm approaching. You'd hear the thunder coming closer, then it would start pouring rain. Then he'd have tape recordings from the Second World War: Messerschmitts over Buckingham Palace, the radio report. Sophy would be in the other room, flopped down knackered.'

'It fell into a rhythm', says Merlin. 'Takeaways would be consumed, spliffs would be smoked, and diamonds would be exhibited,' referring to the curious case of Rainbow George's rose diamond collection, which became mysteriously depleted one hazy afternoon when Ian and Chaz were shown the jewels. 'The singer Ronnie Carroll, who lived round the corner and was a friend of George's, would sometimes appear,' continues Merlin. 'Ian used to get people to do their party piece, and Sophy would sing a folk song. Ian would play hand drums and tell endless jokes and stories. He would get you to sit next to him in that little back room. You'd be his best friend for a while and he would whisper in your ear.'

Then one morning the postman delivered Ian a reminder of his tortured schooldays. 'I got a letter from the Royal Grammar School Debating Society,' said Ian. 'It read: "Dear Ian, as a former pupil and art lecturer and punk rocker, you would have interesting things to say to the Debating Society." I was going to write back and say: "As an art lecturer it interests me very much but as a punk you can go fuck yourselves. " In 1982 they did *Top of the Form* on Radio 4. "Here we are at High Wycombe Royal Grammar School, whose most famous pupil was Ian Dury." I think Leonard Cheshire VC might have been one of 'em an' all [old boy] but the only one they mentioned was me! I couldn't believe it. I was their most famous fucking pupil!'

Ian flew to Johannesburg in July 1997, en route to Zambia for his debut as a UNICEF representative, accompanied by minder Derek Hussey, Jo Bexley and Claire Williams from UNICEF and a sprinkling of journalists. As one might expect, the trip was not without humorous incident. At Lusaka Airport, Ian passed

Derek a bank note with which to bribe the immigration officer, in the hope that they might jump the queue. 'They're bound to take a drink here,' said Ian. 'We won't be fucking around with that lot over there, we'll be round the back, bosh!' It wasn't that simple, as Derek recalls: 'The geezer put the money in his pocket and then pressed a button. The airport came to a standstill. Who's greased the geezer? Me! That caused a two-hour delay. The UNICEF lot had gone straight through with their parcels, but I'd greased the geezer and had to go through this explanation. I told them, "The bloke I'm with is disabled, he wasn't feeling very well." They went through my pockets.'

At the United Nations building in Lusaka, Ian was shown round a number of departments dealing with different aspects of UNICEF's work to prevent the spread of AIDS and other diseases amongst young children. It was a crash course in field medicine, and Ian took great interest. Over the next five days, the party toured the region, putting in eighteen-hour days to see first-hand the scale of the problem and UNICEF's initiatives to control it.

'Ian was sussing us out,' says Jo Bexley. 'He and Derek were being slightly mischievous. They performed when they needed to but, left to their own devices, they could be a bit naughty. I was quite heavily pregnant and making a radio programme, trying to look after these celebrities *and* get the coverage. I was doing too much and one night I broke down, physically. I thought I was about to give birth. And Ian was trying to get me to run around for him. I walked into the bar and said to Ian: "Look, mate, I'm absolutely knackered!" From that minute his attitude to me and the trip changed. He'd been having a few drinks and being slightly rude to people, seeing how far he could push it with the journalists and not quite delivering. When I reminded him why he was there, he changed immediately. I now realize he wanted me to stand up to him. From that point I had his respect and he had mine.'

I visited Ian shortly after he returned from Zambia, and he

gave me his impressions. 'I was at this airport at six in the morning. I was with the flying doctor, who's also got polio . . . waving the plane off. They strip out all the heating and the silencers 'cos it makes the plane lighter – fuckin' great refrigerator and about nine people all with overcoats on, 'cos it's so cold, and it's taking the gear off into the middle of nowhere. We went to the place where they make the callipers and wheelchairs, which was started by these young people who realized the only way they'd get their shit together was to make them themselves. They've got a little foundry, they make wheelchairs from old bits of pipe, they get a bit of help from Denmark, a big compound and they're slowly hacking out a life.

'Zambia's not a war-torn country by any means,' continued Ian. 'The bottom fell out of the copper market because of fibre optics and what-have-you in about 1970, so they've slowly gone a bit broke, and they had a fantastic health service and education system but they've slowly got poorer and poorer because the copper's not so valuable, and they're suffering. You don't see many people over the age of fifty. We went to one place where they're advertising the day of immunization and we said, "How do you advertise it?" There's eight million people and they're going to immunize two million children, which is basically all the children under four. We said, "Do you put a poster up?" and they said, "No, you put a poster up, it'll be there twenty minutes and someone will nick it, for the paper."

'We were in the UNICEF trucks, and the driver slings his bottle out the window. I said, "Why did you do that, ain't that a bit ecologically unsound?" He said somebody would run out of the bush and nick that bottle and use it for the next three years. They get overlap from the Zairian border, where there's a fucking shocking war going on. They encourage them to cross the border from Zaire to get the injections. The aim is in another two or three years to isolate polio specifically to pockets where it can't jump to another place so they can eradicate it.

'I can go to Zambia, have a look around, meet a few people.

It's very useful for me to be a disabled person in a disabled kid's school in Zambia, for instance. They climb all over me and ask me straight questions and compare legs and all that. Those aspects of it are brilliant. I'm out there as an observer, seeing what goes on and come back and use my so-called abilities to be able to talk about it. That's my job.'

Recalling key events from the Zambia trip, Jo Bexley says, 'We were in the bush and all these expectant mothers were sitting waiting for the vaccine for their children, flying doctors, boats coming up river, bikes, motorbikes, and the doctor was giving a chat through a translator and he said, "If you don't take this vaccine, your children might get polio. It even happens to white men. Can anyone see somebody here who might have polio?" A little kid pointed to Ian, who was close to tears, not embarrassed or ashamed or pissed off. He didn't feel singled out. He was absolutely proud that he had been used in that way. I put the microphone to his mouth and he said, "It's the most humbling moment of my life." We both broke down in tears.

'The flip side of that was when we went to another orphanage for disabled children. The disability thing in Zambia is not quite how it is here, they still call them "handicapped" and put them in homes so they don't become street children. They are well funded, run by Italian nuns, with a hydro pool. The kids want to become doctors and solicitors. They set up this performance for us, the visiting dignitaries. We were sat at this top table and they brought on the little boys, the middle-size boys and the big boys to perform, all severely disabled. There were kids with huge heads, it was pretty bad. Ian was getting more and more angry. He saw them as performing monkeys. "It's a fucking freak show," he said. He was getting so angry I had to hold him down. I told him to just get through it. He did hold it together, but I think it hit a note with Ian. Maybe it brought back memories of Chailey.'

22

Sweetness and Light

Harley Street, London, 29 January 1998. It was a routine 3.30 appointment at the London Clinic, but the outcome was not good. Tests showed that secondary tumours had started to appear on Ian's liver. The prognosis was harsh: terminal cancer.

'How long have I got, doc?' asked Ian.

'Between eight months and eight years,' replied the doctor.

'That'll do,' said Ian. 'Bosh!'

Sophy was slightly less flippant. It was the hardest moment when the doctor told her that the cancer would kill Ian. 'It was like a storm descending,' says Sophy. 'There was nothing the doctors could do, but they *could* offer Ian something that would prolong his life.'

Oncologist David Gueret-Wardle recommended chemotherapy using a Hickman line – a thin plastic tube that would run between Ian's body and a small container – to deliver anticancer drugs into his bloodstream. It was a pricey option, but Ian was willing to dig deep. 'A nozzle is implanted in my chest, straight into the main artery,' Ian told me, genuinely fascinated by the technology. 'I plug it in Tuesday morning and take it off Thursday night. It's exceedingly expensive but exceedingly gentle. The other end is attached to this bottle in a bum-bag round my belt. When I go out for a walk, I'm worried someone's gonna think it's a money belt and nick it!'

The liquid was kept in the fridge, and Sophy was taught how to connect the Hickman line, flush it out, disconnect it and clean it, allowing her and Ian to manage the programme and live as normal a life as possible. 'It doesn't make you hair fall out, no nausea,' added Ian. 'I get a little bit tired the day after I've unplugged. When I go to the London Clinic I'm a noisy bastard, telling jokes all the time. I have to try to keep my mouth shut 'cos some people are in a terrible state. My surgeon is a joker. He said he's on the cutting edge! Not ten feet in front of the cutting edge – they're the ones who kill you! There's a lot of humour in the trade. I've got a certain equilibrium about it 'cos I'm with good people, but it's a snaky bastard, cancer. It can become immune, run away, hide, pop up somewhere else. It's quite an exciting time.'

But, for Ian, time was running out. On 2 March, he and Sophy were married at Camden Town Hall in a modest ceremony. 'It was all very moving,' says Sophy. 'Ian had his chemo bag on, but it was a lovely day. Then we had an Indian takeaway and a nap!' The chemotherapy forced Ian to take things easy, but his work rate didn't slow down. At the end of April, he flew to Spain to promote *Love Pants* with Blockheads Gallagher and Turnbull, playing as an acoustic trio in Madrid and Barcelona. In a reference to the Hickman line and his musical performance, Ian joked, 'I unplugged on the Thursday night and we were unplugged on the Friday. A double unplugged! The adrenalin keeps you up. My hands go a bit like lobsters. That's all, though. So far, touch wood, the chemotherapy is keeping it at bay.

'The secondaries are much diminished from what they were. You can only measure them every three months 'cos they have to scan me, in the big tunnel, at the London Clinic. I'm having a lecture about it next week from the specialist so I can learn about it and not talk bullshit when I'm doing interviews! He came in to see me when I had the line put in and he said he hadn't decided what to give me yet. He'd have to look on the Internet. He said it sounded frivolous but it's not, because all around the world there's thousands of people working on the disease and they post their findings on PubMed. Something might come up tonight.'

Despite his illness, Ian kept in touch with developments in the art world and had visited the 'Sensation' exhibition at the Royal Academy of Arts, in which many of the new and controversial young British artists were represented. Ian was not a big fan of conceptual art. 'I'd rather see "Swans at Play",' he said. 'I'm a great believer in going out and drawing and painting, but there's room in the world for Andy Warhol.' That spring Ian visited the Kapil Jariwala Gallery in Mayfair, where Humphrey Ocean's and Jock McFadyen's two-man 'Urbasuburba' exhibition was showing. Whilst perusing the works, he unexpectedly encountered Keith Lucas, the guitarist he had forced out of the Kilburns some twenty-three years earlier. Once close friends, they hadn't spoken since the day that Ian and Spider paid Keith a visit in an attempt to recover some money, following the group's dissolution.

Ian was still beset with guilt – in fact, he'd told Sophy it was 'the only time he'd ever been really naughty'. But Keith was prepared to forget the fact he'd once been threatened with having his legs broken. Attempting to break the ice, he approached Ian. 'I'm very sorry to hear about Betty,' said Keith. 'Oh, we're talking again, are we?' Ian replied, as if only hours, not decades, had elapsed since their showdown.

Seeking a UK outlet for *Mr Love Pants*, Ian entered into discussions with East Central One, a record label run by Steve Fernie and Jamie Spencer, who had worked for Stiff Records back in 1981. 'I was always a fan,' says Jamie, 'and when the opportunity arose to work with Ian, it seemed a natural development.' To discuss their plans for the album, Steve and Jamie met with Ian at a Hampstead restaurant, accompanied by Andrew King and Mickey Gallagher.

No sooner had Ian signed his new contract than there was a knock on his front door. It was a reporter from one of the Sunday tabloids. 'We've heard Ian's dying of cancer,' said the hopeful scribe. Sophy turned him away, but now there were more reporters gathering on the doorstep. Sensing that somebody had leaked the news, Ian immediately took pre-emptive action. 'The tabloids were on the phone,' he told me, 'threatening to print an "Ian's dying of cancer" story. I thought the obvious thing was to go to Neil Spencer at the *Observer* and Janie Lawrence on the *Independent on Sunday* and do a spoiler. Neil came round that evening and so did Janie. We did the interviews and they wrote lovely articles.'

When writer Neil Spencer visited, he found a mellower Ian, not the fiery character he recalled from the 1970s, 'earring . . . mascara . . . all in black and scary'. They sat over glasses of Boddingtons ale, which Ian liked because 'it fitted nicely in the glass', and Neil learnt all about recent developments, including Ian's irritation at being disturbed by a journalist from the popular press when he was trying to put the boys to bed. 'He wanted to have a sensible discussion about his illness,' says Neil. 'He was spooked because Charley Charles and his first wife had died from cancer. He said he wasn't in any pain and was all right with it really. By talking about it, he thought he may be able to cheer up someone else, and that was the theme of the interview.'

'Two photographers came round on the Saturday,' recalled Ian. 'I got the most beautiful pictures I've seen of my kids, and that was that. It worked 'cos they didn't print anything in the tabloids that Sunday. But they cannibalized the two broadsheet interviews and did a nasty on the Monday! Apparently, I'm dying of cancer but I've still got reasons to be cheerful! I never said that. I'd never dream of it. They're slime.' Ian had kinder words for his medical team and his fans. 'My doctor's very pleased with me for coming out, as it were, 'cos it's good to come out. If you're going out gigging, the last thing you need is sympathy from people, but it is quite gratifying when people are so nice. I've had some quite breathtakingly warm letters – one that said: "You are a tremendous little canary."'

Despite this huge setback, Ian continued to honour his acting commitments, taking the part of 'Rat's Dad' in *Underground*, a story of small-time drug-dealing in south London. 1998 also saw the much-delayed release of *Middleton's Changeling*, for which Ian had filmed his part back in 1993, reuniting him briefly with his old college mucker, Vivian Stanshall. When I asked Ian to reflect on his movie roles, he replied, 'Something I should have got was *Mona Lisa*, the Robbie Coltrane part. I'm not saying I would have been better than Robbie, but it would have been less Mickey Mouse. I shouldn't say that. I don't phone my agent and say, "Where's my next part, darling?"'

Ian and the Blockheads, now with Dylan Howe on drums, released *Mr Love Pants* that summer on Ronnie Harris Records. 'Ronnie is my accountant,' said Ian. 'I asked him if he would mind me naming the label after him. I thought he might keep an eye on it. He asked, "Is there any blasphemy on it?" I said, "I'll ask Mickey, he's a good Catholic."' It was their first studio album together in eighteen years. The material had been written over a lengthy period, Ian insisting that this was the only way to craft songs of lasting quality. When I asked him for his thoughts about the new album for *Mojo*, he immediately compared it to *New Boots and Panties!!*, hoping that it could be just as successful. 'I've been accused by the Dutch record company of delivering a very short album,' said Ian. 'I said, "You like falling asleep halfway through the ninth verse, do you, mate?" Seventy-two minutes of Verve? This [*Mr Love Pants*] is exactly forty-five minutes to the dog barking at the end. Half a C90. Exactly. Ten pieces is all you need. Ten's enough, a perfect length. I always think in terms of vinyl.'

The opening cut, 'Jack Shit George', was a wry comment on the English education system and in time-honoured Block-heads fashion includes some swearing. 'It's probably about my attitude from being at school,' said Ian. 'A certain party, who shall have to remain nameless, but is an education officer [Ian was referring to his Aunt Molly], once told me that the unofficial statistic for teachers who are maladjusted is about 48 per cent. The unofficial, unofficial is nearer 80 per cent. I think that's probably true. There's always an exception to that. I can think of one, possibly two, teachers I had at the Royal Grammar School who weren't total roll and butters [nutters]. Others were dangerously barmy, hitting you over the head with something . . . striking out . . . the knuckle treatment. It's a very dangerous occupation, being taught. I guess the song is about that. It's quite sentimental in the choruses.'

I commented that the album's closing track, 'Mash It Up Harry', reminded me of the Kinks. Ian: 'It started out as "He's got a little problem up his you know where." [It was] nothing to do with me having cancer of the colon. I thought that was a bit strong, I was being real horrible to this geezer. I don't hate him. I think he's regimented. It's like [Tony] Hancock was in *The Rebel*, before he became an artist – the bowler hat and the routine. He may well have piles, but that's not where I'm at. Then I had a friend round, and we were playing it, and I started singing the "We're on our way to Wembley" bit and I thought, "He wants a bit of Wembley up his . . ." You know, he wants that euphoria, Shearer scoring a goal vibe. He's got his lounge and his shed and he needs that excitement. So I just put Wembley in to be nice to him, because I do like him. Then mash it up . . . don't call him a potato, but mash it up because he *is* a potato. It's want your cake and eat it time.'

I asked Ian about other songs on the album and learnt that he had written 'You're My Baby' for his son Bill. 'It was about a little kid,' said Ian, 'but it had to be about anybody. Which it is . . . the idea about protecting somebody.' 'Honeysuckle Highway' seemed to be about relaxing and having a mellow time. 'Yeah,' said Ian, 'and a few tributes. I do like making tributes. There's a tribute to the Troggs in there. "Everything's groovy." At the death, there's: what rhymes with polka and hoops?

"Oscar Homolka and Marjorie Proops" – I went into raptures when I thought up that. And, in fact, Marjorie Proops died later that week. I didn't know she was ill.

'"Itinerant Child" is about the boys in the old caravans and trailers and getting bashed up in that bean field . . . The travellers – gypsies cum pikeys cum geezers with Strangeways haircuts – not New Age. I associate New Age with the geezers with crystals on their heads and holistic medicine. It's the guys with the dogs and the women with dirty faces, with their little kids in those big old buses with the windows painted black. The old lorries in the convoys and then the old Rule 98 came out and stopped them. There were a couple of really savage episodes with the old bill attacking them and burning up their homes. I felt a lot of sympathy towards those people. I like the ones who wear it on their sleeves, the sartorial affair, the grime, the ones who can scrape a pink line on their necks, it's brilliant. You need a lot of bottle to do that. I'm an old home bird. I've only ever spent about two nights out. Vagabonding. I can't stand it. Where's me bed, where's me jim-jams and me duvet? I admire it, the free life. There's a bit of fresh air involved.'

Commenting on 'Geraldine', Ian said, 'When I was in Reading the nearest lovely town was Henley so me and Mickey used to drive over there to do our shopping in Waitrose and have a wander about. There was a little sandwich shop on the side of the marketplace where there was a double gorgeous ginger-haired person knocking out the sandwiches. It was a figment of my imagination that her name was Geraldine, but she was a gingham-clad person, hair tied back. There was a very fresh and clean schmeer to her. That combination of cleanliness and hunger, you can't go wrong. There's a bit of innuendo in there . . ." When she's buttering my baguette" – it's blatant filth of the Max Miller school. I'm very proud of it.'

Mr Love Pants was without doubt Ian's strongest collection of songs since *New Boots* and sold in respectable quantities. Shortly after meeting with Ian to discuss it, I hooked up with

Dave Robinson, who told me he had received a call, inviting him to go round to Fitzjohn's Avenue for a chinwag. Several days later, Dave told me that the meeting with Ian had taken place and had been 'a religious experience', sitting with him after so many years and reminiscing about pub rock, Stiff Records and the tribulations of Spider Rowe. 'Ian was quite ill,' says Robinson, 'and he wanted a couple of bottles of white wine, so I went and got them. The kids had gone to bed, and we proceeded to reminisce until about 4 a.m., and he rolled some big spliffs. His spirit was quite remarkable. I didn't get the feeling that here was a man who was worried that he didn't have too much time left.'

However ill Ian was, he never forgot he was the star of the show. Inevitably, some of the old tensions between himself and the Blockheads resurfaced. Certain members of the band were still dissatisfied with the financial arrangements. Davey Payne was fast becoming group spokesman, observing that his colleagues would complain about the pay, but 'clam up' if Ian walked into the room. 'I knew him better than the others, we went way back,' says Davey, 'so they would always phone me and say, "Oh, Ian's at it again . . . there's all this money from *Love Pants* . . . it should be shared out, but Ian wants to pay Storm Thorgersen 15,000 for a video." The record company had agreed to pay for it if they could use their people, but Ian insisted on Storm. We all needed money, we could have had ten grand each, but Ian was just spending it, wasting it even, because he knew he'd be getting publishing money. After all those years, it was happening again.'

When I pressed Ian on the subject, he commented, 'Groups are an ecological miracle, given the egos involved. In any group of six people you will always find five bad apples! It's never equal. I'll tell you what I really like about U2, REM – they share the dosh. The drummer may not write anything but he gets a quarter. It's a bit harder to do with seven people. The reason the Blockheads have survived ain't because of that, because we don't do that. We stayed together because we're proud of ourselves, we think we're the best band there is. There's a cross-fertilization of friendships and working relationships.'

Davey Payne was not impressed. His final showdown with Ian occurred on 8 August, when the group opened for Paul Weller at London's Victoria Park. The day started well; Davey had driven up from Cornwall and arranged for his family to attend the concert, but was later told there was not enough room on the tour bus for all of his children. Davey exploded and reached for the whisky bottle. 'It was late and I went to speak to Ian,' says Davey. 'There was this last bit of money from *Love Pants*. We could have shared it out. I said to Ian, "The problem is, Ian, I'm poor and you're rich." He started saying, "I'm dying, I'm dying." I cared, but I didn't want him to use it as an excuse every time.' A fracas ensued and Ian fired Davey.

'It is with great sadness that I have to report the death from cancer of Ian Dury,' announced Bob Geldof on 25 August, in his new role as deejay on radio station XFM. Minutes later Geldof was forced to retract the statement, blaming it all on a 'hoax caller'. The *NME* quickly dubbed Geldof 'the worst DJ of all time'. Ian was, in fact, happy to be alive and preparing for his second UNICEF trip, this time to Sri Lanka. 'The Tamil Tigers have agreed to stop shooting to witness the immunization programme,' said Ian, anticipating the Asian jaunt. He had been having discussions with UNICEF about introducing other pop celebrities to the cause, and one very big name had cropped up. 'I got hold of Robbie Williams to come to a meeting,' said Ian. 'I like Robbie because of his song "Let Me Entertain You". I also think he is a genuine bloke. Plus I've got a mutual friend who says he's a nice geezer. I wouldn't have asked him if I didn't think he was. I wrote to him, and he took the trouble to write back. We did some photos together, the "Give us your money" shots for UNICEF, and he's gonna come to Sri Lanka with me if we get it together.'

Robbie Williams nailed his colours to the mast, and the trip got under way in the second week of September. Ian and Robbie, together with Jo Bexley and the UNICEF team, headed east, enjoying an upgrade to first class on the flight, apparently due to Robbie's celebrity. Ian had hoped that he could travel without his Hickman line but was advised against it. Prior to the trip, Jo had received instruction from Sophy on changing and cleaning Ian's dressing. 'I would have done anything to keep Ian happy and take him on the trip,' says Jo. 'We were in the Galle Face Hotel in Colombo, in Ian's suite overlooking the ocean. I had to change the Hickman line. He had it all laid out meticulously. I couldn't believe it; here I was, a press officer on a field trip and I'm administering chemotherapy! I had the rubber gloves on when room-service knocked on the door with a tray of tea!

'Robbie was on the brink of becoming a huge star,' continues Jo. 'The week we were in Sri Lanka, "Millennium" went to number one. Ian and Robbie were not an obvious combination to manage. Robbie was a good boy, keeping himself to himself. He was in his room, talking to his girlfriend. Ian asked the right questions, looked intelligent, whereas Robbie had to have the two-hour briefing, but what he did bring to it was an interaction with the people. We were in refugee camps – vaccination in wartime – and Robbie would get a football and run off with the kids. He sang "Angels" at a school we visited. Ian played to his strengths, Robbie was the showman. In a way, Ian was handing over the mantle quicker than he would have liked.'

A flight to Jaffna, to witness 'the day of tranquillity', was called off following a terrorist threat. Instead, the party visited Vellankulam to witness an immunization programme. Despite Ian's relatively placid mood, he could still be relied upon to act the naughty schoolboy. His patience was tested when *Sunday Times* writer Ann McFerren repeatedly asked him, 'Are you all right, dear?' Derek Hussey recalls: 'She was patronizing Ian for a couple of days, and it was getting up his hooter. He arranged a cocktail party with the film crew so we could get to know each other. All of a sudden there was a huge rumpus. Ian has called Ann McFerren "a cunt". She turns round and says, "I've never ever in all my life been called a cunt before." Ian didn't stop there. The next day she was going to be travelling in the back of our Mercedes. After breakfast, we went out into the garden. I let Ian walk a little bit ahead with Ann. They stopped for a moment, and he looked round and gave me a wink. Then he said to her, "Ann, I promise you I will never ever call you a cunt again." He liked getting people at it.'

Shortly after the Sri Lanka trip, Ian was summoned to the UNICEF headquarters, where he was made a 'UNICEF UK Special Representative', alongside his old pal Vanessa Redgrave and Lord Bill Deedes. 'He really was an ambassador on behalf of the world's children,' says Jo. 'Despite a punishing work schedule and poor health, Ian was an unstoppable advocate on UNICEF's behalf, putting his name to things where his celebrity made the difference between failure or success.'

Ian attended the Cheltenham Festival of Literature in October 1998 at the invitation of editorial director and writer John Walsh. 'I invited Ian to come and discuss whether music lyrics could ever be regarded as poetry,' says Walsh. 'We had a riveting talk for an hour on stage and hung out together later in the bar of the Queens Hotel.' Walsh wrote about the event in the *Independent*, where he reported that Ian had said he hated seeing his songs written down because it made him realize how far behind true poetry they fell. 'Whereupon,' wrote Walsh, 'he lifted his vast, grizzle-haired bonce to the hot lights and, with closed eyes, recited the beginning of Keats's "Ode to Autumn", word-perfect. A shiver crept up the audience's spine. Mr Dury, from being the Cockney-roughneck-music-hall-Gypsy-showman as advertised, stood revealed as a thinker, a modest well-read poetry-loving cove.'

The autumn of 1998 also saw Ian and the Blockheads on tour, with new saxophonist Gilad Atzmon replacing Davey Payne. An appearance on *Later with Jools Holland* on 29 September reminded viewers that Ian and his band were still a formidable force. On 3 November the group played a showcase at Ronnie Scott's, which was filmed for television. Dates in Ireland and the UK plus forays into Holland, France and Dubai in the run-up to Christmas kept the cash rolling in and continued to promote *Mr Love Pants*.

As Ian's tour manager, Derek Hussey had by now experienced all of his various tricks and behaviour traits. 'When we checked into a hotel,' says Derek, 'Ian would give the first room-service geezer a big tip, a twenty or a fifty, depending on what he had in his pocket. The next time Ian rang room-service, the geezer was at the door before you'd taken your hand off the button. Also, he liked to wind himself up before he went on stage, something to get him going. He would have half a nip of brandy to sharpen the tonsils up and three or four olives for their salt content because he used to sweat a lot during a show. If there were no olives on the rider or a rotten drop of brandy we'd get the promoter and send him down the road for some good brandy or some olives. Then it would be: "Ain't he back yet, where the fuck is he?" an hour before the show, just enough to get the tension going. Some nights, it would have been worth hiding the olives.'

Although there would be a number of shows in the spring of the following year, the 1998 tour was Ian's last flurry of highly intensive road work. Due to his illness, he no longer had the energy of old, although he never disappointed his fans. His nightly stage entry, in which he would be escorted to the microphone by Derek as the band played the opening strains of 'Wake Up and Make Love with Me', was a guaranteed show-stopper. He still managed a few of the old visual tricks, deploying various props, but off stage his behaviour had become comparatively mild. Except, that is, for the events of 13 December.

23

The Diamond Geezer

Amsterdam, December 1998. Marijuana fumes stifled the air at the Paradiso, a legendary music venue in a former church packed with ageing hippies, new-age bikers and young Dutch punks. Tonight would see a performance by Ian Dury and the Block-heads, promoting their new album *Mr Love Pants* and reprising classics from their 1970s heyday. Expectations were high. Ian had flown into town the previous evening to conduct a number of press interviews and was sitting in his hotel bar when the Blockheads arrived on the afternoon of the show. 'Letting Ian go over on his own, the day before the gig, was a big mistake,' says Mickey Gallagher. 'When we arrived at the hotel, there he was, in the foyer, doing an interview at three in the afternoon and was already rat-arsed. Absolutely pissed, glowing. We poured coffee into him, trying to get him sobered up, and he was still having a sly drink.'

The Paradiso was noted for its very high stage, notoriously difficult to negotiate. It was not ideal for Ian, but back in the day, when he was like a matchstick, Spider would simply carry him up the ladder on his back. But now, Ian had grown in size and was bloated with chemo. There appeared to be no way of getting him up onto the stage until the promoter suggested the hydraulic lift that was used for loading the equipment. It was decided that the hoist would be positioned in front of the stage and that Ian would make his entrance from the back of the hall, with two big minders and then be put on the hydraulics.

As the Blockheads began 'Wake Up', Ian was placed on the lift and slowly raised into position. 'He was completely drunk,' recalls Mickey, 'and as the lift went up, the spotlight hit him. He was facing the crowd with his captain's hat on, giving it the old Benny Hill salute. Beautiful. The crowd were going bonkers. Ian walked up to the microphone and couldn't remember a single word of the song. He was completely gone. We were contracted to do ninety minutes, but after about forty we all realized it had gone terribly, terribly wrong. Derek was standing with his hand up Ian's back, keeping him on the mic. Then Ian told the crowd, "We're gonna have to leave you now." We came off completely ashen-faced, in trauma. It was the worst gig we'd ever done. The next day, the reviews were fucking tremendous!'

The following year, 1999, would be a harrowing one, not least for Jemima and Baxter. Having lost their mother four years earlier, Ian may have been seeking to protect them from undue grief when it came to his own predicament. He certainly found communication with his grown-up children difficult. 'It was hard to know what was going through his mind,' says Jemima. 'We were desperate to be part of his situation, but even the day he married Sophy he didn't invite us back to the house. They got married in a register office and didn't really talk to anybody. It was weird. He knew he had terminal cancer, but it was too difficult for him to face his family and tell them. He was finding it difficult to be close.'

Ian didn't know how much time he had left and resolved to cram in as much as he could, believing that hard work would pull him through. 'It was amazing to watch because he was refusing to die,' says Baxter. Looking back, Ian's achievements were remarkable. He became a vociferous supporter of the charity CancerBACUP, raising money for the cause at every opportunity. He once again offered his services to UNICEF, even though he was not really up to flying long distances and arduous daily travel. Voice-over work on TV commercials for the *Sunday Times* and the Halifax Building Society kept Ian's 'dark brown voice' in the public ear and helped to pay his relentless medical bills. With Mickey Gallagher he came up with theme music for the BBC TV situation comedy *Starting Out* and, in April, convened with the Blockheads to record tracks for a possible follow-up to *Mr Love Pants*.

In May, the BBC filmed Ian for the TV documentary *On My Life* (one of two titles he had considered for his aborted autobiography, the other being *It's All Lies*). The programme makers took Ian back to his roots, resulting in an outing to Essex, a journey to Ireland and a night at the dogs, raising money for CancerBACUP at Walthamstow greyhound stadium. In Upminster, Derek drove Ian to Waldegrave Gardens, where Ian reminisced about a local girl he'd taken to see *Baby Doll* at the London Pavilion in 1957. In Ireland, at the Walker ancestral seat in County Donegal, Ian showed the cameras around Kilcadden, the country house that was home to his great grandparents, William and Margaret Walker, and their family.

Other than in his 1992 song, 'O'Donegal', it was the first time that Ian had publicly opened up about his Irish roots. 'You know why?' opines Derek. 'It's because he was Protestant. I think he would have liked to have been on the other side, with the Catholics. He had the IRA rule book for 1936 in his book collection. He liked the rascally side of it.' Sophy was impressed by Ian's ability to make all the travel arrangements for the Donegal trip, recalling, 'It was us and the kids and Derek and his wife, Annie. We travelled to Belfast, got the van and drove to Donegal Bay. It was Albert's second birthday. I was at my saddest because I realized what was happening and I could see that it was all coming to an end. He was quietly very ill.'

Ian was 'quite chipper' on 1 June when he and the Blockheads played the Hay-on-Wye literary festival; however his condition would quickly deteriorate. He was due to perform at Glastonbury at the end of the month, but was forced to cancel following two warm-up dates in Ireland. After a show at Clarendon Docks, Belfast, on 19 June, his complexion turned yellow. Later that night he awoke in his hotel bed sweating profusely, his left leg badly swollen. At 3 a.m., Mickey Gallagher rushed him to the nearest hospital, only to find the emergency department full of accident victims and drunken revellers. 'There was blood everywhere,' recalls Mickey. 'Ian was saying, "That guy looks worse than me, let him go in next." I said, "Ian, let's see the doctor NOW!" Ian wanted to cancel the following night's gig in Dublin right up until the moment the doctor said, "We're going to have to keep you in." Ian suddenly protested, "But I've got a gig to do tomorrow!" The Dublin show went ahead, but Ian's liver was malfunctioning, causing him to go an even deeper yellow.'

Returning to London on the Monday morning, Ian went straight to hospital and learnt the awful truth. Ever since being diagnosed he believed he would beat the cancer, but the doctors were no longer able to do any more for him. 'He was absolutely jaundiced,' remembers Sophy. 'We asked Dr Wardle if there was anything at all that could be done, and he told us there was only one option, which was for Ian to go to Egypt for gene therapy.' Within twenty-four hours, Ian and Derek had booked their flights to Cairo, where a new, controversial treatment – illegal in the UK – was available. 'He was so bad I'm amazed they let him fly,' says Sophy, 'but he got on the plane somehow.'

The Egyptian gene therapy involved a daily injection of serum for five days. Forty-eight hours in, Ian started to regain his colour. Cautiously elated, he and Derek decided to fit in a trip to the great pyramid of Giza for photographs. At the end of the week, Ian's blood was measured to assess the behaviour of the cancer cells. 'Everything had quietened down,' says Derek. 'We thought we might have had a little result.'

He somehow managed to continue recording with the Blockheads and also worked with Madness, contributing a vocal to

'Drip Fed Fred'. 'In the "Drip Fed Fred" video Ian looks like a skeleton because he was dying,' says Sophy. 'Ian and Baxter and Madness were all in a little theatre at the top of the road. It was very moving. He was yellow and skeletal but still found the energy to make the film with Madness, a great group of men.'

In recognition of their hit-making career, Ian and Chaz were awarded the *Q Magazine* 'Classic Songwriters Award' at a ceremony at the Park Lane Hotel in November. Anticipating that he would not be well enough, Ian taped an acceptance speech at home, but at the eleventh hour he summoned the energy to attend, along with Chaz Jankel. Due to his fragile state of health, arrangements were made for Ian to enter the ballroom via a service lift, unlike attendees Keith Richards and Ron Wood, who had to endure a big public entrance in the full glare of the media spotlight. *Q* and *Mojo* writer Paul du Noyer, a Kilburns fan of old, was tasked with looking after Ian and ensuring his needs were catered for. 'Due I suppose to his illness he was quite terse and subdued,' recalls du Noyer, 'but he became much happier once we'd settled him into a corner table, his back to the wall, very near the stage. From there he gave his acceptance speech into a microphone hand-held by Suggs from Madness. I did a brief interview with him and recall praising the new CD edition of the Kilburns' *Handsome* and finding Ian very unhappy about the music itself and his lack of involvement in the reissue. As the room began filling up, he clearly started enjoying himself and got into the spirit of things. I especially liked the way that he kept passing comment on each good-looking female who walked by.'

Ian's outings were becoming extremely rare and most of his time he was confined to bed. Sophy stayed near to attend to his needs and installed a television in the bedroom so that he could enjoy late-night showings of *The Sopranos* in between naps. He also listened to his favourite music and throughout that winter read the novels of Patrick O'Brian. He studied the whole of the Second World War, believing that what people had to endure during wartime was considerably worse than the pain he was going through. Friends like Humphrey Ocean, Wreckless Eric and Ingrid Mansfield-Allman would call round, often bearing records and books. A nurse by the name of Trish Owen called weekly to check for minor infections, and there were regular visits to the hospital for tests. 'There was an emergency one night when his temperature was soaring,' recalls Sophy. 'He got in a cab and went to the hospital on his own – amazing.'

The great and the good collected at Ian's bedside to pay their respects, Labour cabinet minister Mo Mowlam and Paul McCartney among them. 'Ian said McCartney's visit was like having the Queen Mother coming round for tea,' says Sophy. 'He turned up looking like an estate agent, but he was very sweet, it was a lovely gesture. Mo Mowlam invited Ian, me and Derek round to her house for supper. It was a brilliant evening, she opened the door in her pyjamas. Ian found it fascinating to meet a true politician in the best sense of the word, a person who wanted to change the world and make it a better place. It was a great meeting of the minds. It was great affirmation for Ian to get a nod from someone like her.'

One person who regretted not visiting Ian was Fred Rowe, but they did speak on the phone. Fred remembers a particularly sad call from Ian. 'I asked him how he was, and he said, "I ain't got long to go now, will you come up and see me?" I never went up. I don't know why. I remembered him back in the old days when he was at number one, but he feared he wouldn't come up to scratch. To see him like a little boy who didn't know what to do used to make me ever so sad. I would cuddle him and tell him it was all right. He told me about his early life and said, "They never knew where to put me. There was never anything wrong with my brain but they put me in a nuthouse instead of a hospital." Because he had a bad leg, people would say, "ARE – YOU – O – K?"'

As Christmas approached, Ian was looking forward to seeing his family, but Jemima was hurt and frustrated by the way she felt her father had been keeping her and Baxter at arm's length throughout the year. 'I was so pissed off with the situation, so fed up with all this constant rebuffing,' says Jemima. 'You could tell he was dying and I think he knew that we knew, so it was all very tense. I told him on the phone I wasn't coming over for Christmas. He said, "This might be my last one," and broke down in tears.' Baxter adds, 'It was a very strange thing; he couldn't quite handle involving Jemima or I and possibly made the worst decision ever by just hiding away. He didn't answer the phone, and Sophy didn't answer the phone. I think he was realizing that he wasn't going to come out of it.' Jemima continues: 'Baxter was phoning me, telling me I had to come, but by that point I was so angry with dad. But at the same time you can't be angry. If I was dying I don't know how I would relate to everyone. I said, "Of course I'll be there." He started to stop fighting so much and we did see a bit more of him.'

At the start of 2000 Ian was in no fit state to work, but there were still dates in the diary. These included a prestigious show at the London Palladium on 6 February (with a warm-up at the University of East Anglia two nights earlier). The ninety-year-old Palladium held great childhood memories for Ian, and he was determined not to miss it. The prospect of playing the legendary venue kept his spirits up throughout January, despite his being bedridden most of the time. Getting himself into an entertainment frame of mind required a superhuman effort.

On the day of the Palladium show Sophy wrapped Ian's fingers in Elastoplast, his fingernails now brittle from huge doses of chemotherapy. She got him dressed, and Baxter carried him down the ten steep steps outside their front door that in earlier years had never been a problem for Ian. Derek's car was waiting. Arriving at the Palladium, Ian disembarked in Great Marlborough Street and plonked himself into a wheelchair. He was pushed up a ramp to the stage door and taken directly into his dressing room. He hardly spoke a word all afternoon as he focused on the task in hand – to entertain an audience of 2,000, many of whom would sense it was the last time they would glimpse the diamond geezer.

Phill Jupitus warmed up the crowd with comedic banter, followed by a set from Kirsty MacColl, for whom Ian sent out for flowers and champagne. Anticipation was high during the interval, then, shortly after 9 p.m., Ian was walked onto the stage by Derek the Draw and Mick the Ted to a rapturous reception. His set with the Blockheads, billed as 'New Boots and Panto', was a little briefer than usual, but did include the demanding 'Spasticus Autisticus', which he delivered perched against a strategically positioned flight case. For much of the performance he sat, causing Chaz Jankel to reflect, 'His pitching was note perfect. I suddenly realized after all those years that all he needed to do was sit down and he would have been in tune. But he used to like to stand with a straight microphone stand, like Gene Vincent.' Ian's family occupied one of the boxes overlooking the stage, from where they could see Mo Mowlam on the opposite side of the auditorium. 'It was one of those moments,' says Baxter. 'You could tell by Mo's face that she was in awe of the effort dad was putting into singing his songs that night.'

After the show, Ian sat quietly in his wheelchair until Sophy arrived backstage. Unlike the old days, there was minimal socializing, but Ian managed a few brief conversations with well-wishers. Old friends who had not seen him in recent months were shocked and distraught by his gaunt appearance. 'He suddenly said, "I've got to go home now,"' remembers Sophy. 'He started dying from that night. He went to bed and was in more and more pain. His morphine doses were increased, but he remained quite lucid. All of the remaining dates in the diary were cancelled.'

By the end of February, Ian's condition had worsened. Nurse Trish Owen now visited more frequently to assist Sophy, who slept with Bill and Albert in a double bed in the same room as Ian. He had no physical strength left at all, but his mind was still active; sitting up in bed one morning, he thought that now was the perfect opportunity to start writing his autobiography. An Apple laptop was obtained, and Jemima showed her father how to turn it on and start a document. Ian sat in bed with the computer in front of him and began writing his story, but sadly couldn't summon the energy to get past his first two words: 'Hallo sausages . . .'

Baxter and Jemima remained on hand to nurse Ian in shifts with Sophy, who would take care of the boys and their school runs. In mid-March, Doctor Adrian Whiteson visited and noted how quickly Ian had deteriorated since his last visit. Palliative care was all that could be offered. 'What should he eat or drink?' asked Sophy. 'He doesn't need to eat or drink, just make him comfortable,' advised the doctor. Sophy was devastated to hear that Ian didn't need to eat any more and prepared herself for the inevitable. Accompanied by Baxter, she broke the reality to Ian that he was dying. 'Shit,' Ian replied.

Wishing to remain as lucid as possible, he refused further morphine. From now on, not so much as an aspirin would pass his lips. He sipped only water and sucked ice cubes to stay hydrated. He tried to sit up as much as possible, relentlessly fighting his pain, but found it hard to stay upright. Everyone prayed that he wouldn't contract pneumonia. Ian's words were few and far between, but he managed to tell Sophy, 'You've got to keep the rhythm going.'

On Friday 24 March, Doctor Whiteson visited again and indicated that it wouldn't be long. Sophy beckoned to Jemima, who handled the night shift, and they took it in turns to massage Ian's feet to help him relax. Baxter came over to assist. The last weekend of March was a sombre time, with Ian now drifting in and out of sleep and who knows what colourful memories passing through his conscious and subconscious mind? When his eyes opened, he could see from his bed the sun shining through the trees and a last, beautiful glimpse of the old-fashioned garden that Peggy had tended when she lived in the flat.

By the early hours of Monday 27 March, he was fast losing his fight. 'He was letting go,' says Sophy. 'As his friend, I couldn't wish for him to have lived any longer.' Release soon came. At around 7 a.m., just as Jemima was finishing the night shift and Sophy was thinking about getting the boys ready for school, Ian's breathing weakened considerably. There would be no school that day. Shortly after 9 a.m., with Jemima and Baxter sitting by his side, Ian slipped away. Gone . . .

In the hours following Ian's death, his nearest and dearest experienced a strange kind of elation. They had managed to nurse him through a wretched illness, and their tender care allowed him to die at home, surrounded by those he loved. No one had panicked, and Ian had died peacefully. A calm 'home death' is how they saw it. Sophy asked the nurse what they should do next. 'He's yours, you can do what you like with him; you can even dress him up in a gold lamé suit!' she replied. Jemima and Sophy gathered together Ian's best clothes and dressed him, ready for the doctor to visit and certify his death. Ronnie Harris, who was in Israel, called and said, 'Keep him. I need twenty-four hours to get back. I've got to say goodbye to him.' That night, after Baxter left, Sophy and the boys sat with Ian, his coat pockets stuffed with chocolates, joints and goodbye notes. Ronnie Harris arrived just in the nick of time to bid Ian farewell.

Baxter remembers returning to his flat near Baker Street. 'I was on the tube with a bag of washing, and everyone was reading the evening paper with a big picture of dad and Bill and Albert on the front, all along the train. They had no idea who I was. It was very a strange time, but all totally positive, very moving.' The following morning the undertakers arrived at Fitzjohn's Avenue, telling Sophy, 'You might not want to watch this bit.' 'He's mine,' said Sophy, 'I'll watch if I want to!' They put Ian in a body bag and carried him out. At that moment Sophy had the realization that Ian's funeral was going to attract a great deal of press coverage.

She was right. Outside of royalty, it was probably the most widely reported send-off London had seen in many a year. The capital had taken the little guy to its collective heart, and his death, aged fifty-seven, was mourned by family and fans, colleagues and cabinet ministers. The funeral had been planned, in part, by Ian, with Jemima and Baxter working out the fine detail. 'We're gonna have it proper,' Ian had told his friend Jock Scot some weeks earlier. 'I want the horses with the plumes and the glass-sided carriage.' North London funeral directors Levertons had been appointed, as was Ian's wish. They had administered Peggy's funeral and, in 1930, that of Henry Croft, the original Pearly King of London, whose coffin had been transported through the streets in the same horse-drawn hearse.

On the morning of 5 April the funeral cortège stopped outside Ian's and Sophy's home before making its onward journey to Golders Green crematorium. Floral tributes adorned the carriage, including a huge wreath spelling 'Durex', curiously appropriate for someone who had died within twenty-four hours of Dr Alex Comfort, author of *The Joy of Sex*. Hampstead traffic came to a standstill, with police in attendance to maintain order. 'It was one of the most amazing days of my life,' remembers Baxter. 'It was such amazingly weird fun, and we were lucky to be involved. From the moment we woke up, there were a million incidents.'

An old gangster friend of Ian's 'with a name like Stanley Stichett' turned up bearing a huge smoked trout, which was consumed al fresco. Two motorcycle police arrived to accompany the funeral procession, saying that they were big fans of Ian's, and apologized for the fact they were unable to provide police horses. 'They stood outside the house with their huge bikes,' remembers Baxter, 'and there's Derek the Draw in the middle of them with a massive spliff on. The paparazzi were on the other side of the road, and the gangster was slicing up the fish. It was as if all of Ian's life started to appear before us. Then me and Jemima and Aunt Moll and Sophy and the kids got in the funeral car. Aunt Moll was wondering what the fuck was going on.'

The journey to Golders Green crematorium took a little longer than expected, and by the time the cortège arrived, hundreds of mourners were gathered outside the chapel. They included Mo Mowlam, Robbie Williams, Neneh Cherry and Nick Lowe. It was arranged that Blockheads Norman, Mickey, Johnny and Chaz would be pallbearers, assisted by members of Madness, whose Chris Foreman recalls, 'They wanted some of us, and I assumed it would be Suggs and Carl, but the Blockheads are kind of small, so they chose Lee Thompson and myself, as we are of similar height. I was quite surprised to be asked, but it was an honour.'

Jock Scot remembers, 'There were more people than could be fitted into the chapel. People who had every right to be there couldn't get in and had to watch the service on television screens. I was standing outside talking to Suggs and asked him if he was carrying the coffin. He said, "No, I'm too tall." A guy came out of the chapel and said, "Full up." Suggs said, "Come with me," and we walked in behind the coffin.'

Annette Furley, from the British Humanist Association, conducted the service, telling the congregation how Ian battled polio and fought cancer with strength and good humour. 'What made him sad,' said Ms Furley, 'was knowing that he would not see Billy and Albert grow up.' One of the most moving parts of the service was the Blockheads' rendition of 'You're the Why', a song Ian had written with Chaz and recorded during the last year of his life.

Later that day, a huge wake took place at the Forum in Kentish Town. 'It was a sad occasion but it was spectacularly sad,' says Jock. 'He wanted an Irish-style wake where everyone gets together and gets pissed.' My personal recollection of the event was that there was indeed much alcohol consumed throughout the afternoon and evening, leaving many 'tired and emotional'. But the musical entertainment was superb, and the affection for Ian immense. The stage was adorned with Tom Sheehan's 'Paddy' portrait of Ian, enlarged as a giant backdrop. The Blockheads supplied accompaniment for a succession of guest vocalists, including Baxter, who performed a poignant 'My Old Man'. Ronnie Carroll appeared in an overcoat and sang 'Danny Boy' *a capella*, adapting the words to 'Oh Ian Boy'. 'Reasons to Be Cheerful' provided a fitting finale to a long and moving day.

Baxter was adamant that his father's ashes had to be disposed of properly and promptly. 'We've got to do it now,' he exclaimed. Everyone agreed. 'Derek went to pick up the ashes and brought them back here,' recalls Sophy. 'We had a look. Bill couldn't understand what happened to Daddy between being here, dead, and suddenly being in a box. He wanted to know what happened to the box. I had to explain about the magic fire.'

The family hired a car and driver to take them to Hammersmith, where they hooked up with the sage-like Derek the Draw outside Digby Mansions. Sophy, Jemima, Baxter, Bill, Albert and Derek walked up onto Hammersmith Bridge and ceremoniously threw one of Ian's old callipers into the river. It was swiftly followed by one of his favourite sticks. Then, on their way to the Blue Anchor pub, where they would remember their loved one over port and lemonade, they strolled down to the riverbank. Knowing that the tide was going out, Jemima and Derek took Ian's ashes and sprinkled them into the Thames, along with some flowers and pieces of poetry. 'He was now free and free of disability,' says Sophy.

Ian's ashes floated down river, winding their way through his beloved London, where ribald tales of 'Billericay Dickie' and 'Plaistow Patricia' were born, to be carried on the outbound tide past the Medway towns where, thirty years earlier, he had cut his musical teeth with the Kilburns and then past Southend and the site of the swimming pool where, on that fateful day in August 1949, he was tragically afflicted with the poliovirus that wasted the left-hand side of his body and dominated his life, yet in some magical way inspired him to enrich the lives of us all.

Acknowledgements

Shortly after Ian's death, I learned that his widow Sophy and daughter Jemima might be interested in collaborating with me on a book. They thought that there was an important side to Ian that had not been fully explored or written about. I shared their views, but after various discussions about the concept of an 'authorized biography', we did not proceed, not least because the family were not even sure if they had much material to contribute. There were even rumours that Ian had burnt much of his archive before he died. Sophy and Jemima did, however, put me in touch with other family members, crucially Ian's Aunt Molly.

I arrived at Molly Walker's cottage in the spring of 2001 to hear stories of Ian's post-war childhood. Molly, then eighty-seven, was Ian's oldest surviving relative. I had phoned her some days earlier to arrange the meeting and seek confirmation of her address. 'It's opposite the Black Boy pub,' Molly advised. 'Does your house have a name or a number?' I enquired. 'Oh, I don't know,' she said, a little irritably, 'it's opposite the Black Boy pub!' Molly greeted me with a sprightly step and I was ushered into the parlour. A framed photo of Ian, circa 1990, sat on the mantelpiece. Molly was obviously proud of her nephew and happily trawled her memory for little nuggets of information and personal reminiscences. Subsequent telephone conversations found her less lucid. Sadly, Molly died in 2004.

After visiting Molly, I met Ian's cousin Margaret Webb (née

Dury), who filled in some of the missing detail from her side of the family and reminisced about her 'Uncle Billy' (Ian's father). This put me on course to research Ian's genealogy at the Family Records Centre and various online resources. Margaret continued to verify genealogical detail relating to Ian's paternal roots and to her I am indebted. Finding information about the Walkers' Irish roots was somewhat more difficult, but I am grateful to Robert Williams at Ulster Ancestry who helped me uncover details of Ian's mother's family going back to the mid-nineteenth century.

I would specially like to thank Jemima, Baxter and Sophy Dury for all their help: granting me interviews; verifying family and domestic detail; letting me view photographs and documents and granting me permission to quote from Ian's lyrics and correspondence. This would be a much lesser book without their blessing.

Acquainted with many of Ian's former music business associates and musicians, plus one or two of his old friends, I planned a series of interviews that took rather longer to complete than originally envisaged, but the passage of time helped me to reflect on Ian's life and go back to various participants with hopefully new insights and questions. I would like to make special mention of the following persons, who went the extra mile and provided me with truly invaluable stuff: Mick Gallagher of the Blockheads, who dug out his diaries from a twenty-three-year association with Ian and confirmed dates, times and places, plus possibly *the* most candid view of 'Dury-world'; Alison Chapman Andrews (née Armstrong), who was at the Royal College of Art with Ian and supplied me with copies of mementos from that era; Barry White, for furnishing a tape of Gordon Law's 8mm home movies and Gordon Law himself for sending me copies of mid-sixties correspondence from Ian; Kees Bakker for supplying numerous photographs; Davey Payne of the Blockheads for providing me with tour itineraries, and Paul Phear, a Dury fanatic with an almost comprehensive archive of Ian's radio, television and press interviews. Paul let me raid his treasure trove of Dury media and I am very grateful.

Special thanks go to Roberta Bayley, who allowed me to view dozens of personal letters written to her by Ian during the mid-seventies when he was struggling for recognition. Ian once commented to Roberta about his correspondence in general, saying: 'These manuscripts will be of value only to my dear old mum as an insight and she may publish them privately in pamphlet form and distribute them with a shawl and a cackle.' Needless to say, the letters have contributed greatly to my research.

I am indebted to everyone who granted me interviews and provided information or clues. Only a couple of people declined to be interviewed. Some, when interviewed, 'sat on the fence', either out of loyalty to Ian or perhaps inhibited by his relatively recent demise. They may have been less circumspect if Ian had been alive to defend himself, but others wasted no opportunity in telling it like it was. Would these stories have been any different if Ian were still alive? Possibly, but either way, attitudes to him were wild and disparate, ranging from those who remember him as a warm and wonderful human being, to those who thought him a cantankerous old git. Hopefully, a balance has been achieved and this is a fair portrait of the man, reflected in the personalities of those who knew him well.

I therefore thank: Barry Anderson; Kees Bakker; Roberta Bayley; Jo Bexley; Sir Peter Blake; Chris Brown; Paul Bura; Joe Cang; Pat Carson (née Few); Alison Chapman-Andrews (née Armstrong); Martin Cole; Glen Colson; Jenny Cotton; Lucy Cresswell (née Walker); Clive Davies; Terry Day; Germaine Dolan; Baxter Dury; Brian Dury; Jemima Dury; Sophy Dury (née Tilson); B. P. Fallon; Chris Foreman; Jenny Forrest; Chris Gabrin; Mick Gallagher;

Charlie Gillett; Nicola Gooch; Eric Goulden; Angela Hardy; Russell Hardy; Ronnie Harris; Charlie Hart; Mick Hill; Ian Horne; Derek Hussey; Chaz Jankel; Peter Jenner; Wilko Johnson; Andrew King; Gordon Law; Belinda Leith; Laurie Lewis; Chris Lucas; Keith Lucas; Tracey MacLeod; Ingrid Mansfield-Allman; Pippa Markham; Roy Marsden; Glen Matlock; Mike McEvoy; Malcolm McLaren; Rod Melvin; Gordon Nelki; Stephen Nugent; Humphrey Ocean; Graham Parker; Davey Payne; John Plumb; Warwick 'Rocky' Prior; Merlin Rhys-Jones; Clive Richards; Geoffrey Rigden; Tommy Roberts; Dave Robinson; Franco Rosso; Denise Roudette; Fred 'Spider' Rowe; Jock Scot; Ed Speight; Jamie Spencer; Neil Spencer; Max Stafford-Clark; Leslie Tipping; Paul Tonkin; Kosmo Vinyl; Molly Walker; Margaret Webb (née Dury); George Weiss; Barry White. Thanks also to Andrew Motion for his comment about Ian.

I am grateful to the following persons who provided me with information and comments: the residents of Weald Rise, then and now: Maurice Cattermole, Diane and Gwendoline Hill and Ivy and Robert Trueman; former pupils of the Royal Grammar School, High Wycombe: Nicholas Avery, Michael Claridge, Tony Hare, John Owen Smith and Graham Watson. For valued advice, input and help: Stuart Batsford; Paul Bradshaw; Paul Conroy; Dave Cronen; Nigel Cross; Chas de Whalley; John Delany; Paul du Noyer; Bill Ellis; Ian Flooks; David Gentle; Ray Gillon; Paul Gorman; Lee Harris; Mark Kidel; Lizzy Kremer; Nick Lowe; Barry Payne; Paul Pierrot; Rebecca and Mike; Karl Rehse; Jake Riviera; Alan Robinson; Keith Smith; Simon Ryan; Mat Snow; Chris Taylor; Richard Terry; Justin Tunstall; Nick Vivian; John Walsh; Carol Watt; John Whyton; Valerie Wiffen. My thanks also to Pete Frame, for reading and commenting on draft chapters and general encouragement.

I would also like to thank photographers Ed Baxter, Jill Furmanovsky, Chris Gabrin, Mick Hill, Alain Lekim, Tom Sheehan, Kate Simon and Pennie Smith, as well as the following people who were immensely helpful with my research: Angus Fulton at Warner Chappell Music; Charlie Gillett at Oval Music; Jen Willis at Andrew Heath Music; Jonathan Simon at London Publishing House; Sarah Edis at Harrow Civic Centre Library; R. W. Thomson, Local History Librarian at Harrow Civic Centre Library; David Lovett at Harrow Register Office; Ian MacGregor, Library & Archive Services Manager at The Meteorological Office, Bracknell, Berkshire; the staff of the Family Records Centre, London; the staff of the British Library, St Pancras and the Newspaper Library at Colindale; Duncan Drury, Ian Lewis and Wendy Butler in the Records Office at University College London; Maria Ohlson, Administrative Assistant at the registry of the Royal College of Art; Kathleen Dickson and Veronica Taylor at the British Film Institute; Dan Mills at ITN Source.

Last but not least: heartfelt thanks to Lesley and Rupert who allowed me to live in my study for hours on end; Julian Alexander, my literary agent at Lucas Alexander Whitley and Ingrid Connell, my commissioning editor at Sidgwick & Jackson for her inspired editing and, most importantly, believing in this story.

And, once again, thank you Ian.

Bibliography

Books

Air Ministry – The Daily Weather Report of the Meteorological Office,
    Monthly Supplement, August 1949.

Arscott, David – *Chailey Heritage, A Hundred Years*. S. B. Publications,
    2003.

Balls, Richard – *Sex & Drugs & Rock & Roll*. Omnibus, 2000.

Berry, Chuck – *The Autobiography*. Harmony Books, New York, 1987.

Birch, Will – *No Sleep Till Canvey Island*. Virgin Books, 2003.

Bracewell, Michael – *Remake/Remodel*. Faber, 2007.

Bura, Paul – 'Chailey Heritage' (poem) from *The Drunk On The Train*.
    Bosgo Press,1997.

Brown, R. S. – *On The Suburban Trail Again*. Histories of Harrow Weald
    Highways Vol 2, 1975.

Drury, Jim – *Ian Dury & The Blockheads Song By Song*. Sanctuary
    Publishing, 2003.

Dury, Ian with Mickey Gallagher – *Apples The Musical*. Faber, 1989.

Dury, Ian etc. – *The Ian Dury Songbook*. Wise Publications, 1979.

Farren, Mick – *Gene Vincent: There's One In Every Town*. The Do Not
    Press, 2004.

Frame, Pete – *Rock Family Trees*. Omnibus Press, 1980.

Frame, Pete – *The Restless Generation*. Rogan House, 2007.

Gilbert, Pat – *Passion Is A Fashion – The Real Story Of The Clash*. Aurum
    Press, 2004.

Gimarc, George – *Punk Diary 1970–1979*. Vintage, 1994.

Glazier, Ken – *London Buses Before The War*. Capital Transport
    Publishing, 1995.

Gorman, Paul – *The Look – Adventures In Pop & Rock Fashion.* Sanctuary Publishing, 2001.

Gorman, Paul – *Reasons To Be Cheerful – The Life And Work of Barney Bubbles.* Adelita, 2008.

Goulden, Eric – *A Dysfunctional Success.* The Do Not Press, 2003.

Heylin, Clinton – *Babylon's Burning.* Viking, 2007.

House, Gordon – *Tin-Pan Valley, A Memoir with Paintings.* Archive Press, London, 2004.

Muirhead, Bert – *Stiff, The Story Of A Record Label.* Blandford Press, 1983.

Partington, Angela, ed. – *The Oxford Dictionary of Quotations – Revised Edition.* Oxford University Press, 1996.

Sann, Paul – *The Lawless Decade.* Bonanza Books, New York, 1957.

Sondhi, Madhuri and Mary M. Walker – *Ecology, Culture And Philosophy.* Abhinav Publications, New Delhi, 1988.

Stewart, Tony, ed. – *Cool Cats – 25 Years Of Rock'n'Roll Style.* Eel Pie Publishing, 1981

Vanhecke, Susan – *Race With The Devil – Gene Vincent's Life In The Fast Lane.* St Martin's Press, 2000.

Vyner, Harriet – *Groovy Bob – The Life And Times of Robert Fraser.* Faber, 1999.

Woolrich, Cornell – *Two Murders One Crime* – appears in the anthology *Pulp Fiction, The Crime Fighters,* Otto Penzler (ed.). Quercus, 2007.

Yearsley, Ian – *A History Of Southend.* Phillimore & Co, 2001.

Barnett's Street Plan of Aylesbury, Tring and Wendover. G. L. Barnett, 1973.

Newspapers and Magazines

Allott, Serena – 'Old boots and new panics for Dury'. *Sunday Telegraph,* 12.5.91.

Anon. – 'Singer Dury in divorce'. *Sun,* 22.10.85.

Anon. – 'Ian wrecks bash in rhythm stock row: another belting exclusive'. *News of the World,* 19.5.91.

Anon. – 'Geldof makes a grave mistake'. *Evening Standard,* 26.8.98.

Baker, Danny – 'Ian Dury – a turn for the verse'. *NME,* August 1981.

Boucher, Caroline – 'Ian Dury picks his favourite films'. *Daily Telegraph*, 15.10.89.

Brown, Glyn – 'Baxter Dury: Chip off the old Blockhead'. *Independent*, 2.8.02.

Cain, Barry – 'Hats off to Ian'. *Record Mirror*, August 1979.

Case, Brian – 'Billericay Dickie vs. Uncle Sam'. *NME*, April 1978.

Clarke, Jeremy – 'Sex, drugs and rock'n'roll in Zambia'. *The Weekly Telegraph*, July 1997.

Cooper, Tim – 'Blockheads bid Ian Dury farewell with his final tune'. *Evening Standard*, 5.4.00.

de Whalley, Chas – Live review of 'Kilburn and The High Roads' at the Hope & Anchor. *NME*, December 1975.

Doyle, Tom – 'Famous Last Words'. *Q*, September 1998.

Dury, Ian – '8 Days a Week'. *Melody Maker*, June 1976.

Errigo, Angie – 'Ian Dury is not finished yet'. *NME*, September 1976.

Erskine, Pete – 'Leery, Beery, Gruff and Sneery'. *NME*, October 1973.

Fuller, Steven – 'You don't have to have a leg iron but it helps'. *Penthouse*, April 1974.

Henke, James – 'Ian Dury hits the high road in Britain'. *Rolling Stone*, September 1979.

Hind, John – 'He knew how to make you laugh'. *Independent*, 8.4.01.

Kent, Nick – 'Hardened criminals plan big break-out'. *NME*, September 1973.

Kretzmer, Herbert – 'Rough, risky, heroic' – a review of *King Of The Ghetto*. *Daily Mail*, 2.5.86.

Lawrence, Janie – 'Sex and drugs and rock and roller Dury battles cancer'. *Independent on Sunday*, 1998.

Lynch, Declan – 'Ian Dury gets the needle'. *Record Mirror*, January 1981.

Martin, Gavin – 'Too much Noddy business'. *NME*, October 1983.

Morley, Paul – 'The Ian Dury interview'. *NME*, June 1979.

Nugent, Stephen – 'Taking the low road'. *Let It Rock*, April 1973.

Pratt, Stephen – 'Mary's true confessions' – a review of *Talk Of The Devil*. *Watford Observer*, February 1986.

Romney, John – 'Ian Dury/Kilburns'. *Negative Reaction*, 1978.

Ross, Deborah – 'Great sense of tumour'. *Independent*, 17.8.98.

Salewicz, Chris – 'At the sign of the jolly Blockhead'. *NME*, July 1980.

Schruers, Fred – 'Tales of Sex & Drugs & Rock & Roll. *Rolling Stone*, June 1978.

Seal, Rebecca – 'What I know about men' – an interview with Jane
Horrocks. *Observer*, 27.9.09.

Shaar Murray, Charles – 'How not to get lumbered (part three)'. *NME*,
December 1980.

Silverton, Pete – 'America (well some of it) wakes up and makes love to
Ian Dury'. *Sounds*, May 1978.

Smith, Monty – 'All I want for Christmas is a new left leg'. *NME*,
December 1977.

Smith, Monty – 'Blocks Mental'. *NME*, August 1979.

Spencer, Neil 'Ian Dury – Despite cancer, still with reason to be cheerful'.
Observer, 1998.

Sutcliffe, Phil – 'Hello tosh, got a new career strategy?'. *Q*, June 1991.

Sweeting, Adam 'Triffic – Ian Dury returns to the stage'. *Q*, February
1987.

Tinker, Jack – 'Under fire from a half-baked barrage' – a review of
Apples. *Daily Mail*, September 1989.

Walsh, John – 'Literature by association'. *Independent*, 22.10.98.

Widgery, David – 'The man from Walthamstow'. *Sounds*, December
1978.

Internet

Websites that may be of interest include:
www.iandury.co.uk – Ian's website
www.iandury.com – a fan site presented by Roger Harris
www.theblockheads.com – for news on current Blockheads activity
www.blackmarketclash.com – great Clash site
www.paulbura.co.uk – poet Paul Bura also attended Chailey Heritage
Craft School
www.rocksbackpages.com – a library of music press articles and writings
www.bestiff.co.uk – sharing knowledge and the history of Stiff Records
www.terryday.co.uk – the Kilburns' first drummer and member of the
People Band
www.willbirch.com – the author's site, through which he can be contacted
by email

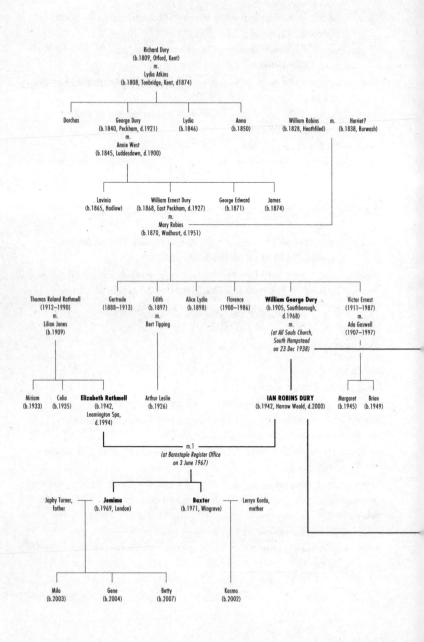

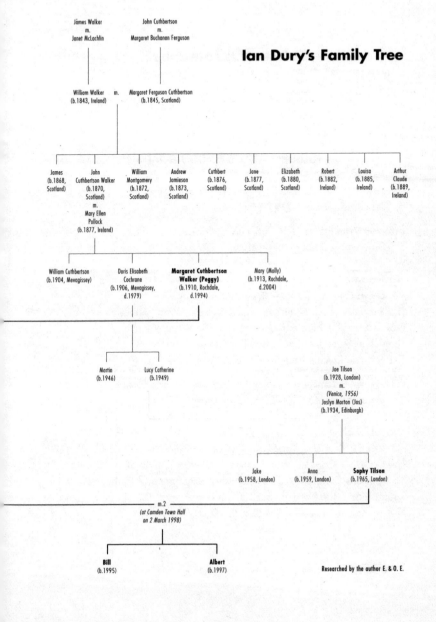

Ian Dury's Family Tree

James Walker
m.
Janet McLachlin

John Cuthbertson
m.
Margaret Buchanan Ferguson

William Walker   m.   Margaret Ferguson Cuthbertson
(b.1843, Ireland)   (b.1845, Scotland)

| James (b.1868, Scotland) | John Cuthbertson Walker (b.1870, Scotland) m. Mary Ellen Pollock (b.1877, Ireland) | William Montgomery (b.1872, Scotland) | Andrew Jamieson (b.1873, Scotland) | Cuthbert (b.1876, Scotland) | Jane (b.1877, Scotland) | Elizabeth (b.1880, Scotland) | Robert (b.1882, Ireland) | Louisa (b.1885, Ireland) | Arthur Claude (b.1889, Ireland) |

William Cuthbertson
(b.1904, Mevagissey)

Doris Elisabeth Cochrane
(b.1906, Mevagissey, d.1979)

Margaret Cuthbertson Walker (Peggy)
(b.1910, Rochdale, d.1994)

Mary (Molly)
(b.1913, Rochdale, d.2004)

Martin
(b.1946)

Lucy Catherine
(b.1949)

Joe Tilson
(b.1928, London)
m.
(Venice, 1956)
Joslyn Morton (Jos)
(b.1934, Edinburgh)

Jake
(b.1958, London)

Anna
(b.1959, London)

Sophy Tilson
(b.1965, London)

m.2
(at Camden Town Hall
on 2 March 1998)

Bill
(b.1995)

Albert
(b.1997)

Researched by the author E. & O. E.

Selected Discography

KILBURN AND THE HIGH ROADS

Rough Kids / Billy Bentley (Promenades Himself In London)
Dawn 45 – DNS.1090 – November 1974

Crippled With Nerves / Huffety Puff
Dawn 45 – DNS.1102 – February 1975

Handsome

Dawn LP – DNLS3065 – June 1975
The Roadette Song / Pam's Moods / Crippled With Nerves /
Broken Skin / Upminster Kid / Patience (So What) / Father /
Thank You Mum / Rough Kids / The Badger And The Rabbit /
The Mumble Rumble And The Cocktail Rock / The Call-Up

Billy Bentley (Promenades Himself In London) / Pam's Moods
Warner Bros 45 – K17225 – September 1978

Wotabunch

Warner Bros LP – K56513 – October 1978
The Call-Up / Crippled With Nerves / Patience (So What) /
You're More Than Fair / Upminster Kid / Billy Bentley / Huffety Puff /
Rough Kids / The Roadette Song / The Badger And The Rabbit /
The Mumble Rumble And The Cocktail Rock / Pam's Moods

IAN DURY

Sex And Drugs And Rock And Roll / Razzle In My Pocket
Stiff 45 – BUY17 – August 1977

New Boots And Panties!!
Stiff LP – SEEZ4 – September 1977 – reached UK chart No. 5
Wake Up And Make Love With Me / Sweet Gene Vincent /
I'm Partial To Your Abracadabra / My Old Man / Billericay Dickie /
Clevor Trever / If I Was With A Woman / Blockheads /
Plaistow Patricia / Blackmail Man

Sweet Gene Vincent / You're More Than Fair
Stiff 45 BUY23 November 1977

Spasticus Autisticus / (Version)
Polydor 45 – POSP285 – July 1981
Polydor 12" – POSPX285

Lord Upminster
Polydor LP – POLD5042 – September 1981 – reached UK chart No. 53
Funky Disco Pops / Red Letter / Girls Watching / Wait For Me /
The Body Song / Lonely Town / Trust Is A Must / Spasticus Autisticus

Really Glad You Came / You're My Inspiration
Polydor 45 – POSP646 – November 1983

Apples
WEA LP – WX326 – October 1989
Apples / Love Is All / Byline Brown / Bit Of Kit / Game On /
Looking For Harry / England's Glory / Bus Driver's Prayer /
PC Honey / The Right People / All Those Who Say OK /
Riding The Outskirts Of Fantasy

Apples / Byline Brown
WEA 45 – YZ437 – October 1989

Profoundly In Love With Pandora / Eugenius (You're A Genius)
        EMI 45 – P553 – October 1989, reached No. 45 on UK chart

The Bus Driver's Prayer & Other Stories
        Demon CD – FIENDCD702 – November 1992
That's Enough Of That / Bill Haley's Last Words / Poor Joey /
Quick Quick Slow / Fly In The Ointment / O'Donegal /
Poo-Poo In The Prawn / Have A Word / London Talking /
D'Orine The Cow / Your Horoscope / No Such Thing As Love /
Two Old Dogs Without A Name / Bus Driver's Prayer

IAN DURY AND THE BLOCKHEADS

What A Waste / Wake Up And Make Love With Me
        Stiff 45 – BUY27 – April 1978 – reached No. 9 on UK chart]

Hit Me With Your Rhythm Stick / There Ain't Half Been Some Clever
Bastards
        Stiff 45 – BUY38 – November 1978 – reached UK chart No. 1

Do It Yourself
        Stiff LP – SEEZ14 – May 1979 – reached UK chart No. 2
Inbetweenies / Quiet / Don't Ask Me / Sink My Boats /
Waiting For Your Taxi / This Is What We Find / Uneasy Sunny Day
Hotsy Totsy / Mischief / Dance Of The Screamers / Lullaby For Frances

Reasons To Be Cheerful (Part 3) / Common As Muck
        Stiff 45 – BUY50 – July 1979 – reached UK chart No. 3

I Want To Be Straight / That's Not All
        Stiff 45 – BUY90 – August 1980 – reached UK chart No. 22

Sueperman's Big Sister / You'll See Glimpses (*12" c/w* Fucking Ada)
        Stiff 45 – BUY100 – November 1980 – reached UK chart No. 51
        Stiff 12" – BUYIT100

Laughter
Stiff LP – SEEZ30 – December 1980 – reached UK chart No. 48
Sueperman's Big Sister / Pardon / Delusions Of Grandeur /
Yes And No (Paula) / Dance Of The Crackpots / Over The Points /
(Take Your Elbow Out Of The Soup) You're Sitting On The Chicken /
Uncoolohol / Hey, Hey, Take Me Away / Manic Depression (Jimi) /
Oh Mr Peanut / Fucking Ada

Juke Box Dury (Compilation)
Stiff LP – SEEZ41 – November 1981
Sex And Drugs And Rock And Roll / Inbetweenies / Common As Muck /
Sweet Gene Vincent / I Want To Be Straight / You'll See Glimpses /
What A Waste / Reasons To Be Cheerful (Part 3) / Wake Up And
Make Love With Me / There Ain't Half Been Some Clever Bastards /
Hit Me With Your Rhythm Stick / Razzle In My Pocket

Warts and Audience (Live)
Demon LP – FIEND777 – 1991
Wake Up And Make Love With Me / Clevor Trever / Billericay Dickie /
Quiet / My Old Man / Spasticus Autisticus / Plaistow Patricia /
There Ain't Half Been Some Clever Bastards / Sweet Gene Vincent /
What A Waste / Hit Me With Your Rhythm Stick / Blockheads

Mr Love Pants
Ronnie Harris Records – DUR1 – June 1998
Jack Shit George / The Passing Show / You're My Baby /
Honeysuckle Highway / Itinerant Child / Geraldine / Cacka Boom /
Bed O'Roses No. 9 / Heavy Living / Mash It Up Harry

Ten More Turnips From The Tip
Ronnie Harris Records – DUR2 – March 2002
Dance Little Rude Boy / I Believe / It Ain't Cool / Cowboys /
Ballad Of The Sulphate Strangler / I Could Lie / One Love /
Happy Hippy / Books And Water / You're The Why

IAN DURY AND THE MUSIC STUDENTS

4000 Weeks' Holiday
Polydor LP – POLD5112 – January 1984
You're My Inspiration / Friends / Tell Your Daddy / Peter The Painter /
Ban The Bomb / Percy The Poet / Very Personal / Take Me To The
Cleaners / The Man With No Face / Really Glad You Came

Very Personal / Ban The Bomb (12″ c/w The Sky's The Limit)
Polydor 45 – POSP673 – February 1984
Polydor 12″ – POSPX673

Radio, Television and Film Appearances

Selected Radio Appearances

It's No Handicap. Ian interviewed by Frances Donnelly. BBC Radio 4,
June 1981.

Mailbag, Ian interviewed by Anne Nightingale. BBC Radio 1, August
1983.

A View from the Top. Ian interviewed by Roger Scott. Capital Radio,
September 1985.

Six Men. Ian interviewed by Ann Brown. BBC Radio 4, May 1986.

Loose Ends. Ian talks to Ned Sherrin about *Apples.* BBC Radio 4, January
1989.

No Triumph, No Tragedy. Ian interviewed by Peter White. BBC Radio 4,
August 1994.

DESERT ISLAND DISCS. Introduced by Sue Lawley. BBC Radio 4,
December 1996.

Ian's eight pieces of music:

    'Small Town Talk' by Bobby Charles – Ian: *'Charlie Gillett played it'.*

    'That's Amore' by Dean Martin – *'I can remember my dad singing this'.*

    'Abdul Abulbul Amir' by Frank Crumit – *'my mum's favourite'.*

    'Woman Love' by Gene Vincent – *'the b-side to "Be Bop a Lula"'.*

    'Music Keeps Me Together' by Taj Mahal – *'I'd always stayed away
from the blues'.*

    'Naughty Lady of Shady Lane' by Alma Cogan – *'it's got a kind of
edge to it'.*

    'I Can't Stand the Rain' by Ann Peebles – *'perfect'.*

    'Ramblin' by Ornette Coleman – *'I've always loved jazz very much'.*

Which record would Ian have selected if he could have taken only one of
  them to his desert island? – 'The Ornette Coleman.'
Which book would Ian have liked in addition to The Bible and
  Shakespeare? – 'The Macmillan Dictionary of Art in all its
  34 volumes at the cost of £5,700.'
What luxury? – 'My luxury would be a working item . . . an 8-track home
  recording studio with a solar panel . . . that would keep me
  happy for ever.'

Selected Television Appearances

The London Weekend Show. With Kilburn and the High Roads.
  LWT, June 1975.
The London Weekend Show. With Kilburn and the High Roads.
  LWT, October 1975.
The London Weekend Show. With Kilburn and the High Roads.
  LWT, January 1976.
The London Weekend Show. Ian interviewed by Janet Street-Porter.
  LWT, January 1978.
The London Programme. Ian interviewed by Yvonne Roberts.
  ITV, February 1978.
To Be an Idiot. Ian meets young people with mental illness.
  BBC2, May 1981.
Michael Parkinson Show. Ian interviewed by Michael Parkinson.
  BBC1, November 1981.
A Better Read. Ian discusses books. ITV, May 1983.
Ian Dury – Spasticus Autisticus. Directed by Franco Rosso. Channel 4,
  November 1983.
The Tube. Ian gives 'the Gene Vincent Lecture'. Channel 4, January
  1985.
Wogan. Ian interviewed by Terry Wogan. BBC1, May 1986.
Metro. Arts series presented by Ian. LWT, 1991–1992.
On My Life. Directed by Mike Connolly. BBC2, September 1999.
Jukebox Heroes – Ian Dury. Directed by Paul Pierrot. BBC1, August
  2002.

Selected Film Appearances

Number One. Directed by Les Blair. 1985.

Pirates. Directed by Roman Polanski. 1986.

Rocinante. Directed by Ann and Eduardo Guedes. 1987.

Hearts of Fire. Directed by Richard Marquand. 1987.

Red Ants. Directed by Vassilis Boudouris. 1987.

The Raggedy Rawney. Directed by Bob Hoskins. 1988.

Die Stemme (aka *The Voice*). Directed by Gustavo Graef-Marino. 1988.

Brennende Betten (aka *Burning Beds*). Directed by Pia Frankenberg. 1988.

The Cook, the Thief His Wife and Her Lover. Directed by Peter Greenaway. 1989.

Bearskin: an Urban Fairytale. Directed by Ann and Eduardo Guedes. 1989.

The Rainbow Thief. Directed by Alejandro Jodorowsky. 1990.

After Midnight. Directed by Shani Grewal. 1990.

Split Second. Directed by Tony Maylam and Ian Sharp. 1992.

Judge Dredd. Directed by Danny Cannon. 1995.

Different for Girls (aka *Crossing the Border*). Directed by Richard Spence. 1996.

The Crow: City of Angels. Directed by Tim Pope. 1996.

Middleton's Changeling. Directed by Marcus Thompson. 1998.

Underground. Directed by Paul Spurrier. 1998.

Permissions Acknowledgements

The author is grateful to the Estate of Ian Dury for permission to quote from Ian's letters to Gordon Law and Roberta Bayley, and to reprint extracts from 'Razors Out at Rock Riot', a chapter written by Ian for *Cool Cats – 25 Years of Rock 'n' Roll Style* (Eel Pie Books, 1981) and 'Eight Days a Week', an article written by Ian for *Melody Maker* in 1976.

Extracts from 'Hardened Criminals Plan Big Break-Out' by Nick Kent and a review of 'Kilburn and The High Roads' by Chas de Whalley are reprinted by kind permission © NME / IPC.

The author is also grateful to the music publishers listed below for permission to reprint extracts of Ian's lyrics from the following works:

'I Made Mary Cry' (Dury / Hardy). Warner Chappell Music Ltd / Oval Music Ltd.

'The Upminster Kid' (Dury / Hardy). Warner Chappell Music Ltd / Oval Music Ltd.

'Rough Kids' (Dury / Hardy). Warner Chappell Music Ltd / Oval Music Ltd.

'Sex and Drugs and Rock and Roll' (Dury / Jankel). Warner Chappell Music Ltd.

'Sweet Gene Vincent' (Dury / Jankel). Warner Chappell Music Ltd.

'What a Waste' (Dury / Melvin). Warner Chappell Music Ltd.

'Hit Me with Your Rhythm Stick' (Dury / Jankel). Warner Chappell Music Ltd.

'There Ain't Half Been Some Clever Bastards' (Dury / Hardy). Warner Chappell. Music Ltd / Oval Music Ltd.

'This Is What We Find' (Dury / Gallagher). Warner Chappell Music Ltd.

'Reasons to Be Cheerful' (Dury / Jankel / Payne). Warner Chappell
Music Ltd. / London Publishing House Ltd.
'Spasticus Autisticus' (Dury / Jankel). Warner Chappell Music Ltd /
Heathwave Music Ltd.
'Futures Song' (Dury / Gallagher). Warner Chappell Music Ltd.
'The Bus Driver's Prayer' (Dury). Warner Chappell Music Ltd.

Additional lyrics referenced by kind permission:

'The Roadette Song' (Dury / Hardy). Warner Chappell Music Ltd /
Oval Music Ltd.
'Crippled With Nerves' (Dury / Hardy). Warner Chappell Music Ltd /
Oval Music Ltd.
'Nervous Piss' (Dury / Melvin). Warner Chappell Music Ltd.
'England's Glory' (Dury / Melvin). Warner Chappell Music Ltd.
'Razzle in My Pocket' (Dury / Jankel). Warner Chappell Music Ltd.
'My Old Man' (Dury / Nugent). Warner Chappell Music Ltd.
'Billericay Dickie' (Dury / Nugent). Warner Chappell Music Ltd.
'Clevor Trever' (Dury / Jankel). Warner Chappell Music Ltd.
'Blockheads' (Dury / Jankel). Warner Chappell Music Ltd.
'Plaistow Patricia' (Dury / Nugent). Warner Chappell Music Ltd.
'I Want to Be Straight' (Dury / Gallagher). Warner Chappell Music Ltd.
'Sueperman's Big Sister' (Dury / Johnson). Warner Chappell Music Ltd.
'Sister Slow' (Dury /Jankel). Warner Chappell Music Ltd / Heathwave
Music Ltd.
'Peter the Painter' (Dury / McEvoy). Warner Chappell Music Ltd.

Picture Acknowledgements

Every effort has been made to contact copyright holders of photographs
reproduced in this book. If any have been inadvertently overlooked the
publishers will be pleased to make restitution at the earliest opportunity.

Page 1: 'Bill and Peggy Dury (with Bella the sheepdog) at Weald Rise,
Harrow, 1940' and 'Little Lord Upminster' courtesy of Jemima Dury.
'On the Beach', and 'King of the Hill', courtesy of Barry Anderson.
Page 2: All photographs courtesy of Margaret Webb.

Page 3: 'At the pantomime, 1953' and 'Elvis has landed' courtesy of Jemima Dury. 'The new boy', courtesy of Margaret Webb.

Page 4: 'Roaming radicals, Newquay 1960' courtesy of Pat Carson. 'The "college" boy' and 'We're arts and crafts' courtesy of Jemima Dury.

Page 5: 'Ian's poster for Kilburn and the High Roads, 1972', photographs © the Mick Hill Collection, lettering and layout Ian Dury. 'Early Kilburns, 1972' © Ed Baxter.

Page 6: 'Humphrey steps out of line; Ian glowers, 1973' © the Mick Hill Collection. 'Gentle, disciplined, self-contained' courtesy of Jemima Dury.

Page 7: All photographs © Alain Le Kim.

Page 8: 'Stiff's stable of stars, 1977' © Chris Gabrin, 'Ian summons the muse; Gene Vincent hovers' © Jill Furmanovsky/rockarchive.com.

Page 9: 'Limousine intererior, New York City, 1978' © Waring Abbot/ Alamy. 'Quiet Reflection' © Kees Bakker. 'A Little Bit of Tommy Cooper' © Pennie Smith.

Page 10: All photographs © Chris Gabrin.

Page 11: All photographs © Tom Sheehan.

Page 12: 'He ain't heavy' © Jorgen Angel/Redferns. 'With "Magic" Mike McEvoy' courtesy Jenny Cotton. 'Barney told me I'd been a horrible piece of work' © Bob Bromide. 'The dramas going on backstage were better than the show' © Kees Bakker.

Page 13: 'A welcome deflection of attention' courtesy of Belinda Leith, © Alan Mercer. 'They want me to have a cigar' © Everett Collection/Rex Features. 'Peggy, so proud of Ian' © Kees Bakker.

Page 14: All photographs courtesy of Sophy Dury.

Page 15: 'UNICEF special representatives, 1998' courtesy of Sophy Dury. 'Jemima and Ian Shepherds Bush Empire, 1999', courtesy of Jemima Dury. 'Magnificent to the end' © Kees Bakker.

Page 16: 'We're gonna have it proper' and 'You're the Why' © Kees Bakker. 'The author interrogates Molly Walker' © Chris Gabrin.

Index

ID indicates Ian Dury.